GOVERNMENT AND POLITICS IN AFRICA

GOVERNMENT AND POLITICS IN AFRICA

WILLIAM TORDOFF

Indiana University Press
Bloomington

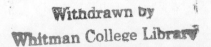

Copyright © 1984 by William Tordoff

Manufactured in Hong Kong

Library of Congress Cataloging in Publication Data

Tordoff, William.
  Government and politics in Africa.

  Bibliography: p.
  Includes index.
  1. Africa—Politics and government—1960–
I. Title.
JQ1872.T67   1984   320.96   84–47769

ISBN 0–253–32611–7
ISBN 0–253–21270–7 (pbk.)

1 2 3 4 5 88 87 86 85 84

For
Audrey and Jane,
Jill and Michael

Contents

Preface		ix
Acknowledgements		xi
List of Abbreviations		xii
Changes in Country Names		xvi
Map		xviii
1	Introduction: African Politics since Independence	1
2	Colonialism and the Colonial Impact	29
3	Nationalism and the Transfer of Power	50
4	State and Society	79
5	Political Parties	102
6	Administration	123
7	The Military	152
8	Revolution and Revolutionary Regimes	181
9	Regional Groupings and the Organisation of African Unity	224
10	Conclusions: Ideology, the Post-Colonial State and Development	261
Notes and References		296
Bibliography		321
Index		338

Preface

This book draws upon my experience of living in Ghana, Tanzania and Zambia for some sixteen years in the 1950s and 1960s, as well as on subsequent visits to these and other African countries. I have been constantly impressed by the courtesy and kindness of the African people, in all walks of life, and their willingness to discuss with me political, administrative and other issues. My debt to them, in all my publications, is very great.

In writing this particular book, I have received valuable help and advice from many friends and colleagues. I am especially indebted to Ralph A. Young, whose willingness to give up his own time for the benefit of others is proverbial at Manchester; his comments on successive drafts were invariably penetrating and constructive. I would also particularly like to thank Barry Munslow who, by his perceptive criticism of the typescript and through discussion, advanced my understanding of the new Afro-Marxist states. I am grateful also to Richard Jeffries, who read the first and final drafts of the typescript for Macmillan with great care and made many suggestions for its improvement, as well as to Macmillan's overseas reader. In addition, I would like to thank the following for their helpful comments on various parts of this work: Dennis Austin, Paul Cammack, Robin Luckham, Keith Panter-Brick, Sam Nolutshungu, and Roger Tangri. It is customary for an author to state, in the preface to his book, that he alone is responsible for the views expressed in the pages which follow. It is important for me to do so on this occasion since my own ideological perspective – that of a democratic socialist – has no doubt led me to express certain points in a way that will not commend itself to all those who have advised me.

The writing and completion of this book have been greatly facilitated by the speed and accuracy with which Gillian Woolley has typed successive drafts; to her, as well as to Jean Ashton and Linda Cooper, my warm thanks. I gladly acknowledge, too, the help given me at all stages of preparation by Chiu-Yin Wong, former publisher of the International College Division, Macmillan, and her successor, Alison Hart, and Kay McCann, Macmillan's Editorial Services Consultant. It remains to add that without the constant encouragement and support of my wife, Audrey, this book would never have been written.

William Tordoff

Manchester
August 1983

Acknowledgements

By kind permission of the author and the editor, table 10.1 in this book has been reproduced from Colin Leys' article 'African Economic Development in Theory and Practice', *Dædalus*: 'Black Africa: A Generation after Independence', issued as vol. III, no. 2 of the Proceedings of the American Academy of Arts and Sciences (Spring 1982), p. 109, table 3. Inevitably, this book draws upon the works of many authors and, under the terms of the agreement between the Publishers' Association and the Society of Authors, I have quoted from several of them, including Colin Leys, Robin Luckham, James Mayall, Barry Munslow, Joel Samoff, Richard L. Sklar, Morris Szeftel, Crawford Young, and the late Thomas Hodgkin. I am grateful to Morris Szeftel, as well as to the Librarian and Director of the John Rylands University Library of Manchester, for allowing me to quote extensively from his unpublished Ph.D. thesis, *Conflict, Spoils and Class Formation in Zambia* (University of Manchester, 1978).

Abbreviations

Note. Where the geographic locus of any organisation is not clear from its title, this has been indicated in brackets.

AAPC	All-African People's Conference
ACP (countries)	African–Caribbean–Pacific
AEF	Afrique Equatoriale Française
AG	Action Group [Nigeria]
ALC	African Liberation Committee
AMU	African Mineworkers' Union [Northern Rhodesia/Zambia]
ANC	African National Congress [Northern Rhodesia/Zambia]
AOF	Afrique Occidentale Française
APC	All People's Congress [Sierra Leone]
ARDP	Accelerated Rural Development Programme [Botswana]
ARPS	Aborigines' Rights Protection Society [Gold Coast]
ASP	Afro-Shirazi Party [Zanzibar]
BNF	Botswana National Front
BP	British Petroleum
BPN	Bureau Politique Nationale [Guinea]
CCM	Chama cha Mapinduzi [Tanzania]
CEAO	Communauté Economique de l'Afrique de l'Ouest

CFAO	Compagnie Française de l'Afrique Occidentale
CIAS	Conference of Independent African States
COREMO	Comité Revolucionário de Moçambique
CPP	Convention People's Party [Gold Coast/Ghana]
CUF	Companhia União Fabril [Portugal]
EAC	East African Community
EACSO	East African Common Services Organisation
ECA	Economic Commission for Africa [United Nations]
ECOWAS	Economic Community of West African States
EEC	European Economic Community
EPRP	Ethiopian People's Revolutionary Party
FLING	Frente para a Libertação e Independência da Guiné Portuguesa
FLN	Front de Libération Nationale [Algeria]
FNLA	Frente Nacional de Libertação de Angola
FRELIMO	Frente de Libertação de Moçambique
GNP	Gross National Product
GRAE	Governo Revolucionário de Angola no Exilio
IMF	International Monetary Fund
KANU	Kenya African National Union
KFL	Kenya Federation of Labour
MAP	Muslim Association Party [Gold Coast/Ghana]
MNR	Mozambique National Resistance
MPLA	Movimento Popular de Libertação de Angola
MRM	Mozambique Resistance Movement
NCNC	National Council of Nigeria and the Cameroons/National Council of Nigerian Citizens
NDR	National Democratic Revolution [Ethiopia]
NLC	National Liberation Council [Ghana]
NLM	National Liberation Movement [Gold Coast/Ghana]
NNA	Nigerian National Alliance
NNDP	Nigerian National Democratic Party
NPC	Northern People's Congress [Nigeria]
NPN	National Party of Nigeria

NPP	Northern People's Party [Gold Coast/Ghana]
OAU	Organisation of African Unity
OCAM	Organisation Commune Africaine et Mauritienne
OLF	Oromo Liberation Front [Ethiopia]
PAFMEC(S)A	Pan-African Freedom Movement of East, Central (and Southern) Africa
PAICV	Partido Africano da Independência da Cabo Verde
PAIGC	Partido Africano da Independência da Guiné e Cabo Verde
PDCI	Parti Démocratique de Côte d'Ivoire
PDG	Parti Démocratique de Guinée
PF	Polisario Front [Western Sahara]
PFP	Patriotic Front Party [Rhodesia/Zimbabwe]
PMAC	Provisional Military Administrative Council [Ethiopia]
PP	Progress Party [Ghana]
PRA	Parti de Regroupement Africain [French Black Africa]
PRL	Pouvoir Révolutionnaire Locale [Guinea]
PRP	People's Redemption Party [Nigeria]
PSS	Parti Socialiste Sénégalais
RDA	Rassemblement Démocratique Africain [French Black Africa]
SADCC	Southern African Development Co-ordination Conference
SADR	Saharan/Sahrawi Arab Democratic Republic
SCOA	Société Commerciale de l'Ouest Africain
SLPP	Sierra Leone People's Party
SMC	Supreme Military Council [Nigeria]
SRC	Supreme Revolutionary Council [Somalia]
SWAPO	South West African People's Organisation
TANU	Tanganyika African National Union
TFL	Tanganyika Federation of Labour
TPLF	Tigre People's Liberation Front [Ethiopia]
TUC	Trades Union Congress
UAC	United African Company [Britain]
UAM	Union Africaine et Malgache

UDEAC	Union Douanière et Economique de l'Afrique Centrale
UDV	Union Démocratique Voltaique
UGCC	United Gold Coast Convention
UGTAN	Union Générale des Travailleurs d'Afrique Noire [Guinea]
UN	United Nations
UNCTAD	United Nations Conference on Trade and Development
UNDD	Union Nationale pour la Défense de la Démocratie [Upper Volta]
UNIP	United National Independence Party [Northern Rhodesia/Zambia]
UNITA	União Nacional para a Independência Total de Angola
UPA	União das Populações de Angola
UPC	{ Union des Populations du Cameroun { Uganda People's Congress
UPGA	United Progressive Grand Alliance [Nigeria]
UPN	United Party of Nigeria
UPP	United Progressive Party [Zambia]
UPS	Union Progressiste Sénégalaise
UPV	Union Progressiste Voltaique
US	Union Soudanaise [French Soudan/Mali]
WSLF	Western Somalia Liberation Front
ZANLA	Zimbabwe African National Liberation Army
ZANU	Zimbabwe African National Union
ZANU(PF)	Zimbabwe African National Union (Patriotic Front)
ZAPU	Zimbabwe African People's Union
ZIPA	Zimbabwe People's Army
ZIPRA	Zimbabwe People's Revolutionary Army

Changes in Country Names

Note. Throughout the text, I have used the name by which the country was known at the date relevant to the discussion. Changes of name usually occurred at independence; post-independence changes are indicated in brackets.

Present	Pre-independence
Benin (1975)	Dahomey
Botswana	Bechuanaland
Burundi[1]	Ruanda–Urundi
Cameroon	{ French Cameroons British Southern Cameroons[2]
Cape Verde	Cape Verde Islands
Central African Republic	Oubangui Chari
Congo	French Congo[3]
Djibouti	French Territory of the Afars and Issas[4]
Equatorial Guinea	Spanish Guinea
Gambia/Senegambia[5]	Gambia
Ghana	Gold Coast and British Togoland
Guinea-Bissau	Portuguese Guinea
Lesotho	Basutoland
Malagasy Republic/ Madagascar	Madagascar
Malawi	Nyasaland
Mali[6]	French Soudan
Namibia[7]	South West Africa

Present	Pre-independence
Rwanda[1]	Ruanda–Urundi
Saharan Arab Democratic Republic[8]	Spanish Sahara/ Western Sahara
Senegal/Senegambia[5]	Senegal
Somalia/Somali Democratic Republic	{ British Somaliland { Italian Somaliland
Tanzania (1965)[9]	{ Tanganyika { Zanzibar
Togo	French Togoland
Zaire (1971)	Belgian Congo [10]
Zambia	Northern Rhodesia
Zimbabwe	Southern Rhodesia/ Rhodesia

Notes

1. Ruanda–Urundi was a Belgian-administered trust territory which became independent in 1960 as two separate states.
2. The Southern Cameroons, a British-administered UN trust territory, joined the Republic of Cameroon following a plebiscite in 1961: the people of the Northern Cameroons opted for integration with Nigeria.
3. Often referred to as Congo-Brazzaville.
4. Often referred to as French Somaliland.
5. The names 'Gambia' and 'Senegal' are retained, but in 1981 the two states formed the confederation of Senegambia.
6. The Mali Federation was formed by Senegal and Soudan in 1959, but survived for less than three months after being granted political independence by France in June 1960. France then recognised the separate independence of Senegal and Soudan, and the Union Soudanaise changed the name of Soudan to the Republic of Mali.
7. Not yet independent.
8. Also known as the Sahrawi Arab Democratic Republic. Its international status is in dispute.
9. The United Republic of Tanganyika and Zanzibar came into being on 26 April 1964, as a consequence of the union between Tanganyika and Zanzibar; the name 'United Republic of Tanzania' was officially adopted a year later.
10. Often referred to as Congo-Léopoldville and subsequently (from 1 July 1966) as Congo-Kinshasa.

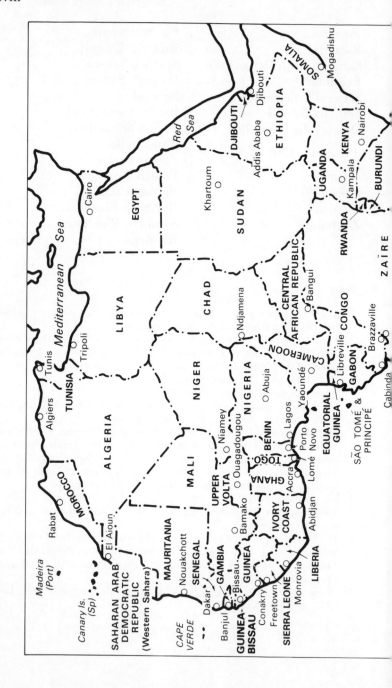

Political Map of Africa

1

Introduction: African Politics since Independence

Africa is a vast and diverse continent, comprising fifty or (if the Saharan Arab Democratic Republic is included) fifty-one independent states. With only a few exceptions, such as Egypt, Ethiopia and Liberia, they are 'new' states: most of them achieved independence in 1960, which was the *annus mirabilis* of African independence, or within a few years of that date. To lump these states together and talk about 'African politics' is somewhat misleading because there are important differences between them. There is, for example, a wide cultural gap between the North African states and the Black African states south of the Sahara. The geographic and demographic differences are often striking, as witness the huge Sudan and Zaire on the one hand and the tiny Rwanda, Burundi and Swaziland on the other; within West Africa, oil-rich Nigeria – four times the size of Britain and with a population probably exceeding 100 million – contrasts sharply with the Gambia which, with an area of just over four thousand square miles and a population of approximately 600,000, was once (in pre-independence days) described as 'an eel wriggling its way through a slab of French territory'.

None the less, at independence these new African states had several things in common. First, they were ex-colonial, that is, with only a few exceptions (such as Liberia) they had been subjected to rule by one or another of the colonial powers –

Britain, France, Germany, Belgium, Italy, Portugal and Spain. But colonial rule was brief (often less than a hundred years) and these new states were also old societies, with a pre-colonial history of their own. Secondly, they were searching for a new identity as nation-states. At independence, they acquired statehood and, as members of the United Nations, international recognition, but (with the odd exception such as Somalia) the task remained of welding into a nation a variety of different peoples, speaking different languages and at different stages of social and political development. Nowhere was this task more demanding than in Nigeria, which has been aptly described as 'the linguistic crossroads of Africa'. Thirdly, these states were mostly poor, predominantly rural and over-dependent on the vagaries of the world market. Any benefits which they received from foreign aid, for example, might be swiftly eroded if the terms of trade turned against them through a fall in the price which they received for their primary produce. The leaders of many of these states have, therefore, sought to diversify the economy away from reliance on a single cash crop or mineral product (for example, Ghana on cocoa, Senegal and the Gambia on groundnuts, and Zaire and Zambia on copper). However, in trying to industrialise they faced immense problems – of technology and manpower, of the cost of imported machinery, and marketing. Moreover, as Michael Lofchie has pointed out,[1] in the West industrialisation took place before full democratic practices were introduced into the political process, and this meant that resources were available to meet the most pressing demands of the enfranchised workers. In Africa, as in Asia and the Caribbean, there was no such time-lag: universal franchise was granted just before, at, or immediately after independence before economic policies could even be formulated. The expectations of the electorate, heightened by promises made during the independence struggle, far exceeded the governments' capacity to provide.

In the fourth place, the newly independent states had an unsettled political culture. Not only had the political leadership next to no experience of operating a governmental system on a national scale, but the institutions (such as parties, parliaments and civil services) through which they had to work were also relatively new and weak. Thus, with the exception of Liberia's

True Whig Party, which was formed in 1860 as the Whig Party, political parties were mostly post-1945 creations; they therefore lacked the political experience of the Indian Congress Party. The weakness of the inherited institutions was serious because the private sector was under-developed and the state itself had to assume a major entrepreneurial role. The result was an increase in the number of public enterprises, in bureaucratic power, and in a further widening of the élite-mass gap, with educated, mostly urbanised élites existing side by side with conservative and illiterate chiefs and villagers. Finally, in the international context, the new states were no match, either diplomatically or militarily, for the developed states; in the 1960s especially, most Francophone states took shelter under the wing of the former metropolitan power. It was only in the next decade that the oil weapon gave a few states a significant economic, and therefore diplomatic, leverage.

And so one could go on, adding to the list of common characteristics of the new African states and pointing to shared problems. Of course, these common characteristics masked important differences. In relation to the industrialised Western countries, the new African states were indeed poor; but, as between themselves, some were much better off than others – the Ivory Coast than neighbouring Upper Volta, for example. There were also often glaring disparities between one part of a country and another: for instance, between Zambia's line-of-rail and outlying rural provinces, and between Nigeria's Northern Region and the two (after 1963 three) southern regions; these disparities underlined the differential impact of capitalist penetration during the colonial era. There were differences between the states in manpower terms: in this respect, West Africa was much better off than East Africa; educationally, there was almost a generation gap between them. Mainland Tanzania, like Zambia, faced independence with barely a hundred graduates and a totally inadequate number of secondary-school leavers; but both states were better off than Angola and Mozambique, though less so than Zimbabwe. Finally, despite the briefness of colonial rule and the fact that the characteristic, 'ex-colonial', is obviously a dwindling distinction the further one moves away from independence, colonialism has left a deep imprint on the new states of Africa. Thus, there are important differences in the system and style of administration between (say) Francophone and Anglophone Africa, so that a Sierra Leonean civil servant trained in the British tradition, would feel more at home in distant Kenya or Botswana than in nearby Senegal, Guinea or the Ivory Coast. Moreover, as we have suggested, some of the differences arising from the colonial legacy were reproduced in the external sphere, with ex-French colonies tending to maintain closer ties with France than ex-British colonies did with Britain.

It might be objected that what we have depicted as characteristics of the new states at independence were not peculiar to those states, but were shared by some of the developed states also. This is true, regional imbalances in a country's economy being a case in point. The main difference lay in degree – the greater severity of these problems in the new states – and especially in the concentration of these problems. If it is accepted that these characteristics are valid (subject to the *caveat* that they mask important underlying differences), we must ask next: what has happened since independence? Obviously, a great deal: *ex-Africa aliquid semper novi*. Since we are faced with so much that is new in African politics, we identify a number of trends.

An obvious trend, in most of Africa in the 1960s, was the move away from pluralism towards the centralisation of power in the hands of a single party. By the early 1970s few countries retained multi-party systems and, with the odd exception (such as Botswana), we had – as political scientists – to talk in terms of competition within the single-party system rather than of competition between parties. There were, of course, important differences between one-party systems: how they came into being; whether they rested on a *de facto* or *de jure* basis; whether they had a strong ideological base, as in Guinea, or a weak one, as in Kenya; whether they made provision for inner party democracy, as the Tanganyika African National Union (TANU) did in Tanzania and the Convention People's Party (CPP) in Ghana increasingly did not. It should, of course, be noted that to a limited extent this trend was reversed from the mid-1970s with the restoration, following military withdrawal, of multi-party politics in Ghana and Nigeria in 1979, and new constitutional and political experiments in Francophone states such as Mali, Senegal, Tunisia and Upper Volta.

A second and related trend was not only for power to be centralised in a single party, but also for it to be personalised in the hands of the party leader, who became State President. This phenomenon, referred to by one Zambian minister as the 'divine right of Presidents', carried obvious disadvantages: sometimes, as in Ghana between 1960 and 1966 and in Malawi, it meant the heavy concentration of powers in the President's own office, to the detriment of other ministries; the virtual monopoly of policy-making by the President, without adequate consideration of alternative policies, and the erection of the President's own thought into the official ideology; and, the cases of Kenya, Senegal, and Cameroon notwithstanding, it carried the danger of succession crises which, as Morris-Jones has pointed out, 'are the moments of truth in a political system's life'.[2] On the other hand, in new state conditions the personalisation of power may have advantages where an exceptional leader holds office – perhaps Julius Nyerere in Tanzania, Kenneth Kaunda in Zambia, and Samora Machel in Mozambique. Take Nyerere. In the pre-independence period, Nyerere – like Kwame Nkrumah in Ghana and Ahmed Sékou Touré in Guinea – emerged as a charismatic leader, not only because he possessed those 'exceptional powers or qualities' which (according to Weber) anyone with charismatic authority must have, but also because the message of freedom which he conveyed was relevant and meaningful within the prevailing social context. It can be argued that Nyerere retained his appeal after independence because he realised that charisma must be socially validated; in practical terms, this meant that he was able to assess the changing social situation and adapt himself and his policies to it.[3] This is what he did, for example, when he resigned as Prime Minister in 1962 and when he formulated the series of resolutions which made up the Arusha Declaration in 1967. On the first occasion, he was acutely aware that TANU had lost its sense of direction and purpose and that he alone could help it, as well as the country as a whole, to make the psychological readjustment to independence. On the second occasion, in issuing the Arusha Declaration, he took account of the mounting discontent among up-country workers and farmers at the growing detachment of the ruling élite. His subsequent actions helped to dispel that discontent and, through the adoption of equalisation measures, to share out the 'burden of development'. It must be added, however, that there is evidence in Tanzania, as in Zambia, pointing in an opposite direction. In each case, the leadership has displayed authoritarian tendencies which have resulted in a less than critical assessment of questionable presidential initiatives in, for example, rural development policy.

A third trend, also related though not confined to one-partyism, has been the espousal of some form of socialism. In the 1960s, the range among African states in this regard was very wide, thereby underlining the fact that socialism was a loose concept in Africa and subject to varying interpretations. It usually had nationalist overtones, and many African leaders would have subscribed to the statement made by Aimé Césaire, the West Indian who was influential in the intellectual circles of Francophone Africa, when he resigned from the French Communist Party in 1956:

> I think I have said enough to make it understood that it is neither Marxism nor Communism that I renounce, but it is the use that certain people have made of Marxism and Communism of which I disapprove. What I want is Marxism and Communism to be placed in the service of the black peoples and not the black peoples in the service of Marxism and Communism.[4]

In fact, few African leaders were orthodox Marxists. They rejected key tenets of Marxist orthodoxy, such as the notion of the class struggle. This applied to Sékou Touré of Guinea as well as to less obviously radical leaders. They refused to espouse atheism but remained (for example) Christians and Muslims. They adapted Marxist and other ideas to suit African conditions and their interest in socialism was often accompanied by an affirmation of traditional values. We are, said Nyerere, 'groping our way forward towards socialism', but he warned of the danger 'of being bemused by this new theology'.[5] Of course, there were other African leaders, such as the Ivory Coast's Félix Houphouet Boigny, who did not draw on

Marxism at all, and some who, under the broad umbrella of African socialism, pursued (as in Kenya and Senegal) capitalist-type policies. Some states, including many of those under military rule, either shunned ideology or rested on a weak ideological base.

In the immediate post-independence period, most African leaders stressed the 'social responsibility' dimension of socialism, pointing (for example) to the social obligation to work and the need to convert labour unions from consumptionist to productionist associations.[6] From about the mid-1960s, they also emphasised the economic aspects of socialism by taking under public ownership and control import–export houses, mines and industries, banks and insurance companies, farms and other properties; these enterprises were predominantly foreign-owned. It is well to remember, however, that such measures were taken by states, such as military-ruled Ghana and Uganda, which did not claim to be socialist as well as by states, such as Tanzania, whose rulers did pursue broadly socialist strategies.

Further changes took place in the 1970s, though their effect was not everywhere to reverse the earlier trend towards an eclectic brand of African socialism. This resulted from the emergence in several states of a more scientific form of socialism than had previously existed, except perhaps in Guinea in the late 1960s. Thus, revolutionary regimes emerged from below in Guinea-Bissau, Angola and Mozambique following protracted wars of independence, and were imposed from above in Somalia, Ethiopia, and the People's Republics of Benin and Congo following military coups. These regimes shared a commitment to Marxist–Leninist principles, but differed in the way in which they set about the task of socialist transformation.

A fourth post-independence trend, which was observable in many states before the rash of military coups, was the progressive decline of the party as the centre of power and decision-making and the corresponding rise of the bureaucracy. Thus, Aristide Zolberg, in *Creating Political Order: The Party-States of West Africa*, referred to 'a common tendency toward the emergence of regimes in which governmental and administrative structures are at least as salient as parties'. Writing in 1966, he said of Ghana, Guinea, Mali, Senegal and the Ivory Coast that 'within a short time . . . it is likely that these regimes will be composed of a senescent party and of a young, vigorous governmental bureaucracy which will not hesitate to assert its place in the sun.'[7] He pointed to the movement towards the emergence of the administrative state, with the party reduced to a symbolic role. In fact, the CPP in Ghana and the Union Soudanaise (US) in Mali soon suffered a worse fate, being proscribed with the advent of military rule. In respect of the other three states, Zolberg was perhaps unduly pessimistic. In Guinea the party has not been eclipsed by the state structure, but, according to R. W. Johnson, exists in parallel to it, subsuming it at the lower levels. In the Ivory Coast Richard Stryker, while admitting the pre-eminence of the governmental bureaucracy, thought that by 1971 the Parti Démocratique de Côte d'Ivoire (PDCI) had stemmed, if not reversed, 'the trend . . . toward inanition' which Immanuel Wallerstein, as well as Zolberg, detected generally in West Africa. More recently, Donal Cruise O'Brien has stated that Senegal's ruling party – the Union Progressiste Sénégalaise (UPS), now renamed the Parti Socialiste Sénégalais (PSS) – is 'a remarkably efficient organization in its own unedifying way' and 'quite a formidable agency of national political power'.[8]

What is certain is that the ruling party nowhere became the mobilising agent projected at independence. Sometimes, this was because the political leadership turned purposely to the administration rather than the party as the 'agent of development'. This happened in Kenya, where the party organs tended to atrophy through lack of use. It happened to some extent, too, though not intentionally, in Tanzania and Zambia. In Tanzania, Nyerere and the TANU national executive committee became increasingly concerned at what they identified as 'the dominance of the government bureaucracy' and in the early 1970s took steps to reduce it. Structural changes in TANU were designed to improve the party's ability to secure its socialist goals, and TANU executive committees at the various levels were to oversee the activities of all government departments in their areas. However, bureaucratic dominance at regional and district levels was not thereby reduced and may even have been increased as a result of 'decentralisation' measures introduced in 1972. In Zambia, also, the bureaucracy rather than the ruling party increasingly spearheaded the development effort: following the creation of the one-party state in 1972 and the down-turn in the country's economy, the United National Independence Party (UNIP) suffered a loss of vitality and its officials, especially at constituency and branch levels, became demoralised. The Local Administration Act of 1980 is, in part, designed to reverse that trend. Again, the fact that the Partido Africano da Independência da Guiné e Cabo Verde (PAIGC) in Guinea-Bissau was ill-equipped to play a mobilising role is evident from Barry Munslow's comment that 'One of the main reasons for the November 1980 military coup in Guinea-Bissau was the growing weakness of the party which had tended to atrophy since independence'. In Senegal, too, the PSS is effective as an agent of control and patronage, but it is not a machine designed for mass mobilisation.[9]

Another post-independence trend in African politics has been the move away from federal and quasi-federal systems of government to unitary structures; Nigeria, under civilian rule, and the Sudan after 1972, were the only important exceptions to this pattern. Thus, the federal elements in the independence constitutions of Ghana and Kenya were removed in 1959 and 1964 respectively; French West and French Equatorial Africa did not survive as quasi-federal apparatuses; the Mali Federation collapsed in 1960; and Buganda's federal relationship with the rest of Uganda was ended forcibly in 1966. The feeling was widespread that federal and quasi-federal constitutional arrangements would encourage sub-nationalist sentiments and render more difficult the daunting task of achieving national integration. As part of the colonial legacy, many African states faced this problem of sub-nationalism – the problem of widespread, popular attachment to a unit (whether tribally, linguistically or regionally defined) which was within, but not coterminous with, the boundaries of the new state. Thus, we had the problem posed by (among others) the Ashanti in Ghana, the Baganda in Uganda, the Eritreans in Ethiopia, the Katangese in Zaire, the Ibos in Nigeria, the Southern Sudanese in Sudan, and the Barotse in Zambia. Where the problem was solved and the integrity of the state maintained, different means were utilised; mainly constitutional amendment in Ghana, the Sudan and Zambia, force in Zaire and Nigeria, and a mixture of constitutionalism and force in Uganda. The Sudan was one of the very few African states which, following the agreement reached at Addis Ababa in February 1972 between the central government and the Southern Sudan Liberation Movement, created representative assemblies and governments at a level intermediate between the centre and the locality. Most states shied away from such sweeping decentralisation measures. Thus, the so-called decentralisation undertaken by Zambia in 1968–9 and Tanzania in 1972 really amounted to a deconcentration of administrative authority, whereby civil servants working in central government ministries were posted to the field. Though these civil servants were subject to increased local pressure, the reality of central government control was in no way diminished. In Zambia, the Local Administration Act of 1980 increased the role of UNIP office-holders in the local authorities, at the expense of popular participation; however, this Act has not yet been fully implemented. Most of Francophone Africa has retained a French-style prefectoral system. 'This administrative "deconcentration is only another form of centralization" ', Stryker wrote of the Ivory Coast, 'and must not be confused with any devolution of central authority to autonomous local bodies.'[10]

Another trend has, of course, been the supplanting of civilian governments by military regimes in a large number of African states. Why has the military intervened? Why has it intervened in some states, but not in others? Generalisation is risky. Sometimes the military has filled, or has claimed to fill, a guardian-type role and, as custodian of the national interest, has intervened to save the country from corrupt and inefficient politicians who had brought the country to the verge of bankruptcy. This was the claim made in Ghana, for example, in 1966. Sometimes, the military has intervened to safeguard its own interest against a rival force being created by the President – a motive (among others) in Ghana and Uganda. Sometimes, elements of the military have political objectives; this encouraged intervention, for example, in Nigeria in 1966, when the principal coup-makers sought to put an end to regionalism. Some of the coups have, of course, been counter-coups, one set of officers displacing another, thereby reflecting a breakdown in the army's internal command structure; Benin (formerly

Dahomey) was the classic case. A common feature of the coups has been the ease with which they have been executed, often by only a small force of men. Most have not involved any fundamental restructuring of society, though this pattern was sometimes broken where revolutionary military regimes were established, as in Ethiopia and Somalia. The change has generally been a change at the top – in the élite running the country – rather than (in Sklar's words) 'a change in the class content of power'.[11] Though the military proscribed political party activity and found new allies among civil servants, chiefs and professional groups (as in Ghana under the National Liberation Council between 1966 and 1969), life in the village went on substantially as it had done before the coup.

On assuming power, the military has sometimes promised that it will yield to a civilian government and withdraw to the barracks once constitutional integrity has been restored, corruption eliminated, and the economy revived. The military has in fact withdrawn in a number of cases, including Ghana and Nigeria in 1979; following the holding of multi-party elections, a form of parliamentary democracy under presidential leadership was established in both countries. Sometimes, however, the military has withdrawn only to return, often within a short period of time, as in Dahomey on several occasions, Sudan in 1969, Ghana in 1972 and 1981, and Nigeria in 1983. From the mid-1960s, the nature of military coups seemed to alter, with the soldiers coming to stay for indefinite periods. Withdrawal in favour of civilian rule has been more frequent in Anglophone than in Francophone Africa. The tendency in the latter has been for the incumbent military regime to seek to legitimatise its rule by forming a political party and then holding presidential and parliamentary elections. Though multi-party elections and a competitive presidential election were held in Upper Volta in 1978, elections in such states have normally been of the plebiscitary type at which the electorate massively endorsed the regime's right to rule; Mali in 1979 afforded a good example of this process. Despite their civilian garb, these remained essentially military regimes.

Another post-independence trend is more socio-economic than political, but has important political repercussions. It is the drift to the towns in many African states, leading to the growth (as in Zambia and Nigeria) of sprawling, insanitary shanty-towns around the main urban centres, and the increase in the number of school-leavers, educated at least to the primary-school level, for whom jobs are not available because the economy cannot expand fast enough to absorb the rising school output. Thus, in Botswana, the stark facts at independence in 1966 were that only about three out of every ten primary school-leavers could hope either to find salaried jobs within the country or to obtain further training or education; the remainder had to find employment in the rural economy or enlist for work in South Africa. Hence the attempt made in Botswana, Tanzania, Mali and elsewhere to develop an educational system more relevant to the needs of predominantly rural societies. In many states, too, despite the increasing emphasis given to rural development, the rural–urban gap has widened since independence and regional imbalances in the economy have grown. It is in this context that one can see the relevance of the argument (often applied to Kenya and the Ivory Coast) that economic growth does not necessarily equal economic development, and assess attempts made to check social stratification through the adoption of equalisation measures. In Tanzania President Nyerere's government has imposed severe restrictions on private enterprise and, by taxation and in other ways, has clipped the privileged wings of the political leadership and state bureaucracy. The result has been not to halt the process of class formation, which is the inevitable corollary of modern education and public employment, but to prevent the ruling class (the 'managerial bourgeoisie') from consolidating its power at the expense of other emergent classes. The Tanzanian experience contrasts sharply with that of Nigeria, where, as Richard L. Sklar has pointed out, 'the indigenisation of capitalist enterprise . . . is a leading nationalist goal', and the dominant class, committed to capitalist development in alliance with private investors, is quickly consolidating its power.[12]

A final trend – among others which could be isolated for comment – has been the determination of African states to pursue an independent foreign policy, however weak their bargaining power. Many have sought to widen their trading links and diversify their sources of foreign aid away from the former colonial power, often in favour of middle-ranking powers such as Canada and Sweden. Such changes in trade and aid patterns have not of course ended the external economic dependency of African states. Take Mali, for example: though she has developed important diplomatic and military links with the Soviet Union, France remains easily the most important of her trading partners and, through the control of cotton, still dominates the Malian economy.[13] Even revolutionary regimes, such as those in Angola and Mozambique, cannot seriously contemplate short-term disengagement from the world capitalist economy – Angola is dependent on oil revenues and must therefore work with the multinational oil companies, while Mozambique remains dependent on the regional sub-system, centring on South Africa. Such stark facts have led some scholars to conclude that socialism in one state can achieve little and that world revolution must precede any meaningful transition to socialism. Yet continuing external dependency, as well as unfavourable geographical position and internal economic weakness, have not prevented African states from vigorously asserting their national interest and/or upholding revolutionary principle. This was shown when Zambia took majority control of the copper companies in 1969–70 against the wishes of the multinationals concerned, Mozambique closed her border with Rhodesia in 1976 at enormous cost to herself, and Nigeria nationalised British Petroleum holdings in 1979 in protest against the company's dealings in Southern Africa. Such incidents serve to reinforce the conclusion reached by Professor Sklar that:

> The idea of foreign domination by proxy, through the medium of a clientele or puppetised upper class, is controverted by a large body of evidence. In many post-colonial and newly developing countries, governments, businessmen, and leaders of thought regularly defy the demands and frustrate the desires of their counterparts in the industrial countries.[14]

Though post-independence attempts to create regional political unions have come to little, there has been widespread recognition among African leaders that 'in unity lies strength'.

They have continued to meet in the Organisation of African Unity, whose 1963 charter represented a compromise between the different interests involved, and they have joined together in regional functional groups, such as the long-standing Union Douanière et Economique de l'Afrique Centrale, the 16-nation Economic Community of West African States, founded in 1975, and the 9-state Southern African Development Co-ordination Conference, established in 1979. Francophone associates and Anglophone associables maintained a united front in negotiating a new Lomé Convention between the African, Caribbean and Pacific group of countries and the European Economic Community in 1978–9. African states have also joined other less developed countries in presenting a 'Third World' view at international forums such as the general assembly of the United Nations and at various meetings of the United Nations Conference on Trade and Development (UNCTAD). Whereas in the 1960s the African states lacked any significant leverage which they could apply in negotiations with the developed states, in the next decade the oil-weapon strengthened the diplomatic bargaining power of oil-rich states such as Algeria, Libya and Nigeria. However, for African states as a whole the oil-weapon proved double-edged, since they faced enormous increases in the cost of importing petroleum products and manufactured goods. Unfortunately, too, many efforts at working together have been vitiated by divisions between African states. Some disagreements have been so serious that they could not be reconciled, resulting in the collapse of fruitful experiments in regional economic co-operation; the demise of the East African Community in 1977 is a case in point. Other disputes have ended in open warfare, including those between Somalia and Ethiopia in 1977–8 and Tanzania and Uganda in 1978–9.

What has been said so far represents a simplified over-view of political developments in Africa since independence. The following chapters will take up some of these themes and elaborate them both theoretically and in greater empirical detail. Before doing this, however, it might be useful to outline and comment on the general models of 'development' which have been employed in much of the literature on African politics.

The Study of Development

Two main schools of thought can be identified in the study of development – the modernisation school and the 'development of underdevelopment school'.[15] The predominantly American modernisation school blossomed in the mid-1950s and owed much to Marion Levy and Talcott Parsons and ultimately to Max Weber. Strongly behavioural, it was the product of a search for a comparative approach to politics that was extended to the developing areas and was conducted with the aid of various models, including structural-functionalism and systems theory. Among its central concerns are problems of national integration, democracy and institutional stability, and cultural problems such as ethnicity, the impact of Western education and role conflicts. Its early 'African' exponents included James Coleman, David Apter and Aristide Zolberg. This school has had behind it much of the weight of the American academic establishment and, having been well financed, has resulted in a vast literature, including the Princeton Political Development series. It does not, however, represent a closed system, being subject to criticism and revision from within.

The founder of contemporary underdevelopment theory, whose origins go back to Marx and Lenin, is Paul Baran; his *Political Economy of Growth* was published in 1957. More internationally diverse than the modernisation school, its exponents include André Gunder Frank, Celso Furtado, James Petras and Fernando Henrique Cardoso for Latin America, and Frantz Fanon, Samir Amin, Walter Rodney and John Saul for Africa. They place a common emphasis on economic-based patterns such as modes of production, social formations and class conflict; they see colonialism as essentially exploitative, and seek to explain the continuing predicament of underdevelopment in terms of the international capitalist environment. However, this school, too, does not constitute a closed system and two strongly contrasting viewpoints are to be found within it: the first, represented by Frank, denies the possibility of capitalist development in the periphery and the second, represented by Cardoso, focuses explicitly on the process of such development and shows how it differs from 'classic' capitalist development.

Modernisation theory

According to Claude Welch, 'Modernization is a *process*, based upon the rational utilization of resources and aimed at the establishment of a "modern" society.' Its most important characteristic is 'a core belief in rational or scientific control'.[16] If we make an artificial division, we can say briefly what modernisation involves in the economic, social and political spheres. It entails, in the economic sphere, the application of technology and industrialisation, and in the social sphere, changes in traditional patterns of behaviour and values, with urbanisation, literacy and social mobility as characteristic indices of levels of change. In the political sphere, modernisation involves the development of an institutional framework that is sufficiently flexible to meet the demands placed upon it; the centralisation of power in the state, coupled with a weakening of traditional sources of authority; differentiated political structures, sub-system autonomy, and widened political participation; and an instrumental ideology to give purpose and direction to the process of change. It needs to be emphasised that such compartmentalisation is artificial: thus, industrialisation alone does not equal modernisation, but is rather a special aspect of it. Moreover, Lucian Pye's study of Burma, published in 1962, underlined the fact that development is a complex process, amounting to a good deal more than the achievement of the self-sustaining economic growth earlier projected by Rostow.[17]

Modernisation theory is subject to a number of criticisms. The initial stress on the key role of industrialisation was in practice irrelevant to the many underdeveloped countries which lacked mineral resources, sources of energy, technical skills and accessible markets. Economically, it was more advantageous for them, and indeed for some of the countries which were well endowed with natural resources, to base their development on a sound agricultural base – this was the advice given by Professor Arthur Lewis to Ghana in 1951 and the policy adopted by Tanzania in the Arusha Declaration of

January 1967. By the 1970s, when many countries could not even grow enough food to meet their own needs, the lesson was being learned and increased attention was then given to rural development programmes and poverty-focused strategies, which stressed the need to redistribute the benefits of growth.

In the second place, the emphasis placed on weakening traditional authority and behavioural patterns proved socially disruptive in some instances. This was because it not only denied what was often a rich cultural heritage that could be harnessed to the process of change, but it also ignored the fact that legitimacy lay at the base, rather than the apex, of the political system. Many new states, including Zambia and Botswana, which soon after independence stripped the traditional authorities of most of their formal powers, have looked to these authorities subsequently for assistance in implementing their rural development programmes.

A third criticism of modernisation theory was put forward by Samuel Huntington, who can be regarded as a revisionist within the modernisation school. In a seminal article which first appeared in *World Politics* in 1965, he maintained that 'Most modernizing countries are buying rapid social modernization at the price of political degeneration'; a concept of political development should, he said, be matched by a concept of political decay. As against Myron Weiner and others who argued that political modernisation, social change and political development were intimately related processes of change which tended to go together, Huntington maintained that rapid modernisation led to the weakening of political institutions and that the latter could not sustain the heavy demands placed on them by mass, mobilised and increasingly literate electorates in the post-independence era. In the language of systems theory, inputs could not be matched by outputs. Moreover, a paradox of modernisation was that as the state assumed the trappings of modernity, the scope and intensity of communal conflict increased. In these circumstances, strong political institutions were (said Huntington) essential for stable and eventually democratic government and were a precondition of sustained economic growth. His solution was to strengthen key political institutions and the instruments of control, and to slow down popular mobilisation by increasing the complexity of the socio-political structure, limiting or reducing communications in society, and minimising competition among segments of the élite by, for example, adopting the one-party system of government. (In the second half of the 1960s, as America continued to be troubled by anti-Vietnam War demonstrations and civic disturbances, Huntington, in common with other modernisation theorists, carried his arguments further and attached much greater weight to the maintenance of order and stability than the achievement of democracy; the underdeveloped countries needed strong governments as did America itself.)[18] Huntington was right to stress the importance of institution-building in new states; however, he grossly overestimated the extent of popular political mobilisation and his arguments relating to its politically deleterious effects were of doubtful validity, as Paul Brass showed in his study of the Indian states. Political instability in Africa was to result less from such mobilisation than from conflict between sections of the political élite.[19]

Huntington was also justified in challenging the identification of political development with modernisation since, as he pointed out, the effect of this identification was to limit the concept both in time and space and, thus, to deny the political achievements of fifth-century Athens and the third-century Roman Republic. What he did not do was to extend his own theory of political decay to the economic and social spheres and to point out that economic and social modernisation might also, in certain circumstances, be inimical to social development. Take, for example, urbanisation: this is accepted by Huntington as a social index of modernisation, though its effects might not only be imposing buildings, paved and lighted streets, and a pipe-borne water supply but also overcrowding in insanitary shanty areas and unemployment.

Another criticism of modernisation theory is that it is based on a Western (and predominantly American) outlook and values. 'Historically', writes Eisenstadt,

> political modernisation can be equated with those types of political systems which have developed in Western Europe from the 17th century and have then spread to other

European countries, to America and in the 19th and 20th centuries to Asian and African continents.[20]

It is of course substantially true that the vehicle of modernisation is the state bequeathed by the colonial power; that the ruling élites at independence had mostly been educated in, or by academics drawn from, the metropolitan country; and that the latter remained the dominant trading partner for many years after independence. Inevitably, therefore, Western influences on the new African states were strong. Nevertheless, there is a disturbing arrogance underlying the modernising concept. It involves, as Eisenstadt, La Palombara and others have pointed out, transplanting Western political institutions, emphasising the virtues of stability and democracy, and inculcating Western and non-traditional values. It takes insufficient account of what Edward Shils has called the 'ongoing culture' and assumes too readily that traditional values and patterns of authority (often communal rather than individual in the Western sense) should, or indeed necessarily can, be discarded, when what matters is to harness the best of the old to the service of the new.[21] A major problem for African, and indeed for most Third World leaders is how to adapt selected modernising methods (organised parties, for example, or disciplined and cohesive bureaucracies) to fit a social context very different from that in which these methods were originally devised. This problem is recognised in the work of Fred Riggs, a modernisation theorist who sought to apply some of the insights gained from the study of comparative politics to development administration and founded the 'ecological school'. Riggs stressed the need to look at the administration in the context of a country's entire cultural and social system – an acceptable proposition which is then developed within a complicated theoretical framework. The resultant 'prismatic' model does not easily fit African conditions (Riggs' experience is in Asia), but is, in Donal Cruise O'Brien's opinion, 'perhaps the most successful attempt to conceptualise the problems of political underdevelopment at a general level'. Be that as it may, O'Brien is right to point out that 'Riggs is virtually unknown on the Left', despite the fact that he has given 'serious intellectual substance to Gunder Frank's influential slogan, "the development of underdevelopment" '.[22]

A final and weighty criticism of modernisation theory is that it gives insufficient attention to the socio-economic basis of society: specifically, it says little about social formation, modes of production, and class conflict. This criticism is valid, especially of early exponents of this school. The contrast is sharp between the radical treatment of Nigerian political parties given by Richard L. Sklar in his 1963 volume bearing that title and that by James S. Coleman in his earlier *Nigeria: Background to Nationalism* (both, in their different ways, excellent books). However, later writers who fall within the modernisation school (sometimes, admittedly, uneasily) have not so much neglected socio-economic issues as challenged the Marxist interpretation of them. Thus Cranford Pratt, writing from a democratic socialist perspective, examines the arguments relating to the 'bureaucratic bourgeoisie' in Tanzania put forward by Issa Shivji and John Saul, only to reject them as insufficiently grounded in empirical evidence. Again, Walter Ilchman and Norman Uphoff, the post-behaviouralist authors of *Political Economy of Change*, stress the linkage between political and economic variables in policy-making and draw an analogy from the market-place in presenting what Jonathan Barker has called 'an allocation-support model of politics'. They offer a mild challenge to the modernisation school, without, however, attacking its basic tenets; despite the title of their book, they must be counted as revisionists within that school.[23]

Underdevelopment Theory

Colin Leys has provided a succinct account of the main tenets of underdevelopment theory. The latter is, he writes,

> partly a correction and partly an expansion of Marx's interpretation of history, an extension of his method and central ideas to a problem which, in a world scale, was still in embryo at his death: the failure of the countries of Asia, Africa and Latin America to follow a path of autonomous capitalist development, leading to their 'regeneration' after

they had been brought within the capitalist world economy.[24]

The theory traces the relations between the Third World and the expanding capitalist economy. From the outset the latter benefited at the expense of the former: even where plunder and extortion – euphemistically called 'trade' (thus the slave 'trade') – gave way to exchange, this exchange was conducted on very unequal terms because capitalist 'traders' could reinforce their bargaining position with superior force. Investment, for example, in gold-mining or plantations, followed, sometimes at an early date, and had then to be protected by colonialism. Internal commerce, banking and shipping, and external markets were monopolised by overseas firms. Industrial development, mainly in the form of import substitution, might also take place, especially after political independence was achieved, but on terms very favourable to the foreign companies which, in Leys' words, set up 'highly protected subsidiary factories to manufacture in the periphery what they formerly exported there'.[25] This new manufacturing sector tended to be capital-intensive and dependent on the industrial technology provided by the companies.

Underdevelopment theory traces both the short- and long-term effects of this unequal relationship, which characterises both the colonial and post-colonial (or 'neo-colonial') periods. The surplus of the peripheral countries is extracted for use in the metropolitan countries: the latter manufacture the raw materials (for example, copper, cotton and tobacco) which they have imported at prices determined on the international market and export these manufactured goods at prices determined by themselves. Even when processing does take place in an underdeveloped country, the foreign corporation concerned may find it more profitable to import the raw material needed rather than use domestic supplies, however, plentiful – thus, the Volta Aluminium Company makes little use of local bauxite to fuel the alumina smelter in Ghana. As Leys points out, a second consequence of this unequal relationship was that new relations of production developed in the peripheral countries, 'based on their progressive exposure to, and domination by, capitalism'. New social strata or classes also emerged and were engaged in trade, mining, crop production and other economic activities; since their interests coincided with those of the metropolitan country, the latter granted political independence in the knowledge that these 'comprador elements', who came to acquire a large measure of political power in the new states, could maintain the existing patterns of trade and industrial dependency. The bulk of the surplus therefore continued to be extracted for use in the metropolitan countries, which enjoyed a monopoly in industrial technology as well as in international commodity markets. The demands of the puppet class (sometimes called the 'bureaucratic bourgeoisie') were satisfied by importing manufactured goods and the peripheral countries remained substantially producers of primary commodities for export. The result, Professor Leys notes, was that 'The economies of the periphery acquired their well-known "external orientation", with very weak links between the different domestic sectors, and very strong links between the primary-producing sectors and overseas markets and suppliers.'[26]

Among the merits of underdevelopment theory are that it offers a rational explanation of the continuing predicament of underdevelopment; moreover, by stressing the importance of setting the politics of new states in their socio-economic context, it has been better able than (say) structural-functionalism to capture the dynamics of the political process. However, the underdevelopment school can also be challenged on a number of grounds.

First, underdevelopment theory has often been applied uncritically, without sufficient recognition of the fact that Third World countries cover many different stages and forms of development. Some of its exponents have asserted a position somewhat crudely, without supporting evidence. In this category can be placed Issa Shivji's argument that Tanzania's Arusha Declaration of 1967, with its accompanying nationalisation programme, was not 'a product of nationalist and socialist concerns', but merely 'a selfish, class-motivated intervention manipulated into being by the bureaucratic bourgeoisie', which was out to promote its own interests and protect the interests of international capitalism with which this bourgeoisie was closely linked. Again, Timothy Shaw has drawn upon dependency theory to argue that Zambia's bureaucratic bourgeoisie has been so bent on maintaining its own dominance, as the lackey of foreign companies, that the Zambian government has been lukewarm in its support of liberation movements in Southern Africa.[27] No empirical evidence is advanced to support this statement; what can be said, and empirically validated, is that Zambia has sometimes backed the 'wrong' liberation movement – 'wrong' in the sense that, in Angola as in Zimbabwe, it has lacked popular support. In fairness to Shaw, it must be conceded that, if viewed from another angle, the Angola and Zimbabwe cases can be used to justify his contentions to the extent that Zambia in the end committed itself to the least radical (and most 'dependency'-inclined) of the alternatives.

A second criticism is that references to the bureaucratic bourgeoisie, as the pivotal comprador element in society, tend to underestimate the nationalism of that class. Nationalism is a deep-rooted sentiment, not to be sacrificed for a mess of pottage so readily as underdevelopment theorists suggest. Richard L. Sklar, himself a radical scholar of distinction, says of the national bourgeoisie that it 'yields to no group or class in the intensity of its nationalism'.[28] It was the nationalist sentiment to which Sklar refers that led the Zambian government in 1969–70 to take majority control of the copper mines. 'Nationalisation' was not at the time perceived by the mining companies – the Anglo-American Corporation and the Roan Selection Trust – to be in their own best interests, and they were strongly opposed to this unexpected move. However, they were quick to accommodate themselves to the new situation and, indeed, were able to do well out of it through the arrangements for compensation and management and sales contracts.

A third criticism is put forward by Bill Warren in *Imperialism: Pioneer of Capitalism*, where he argues that capitalism can, and does, perform a progressive function on the periphery by developing productive forces and can thus serve as a bridge to socialism. Indeed, the point that despite imperialism, a significant degree of capitalist development could occur, and a bourgeoisie emerge, in peripheral countries is conceded by Colin Leys writing in *The Socialist Register, 1978*, following a short return visit to Kenya in 1977 and after studying the evidence assembled by Michael P. Cowen in a number of unpublished papers and by Nicola Swainson in her London University doctoral thesis on corporate capitalism in Kenya (published by Heinemann in 1980).[29] Thus, those scholars who are taking part in this (ongoing) debate on Africa, with Rafael Kaplinski and others challenging Leys' revised view, are now addressing themselves to the same issues and, in some cases, are adopting essentially the same perspective as was adopted earlier by writers such as Cardoso working on Latin America.[30]

Further criticism of underdevelopment theory is offered by Goran Hyden in his study *Beyond Ujamaa in Tanzania*. Dr Hyden taxes its exponents with exaggerating the extent of capitalist penetration of the rural areas of colonial Africa and with failing to realise that pre-modern social formations still hold capitalism at bay in the independent state. Thus, it follows that those with power are not necessarily those in control of the state but those who remain outside its control – the 'uncaptured' peasantry, who are linked in an 'economy of affection' and who, rather than the international system, are to blame for underdevelopment in Africa. Though Hyden may be guilty of generalising on the basis of limited (Tanzanian) experience, his arguments point the way to further criticism of underdevelopment theory, namely that, because of its emphasis on class, it tends to neglect cultural factors as determinants of political behaviour. As Crawford Young, drawing upon a wealth of illustrative material from various parts of the Third World, has pointed out, class and cultural factors are not necessarily incompatible in this respect.[31]

Other criticisms of underdevelopment theory may be stated briefly. While the theory is, almost by definition, anti-Western, it fails to differentiate between the different attitudes of the Western powers; moreover, it is over-generous in its interpretation of the motives of leading socialist countries, such as the Soviet Union. Finally, the theory looks at the effect of international capitalism on Third World countries but, as Leys has pointed out, says less about the struggle against it.

In view of the substantial revisions of modernisation and underdevelopment theories made from within each school, the original theories no longer have much utility. From the outset, comments John Lonsdale, there was 'too much theory chasing too little empirical data': 'The behavioural circularities of modernization theory . . . were as difficult to *use* as have been, more recently, the market determinisms of underdevelopment theory – which perhaps explains their incandescent brevities of life.'[32] Certainly, there has been some convergence between the two schools in the sense at least that 'modernisers' now pay more attention to socio-economic dynamics than they did and underdevelopment theorists are less neglectful than formerly of cultural factors. Although the underdevelopment school falls broadly within the Marxist tradition of scholarship, it has (as the quotations from Sklar reveal) been subjected to very sharp criticism by Marxist writers. The result has been that the external dependency arguments, which dominated the English-speaking debate, have been refined and that increased attention has been given to relations of production and power-holding within the post-colonial state. In round terms, this represents a shift from neo-Marxism back to Marxism. We summarise some of the main developments, concentrating on a number of controversial propositions which have been advanced by Marxist scholars in recent years and which bear directly on the politics of African states.

Immanuel Wallerstein has maintained that socialist transition in backward, peripheral countries can only take place when the world capitalist system collapses. From a Marxist perspective, this is a gloomy prognosis and one which would render futile attempts at socialist construction in states such as Angola and Mozambique. Wallerstein's argument is carried further by Callinicos and other authors who adopt what Munslow has characterised as 'the worker spontaneity / internationalist approach' and argue that only after a world-wide revolution has taken place will the conditions exist for a socialist transition. For them, therefore, the solution lies in smashing the world economy – it is not enough just to opt out of it; however, they see little prospect of this happening so long as the revolutionary parties retain their petty-bourgeois leadership.[33]

This view parallels that previously adopted by André Gunder Frank in the Latin American debate. However, the work of Cardoso and others is far more compatible with the earlier Marxist view that capitalism performs a progressive function in peripheral countries and thus facilitates the transition to socialism. This 'capitalist roader' view (as Munslow calls it) has been followed by Susanne Mueller, who writes in favour of 'letting the kulaks run' in Tanzania, and by one side in the 'Kenyan debate' which came to a head in 1980.[34] Barry Munslow, following Bettleheim in his earlier writing, accepts that 'an intermediate phase is necessary to create the conditions for a transition to socialism'; this phase, which is *not* capitalist but is oriented towards socialism, is identified in Angola as a 'revolutionary democratic dictatorship' and in Mozambique as the 'popular democratic phase'. During this interim stage national independence is consolidated, the national movement is transformed into a vanguard-type party, structures of *poder popular* (people's power) are established, and control of the economy is transferred to the workers and peasants. As Munslow argues, and as the empirical material in chapter 8 goes some way to confirm: 'The problems for such a transition are multiple and involve considerations of party, state, class structure and the political economy, both internally and in its relations with the world system.'[35]

From a non-Marxist perspective, the difficulty with the concepts of 'socialist transition' and 'socialist construction' is that they describe what is potentially a never-ending process; 'success requires anywhere from one to several centuries', said Mao. Moreover, it is a process which may involve the concentration of political power in order, Goodison notes, 'to overcome the obstacles to socialism inherited from capitalism'.[36] The danger to socialist thought and practice arises when this concentration of power becomes tyrannical dictatorship and the upholders of liberty are denounced as 'class enemies of the revolution'. In these circumstances, which have prevailed in Sékou Touré's Guinea for much of the post-independence period, it becomes almost meaningless to talk of socialist construction (chapter 8); for ultimately, socialism and authoritarianism are incompatible.

*   *   *

This book takes account of such theoretical considerations as those outlined above, without however being closely tied to any one approach. While it accepts that the exchange between the developed and underdeveloped countries is unequal – a central tenet of underdevelopment theory – it does not concede that Africa's underdevelopment is to be explained exclusively or even primarily in terms of the international capitalist environment. If that was so, the book's focus on the domestic political scene, supplemented by a discussion of inter-African relations (chapter 9), would not be justified. Again, while it recognises the importance of understanding the nature of class domination in Africa, it asserts with Crawford Young that 'it is not necessary to deny cultural pluralism in order to assert class'.[37] The fact that modernisation theorists were right to stress the importance of cultural factors was shown dramatically by the Islamic revolution in Iran and is illustrated at several points in this volume – for example, by the communal resistance to the land and increasingly pro-Amhara policies pursued by Ethiopia's military government (chapter 8; see also chapter 4). The book proceeds on the assumption that while class is often an important determinant of political behaviour, it is not the only determinant. The author is at pains to stress the variety and complexity of the socio-economic process in Africa: thus, in some states identifiable classes have emerged – the middle class in Gabon, Kenya, the Ivory Coast, Nigeria and Zambia, for example – while in others they are only incipient. Again, we believe that in many rural areas of the continent, either because of the limited penetration of capitalism (as Hyden asserts) or because of the breakdown of the market economy in the face of severe economic recession, the peasantry has a poorly developed sense of class consciousness and is preoccupied with meeting immediate family needs and with other local concerns. This phenomenon, which may be temporary and may change when economic conditions improve, need not be surprising – as we shall see, it was what Amilcar Cabral foresaw.[38] In a situation where 'all classes . . . are incompletely formed and poorly organised', as Goodison has recently written of Mozambique, one must conclude either that his statement that 'class struggle is ubiquitous in the construction of socialism' is mistaken or that the state in question (in this case Mozambique) is at a very early stage of the transition to socialism. Dr Munslow subscribes to the latter view and argues that an intermediate phase is necessary to create the conditions for a transition to socialism; the latter is not 'on the immediate agenda' in Angola, Mozambique and 'similar peripheral formations'.[39]

Finally, the author finds persuasive Professor Sklar's argument that in Africa 'class relations, at bottom, are determined by relations of power, not production';[40] this is illustrated by Zambian experience following the post-1968 reforms (chapter 4). Sklar's statement has a further importance: it underlines for this writer the need to study the institutions, including political parties and interest groups, through which power is expressed and to understand why such institutions have tended to be superseded by instruments of control, notably the military and the bureaucracy (chapters 5–7). It would be a fundamental error not to take account of institutional weakness – notably the lack of skilled and highly trained manpower to run an expanded state sector – in explaining the disappointing record of most African states in the post-independence era.

Further Reading

Austin, D., *Politics in Africa* (Manchester University Press, 1978).

Dædalus, vol. iii, no. 2 (Spring 1982): 'Black Africa: A Generation after Independence'.

Goulbourne, H. (ed.), *Politics and State in the Third World* (London: Macmillan, 1979).

Grew, R. (ed.), *Crises of Political Development in Europe and the United States* (Princeton University Press, 1978).

Gutkind, P. C. W., and Wallerstein, I. (eds.), *The Political Economy of Contemporary Africa* (Beverly Hills: Sage, 1976).

Huntington, S. P., *Political Order in Changing Societies* (New Haven: Yale University Press, 1968).

Leys, C., *Underdevelopment in Kenya: The Political Economy of Neo-Colonialism, 1964–1971* (London: Heinemann, 1975).

Limqueco, P., and McFarlane, B. (eds.), *Neo-Marxist Theories of Development* (London: Croom Helm, 1983).

O'Brien, D. B. Cruise, 'Modernisation, Order and the Erosion of the Democratic Ideal', *Journal of Development Studies*, vol. 8, no. 4 (July 1972).

Rosberg, C. G., and Jackson, R. H., *Personal Rule in Black Africa: Prince, Autocrat, Prophet, Tyrant* (Berkeley: University of California Press, 1982).

Swainson, N., *The Development of Corporate Capitalism in Kenya, 1918–1977* (London: Heinemann, 1980).

Warren, B., *Imperialism: Pioneer of Capitalism* (London: Verso, 1980).

2

Colonialism and the Colonial Impact

The pre-colonial history of Africa has been pieced together from archaeological findings, oral tradition, and the records of Arab and other alien chroniclers, such as Ibn Battuta, who travelled widely in the Muslim world in the fourteenth century. A good deal is now known, for example, of the richness of the Egyptian civilisation of the pre-Christian era, of the medieval empires of the Western Sudan – Ghana, Mali and Songhai – and of the forest kingdoms which subsequently emerged in West Africa. Some of these kingdoms extended at the height of their power over a wide area and were underpinned by a centralised bureaucracy. Such was Ashanti, which was founded at the end of the seventeenth century, but about whose internal organisation little was known until Thomas Bowdich and Joseph Dupuis visited Kumasi, the Ashanti capital, in the first quarter of the nineteenth century. Benin (in present-day Nigeria) was another powerful kingdom, which, according to oral tradition, had been founded by immigrants from Ife some three centuries before the coming of the Portuguese; possibly these immigrants brought with them the technique of casting in bronze which in Benin, as in Ife, resulted in sculpture of world renown. The capital city seemed to a Dutch visitor to be comparable in many ways with Amsterdam. Writing in 1602, he observed of Benin City:

> The town seemeth to be very great; when you enter into it, you go into a great broad street, not paved, which seems to be seven or eight times broader than the Warmoes street in

Amsterdam; which goeth right out and never crooks . . .; it is thought that that street is a mile long [a Dutch mile, equal to about four English miles] besides the suburbs . . . When you are in the great street aforesaid, you see many great streets on the sides thereof, which also go right forth . . . The houses in this town stand in good order, one close and even with the other, as the houses in Holland stand . . .

The King's Court is very great, within it having many great four-square plains, which round about them have galleries, wherein there is always watch kept. I was so far within the Court that I passed over four such great plains, and wherever I looked, still I saw gates upon gates to go into other places . . .[1]

While there is no doubt that many such states existed in pre-colonial Africa – in the Sudan, deep in the West African forest, and in Southern Africa, for example – they were not typical of pre-colonial Africa as a whole. Many Africans lived in stateless societies, organised around the family, kinship group and clan, though this did not necessarily mean that they were more 'backward'. John Iliffe has pointed out that Tanganyika was not composed of tribes; indeed, at least in parts of Eastern and Central Africa, it can be argued that the unit of organisation called the 'tribe' was largely a European invention and that the reality was vastly more complex. Moreover, Africa was a continent on the move in the sense that migration from one area to another was frequent, as a consequence of war, disease, drought, and economic need. Almost everywhere, the African was engaged in a constant struggle with a harsh environment.[2]

European contact with Africa – through missionaries, traders and explorers – long preceded the establishment of European rule. Thus, the Portuguese began to trade to the west coast in the fifteenth century and, in a vain bid to exclude other European seafarers – the Dutch, the Brandenburgers, the Danes, the British and the French – established a number of coastal forts from which they conducted a profitable trade in gold and ivory and, especially from the seventeenth century, in slaves. They also traded southwards to Angola, which (in the words of Roland Oliver and John Fage) was reduced by the slave trade to 'a howling wilderness', rounded the Cape of

Good Hope, sailed up the east coast, where they encountered fierce Arab competition, and so to India.

Until the nineteenth century, Portuguese and other European traders dealt almost exclusively with African middle-men in their coastal stations; nevertheless, they succeeded in diverting African trade away from the trans-Saharan route, which linked Africa with the Maghreb, and thus increased the power and wealth of the coastal states at the expense of the states in the Western Sudan. This pattern of coastal trading began to change, however, when the slave trade was supplanted by legitimate commerce and the interior of the continent was gradually penetrated by explorers and missionaries, culminating in the period of European empire building.

In most of the continent the establishment of colonies did not take place until the last quarter of the nineteenth century; before that time, only a relatively small part of Black Africa was under European rule. European colonisation of West Africa long preceded that of East Africa, but by 1875 only the 'colony' areas of Sierra Leone and the Gold Coast and the areas adjacent to Bathurst and Lagos were ruled by Britain, while France was firmly established only in Senegal. The partition of Africa was precipitated by the ambition of King Leopold II of the Belgians to absorb the whole of the Congo basin into a personal empire and the annexation by Germany, in 1883–5, of the Cameroons, East Africa, South-West Africa, and Togoland, thereby projecting the rivalry of the European powers into Africa. The Berlin conference of 1884–5, by recognising the existence of a 'Congo Free State', was the signal for France and Britain to extend their spheres of influence, preliminary to creating new colonies and protectorates. The boundaries between one colony and another were often drawn arbitrarily, with scant regard for traditional allegiance; thus, the Bakongo were split between the French Congo, the Belgian Congo and Angola.

What prompted this insatiable desire on the part of the various European powers – Portugal and Belgium, Britain and France, Germany, Italy and Spain – to establish colonies in Africa? Was it part of a civilising mission, as the Portuguese claimed? Brett observes, for example, that the colonialists

generally saw themselves 'as the advance guard of a civilization
with a universal message equally applicable to the whole of the
underdeveloped world'.[3] Was it for purposes of trade, conducted for the mutual benefit of coloniser and colonised? Was it
for economic gain and exploitation, or were strategic considerations paramount? The answer to such questions depends
on many factors, and not least the analyst's own ideological
perspective.

In West Africa, in the latter part of the nineteenth century,
British missionaries and traders pressurised their home
governments to extend the colonial boundaries inland as a
means of protecting their interests and gains against French
and German competition. At first, British ministers held back,
being doubtful whether the economic gains of empire in this
region would compensate them for the cost of maintaining it.
They also took account of strategic considerations. Indeed, in
their book *Africa and the Victorians*, Ronald Robinson and John
Gallagher argue that such considerations were uppermost in
Britain's attitude to tropical Africa:

> Nothing is more striking about the selection of British claims
> in tropical Africa between 1882 and 1895 than the emphasis
> on the east and the comparative indifference to the west. The
> British chose to concentrate on the Nile and its approaches.
> Their over-riding concern was not with tropical Africa as
> such but with security in the Mediterranean and the Orient.
> To this supreme purpose, the reserving of so much of tropical
> Africa had been largely incidental. The concentration on
> east Africa shows the preoccupation with supreme strategic
> interests. The neglect of west African claims on the other
> hand, shows a relative indifference to tropical African
> commercial gains.

The authors conclude that the late-Victorians 'preferred to
make the empire safer in poorer east Africa than to make it
wealthier in the richer West'. It was left to Joseph Chamberlain, who became Colonial Secretary in 1895, to break with this
tradition and to try 'to make a business of the tropical African
fields which others had staked out mainly with an eye to
security'. He pressed the need for state enterprise in building

roads, railways and harbours and sought new opportunities for private enterprise and new markets for British industry. In August 1895 he told a West African Railways' deputation that progress and prosperity in Britain depended upon developing the empire.[4]

On another view, colonies were established to prolong the life of moribund European capitalism; as a French saying has it: 'the colonies have been created for the metropole by the metropole'.[5] While this view does not sufficiently encapsulate the complex motives which sometimes underlay the creation of colonies, there is no doubt that the European powers were anxious to secure easy access to the raw materials needed to fuel the manufacturing industries established following the industrial revolution and to obtain a protected market for their manufactured goods. Thus, the cotton grown by African (and Asian) peasant farmers was fed into the Lancashire textile mills, via the flourishing port of Liverpool, and the cloth which the mills produced was exported back to Africa by European trading companies. However, while the price which the producer received for his cotton fluctuated widely, and often downwards, the price which he had to pay for imported cloth constantly increased. The unequal nature of this exchange furnished for the late Walter Rodney an example (one out of many) of colonial exploitation. Colonialism, he believed, contributed to the capitalist development of Europe, while leaving Africa underdeveloped:

> Colonialism was not merely a system of exploitation, but one whose essential purpose was to repatriate the profits to the so-called 'mother country'. From an African viewpoint, that amounted to consistent expatriation of surplus produced by African labour out of African resources. It meant the development of Europe as part of the same dialectical process in which Africa was underdeveloped.[6]

That colonialism had many negative aspects is not in question. It is certainly not easy to sustain Chamberlain's argument that colonial development and metropolitan prosperity went hand in hand in view of the unequal nature of the relationship between the two sides. But it can also be argued, against

Rodney, that colonialism had also certain beneficial effects: for example, in checking (if never entirely eliminating) inter-communal fighting and establishing a framework of territorial unity out of disparate social elements; in creating an essential infrastructure of railways, roads and harbours; in providing schools, churches and hospitals; in introducing new food plants, such as cassava, maize and sweet potato (imported by the Portuguese from South America); and in controlling disease among cattle through the use of veterinary skills. Whatever assessment is made of colonialism and its impact on Africa, it is important to remember that many different colonial powers were involved. These powers differed, often widely, in their specific policies and overall approach to colonial development.

Policies of the powers

Following the Berlin conference of 1884–5, French troops sought to establish effective political control over the hinterland in West and Equatorial Africa. Each of the new colonies thus established – there were eventually eight dependencies in Afrique Occidentale Française (AOF) and four in Afrique Equatoriale Française (AEF) – had its own governor and budget and, from 1946, its own elected assembly. The governors were subject to the general direction and authority of a governor-general (AOF headquarters were in Dakar and those for AEF in Brazzaville), who controlled a general budget and was advised by a 'grand council', made up of elected territorial representatives. Ultimate control was vested in the Minister for Colonies in Paris.[7]

Each colony was divided for administrative purposes into *cercles*. A *cercle* was administered by a political officer, the *commandant de cercle*, and was in most cases divided into sub-divisions, each headed by a *chef de subdivision* (also a political officer). In what amounted substantially to a system of direct rule, traditional rulers were often replaced by 'straw chiefs' – frequently old soldiers and retired government clerks – who constituted the bottom tiers in the administrative hierarchy (*chefs de canton* and *chefs de village*) and served as agents of the administration. The system was more indirect where relatively strong traditional rulers were well established, as the Mossi chiefs were in Upper Volta and the Fulani Emirs in the northern provinces of the Cameroons (a French-administered trust territory which, like Togoland, did not belong to AOF), though in certain cases, as in Guinea's Fouta Djalon, the French deliberately broke up the old political units. It was, overall, a highly centralised system, characterised by parallel administrative structures in each territory and staffed by a remarkably mobile public service, which ruled the vast French African territories with the aid of 'chiefs'.

Until the collapse of the Vichy regime and the Brazzaville conference of 1944, the French system of administration was also strongly paternalist: the mass of Africans were French subjects, not citizens, and were exposed to *indigénat* (a form of summary administrative justice) and *travail forcée* (forced labour). Following the Brazzaville conference, French policy moved increasingly from paternalism to what Kenneth Robinson has called a policy of identity – 'the policy seeking in principle to establish in the colonial country institutions identical with those at home'. (Some writers prefer to distinguish between policies of 'assimilation' and 'association'. Michael Crowder points out that the administration retained assimilationist characteristics even after assimilation had ceased to be official policy. French political officers still believed in France's civilising mission and established more amicable relationships than their British counterparts with educated Africans – the latter, after all, had been taught in French, in schools based on the French pattern).

Africans, as French citizens, were no longer subject to the *indigénat* or to compulsory labour; they were granted the right of free association and meeting; they could serve, in each territory, on local government organs called *conseils généraux* (later renamed *assemblées territoriales*); and they were allowed to send representatives to the French National Assembly and the Council of the Republic in Paris. As Thomas Hodgkin has pointed out, 'the pull of the metropolitan axis' in the post-war period was so strong that African political parties and trade unions tended either to be linked with, or to function within the orbit of metropolitan parties and unions, and nationalism lost some of its force amidst the welter of other ideas to which French theorising gave rise.[8] For at least ten years after 1945 the main thrust of most nationalist activity was to secure equal rights for Africans as citizens of an 'indivisible' Fourth Republic. But, ultimately, equality was not enough. Though the *loi cadre* reforms of 1956, which conferred territorial autonomy, constituted on France's part a holding operation without any commitment as to the final outcome and may actually have been designed to prevent independence, they set in motion a train of events which resulted in the independence of Guinea in 1958 (by a 'No' vote in the constitutional referendum in September of that year) and of the other territories in French West and Equatorial Africa in 1960, following individual negotiations with France.

British colonial policy was more pragmatic than the French and often seemed to be formulated as a reaction to extraneous events, such as the post-1945 challenge of African nationalism. British rule was also less centralised. Colonial governors were allowed considerable discretion, within the framework of policy laid down by the Colonial Office in London, in initiating policy deemed suitable for their individual territories. Indeed, this discretion extended to senior officers within a colony's administrative hierarchy. Thus, the proposal in the early 1930s to restore the Ashanti Confederacy was put forward initially not by the Gold Coast Governor, who was considering the case for amalgamating the administration of the Colony and Ashanti in the interest of economy, but by the Chief Commissioner of Ashanti.[9]

Restoration took place (in 1935) to further indirect rule, which from the 1920s was a cornerstone of British colonial policy and, together with the concept of preparation, gave it a certain theoretical basis. The chief architect of indirect rule was Lord Lugard, whose book *The Dual Mandate in British Tropical Africa* appeared in 1922. This approach entailed the British administration ruling through indigenous political institutions – chiefs and their councils, who were constituted into native authorities and supported by native courts and, eventually, by native treasuries. The system worked best in areas where chieftaincy was strongly entrenched; Northern Nigeria served as the model and the northern Emirs were subject to minimal interference by British administrative officers. Indirect rule proved least satisfactory in areas where traditional institutions were weak or non-existent and therefore depended, as in south-eastern Nigeria and parts of the Northern Territories of the Gold Coast, on government-created chiefs; closer administrative supervision was exercised over these areas. The experience was widespread – in the Ivory Coast and certain other parts of French Africa, as well as in British Africa – that a chief who was not selected according to customary procedures or was elevated to a status to which he was not entitled by tradition, lacked legitimacy and had difficulty in securing the respect and co-operation of his people. In the Gold Coast in the early 1930s this consideration reinforced the case for restoring the Ashanti Confederacy.

While indirect rule, at its best, was a worthwhile exercise in local self-government and resulted in the preservation of certain wholesome African traditions and customs that might otherwise have been lost, it also had negative consequences. It exacerbated existing communal differences (based on ethnicity, language or geographical region) to such an extent in some territories, for example Nigeria, as to warrant the designation of 'divide and rule'. These communal sentiments were sometimes fanned by the chiefs themselves: thus, in the Ashanti region of the Gold Coast, the Asantehene and the great majority of Ashanti chiefs gave open backing to the National Liberation Movement (NLM) – a movement of revolt directed against the CPP government, on the main ground that it was discriminating unfairly against Ashanti interests. The strength of such sentiments made it necessary to incorporate power-sharing arrangements into the independence constitutions of several states – a federal constitution was retained in Nigeria (its adoption in 1954 was the inevitable sequel of the Richards Constitution of 1946), federal elements were incorporated into the constitutions of Ghana, Kenya and Uganda, and Barotseland secured a privileged position for itself in Zambia under the 1964 agreement. Again, in the post-1945 period, the effect of indirect rule was often to drive a wedge between chiefs and those of their people who joined mass-based political parties, which castigated the chiefs as 'government stooges'. (Resentment of chiefs in French Africa was even stronger and more widespread than in British Africa). Moreover, indirect rule made a nonsense of the concept of preparation which, at least in principle, was the second pillar of British colonial policy in non-settler Africa.

This concept, according to which the territories ruled by Britain were held in trust until their people could stand on their own feet, involved the early creation of legislative and executive councils, and a steady expansion in the local composition of these bodies. However, it was not until 1946 that the legislative councils of the Gold Coast and Nigeria contained a majority of African representatives and even then the writ of the Gold Coast legislative council did not extend to the Northern Territories. This change came in 1951, when also the executive councils of both countries finally secured unofficial majorities. The attempt to marry the principles of indirect rule and crown colony government through the inclusion in the legislature, and subsequently in the executive, of representatives of the traditional councils of chiefs came to nothing when, in the 1950s, it was decided to allow political parties to compete in national elections held under an expanded franchise. Thus, it can be argued that the British had trained the wrong people; certainly, as Bernard Schaffer has pointed out, meaningful preparation for independence began 'very late indeed' and was 'all along rivalled and hindered by other values, which were predominantly bureaucratic'.[10] Preparation was seriously distorted in areas of substantial white settlement such as Kenya, Northern Rhodesia and above all Southern Rhodesia. Nevertheless, it remains true that Britain did more to prepare her colonies for independence than any other European power; the contrast with Belgium and Portugal is sharp.

The Congo Free State, created in 1885 as the personal fief of King Leopold II, became a Belgian colony in 1908. Belgian rule was extremely centralised – on Leopoldville and Brussels, where policy was formulated by the Minister of the Colonies, advised by a Colonial Council. It was a strongly paternalist system of rule, resting on three main pillars – the state, the Roman Catholic Church and big business, such as Union Minière du Haut-Katanga. Its object was to create a materially prosperous and contented people, educated (mainly by missions – Protestant as well as Catholic) to the primary level, and subject to close European supervision. It rested on the conviction that social and political change could be arrested and Belgian middle-class values inculcated. The attempt failed and in the post-Second World War period Congolese évolués came increasingly to resent restrictions on their civil liberty – political parties, independent African trade unions, and a free press were proscribed, and the social status of Africans was subordinate to that of Europeans. The latter, too, enjoyed few political rights, and executive power remained firmly in the hands of the Administration.[11]

Portugal, Africa's oldest colonial power, conceived itself as a small nation in Europe, but a great nation in the world: she was the hub of a pan-Lusitanian community, geographically scattered over the globe, but held together by the bonds of Portuguese culture. According to this image, Portugal's overseas possessions were not colonies, but overseas provinces, indissolubly linked with metropolitan Portugal and forming an integrated whole. Portugal claimed to be undertaking in Africa a non-racial, Christian civilising mission, but in fact her colonies (Angola, Mozambique, Guinea-Bissau, Cape Verde, São Tomé and Principé) were subject to long years of neglect. In part, this neglect resulted from the poor state of Portugal's own economy – the industrial revolution in Europe passed her by – and, as far as Mozambique was concerned, from the collapse of the spice trade with India in the eighteenth century. But neglect it was: according to official government statistics, the illiteracy rate in 1959, after some 500 years of Portuguese presence, was 97.8 per cent in Mozambique, 96.97 per cent in Angola, 98.85 per cent in Guinea and 78.5 per cent in Cape Verde. Moreover, economic exploitation and racial discrimination were cardinal features of Portuguese colonial rule.[12]

Economic exploitation on a more systematic scale took place in the 1930s following the introduction in Portugal of the corporatist New State (*Estado Novo*), and was accompanied by a significant increase in forced crop cultivation, notably of cotton, and forced labour. In the post-war period, and especially after the outbreak of the African colonial wars in 1961, Portugal opened up both the metropole and the colonies to foreign investment. The Portuguese economy received a much-needed boost, but Portugal, still an underdeveloped country, could only make her manufactured goods competitive in the European market if she retained a cheap supply of raw materials. For this she looked to her colonies, which also imported more than a third of her cotton manufactures, served as a refuge for unemployed Portuguese peasants, and acted as a major source of foreign exchange. Throughout the period of colonial rule and up to the *coup d'état* in 1974, these socio-economic policies were worked out within a framework of rule that, in Portugal as in the colonies, was both highly authoritarian and subject to tight bureaucratic control.[13]

Not only did the various European powers with colonies in Africa pursue different policies, but the colonial period as a whole can be divided, from an economic and social standpoint, into three overlapping phases: the period from the establishment of colonies in the 1880s and 1890s until the First World War; the inter-war period; and the period from the Second World War to independence.[14] It should be emphasised, however, that this periodisation is inexact and more relevant to France and Britain than the other European powers. For Portugal, which is substantially a case apart, Dr Munslow has suggested a different periodisation: the period to 1926, when the colonies were neglected and left to foreign capital to exploit; 1926–50, when 'nationalist' economic policies were pursued, the colonies were more systematically exploited and intensively 'labour-repressive' policies were adopted; 1950–60, when Portugal was again opened up to foreign capital and industrial production increased while remaining dependent on the supply of cheap cotton from the colonies; and 1960–74, a period mainly characterised by the impact of the nationalist struggle in the colonies leading to the encouragement of foreign investment. Throughout, colonial rule was authoritarian and even the tiny number of *assimilados* was denied any meaningful outlets for political expression. Munslow argues, with some force, that Portugal took no steps to decolonise because, unlike the other European powers, she was 'unable to neocolonise': that is Portugal, an economically backward country, could not be certain that she could exploit her ex-colonies economically after granting them political independence.[15]

For more than thirty years, after the intense diplomatic activity associated with 'the scramble for Africa', the colonial powers largely neglected their territories. Colonies were expected to be economically self-supporting and were ruled by a handful of men, often with experience as army officers; thus, in Ronald Robinson's memorable description, the British colonial empire was a 'gimcrack effort run by two men and a dog'.[16] Local resistance was overcome, a national administration was established, and inter-communal warfare was prohibited. Taxation was also imposed, railway tracks were laid down both for security and commercial purposes, and cash crops were introduced, eventually to the serious detriment of food production. In territories where Europeans were looking for land and minerals, as in Southern and Northern Rhodesia, the Belgian Congo, Kenya, Angola and Mozambique, African land was alienated – most extensively to the south of the Zambezi river. In these territories Africans were employed as wage-labourers on settler farms and by plantation and mining companies; they were also, especially north of the Zambezi, allowed to grow cash crops, but only to the extent that these did not prejudice the interests of European agriculture. Elsewhere – that is where, as in most of West Africa, Europeans sought to trade and govern rather than to settle – Africans were actively encouraged to grow cash crops, on communally-owned land, for the European market. They were everywhere subject to compulsory labour on which, in one form or another, all the colonial powers relied for porterage and the construction and maintenance of roads, railways and government stations.[17] (The detested *travail forcée* was a feature of the French African scene until the Brazzaville reforms of 1944 and, under the euphemistic title of 'contract labour', of Portuguese Africa until the 1960s and beyond.) Direct governmental activity was minimal and most social development, in the sphere of education for example, was the result of missionary effort.

The inter-war period began with the break-up of Germany's African empire and its partition, under League of Nations' mandate, between Britain and France, Belgium and South Africa. This period was the high water-mark of colonial rule. Civil administrations were served by an increased, though still fluctuating, number of colonial officials, with the district administrative officer as the lynch-pin of the system. The functions of colonial governments were still extremely limited;

medical, educational, agricultural and veterinary services were improved, but remained grossly inadequate for the needs of the bulk of the African (as distinct from the European) population. Roads and harbours were built, but further expansion of the public works programme, as of other forms of development, was curtailed by the world-wide economic depression of 1929–31. In the 1930s and during the subsequent war years neither colonial governments nor Christian missions had the resources to extend throughout the country the educational, medical and other services which they had already provided in areas adjacent to the national capital – for example, in the 'Colony' areas of Ghana and Sierra Leone and the southern part of Nigeria. African peasant proprietors stepped up their supply of produce for the world market and purchased imported goods, thus further linking the African economies to the international environment. In some instances, they adopted the tactic of holding up their produce when the price offered by the buyers fell below the costs of production. This happened in the Gold Coast, where farmers in the Colony and Ashanti areas staged cocoa hold-ups in 1931 and 1937 in an attempt to force the price upwards; they were convinced, with justification, that 'pooling' arrangements among the European companies had artifically depressed the cocoa price. No comparable action was taken in Nigeria, where cocoa played a lesser part in the total economy, but the device of the hold-up was not unknown in that country also. In Senegal, what Donal Cruise O'Brien calls 'peanut-running' – the practice whereby peasants smuggled their produce across the border into the Gambia in order to secure a higher price – had 'a long history', though it only reached its peak in the post-independence period.[18]

European investment (both private investment and public loans) went especially to territories whose economies were based on mining, above all to South Africa, the Rhodesias and the Belgian Congo. Multinational companies began to loom large on the African scene – for example, the South African-based Anglo-American Corporation and the American-controlled Rhodesian Selection Trust (later renamed Roan Selection Trust) in Northern Rhodesia and, through its subsidiary Union Minière du Haut-Katanga, the Société

Générale in the Belgian Congo. There was also limited investment in plantation agriculture – tea in Nyasaland and Kenya, for example – but in general, as Oliver and Fage point out, European investors found it 'more profitable to support companies engaged primarily in buying and selling to African producers, rather than those which themselves engaged in agricultural production'.[19] Among such trading companies were the French-controlled Compagnie Française de l'Afrique Occidentale (CFAO) and Société Commerciale de l'Ouest Africain (SCOA) and the British-controlled United Africa Company (UAC), which was itself a subsidiary of Unilever, the Anglo–Dutch monopoly. These companies had a wide range of interests in Africa and made handsome profits for their European shareholders.

Turning to the third phase, the demand for raw materials during the Second World War and the shortages of foodstuffs and many raw materials in the post-war period brought home to the European powers the great economic value of their colonies. Copper exports from Northern Rhodesia and the Belgian Congo increased enormously, while certain cash crops, including Gold Coast cocoa and Tanganyikan sisal, commanded high prices. Even after purchasing European manufactured goods out of their earnings, many of the richer colonies were left with substantial credit balances in London and the other European capitals (thus easing the credit position of the European powers), and in the 1950s they were therefore able to embark on what then seemed ambitious development schemes. An increased number of functional specialists – in agriculture, education, health and public works – now served at district level, though in most colonies only a small number of them were African.[20]

On the political front mounting discontent outpaced the significant constitutional advance conceded in a number of colonies – the grant of representative government, for example, to the Gold Coast and Nigeria in 1946. Ex-servicemen returning from the war found jobs difficult to obtain and goods as scarce as they were costly. Together with the young men educated to the primary-school level in the rapid educational expansion which had taken place in the inter-war period and who were now either unemployed or under-employed, they became fodder for the new nationalist movements that were springing up in various parts of the continent – in French North and British West Africa, closely followed by British East and Central Africa. The colonial powers seemed oblivious to this growing ferment of unrest and to the inherent contradiction between empire and liberal democracy, in defence of which the Second World War had been fought (though not by neutral Portugal). Even in the case of the Gold Coast – the pacemaker in tropical Africa – Britain gave no serious thought to preparing the country for self-government before the 1948 riots. However, these riots, coupled with pressure from the United Nations and the United States, as well as liberal elements at home, led Britain to quicken the process of decolonisation. For successive British governments, Conservative as well as Labour, the issue in dispute throughout British Africa was not the final end, namely independence, but the timetable by which that end should be achieved. In colonies such as the Gold Coast, Nigeria and Sierra Leone such delay as occurred in the achievement of self-rule in the 1950s was caused, not by British reluctance to transfer power, but by internal communal conflict. The only seriously disputed areas were those where it was not clear who should receive the transfer of power, notably the areas of white settlement in East and Central Africa. In November 1965 the white minority in Rhodesia tried to resolve this issue by declaring their independence unilaterally and, in doing so, precipitated a protracted liberation struggle.

The French faced the dilemma of how to reconcile liberty and empire by stressing equality – the equal treatment of all citizens regardless of origin and colour, including representation at Paris for *départments* like Algeria and overseas territories such as Senegal and the Ivory Coast, Chad and Gabon. When that failed – and the *loi cadre* reforms of 1956 gave legal recognition to that failure – the French then moved in the direction of the British, hesitating only in Algeria which, like Rhodesia, was an area of substantial white settlement. Eventually, the Belgians followed suit: in 1960 they catapulted the Congo to independence in a brief six months, initially with disastrous consequences.

The alternative course to granting decolonisation would have been to attempt to hold the nationalist forces in check through a long process of repression – as the Dutch had tried unsuccessfully to do in the Dutch East Indies. This option, which would have been intolerable to British, Belgian and (following the reverses in Indo-China and the experience in Algeria) French public opinion, was chosen by autocratically ruled Portugal, thus giving rise to a bitter and protracted war of liberation in her African colonies.

The Colonial Legacy

Since Africa was subject to rule by several different colonial powers, the colonial legacy has varied from one part of the continent to another. Generalising, therefore, one can say in the first place that the economies (and the communication networks) of the African states were largely developed in accordance with the needs of the colonial power. Primary products – whether cash crops such as cocoa and coffee or minerals such as copper and bauxite – were exported to European markets in their raw state; in return, the colony imported manufactured goods from abroad, mainly from the 'mother country'. Purchasing and distribution were handled by large European companies, such as the UAC, until at least the terminal phase of colonial rule, when some colonies established marketing boards in an attempt to break the European trading monopoly and to pay the farmer a stable price. The price of African produce on the world market fluctuated widely, sometimes falling dramatically, but the price of manufactured goods was subject to the inflationary pressures of the European domestic economies and these were acute in the immediate post-1945 period.[21] Though political independence was achieved by most African countries in (or about) 1960, economic dependency remained, giving rise to charges, as formulated by Kwame Nkrumah of Ghana for example, of neo-colonialism. A corollary of the monopoly long exercised by the large European companies was that the great majority of indigenous (African) entrepreneurs had scope only at the lowest levels of business activity – private entrepreneurial activity was very extensive at the level of the petty trader. While some Africans did prosper – in Nigeria, for example, Dr Nnamdi Azikiwe established his

'Zik' group of newspapers – few Africans at this time possessed managerial skills and the commercial banks were reluctant to grant Africans credit facilities. The effect was to retard the pre-independence growth of an African middle-class and to vest the leadership of most nationalist movements and parties in the hands of petty-bourgeois elements such as teachers, clerks, storekeepers, and small-scale businessmen and traders. A further effect was to deprive the post-independence state of the experienced manpower required to run the large number of public enterprises which, in the absence of African private business on any large scale, were almost everywhere established.

Secondly, the introduction of cash-crop farming had a profound impact on the rural scene; it led to the emergence of peasant societies integrated into the world economy. Examples of such societies in Tanganyika were the Chagga and Haya. However, there were also in Tanganyika (as in many other countries) intermediate regions which provided migrant labour – in Tanganyika's case, for the European and Indian-owned sisal plantations in the eastern part of the country. Thus, we can observe the differential impact of capitalism on a given country and the juxtaposition within the modern state of advanced economic regions and areas in which pre-colonial patterns of social organisation persist. This juxtaposition was evident in the Gold Coast between the southern regions and the underdeveloped northern regions of the country. Cocoa was introduced at the turn of the century and flourished in the humid conditions of the forest areas. By the 1950s it accounted for 90 per cent of export revenues and vitally affected the lives of southern Ghanaians, as is indicated by the local 'highlife' sung during a 1954 by-election in Ashanti:

> If you want to send your children to school, it is cocoa,
> If you want to build your house, it is cocoa,
> If you want to marry, it is cocoa,
> If you want to buy cloth, it is cocoa,
> If you want to buy a lorry, it is cocoa,
> Whatever you want to do in this world,
> It is with cocoa money that you do it.[22]

While cocoa-growing was essentially a people's industry, the larger farmers employed labour, drawn from the north and neighbouring French colonies, and invested their wealth in buildings in the urban centres. Apart from increased social differentiation, another effect of a cash-crop such as cocoa was to increase social mobility and to help further erode traditional institutions and values.

In the third place, the level of industrialisation was low in colonial Africa, though there were some exceptions. The latter were mainly in areas of substantial European settlement, such as Southern Rhodesia, which was developed as the manufacturing base of the Central African Federation between 1953 and 1963. On the other hand, substantial mining was undertaken (for example, bauxite in Guinea, iron ore in Sierra Leone, gold in the Gold Coast, copper in the Belgian Congo and Northern Rhodesia) with ownership, production and control vested in European (or South African-based) companies. In relation to the total African population, the labour force involved was small, often unskilled or semi-skilled, and mostly migrant. However, after the Second World War a settled labour force began to emerge in many colonies, including the Belgian Congo and on the Northern Rhodesian Copperbelt, and this facilitated trade union organisation. The difference in salaries and conditions of service between African and European workers became an obvious target of trade union attack.[23]

Finally, rapid urbanisation resulted from mining, the growth after the Second World War of manufacturing industry (if as yet on a limited scale), the commercial activity associated with the introduction of cash crops, and an expanding administrative machine. Rural dwellers were attracted to the towns by the prospect of employment and relatively high wages, as well as by urban amenities such as pipe-borne water, street lighting and cinemas. Many immigrants were disappointed and eked out a precarious existence in overcrowded and insanitary compounds in the shanty areas which ringed, for example, Lagos and Ibadan in Nigeria and Nairobi, the capital of Kenya.

Thus, at independence, the political leaders of the new African states inherited dependent economies that were still bound to the former colonial powers by established patterns of trade and by their membership of European currency blocs, notably the franc zone and the sterling area. They faced formidable problems, in the socio-economic as well as the political sphere. Since, as we have seen, there were few large companies owned by Africans, the state itself became the main agent of economic development; yet in most states, skilled manpower was in critically short supply. The growth of a market economy had resulted in economic imbalances between different regions of a country, as well as sometimes within a single region, the central area of Zambia being one example. Social differentiation had also taken place, though as yet on a limited scale: an incipient middle class existed in states such as the Ivory Coast, Kenya, Nigeria and Senegal; the growth of this class was to be enormously facilitated in the post-independence period when the holding of public office – as politicians, bureaucrats, and army officers – gave more people an opportunity for personal advancement. Again, new state leaders headed political parties which had to be transformed from parties of revolt into parties of rule. They also inherited bureaucracies which were doubtfully strong and experienced enough to undertake the immense tasks which confronted them.

Further Reading

Bender, G. J., *Angola under the Portuguese: The Myth and the Reality* (London: Heinemann, 1978).

Brett, E. A., *Colonialism and Underdevelopment in East Africa: The Politics of Economic Change, 1919–1939* (London: Heinemann, 1973).

Crowder, M. (ed.), *Colonial West Africa: Collected Essays* (London: Frank Cass, 1978).

Gifford, P., and Louis, W. R., *France and Britain in Africa* (New Haven: Yale University Press, 1972).

Hallett, R., *Africa to 1875* and *Africa since 1875*, 2 vols. (London: Heinemann, 1974 and 1975).

Hodgkin, T., *Nationalism in Colonial Africa* (London: Frederick Muller, 1956).

Kjekshus, H., *Ecology Control and Economic Development in East African History* (London: Heinemann, 1977).

Robinson, R., and Gallagher, J., with Denny, A., *Africa and the Victorians: The Official Mind of Imperialism* (London: Macmillan, 1961).

Rodney, W., *How Europe Underdeveloped Africa* (Dar es Salaam: Tanzania Publishing House, 1972, and London: Bogle-L'Ouverture, 1972).

Schaffer, B. B., 'The Concept of Preparation: Some Questions about the Transfer of Systems of Government', *World Politics*, vol. xviii, no. 1 (October 1965).

Slade, R., *The Belgian Congo* (London: Oxford University Press, 2nd edn, 1961).
Suret-Canale, J., *French Colonialism in Tropical Africa, 1900–1945*, trans. by T. Gottheiner (London: Hurst, 1971).

3

Nationalism and the Transfer of Power

As we have already observed, colonial states in Africa were created within artificial boundaries which rarely coincided with the boundaries of traditional polities. We are therefore dealing with what Seton-Watson has termed 'anti-colonial nationalism', a nationalism that was predominantly expressed within the confines of the colonial state.[1] As compared with European nationalism, there were no strong historical and social identities upon which African nationalists could build (Somalia, which was culturally homogeneous, was to an extent an exception to this pattern). This is not to suggest, however, that Africa was a *tabula rasa* when colonial rule was imposed: as we saw in chapter 2, many different forms of political organisation existed in pre-colonial Africa, ranging from centralised kingdoms to stateless societies; there was also a rich variety of cultural forms, though no shared culture such as would have been provided by a system of universal primary education.[2] The problem facing anti-colonial nationalists was that popular loyalties tended to gravitate towards a traditional unit which in the great majority of cases lay *within*, rather than being coterminous with, the colonial state boundaries (the Buganda kingdom within the Uganda protectorate affords a good example of this phenomenon). One of the nationalists' most important achievements during the independence struggle was to render loyalty to a sub-national unit secondary to loyalty to the country-wide unit – in other words, to submerge sub-nationalism within a wider nationalism. This chapter seeks to explain why, and how this happened.

The imposition of Western institutions and values upon the colonies disrupted the social structures and cultural life of the subject peoples. European rule, while sometimes psychologically damaging in so far as it instilled a sense of black inferiority and a tendency to imitativeness,[3] also gave rise to a cultural self-awareness and a pride in the African past which found expression in the search for a national language, in literature and history works that both recalled African suffering and glorified in past achievements, and in religious protest movements. In this way, African nationalism acquired a certain emotional content through the assertion of popular identities – identities that sometimes, as with the concept of pan-Africanism, cut across colonial boundaries. There was, however, also another, deeper side to African nationalism. Popular, emotional appeals were buttressed by instrumental arguments, which condemned colonial rule as authoritarian, bureaucratic and exploitative – the colonies, said the nationalists, were the milch-cows of the industrialised West and could only develop when the colonial yoke was removed and political independence was achieved.

African nationalism was most assertive in the post-Second World War period, when jobs were scarce and inflation was rampant, and, at least in French and British Africa, political parties and interest groups were formed to articulate the people's grievances. The conflict which thus developed between nationalist leaders, who had been educated in government and mission schools and occasionally overseas, and colonial administrators was not, over most of Africa, a class conflict – classes, so far as they existed, were only incipient and we cannot talk convincingly in terms of the assertion of the collective interests of an economic class against an exploitative, foreign bourgeoisie. On the other hand, certain economic interests were involved.

Among them was a traditional élite of chiefs and elders, some of whom identified with the post-war nationalist movements while others remained aloof and sought to preserve their own privileged positions as allies of the colonial administration. Next there was a small professional group, especially of doctors and lawyers, who, together with successful merchants and contractors, were prominent in their countries' congresses and early political parties; the fact that members of this group constituted an economically privileged stratum of colonial society did not deter them from political agitation, although it was usually well-mannered – they sought full social status for Africans, as well as political enfranchisement and (ultimately) political power.[4] Thirdly, we identify a thrusting petty-bourgeoisie of teachers, clerks and small businessmen who were impatient to change places with the colonial élite for a variety of mixed, and sometimes contradictory, reasons – to develop the state for the benefit of the people; to enrich themselves; and/or to transform the inherited socio-economic structure according to socialist principles. Fourthly, there was a bureaucracy – hierarchical, compartmentalised and influenced by Western administrative values – whose members expected to profit from government Africanisation policies. In the fifth place, there was an urban work-force, which sought to improve the wages and conditions of employment of workers through trade union activity; within a particular territory the trade union movement was occasionally linked with the dominant political party in a symbiotic relationship (as in Guinea), but more often it preferred to take independent economic or political action. Next, there was a large informal sector in the urban areas, made up of small shopkeepers and petty-traders, sometimes supplementing an inadequate family income. Finally, we identify a community of mostly cash-crop farmers who, in the southern areas of the Gold Coast, in other parts of West Africa and in Uganda, formed quite powerful farmers' associations in the post-Second World War period.

The socio-economic impact of cash-crop farming was often very great. In the Gold Coast, for example, cocoa was 'the people's industry' and led to the emergence of a new influential group of prosperous trading and business interests – the townsman with a number of cocoa farms in nearby villages, the trader with his cloth and general store, the cocoa broker acting as the link between farmer and European firm, and in time, too, the lorry-owner. In addition, there was a very large community of peasant farmers who grew food for themselves, their families and the urban market and who sometimes, as in Tanganyika,

protested loudly against colonial agricultural regulations and
thereby created a climate in which nationalism could develop.[5]
These peasant farmers – constituting the bulk of the population
in virtually all African states – together with urban workers and
the unemployed, were the 'ordinary' people who looked for an
improvement in their standard of living, better health care and
increased educational opportunities for their children. Great
importance was attached to the latter: if an educated citizenry
is a characteristic of the modern nation-state, the lack of educational provision (extreme in Portuguese Africa) was acutely
felt and powerfully reinforced anti-colonial nationalism.

African nationalism was therefore composed of a number of
different elements, representing sometimes interlocking, but
often divergent, economic interests which united temporarily
in an anti-colonial 'struggle'. It appeared in various forms,
according to the particular colonial context. Following Thomas
Hodgkin, in his classic study *Nationalism in Colonial Africa*, we
concentrate on three main types of association through which it
was expressed – separatist churches and prophetic movements,
trade unions, and political parties. We begin by examining
religious associations.

Religious Associations

In the early colonial period, when open opposition to colonial
rule was either impossible or ineffective, religion became a
vehicle for the expression of African dissent. (We focus here on
Christian Africa, though as Hodgkin reminds us, religious
dissent and political radicalism were often also closely related
in Muslim Africa.)[6] Several factors contributed to this outcome.
Though Christian missionaries might exert limited pressure on
the colonial government where they felt that the African was
being unfairly treated or undesirable policies were being
pursued, they were (as James Coleman points out) widely
regarded as 'the front troops of the Government to soften the
hearts of the people and while people look at the Cross white
men gather the riches of the land'.[7] Moreover, the adoption of
Christianity – especially in its Protestant form – involved the
abandonment of many deep-rooted social customs in favour of

Western values and practices. Though the churches made some concessions to local custom (in the Gold Coast, for example, by the Presbyterians over local marriage customs), the force of these concessions was mitigated by the tendency of many missionaries to present Christianity in an alien, Europeanised guise. Isaac Delano, a leading Nigerian Christian, stated: 'Christ and Western Civilization came together; no one could distinguish one from the other. Collar and ties, or the Bible. The early native Christians were known by their western dresses . . .'[8]

Faced with this challenge to their established way of life, some Africans – indeed, many in southern Nigeria – turned to Islam as a more conservative, indigenous religion which both allowed polygamy and was free of racial discrimination. Others accepted Christianity: of these, most remained within the orthodox Christian fold and sent their children to mission schools, without however necessarily abandoning old social habits, such as participation in traditional funeral ceremonies. A minority of Christians refused to conform in this way; they were the Christian nationalists, in whom we are primarily interested and who wanted (in the words of Isaac Delano) 'Christianity without the system that has been built around it in the West'. They broke away from the European-dominated mission churches and founded self-governing, separatist 'Ethiopian' churches which were modelled substantially on the churches from which they had seceded. This process began at an early date. For example, Coleman records that in Nigeria a religious group seceded from the Anglican Church in August 1891, and 'resolved that a purely Native African Church be founded, for the evangelization and amelioration of our race, to be governed by Africans'. Eight years later ministers of this United Native African Church were ordained by visiting black American clergymen. The United Native Church in the French Cameroons was another independent church to come into being – in this case after the First World War and as an offshoot of the English Baptists; its members sang anti-European hymns in the streets of Douala in 1922–3. Though other secessionist religious groups founded their own churches in British and French West Africa in the post-1945 period (the National Church of Nigeria and the Cameroons was a notable example), the number of independent churches in this part of Africa declined as other outlets for the expression of nationalist claims (including political parties and interest groups) emerged. On the other hand (as Hodgkin shows) where, as in settler Africa, such outlets were absent or minimal, the independent church 'as a kind of ecclesiastical instrument of radical nationalism' continued to be important – as it remains today in South Africa. It featured more prominently in colonies where Protestantism, with its stress on individualism and individual interpretation of the Bible, was dominant than in Catholic-controlled areas. However, Catholic missions also spawned a number of separatist churches, and there were numerous churches of the 'Zionist' type in Catholic territories.[9]

'Zionist' churches had a loose organisation, and adopted rituals which were characterised by spontaneity and emotionalism; they were inclined towards puritanism and xenophobia in their outlook.[10] The two types of church sometimes overlapped, but the 'Zionist' church, which tended to centre on a particular prophet who had received a divine 'call' to undertake his mission, was the more likely to inspire a popular movement. (The case of Sampson Opon, a local Methodist 'prophet' who launched a very successful evangelical crusade in the Eastern Province of the Gold Coast in 1920, showed that even an established, orthodox church could benefit from such a movement.)[11] The 'prophet' was usually an ordinary man (or woman) of limited or no education and previously employed in a humble occupation – Simon Kimbangu, who founded in 1921 the movement ('Kimbanguism') named after him in the Belgian Congo, was a carpenter and Protestant catechist. These attributes made for a close identity between the prophet and the people living in the rural areas, and prophetic movements were therefore also mass movements. Where a prophet caught the imagination of the people, his 'message' spread like wildfire – William Wade Harris, the Liberian prophet, was reported to have baptised 120,000 people in the Ivory Coast in 1914–15. That the colonial authorities were right to regard these movements as a threat to their political authority in indicated by the following hymn from the Kimbanguist *Chants du Ciel*:

Jésus, Sauveur pour les Élus et Sauveur pour nous tous.
Nous serons les vainqueurs envoyés par Toi.
Le Royaume est à nous. Nous l'avons.
Eux, les Blancs, ne l'ont plus.[12]

Many prophets were hanged or imprisoned for long terms. Kimbangu spent twenty-nine years in prison before dying in gaol in Elisabethville in 1950, while Mwana Lesa (literally 'Son of God'), who had introduced *Kitawala* – the Katangese version of the Watchtower (millenarian) Movement – into the Belgian Congo, was hanged in Rhodesia in 1926. But such harsh punishments did not prevent the emergence of further prophet movements which, in their messianic beliefs, were paralleled by the Mahdist tradition within Islam; they proliferated in the Belgian Congo in the 1940s and 1950s. Throughout their history, these movements in both the French and Belgian Congos tended to reach their peak at times of economic hardship, thereby underlining their significance as popular channels of social discontent. Though the prophetic movements represented a very early phase in the development of nationalism and had a greater impact in Bantu Africa than in West Africa, they expressed new, if often confused, ideas and asserted an African way of doing things. They thus created a climate in which modern forms of African nationalism – in the shape of congresses, parties and interest groups – could develop. It is to a consideration of these that we now turn.

Interest Groups: Trade Unions

The phrase 'African societomania' has been coined by J. Lombard to describe the process whereby a large number of voluntary associations sprang up in the expanding urban centres of colonial Africa, especially in the post-Second World War period.[13] These associations ranged from youth, student, women's, old boys' and professional bodies to organisations, such as savings clubs, ethnic mutual benefit groups, craft groups and trade unions, which were in large measure a response to the sense of social and psychological insecurity felt by people who had left their rural homes and entered a new and strange urban environment. They served at once as the vehicles of new ideas and a proving ground for political leaders. Though many of the early groups were small and short-lived and had an interlocking leadership, their cumulative effect was vitally important for the emergence of the African nationalist move- ment: the latter, writes Wallerstein, was 'in large part the outcome of the growth of voluntary associations'.

A small number of these associations (such as the Boy Scouts) were inspired by the colonial administration, but the others bore a more distinctly African imprint. Among the latter were craft organisations; many of these were linked with traditional structures, while others occasionally grew out of old boys' associations. One such association at Bamako was instrumental in creating the first trade unions in the French Soudan in 1937.[14] When – at this time, or during and after the Second World War – the British, French and Belgian govern- ments granted trade unions the legal right to organise in their colonies, these early syndical groups were transformed into mass organisations. That these organisations often became linked to the territory's emergent nationalist movement was an unintended consequence – the official advice given by British labour commissioners and French *inspecteurs du travail*, as well as the unofficial counsel of the metropolitan organisations (not- ably the British Trades Union Congress and the French labour federations, which actively supported trade union organisa- tion) was that the trade unions should not become politically involved. Instead, trade union leaders should (they were told) concentrate on strengthening union organisation by replacing, as in Tanganyika, a plethora of small craft unions with nationwide industrial unions affiliated to a central organisation and on using the new structure to negotiate better wages and conditions of work for their members. However, there were forces pulling in an opposite direction: the new nationalist movements that were beginning to emerge in post-war Africa sought to politicise, and bring under their wing, a large number of voluntary associations, including the trade unions. Thus, in the pre-independence period the labour movement was subject to dual pressures – it was both pulled towards political involvement, because of the sympathy of trade unionists with the nationalist movements to which most of them belonged in an individual capacity, and away from it in order to concentrate on industrial relations. The result, perhaps inevitably, was a very mixed picture and one which has evoked a sharply contrasting response from scholars who have studied the political role of African trade unions in the pre-independence period. On the one hand, Stephen Low, Georges Fischer and others have asserted that trade unions were so intimately involved in politics, normally as appendages of political parties and nationalist movements, that they were in a sense party instruments; on the other hand, Elliot Berg and Jeffrey Butler have argued that in the period before independence 'African trade unions were rarely the instruments of political parties' and played in most cases a 'negligible' political role.[15] Clearly, the direct contribution of the trade union movement to the growth of African nationalism is considerably less on the second view than it is on the first.

There is universal agreement that in Guinea the party and trade unions constituted two legs of a single nationalist movement: Sékou Touré, the president of the Parti Démocratique de Guinée (PDG), had a trade union background and the Union Générale des Travailleurs d'Afrique Noire (UGTAN), which was founded in January 1957 as a result of a merger between the country's principal labour groups, played an important part in the achievement of independence.[16] Moreover, it is widely accepted that union–party ties were generally closer in French Africa than in British Africa. British-ruled Kenya is sometimes regarded as a leading exception to the pattern prevailing in the latter. Berg and Butler take Kenya to be a country where the trade union commitment to the dominant political party – the Kenya African National Union (KANU) – was strong. This was a valid assessment of the Kenya Federation of Labour (KFL), the central labour organisation which, under Tom Mboya's leadership, conducted a holding operation for KANU (then the Kenya African Union) during the emergency period of the 1950s when nationally based political parties were proscribed; however, as we show below, it was not valid for the KFL's constituent industrial unions which did not take direct action in support of the 'struggle' for independence. In the French Cameroons, where party–union relations did not follow the typical French African pattern, the issue was not one of political involvement – the trade unions were very active politically in the immediate post-war period – but the fact that relations between the politically significant Union des Syndicats Confédérés du Cameroun and the major political party (then the Union des Populations du Cameroun – UPC) were severely strained in the period after 1955, when the UPC was banned by the French.[17] Ultimately, it was not the UPC but the northern-dominated Union Camerounaise, led by Ahmadou Ahidjo, which took the French Cameroons to independence in 1960.

In some countries a period of intense political activity on the part of a labour movement might be followed by a long period of quiescence. Nigeria was a case in point. As Berg and Butler, writing in 1964, comment:

> In the history of Nigerian labor there is a sharp division between the period 1945–50, when one segment of the labor movement threw itself vigorously into political activity [under the sponsorship of the Zikist movement], and the period from 1950 to the present, during which the labor movement has been altogether outside the political mainstream.[18]

In Nigeria and in several other countries, the labour movement itself was divided over the question of political involvement. In the Gold Coast in January 1950 the politically-minded leadership of the TUC, which had been created as the central organisation of the trade union movement in 1945 with however only limited formal authority over the unions affiliated to it, called a general strike in support of the 'positive action' campaign of the CPP. The strike was suppressed and the TUC disintegrated. Subsequently, the CPP, which formed the government in 1951 under a diarchical arrangement with the British, sought to use a reconstituted TUC to bring the labour movement under its control. It was supported in this move by CPP activists in the TUC, of whom the most prominent was John Tettegah, but was opposed by the leaders of individual unions, notably the Mineworkers, the UAC Workers, and the Railway Employees, who successfully battled to maintain the autonomy of their unions in the period up to 1958, when the Industrial Relations Act cut the ground from under their feet.[19] A similar split within the labour movement occurred in Northern Rhodesia, where the main upholder of the principle of non-involvement in politics was the powerful African Mineworkers' Union (AMU). What Amsden has written of trade unionism and politics in Kenya also applies, *mutatis mutandis*, to Northern Rhodesia/Zambia:

> When examining the relation between trade unions and political life in Kenya, it appears crucial to avoid the pitfall of viewing Kenya's trade union movement as a homogeneous unity. Otherwise, the participation of Kenya's trade unions in politics can easily be distorted. Whereas the top of Kenya's trade union structure, a TUC-like body, was involved in political manoeuvres to a considerable extent, a focus on the activities of the industrial unions affiliated to it reveals an almost entirely different picture. Most of these unions were, and still are, concerned almost exclusively with bread and butter issues . . . It is against this background of predominantly business unionism that the highly publicised political forays at the top of the union structure must be examined.[20]

The relationship between parties and unions often fell short of formal ties until the eve of independence. This was the case in Tanganyika where, as in the Gold Coast and several other colonies, the fact that trade unions antedated the formation of the dominant party gave them an independent basis of power and influence. If this was one factor which led the Tanganyika Federation of Labour (TFL), the central trade union organisation founded in 1955, to resolve at its first annual conference the next year that 'No Trade Union which is affiliated to the TFL should affiliate itself to TANU at the moment', another was the fear that if the government should move against TANU, which it regarded as an extremist organisation, the trade union movement might also be proscribed. By the end of 1958, with TANU's victory in the first part of the 1958–9 general election, that danger was past, and the party and TFL grew closer together, though it was not until February 1961 that the TFL was given two seats on the TANU national executive committee. A review of the history of party–union relations in Tanganiyka, which can be paralleled by the history of the Gold Coast and a number of other British dependencies, reveals periods of co-operation, estrangement and conflict, the tendency for disagreement increasing in the terminal period of colonial rule, when substantial issues (such as Africanisation and citizenship in Tanganyika) divided the two sides.[21]

Berg and Butler rightly challenge the earlier view that African trade unions were merely party instruments in the pre-independence period. Yet their own picture of an apolitical trade union movement narrowly engaged in negotiating improvements in wages and conditions of employment for its members is itself distorted. The most important distortion implicit in their analysis is the assumption that nationalist (or even political) commitment should be equated first and foremost with affiliation to, or association with, a nationalist political party. As Robin Cohen has pointed out, and Richard Jeffries' study of the railwaymen of Sekondi substantiates, there were good reasons for unionised workers, however radically nationalist, to be wary of too close an association with essentially petty-bourgeois dominated parties which threatened to pre-empt their development as genuine workers' organisations. From a somewhat different standpoint, Berg and Butler concentrated too much on the behaviour of the majority of workers (or unions) and overlooked the significance of particular, more radical groups. Dr Jeffries believes that in this way they 'misconstrued the dynamics and direction of union development.'[22]

Radical elements within a country's labour movement may indeed have interests which conflict sharply with those of 'apparatchiks' in the nationalist party. However, it must also be stressed that in the pre-independence period trade unionists generally shared the politicians' resentment of foreign rule, being convinced that the economy was geared to foreign commercial and industrial interests; they believed that the standard of living of the workers could not be significantly improved until political independence was achieved. This belief was perhaps most strongly held in areas of white settlement, such as Northern Rhodesia, where the wages and employment conditions of the white workers were much better than those of the Africans. There is no doubt that the effect of this common (party–union) outlook was often to strengthen the thrust of African nationalism: in Tanganyika, for example, individual unionists joined TANU, while new union members were largely recruited from party ranks, resulting in a rapid expansion in the size of the trade union movement in the second half of the 1950s. However, we need to think predominantly in terms of parallel lines of resistance to colonial rule, with the political party and trade union movement sometimes agreeing, but also often disagreeing, on the appropriate tactics to adopt. Because the political party was avowedly political in a way that the labour movement was not – or could not afford to be – it was above all the political party which aggregated and voiced the demand for independence. Partly in consequence, but also because of the differing functions of trade unions and political parties, it was to be the politicians rather than the trade unionists who were to benefit most when independence was achieved.

Political Parties

The political parties which became the vehicles of African nationalism within a few years of the ending of the Second World War were preceded by loosely structured and mainly urban centred organisations; the latter had a limited appeal and were led in the main by middle-class elements, among whom lawyers and doctors predominated. An early example of such an association was the Aborigines' Rights Protection Society (ARPS): founded in the Gold Coast in 1897 to safeguard African rights to land, it continued in being to champion the African cause after the land issue was settled. Another was the National Congress of British West Africa which, following its foundation in 1920, tried to bridge the communications gap separating the four British West African colonies and to press for moderate constitutional reform in each territory; it was not founded as an anti-government movement and Casely Hayford, a prominent Gold Coast lawyer and one of its leading spirits, conceded that 'our interests as a people are identical with those of the Empire'.[23] The 1930s saw the emergence in British West Africa of territorially based youth movements, congresses and leagues; though better organised and more broadly based than such earlier associations as the ARPS and the Nigerian National Democratic Party (founded in Lagos in 1923 by Herbert Macaulay, a civil engineer and journalist), they put forward programmes of limited reform, appealed above all to a predominantly urban and educated public, and therefore did not attract effective mass support. Despite the radicalising effect of the Second World War – comparable with the effects of the First World War on India – the return of ex-servicemen who could not find jobs at a time when prices were rising sharply, and an increasingly strident African nationalist press, the congress-type organisation continued in the main to dominate the scene in British and French Africa in the early post-war years. The congress claimed to represent 'all the people'; it had a loosely-knit, often federal structure comprising a number of affiliated associations, and pressed its claim to eventual self-rule or (in French Africa) to equality of political and social rights by petitions and deputations, supplemented (when these did not succeed) by mass demonstrations, national boycotts and general strikes.[24]

Notable examples of such congresses were the National Council of Nigeria and the Cameroons (NCNC), formed in August 1944; the Rassemblement Démocratique Africain (RDA), an inter-territorial party established in French Africa in 1946; and the United Gold Coast Convention (UGCC) and the Northern Rhodesia African Congress, founded in 1947 and 1948 respectively. The NCNC was made up of a large number of affiliated organisations (some 180 in 1945), including tribal unions – very important in the growth of Nigerian nationalism – professional associations and social and literary clubs; the decision in 1951 to admit members on an individual basis marked the transformation of the Council into a political party. The RDA, similarly, viewed itself as a 'national front'; in the words of Gabriel d'Arboussier, its secretary-general, it was 'a broad political organisation, including within itself all sorts of ideology; open to every national group, to men of all social conditions, and every Territory, grouped around a programme of concrete, definite aims'.[25]

Some of these congresses proved short-lived, while others gave birth to political parties, either because a new type of organisation was required to fight a general election or as a result of an internal split. The Gold Coast riots of 1948 and their aftermath revealed the sharp disagreement over strategy and tactics between the UGCC's moderate, middle-class leadership and Kwame Nkrumah, its general secretary; in 1949 Nkrumah broke with the UGCC and founded the CPP out of the already existing Committee on Youth Organisation. The CPP was a new type of political party – pledged to 'self-government now' and with a well-articulated structure, it sought to enrol the bulk of the Gold Coast's adult population as individual members; but significantly, too, it retained the word 'convention' in its own title.[26] In Nigeria, as we have seen, the NCNC became more of a political party and less of a congress with the changeover to an individual-member basis of organisation in 1951. It could reasonably claim to be more national than any of the other parties which emerged in Nigeria in the 1950–60 period, but the extent of its support was limited. Though it won the backing of groups in the Christianised Middle Belt of the Northern Region, it made little impact on the Muslim North and yielded the initiative to the Action Group (AG), founded in 1951, in the Yoruba areas of the Western Region. Its strength lay in the Eastern region and the decision of its national president, Dr Azikiwe, to become Premier of that region in 1953 sealed the NCNC's identification as an Ibo-dominated body, no less committed to regional nationalism than its main rivals, the AG and the Northern People's Congress (NPC).[27] As for the RDA, its national front broke down in 1950 over the issue of compromise with the French administration. This was favoured by Houphouet Boigny, its Ivorian president, and the RDA's conservative wing, while continued co-operation with the French communists was advocated by Gabriel d'Arboussier and the radical wing. Houphouet Boigny was left in control of the RDA machinery, but, as the emphasis in French policy shifted in the 1950s towards greater territorial autonomy, the strength of the RDA increasingly came to be located in its individual sections, such as the PDCI and the PDG, rather than in its central organisation; these parties adapted their organisation to fight

elections to the territorial assemblies. The RDA's radical wing
retained strong backing in Senegal and the French Cameroons
and among trade unionists and students.[28]

If some political parties emerged out of 'parent' congresses,
others, like the Bloc Démocratique Sénégalais, were breakaways from existing parties or, like the Ghana Congress Party
and the Sudanese National Unionist Party, came into being (in
1952 and 1953 respectively) as a result of a merger between
minor parties and groups. Some parties, especially in French
Africa, were nurtured by metropolitan parties – thus, the
(French) Movement Républicain Populaire supported the Parti
Républicain du Dahomey, founded in 1951, while the French
Socialist Party (Section Française de l'Internationale Ouv-
rière) established a section in Senegal in 1936, under the
leadership of Lamine Guèye. Other parties, such as the Union
Progressiste Mauritanienne and the Union Démocratique
Tchadienne, received such strong official backing as to be
frequently dubbed 'partis de l'Administration'. Several parties
were of a mixed origin. The NLM, which was founded in the
Ashanti region of the Gold Coast in 1954, contained a number
of former CPP members who imported into the movement
many of the organisational techniques which they had learned
in the CPP; to that extent, the NLM, as well as the Muslim
Association Party (MAP) and the Togoland Congress, can be
regarded as communal parties which were in effect breakaways
from the CPP.[29] But the NLM, which was backed by the
Asantehene and all except one of the leading Ashanti chiefs,
was also powerfully rooted in Ashanti tradition; an emotional
appeal to Ashanti 'nationalism' was invoked to express Ashanti
dissatisfaction with what was perceived to be the region's
meagre share in the nation's resources. Many of the key
members of the NLM, such as its chairman Bafuor Osei Akoto,
linguist to the Asantehene, had not formerly belonged to any
political party, while others, such as Dr K. A. Busia, had
actively opposed the CPP. Finally, a number of political parties
emerged out of cultural or other voluntary associations.
Prominent examples were the PDCI (founded in the Ivory
Coast in 1946), which had begun as a 'comité d'action
politique' of the Syndicat Agricole Africain, an organisation of
African planters; the Action Group, which grew out of Egbe

Omo Oduduwa, a Yoruba cultural association; and the NPC (Northern Nigeria, 1951), a political offshoot of Jam'iyyar Mutanen Arewa, a pan-Northern, predominantly Hausa cultural organisation; the Sierra Leone People's Party (SLPP – 1951), which originated in the Sierra Leone Organisation Society, a body formed to promote co-operatives in the protectorate; and TANU (1954), which had its roots in the civil service-dominated Tanganyika African Association but whose subsequent growth owed a great deal to the strong rural protest against government agricultural regulations.

Whatever their origin – it was extra-parliamentary in nearly every case – African political parties often differed in important respects. There were obvious and sharp differences in the political experience of British and French Africa; as we shall see, these overlay significant differences between parties *within* each region. The 'metropolitan axis' of French colonial policy had its counterpart in the party political sphere since a political party might well affiliate with a French political party, as the PDCI did for a time with the French Communist Party in the late 1940s; the ties were severed in October 1950. The PDCI was itself a territorial section of an inter-territorial political party, the RDA, of which there was no equivalent in British Africa following the Second World War. French African experience was also distinct in that the primary objective of political parties in at least the early post-war period was to secure for Africans equality of rights as French citizens rather than independence; Ruth Morgenthau points out that in 1956 France reacted to the rising tide of nationalism by accepting territorial autonomy 'as a way to prevent independence'.[30] In other countries again, including Algeria as well as the Portuguese territories and the settler regimes of Southern Africa, political parties have had to engage in protracted armed struggle to secure their independence. Such parties, in the pre-independence period, had no (or virtually no) opportunity of influencing and controlling the personnel and policy of government. This also corresponds with the experience of Zaire, though here there was at least an attempt, if mismanaged, at a constitutional transfer of power; but it contrasts with that of a country such as Ghana, where the transition to independence was relatively smooth and the CPP ruled, in a

diarchical arrangement with the British, for six years before
independence in March 1957.

This varying historical experience of Africa's political parties
was supplemented by other distinctions based on differences in
structure, recruitment and the social basis of support, as well as
on ideology and leadership. While some parties, like the CPP in
Ghana and the PDG in Guinea, sought to appeal to the
lower-middle strata of the population, others, such as the NPC
in Nigeria and the Parti Progressiste Nigérien in Niger, had a
narrower appeal, the NPC especially being at the outset the
mouthpiece of the native authorities. Typologically, the former
type of party has been characterised as a 'mass' party, which is
strongly articulated in structure, is ideologically-based, has
leaders who are selected on the basis of political ability, seeks to
enrol as many individual members within its ranks as it can,
and tries to take under its wing such interest groups as trade
and co-operative unions and farmers' organisations. The
NPC-type of party has been described as an 'élite' party, built
up out of associations affiliated to it, with a leadership enjoying
ascriptive status and with a weakly articulated structure.[31]
This categorisation is, however, inexact. The élite and mass
parties represented ideal types and the divisions between them
were never clear-cut. Moreover, parties sometimes grew away
from their origins: thus, as Mackenzie and Robinson foresaw
might happen when it was forced by events to conduct a general
election campaign, the NPC in Nigeria changed its nature and
developed many of the structural features and organisational
techniques of the mass party.[32] Other parties were difficult to
categorise. The PDCI, for example, had many of the characteristics of the mass party but was more pragmatic than
ideological and made formal use of ethnic bases of support in its
organisation;[33] from the outset its policies were geared to the
interests of the wealthy African planter group to which the
party owed its existence rather than to the needs of the peasants
and workers. Moreover, the patron–client relationship, which
is supposed to typify the élite party, has remained important
within several mass-type party organisations, including
KANU in Kenya, UNIP in Zambia and the Parti Socialiste
Sénégalais (PSS, formerly UPS) in Senegal.

The ideological spectrum of Africa's pre-independence

political parties was broad. Few of the parties which led their countries to independence in or about 1960 were revolutionary, committed to the transformation of the existing socio-economic structure, though the Front de Libération Nationale (FLN) in Algeria promised to be one such group and the PDG in Guinea another. Most parties were reformist, including the CPP in Ghana and TANU in Tanganyika, while others – the Ivory Coast's PDCI and KANU, for example – were inclined to be conservative in orientation. The case of KANU is particularly instructive as demonstrating that a liberation struggle (assuming that Mau Mau in the 1950s can be interpreted in this light) does not necessarily have a radicalising effect. More recent evidence from Zimbabwe, where the Zimbabwe African National Union (Patriotic Front) – ZANU(PF) – has been in power since April 1980 and has so far eschewed fundamental change, reinforces this contention. The experience of Guinea-Bissau, Angola and Mozambique suggests that the transition from liberation movement to revolutionary regime can only occur where the movement's leadership embraces socialism during the course of the struggle and mounts an intensive political education campaign among its followers. However, recent events in Guinea-Bissau (discussed in chapter 8) raise the question whether such a transition will necessarily prove permanent.

The quality and style of party leadership also varied. The contrast was sharp between the quiet authority of Milton Margai of Sierra Leone and the showmanship (combined, however, with considerable organisational skill) of Nkrumah or Gamel Abdul Nasser; or again, between the philosophical reflectiveness of Léopold Sédar Senghor and Nyerere and the strident nationalism of Sékou Touré. Many of these leaders are said to have been 'charismatic' in that, in the view of their followers, they possessed 'exemplary' powers. However, as Chinoy has observed, 'no prophet can succeed unless the circumstances are propitious', and in the run up to independence the sociological aspect of charismatic leadership was no less important than the psychological. Innate qualities of leadership might have gone unrecognised if the party leaders had not also had 'the right message to convey at the right time'.[34] In many cases, the message – of 'freedom' and the importance of unity to attain it (*uhuru na umoja* in Tanganyika) – was commonly delivered at a public rally during pre-independence election campaigns. The social context within which a leader such as Samora Machel of Mozambique operated was very different and it may be postulated that charismatic leadership will be less important where there is an ideologically-based liberation movement. In the next section, we examine how the transfer of power took place in British and French Africa.

The Transfer of Power

Nationalist pressure, particularly following the Gold Coast riots of 1948, quickened the tempo of constitutional reform throughout British Africa: the Gold Coast itself progressed from semi-responsible government in 1951 to internal self-government in 1954, and finally to independence in 1957. The progression was much the same in the other three West African colonies, though the adoption of federalism in Nigeria made that country's constitutional arrangements necessarily more complex. There were hiccups along the way, caused however not by the reluctance of the British to transfer power but by the outbreak of domestic political conflict, notably the eruption of communalism in the Gold Coast, the colony–protectorate cleavage in Sierra Leone and (though less fundamental) in the Gambia, and the demand for the creation of more states in Nigeria. The process in each case was punctuated by a series of elections to what, in the Gold Coast by mid-1954, had become an entirely African legislature from which the cabinet was drawn and to which it was responsible. These elections were keenly contested by a number of parties and gave a good indication of how the political system worked. In each pre-independence election the CPP won comfortably in the Gold Coast, as did the SLPP in Sierra Leone and (from 1960) the People's Progressive Party in the Gambia; in Nigeria, by contrast, the operation of the Westminster system of government was distorted because of the absence of truly national parties.

However, it is important to note that several of the parties which spearheaded the 'freedom struggle' and formed the government when independence was eventually achieved, rested on a somewhat slender base of voluntary support. Take, for example, the showing of the CPP in the general election of 1956. The results were as follows: CPP: 71 seats, 57 per cent of the total votes cast; non-CPP: 33 seats, 43 per cent of the total votes cast. Judged by the standards of a multi-party election in the West, this was a convincing win for the governing party. However, when these results are broken down by region, the victory is less impressive: the CPP won only two out of the country's four regions, losing Ashanti to the NLM and MAP and the North to the Northern People's Party (NPP). Again, the figure of 57 per cent of the total votes cast for the CPP reduces to 28.5 per cent if the CPP vote is taken as a percentage of the registered electorate and to a meagre 15 per cent if the eligible electorate (i.e. adults aged 21 and over who were entitled to register) is taken as the basis of calculation.[35] Thus, CPP rule in the post-independence period rested on the *expressed* support of barely one in six of the estimated eligible voters. (It may of course be the case, as Professor Austin suggests, that many people in the two colony regions did not register because they regarded the contest as a foregone conclusion in areas where the CPP was dominant.) Support for the governing party declined further under the Republic inaugurated in 1960, though no free elections were held to test the extent of that decline, and the one-party state created in 1964 rested on flimsy foundations.

This pattern of constitutional advance punctuated by periodic elections was repeated in the rest of British Africa (except Rhodesia), though the early stage of multi-tiered, indirect elections in West Africa was omitted in East Africa. In general 'the stages of British retreat . . . were less widely spaced', to use Dennis Austin's phraseology, and 'the curve of reform was shortening'.[36] Other variations occurred according to local circumstance, such as the constitutionally entrenched position created for Buganda within the Uganda protectorate and the existence between 1953 and 1963 of a Central African Federation embracing the self-governing colony of Southern Rhodesia and the protectorates of Northern Rhodesia and Nyasaland. In East Africa, as in Britain's West African colonies, elections were contested by two or more parties, the challenge to the dominant party being weak in some cases (in Nyasaland, Tanganyika and Bechuanaland, for example) and strong in others, such as Kenya, Northern Rhodesia and Uganda. Multi-party elections even preceded the transfer of power in Rhodesia – under the abortive internal settlement in April 1979 and again under British supervision in February 1980 – ZANU(PF) emerging a more decisive victor the second time than many observers had predicted. In most cases, the Gold Coast lesson was repeated: measured in terms of support among eligible voters, the legitimacy of the party which took the country to independence was not impressive and meant that on this calculation the designation 'mass party' was hardly warranted.

On becoming independent a British-ruled territory – whether colony, protectorate or even trust territory like Tanganyika – in principle became a constitutional monarchy with the British Queen as its Queen, represented by a Governor-General, and with a Westminster model of constitution, providing for an interlocking cabinet and legislature, a separate judiciary, and an independent public service commission. The monarchical arrangement was to prove short-lived, India having earlier demonstrated that republicanism was not incompatible with Commonwealth membership. While Nigeria and Uganda opted for formal, non-executive presidents after the Indian model (encountering some problems in each case, in defining acceptable limits in practice to the scope of presidential influence), the other British territories followed Ghana's lead in 1960 in making constitutional provision for an executive presidency. By 1964 the pattern had been set and on attaining independence that year, Northern Rhodesia immediately became the Republic of Zambia, headed by a President vested with executive powers. At independence two years later, Bechuanaland protectorate became the Republic of Botswana, though the other former High Commission territories (Lesotho and Swaziland) chose to remain monarchies, albeit with their own monarchs replacing the British Queen. The changeover to republican status had in all cases more than symbolic importance since it opened the way to the establishment of personal rule; however, it did not necessarily involve an abrupt change in the practice of government. Thus, for some time after Tanganyika changed from a Westminster-style parliamentary regime to a republic in December 1962, President Nyerere did not impose his own views on his ministers and an attempt was made in cabinet to secure unanimity. However, as the country faced a series of crises both at home and abroad in and after 1964, the President increasingly took important initiatives, often acting without any reference to the cabinet.

The constitutional context within which elections were held in French Africa was very different. Independence was never demanded throughout the Fourth Republic (1946–58) and, as Hodgkin has pointed out, the overseas territories remained 'integral parts of an indivisible Republic, in which legislation was the exclusive responsibility of the French Parliament'.[37] The territorial assemblies established in each French African colony, and in Togo and the Cameroons (both UN trust territories), possessed limited powers, primarily in the budget-ary and financial spheres. It was only under the *loi cadre* reforms of June 1956 that these powers were increased and provision was made for the introduction of universal franchise and elected territorial executives. Although these reforms changed significantly the relations between France and her overseas territories, they were not designed as a prelude to the grant of independence.[38]

A uniform pattern of elections was introduced throughout French Africa and, under the Fourth Republican Constitution of 1946, voters went to the polls frequently – to cast their ballots in elections to the territorial assemblies, the French National Assembly and in referenda. The result, as Ruth Collier shows, was that they had more experience of limited suffrage and universal suffrage elections before independence than their British or Belgian counterparts.[39] (In the Belgian Congo, where the process of the transfer of power was drastically telescoped, there was only one territory-wide election before independence that was comparable to those held elsewhere, and there were only two such elections in Ruanda-Urundi, the Belgian-administered UN trust territory.)[40] Universal suffrage was introduced in French Africa in 1957, and in the general elections held that year the victorious party won so convincingly in many cases that it was able to consolidate its position at the next elections in 1959. Thus, Zolberg records that PDCI candidates obtained 89 per cent of the votes cast and won all but two of the 60 seats in the Ivorian territorial assembly; 54 per cent of those registered voted, representing about 49 per cent of the potentially eligible electorate.[41]

On the other hand, an overwhelmingly dominant party did not emerge in every case, and in Congo–Brazzaville, Dahomey and Niger the party that won control of the government in 1957 lost power at the subsequent elections, leaving the way clear for the new ruling party to make use of the government machinery to strengthen its position. In general, party dominance resulted in high levels of electoral participation in French Africa; in British Africa, by contrast, a high turnout was most likely when, as in the Gold Coast and Nigeria, party fragmentation occurred and inter-party competition increased.[42]

Dr Collier has suggested reasons for the generally higher levels of party dominance in French Africa than in British Africa, one being the different electoral systems in use. Voters chose a party under the French multi-member list system and an individual candidate under the British single-member constituency system; the French system favoured the strongest party and tended to eliminate weak ones. A second explanation was rooted in the nature of colonial rule: the French reduced the power of chiefs and traditional institutions and thus fostered élite cohesion, while the British policy of indirect rule sponsored two systems of authority and legitimacy (the traditional and the modern) and thereby heightened élite fragmentation. Whereas British policy enabled local and traditional leaders to serve as power brokers, there was less opportunity in French Africa to politicise ethnic groups. Moreover, because of the later and more limited provision of education in French than in British Africa, there was less of a split within the modern élite in most French colonies than occurred in British, and especially non-settler, Africa, between an older, predominantly urban élite of doctors, lawyers and merchants and the petty-bourgeoisie of teachers, clerks and small traders which had emerged in the nationalist ferment of the post-Second World War period. Ruth Collier has argued persuasively that

> the greater pressures for fragmentation in British Africa may
> help to explain why the leading parties in these colonies,
> especially in the nonmulti-racial colonies, were rarely able to
> use successive elections to improve their positions in the way
> that many of the leading parties in the French colonies did.
> ... the greater possibility of a bandwagon effect in a
> situation of relatively weak intermediate groups in French
> Africa is a possible explanation of why the strongest parties
> in French Africa mobilized the vote.[43]

The type of franchise in use was also probably important: the
French list system of voting may have exaggerated the extent of
party support. Whatever the explanation, the leading parties in
French Africa were successful in using subsequent elections to
secure very high voter turnouts. As Zolberg shows in his study
of the four French-speaking African states of Guinea, the Ivory
Coast, Mali and Senegal, even countries which experienced
some of the fragmentary pressures referred to above were still
able to control *all* the legislative seats at the time of independence. This was an important outcome and meant, first, that
governing parties in most of French Africa had consolidated
their position by independence to such an extent that *de facto*
one-party regimes already existed; and secondly that, judged
by the high level of electoral support, the legitimacy of
governments in French-speaking Africa seemed in general to be
greater than in English-speaking Africa.

It needs to be stressed however that, though elections were
more frequent and attracted higher voter turn-outs in post-war
French than British Africa, they were less meaningful from a
nationalist perspective. For they were not signposts along the
road to independence but stages in the achievement by
Africans of equality as French citizens. As Dr Morgenthau has
pointed out, 'although article 86 of the 1958 Constitution made
independence possible, it also made it incompatible with
membership in the [French] Community'.[44] In other words, as
General Charles de Gaulle made clear, a territory voting 'No'
in the constitutional referendum of 28 September 1958 had to
'take the consequences', which were that it would receive no aid

from France. Only Guinea chose the independence option, the other colonies in French West and Equatorial Africa electing to become autonomous republics within the Community; powers on certain enumerated matters, including foreign policy, defence and currency, were reserved in practice to France and in effect to her President. However, these arrangements proved short-lived: the French changed their stance in 1959 and the next year amended Title XII of the Constitution in order to make it possible for a state to be independent and yet remain a member of the 'Communauté renovée'.[45] Each French African state negotiated its own independence with France under what Robin Luckham has called a 'dense network of economic and political co-operation agreements'. The latter included new defence arrangements, negotiated (mostly in 1960–1) on a bilateral basis or in the form of collective sub-regional defence agreements like that between France and the four countries of AEF. All the Francophone states, except Guinea, entered into military assistance agreements with France and a nucleus among them, including Cameroun, the Ivory Coast, and Senegal, signed defence agreements also. (By contrast, the Anglo–Nigerian Defence Pact of 1960 was a modest affair, yet was strongly attacked in Nigeria by the Opposition and by radical and other critics, and was abrogated in early 1962.) Thus protected these new, predominantly single-party states inherited the centralising traditions of the French. In general, they possessed strong executives, modelled on de Gaulle's presidency. Except where two political leaders of more or less equal stature dictated a power-sharing arrangement between a president and prime minister – as in Senegal between 1960 and 1963 and in Dahomey and Congo-Brazzaville for short periods – executive authority in the immediate post-independence period was monopolised by the president to a greater extent than in Anglophone Africa, where vestiges of the British cabinet system, with its emphasis on collective responsibility, persisted. Moreover in this period, too, legislatures in French-speaking Africa were considerably weaker than in English-speaking Africa and local authorities were neither so numerous nor as autonomous; within the framework of a prefectoral-type system, the number of government representatives and administrative areas at the lower levels was rapidly increased.[46]

Conclusion

The origins of African nationalism are different from those of European nationalism. Pre-independence Africa did not experience an industrial revolution and class divisions were comparatively weak. African nationalism was anti-colonial nationalism, which lacked deep historical roots and was born out of a protest movement against European rule and exploitation; it represented also the African's claim to human dignity and the right to self-rule. In some cases – in areas of white settlement such as Algeria and Rhodesia, and above all in Portuguese Africa – the African protest went unheeded by the colonial power and violent conflict followed. In the majority of cases, however, even to talk of an independence 'struggle' is somewhat misleading since, in the 1950s, successive British governments seemed to be all too ready to shed themselves of the burden of African empire, while leading French-speaking Africans only themselves raised the issue of independence (as distinct from equal status with Frenchmen) at the end of the decade, when President de Gaulle realised that he could best preserve French economic and other interests in Africa by granting political independence. It is therefore easier to trace, as we have done, expressions of nationalist discontent than it is to assess with any degree of certainty the impact of nationalism upon colonial policy or to determine the extent to which nationalism quickened the tempo of reform. The Gold Coast riots of 1948 certainly seem to have had that effect, though Professor Austin, a close observer of the Ghanaian scene, believes that the Gold Coast itself would probably have moved towards independence even if these riots had not occurred.[47]

While some African leaders, such as Nkrumah, expressed pan-African ideas and had a vision of a united Africa which would become the primary focus of African loyalty, the horizons of the great majority of African nationalists were bounded by the colonial state and of its successor, the post-colonial state. Hugh Seton-Watson points out that 'If national consciousness, based on religion, language and deeply rooted historical mythologies, were not available, then the agent of continuity could only be the central power.'[48]

In juridical terms, the new African state was strong, its political independence being attested by membership of the Organisation of African Unity (OAU) and the United Nations, among other international organisations. In political and indeed sociological terms, however, it was weak:[49] in the great majority of states there was no shared culture, such as a homogeneous and universal educational system would have provided, and the typical state was characterised by ethnic pluralism, linguistic diversity, the strength of communal ties and loyalties, and an educational system which hitherto had benefited only a minority of the population. A vitally important question for the future was therefore whether those who inherited power at the centre – the political leadership, the dominant or single political party, the bureaucracy and, often subsequently, the military – would be able to sustain or create a strong sense of national identity once the cohesive factor of alien rule was removed. As we have just indicated, their ability to do so also depended on the nature of the society within which the new state operated, and it is to a consideration of this issue that we turn in the next chapter.

Further Reading

Anderson, B., *Imagined Communities. Reflections on the Origin and Spread of Nationalism* (London: Verso, 1983).

Austin, D., *Politics in Ghana, 1946–60* (London: Oxford University Press, 1964).

Coleman, J. S., *Nigeria: Background to Nationalism* (Berkeley: University of California Press, 1958).

Collier, R. B., *Regimes in Tropical Africa: Changing Forms of Supremacy, 1945–75* (Berkeley: University of California Press, 1982).

Gellner, E., *Nationalism and Nations* (Oxford: Blackwell, 1982).

Gifford, P., and Louis, W. R. (eds.), *The Transfer of Power in Africa. Decolonization, 1940–1960* (New Haven: Yale University Press, 1982).

Iliffe, J., *A Modern History of Tanganyika* (Cambridge University Press, 1979).

Morgenthau, R. S., *Political Parties in French-Speaking West Africa* (Oxford: Clarendon Press, 1964).

Nolutshungu, S. C., *Changing South Africa: Political Considerations* (Manchester University Press, 1982).

Seton-Watson, H., *Nations and States: An Enquiry into the Origins of Nations and the Politics of Nationalism* (London: Methuen, 1977).

Suret-Canale, J., *Afrique Noire. De la Colonisation aux Indépendances, 1945–1960* (Paris: Editions Sociales, 1972).

Young, C., *Politics in the Congo: Decolonisation and Independence* (Princeton University Press, 1965).

4

State and Society

Communalism

At independence leaders of the nationalist movements in Africa, or of the victorious political parties in the elections of the decolonisation period, came to power and became ministers, MPs and, in some cases, regional and district commissioners. However, they had mostly not been adequately trained by the colonial government and had limited experience of operating a governmental system on a national scale. Initially, the main problems that confronted them were not those 'of economic development primarily, but much more urgently, those of legitimacy'.[1] They had to establish their right to rule culturally diverse societies which were rent by social cleavage and were characterised, as a result of the differential impact of colonialism and capitalism, by varying levels of political and economic development. Faced with a fragile national unity, many African leaders privately echoed the statement made by Jawaharlal Nehru in post-independence India: 'We were simply horrified to see how thin was the ice upon which we were skating.'[2] The communal challenge took various forms, including disaffection on the part of ethnic minorities, regional pressure for a federal form of government or even for secession, and – as with the Somalis in the Horn of Africa – movements for self-determination by people divided by artificial and colonial-imposed boundaries.

As Clifford Geertz has pointed out, the governments to which power was being transferred could not, like the colonial governments, stand outside the societies which they ruled. The imminence of independence often excited demands on the part of particular communities which lacked confidence in the impartiality of the new government, and led them to try and maximise their position, constitutionally or otherwise, within the emergent state. Take the case of the Gold Coast (Ghana), where a strong Ashanti sub-nationalism clashed with Gold Coast nationalism, as represented by the CPP, in the 1950s. By 1954, with independence in sight, Ashanti – rich in gold, cocoa and timber and proud of its cultural traditions – felt that it was not receiving its fair share of political and economic resources at the hands of Dr Nkrumah's CPP government. The NLM was founded with the backing of the Asantehene and the great majority of Ashanti chiefs and linked up with the NPP and other regionally-based parties to demand a federal constitution. Though this movement failed to gain power in the 1956 elections or even to have its demand for a federation accepted, it left behind a legacy of bitterness and probably inclined Nkrumah to adopt after independence what in his autobiography he termed 'emergency measures of a totalitarian kind', including the Preventive Detention Act of 1958.[3] Buganda, the seat of another powerful traditional kingdom, posed an even greater threat to the integrity of Uganda, the state to which it was destined to belong. Barotseland in Northern Rhodesia provides a third example of a community with a strong traditional base seeking to secure a privileged constitutional status within the newly independent Zambian state. These problems were solved differently. In Ghana, the CPP government removed the federal elements which had been incorporated in the independence constitution as a concession to the NLM and its allies by passing the Constitutional (Amendment) Bill, 1959; the latter abolished the assemblies which had been established in the five regions (including Ashanti). The Buganda problem was solved in 1966 by the forcible removal of the Kabaka, the traditional ruler of Buganda, and the dismemberment of his kingdom as a unit of government. In Zambia, in the period between independence in 1964 and 1969, the government used a mixture of persuasion, threats and legal enactment to bring to an end the privileged position accorded to Barotseland under the agreement reached at independence in 1964.

While tradition bolstered regional demands in each of these cases, it is important to stress that factors other than the traditional, or in addition to the traditional, lay behind the existence of sub-national loyalties. Ashanti, Buganda and Barotseland each sought not only to retain its separate customs and traditions, but also to secure access to political power and economic resources. Moreover, the existence of a centralised traditional authority within the boundaries of a new state did not necessarily constitute a threat to the integrity of that state, as the cases of Benin in Nigeria and the Mossi kingdom in Upper Volta illustrate. Again, sub-national loyalties might flourish without there being a centralised traditional unit upon which they could build – though, in general, the absence of strong sub-national units facilitated (as in Tanganyika) the process of nation-building. The Ibo in Eastern Nigeria and the Kikuyu in Kenya both lacked a centralised authority, yet in 1967 the Ibo sought to secede from Nigeria and establish the new state of Biafra, while the Kikuyu not only constituted the spearhead of the nationalist movement but came to dominate Kenyan politics in the post-independence period to an extent which alienated other ethnic groups such as the Luo.

Robert Molteno, in his study of communalism (or sectionalism as he preferred to call it), emphasised that the conflict between contemporary sectional political groups in Zambia was non-traditional in nature. He argued that it was not possible to say that current conflicts reproduced and reflected historic conflicts: thus, the fact that the Lozi exercised hegemony over the Tonga in the nineteenth century was not sufficient to explain why the Lozi and Tonga were on different sides in the 1967 UNIP central committee elections, since the bulk of them were on the same side in the 1968 general election. The conflict, he maintained, was over jobs and access to economic resources, but was expressed in sectional terms. In the Zambian context 'tribes' or, more accurately, regional-linguistic groups (for the Bemba and Lozi, for example, each comprise many different tribes) were vehicles of symbolic expression of political and economic competition; in other words, 'tribalism', which is as unsatisfactory a concept in political science as in social anthropology, was the idiom within which sectional competition took place. Sectional leaders fostered sectional identifications by playing on the emotions of their followers to win support and votes. On this view, sectional groups were interest groups competing for scarce economic resources.[4]

Richard L. Sklar was making substantially the same point when, in 1967, he stated of Nigeria: 'there is often a non-traditional wolf under the tribal sheepskin'. Sklar, a radical scholar who is never afraid of departing from Marxist orthodoxy, was not saying that traditional attachments may not be one factor influencing political behaviour; the danger was in isolating these as the only factor: 'Tribalism', he wrote, 'should be viewed as a dependent variable rather than a primordial political force in the new nation.'[5] In their volume on communalism and politics in Nigeria (to which Professor Sklar contributed three chapters) Melson and Wolpe carried his argument further by pointing out that the weakening of traditional authority and cohesiveness under the impact of modernisation did not result in the decline of communalism in Nigeria; on the contrary, communal conflict increased as new communal groupings emerged. 'In culturally plural societies', they wrote, 'citizens tend to perceive their competitive world through a communal prism and to be responsive to communal appeals.'[6] The validity of this statement is confirmed by experience in many states, for example in Dahomey (now the People's Republic of Benin), where communalism resulted in a three-cornered political conflict and led to unstable power-sharing arrangements in the 1960s.[7]

Richard Sandbrook has observed that while ethnic conflict models help to promote understanding of African political realities, they often understate the degree of inter-ethnic co-operation evident in many new states and also do not explain some forms of intra-ethnic conflict.[8] This is a valid point and one that is carried further in his study of élite conflict in Zambia by Morris Szeftel.[9] In recognising that factionalism at leadership level may entail an attempt to politicise class as well as ethnic interests, Szeftel also agrees with Sandbrook that in the African context, where a broad consensus on goals and values may be lacking and the coercive power at the disposal of the incumbent regime is often limited, bargains are struck at the highest political level, resulting in the accommodation of different factional interests; this bargaining strengthens the hold of the factional leader over followers who, in return for their support, expect a share in the national economic cake. This process can be seen at work in Zambia, where President Kaunda has long sought to maintain a regional balance in allocating cabinet posts to UNIP leaders. The establishment, under the one-party state, of the central committee on a full-time basis both widened the scope of the President's patronage and opened up a new arena of competition between Zambia's factional leaders.[10]

Zambia also affords other examples of inter-factional co-operation. In the UNIP central committee elections of 1967, the powerful Bemba-speaking group ignored language boundaries and struck an alliance with the much weaker Tonga-speaking group within the party; it succeeded in increasing the Bemba share of key posts in UNIP at the expense of the Eastern and Lozi-speaking bloc. Similarly, in the 1959 federal election in Nigeria, Chief Obafemi Awolowo realised that his party (the Action Group) could not win if its support was limited to Yorubas of the Western Region; he therefore sought and secured allies in the minority areas of the East and North (but still lost the election). The 1979 constitution of Nigeria seeks to guard against the domination of the country's affairs by one or more ethnic groups by incorporating provisions which will promote national unity and reflect 'the federal character' of the new Nigeria. Thus, political associations whose activities appear to be confined to a part only of the geographical area of Nigeria are proscribed and the federal cabinet has to satisfy the principle of state equality by incorporating one minister from each state. Anthony Kirk-Greene questions the wisdom of guaranteeing 'areal and ethnic equality' in this way without also making a constitutional commitment to the promotion of 'some form of overt social justice'. As he astutely observes: 'A satisfactory formula to contain Nigeria's critical ethnic arithmetic may prove inadequate in the absence of a complementary theorem for solving her socio-economic mathematics.'[11]

It is also important to note that while patron–client networks may link people exclusively from the same ethnic group, they sometimes cut across ethnic identities. That faction as a technique of élite competition is compatible with contexts where ethnic (and/or religious) ties are not particularly salient, or, at least, are apparently passive in their influence, is indicated among others by Epstein's study of the internal politics of the African Mineworkers' Union in Luanshya (Northern Rhodesia) in the early 1950s, by Sandbrook's analysis of trade union politics in Kenya, by Elhussein's thesis on rural development in the Gunaid area of Sudan, and by Donal Cruise O'Brien's study of the organisation of Senegalese peasant society.[12] Dr O'Brien points out that the workings of patron–client politics permitted some Senegalese peasants, though exploited as a socio-economic category and marginal to the political operation of the state to which they were subject, to secure concrete benefits by giving their support to a local leader who had influential connections in the capital city. The following quotation from his book *Saints and Politicians* shows, alongside the persistence of communal divisions, the crystallisation of shared economic interests transcending the narrow focus of such cleavages:

> . . . in the fragmented social and political structure of Senegal, it is predictable that the effective basis of political trust should to a large extent reflect communal divisions: the trustworthy are one's relatives, one's co-believers, those who share one's local origins ('home-boys'). These bonds are the more effective when (as is frequently the case) they are combined. And they can be reinforced by past experience of reciprocal exchange of favours in politics or business. This obtains for alliances either of equals or unequals: a sense of shared interest is complemented by other shared values.

Leaders of the Mouride brotherhood were particularly effective patrons of the groundnut-producing peasants; they articulated their grievances and persuaded the government to double the groundnut producers' price in a single year (1974). In this way, they 'proved the efficacy of a bizarre and theatrical form of trade unionism'.[13]

While O'Brien's study shows that the key roles in factional politics are played by urban activists who dominate the alliances which they forge with rural notables, it also indicates that the field of operations of these activists is not infinitely malleable, according to the needs of shifting factional alliances, at the centre. Dr Elhussein's Sudanese study also provides evidence that politicians and bureaucrats must be attentive to the parameters which society itself may impose. After coming to power in 1969, the military regime in the Sudan introduced new political and administrative structures which were designed to strengthen the centre and to break the power of the traditional and tribal land-owning élites. In the event, the government was forced to integrate the old social forces into its new structures and could not (in the Gunaid area and elsewhere) prevent merchants and other local leaders from manipulating these structures for the economic benefit of themselves and their followers.

Like inter-ethnic co-operation, intra-ethnic conflict can be largely explained in terms of patron–client politics, where the patron is either a national leader who reaches down to the grass-roots level or a local leader who is himself a client of the national figure. Again, we take examples from Zambia. As is shown further in the next chapter, the solidarity of the Bemba-speaking 'group', which straddled three provinces, broke down in 1969 as the Luapula Province leaders expressed dissatisfaction with Northern Bemba domination of the alliance and their own meagre share of offices and resources. Though the unity of the Eastern Province, with its numerous ethnic groups (including the Cewa, the Ngoni and the Tumbuka), was maintained after 1967 and was reflected the next year in the formation of a 'Unity in the East Movement', alleged Tumbuka domination was resented *within* the province. As Dr Szeftel has pointed out, the creation of the one-party state in 1972 removed the necessity to maintain party unity in order to contest multi-party elections and meant that a faction united at the centre might split into rival sub-factions at a lower level:

In Livingstone . . . this Tonga–Lozi alliance, which had been a feature of politics between 1968 and 1973, was replaced by bitter factional competition between the two groups when confronted by a candidate from each in the 1973 elections. In Nkana constituency in Kitwe, the presence of three Bemba-speaking candidates did not prevent 'tribalism' from becoming a major issue in the campaign: brokers and supporters developed a concern with the districts and ethnic origins of the candidates – Lala, Namwanga and 'true' Bemba – despite the fact that two candidates came from Northern Province and the other had lived most of his life among the Copperbelt Bemba. In Sinazongwe constituency in the Gwembwe Valley of Southern Province, three candidates were from the same ethnic and linguistic groups, but nevertheless managed to polarise the constituency in terms of the three chiefs areas from which they variously came. There were numerous other instances of the same process occurring throughout the country.[14]

That leaders and their followers tended to act situationally was not only a characteristic of political behaviour in Zambia; the same phenomenon was also to be observed in other African states. For example, in Nigeria the Ibos of the former Eastern Region retained their identity in relation to the country's other cultural–linguistic groups, being linked in this respect with Ibos in the Mid-West, but were themselves split over local matters between the land-locked Owerri Ibo interior and the better-off Ibo riverain groups (Onitsha, Oguta, and Aro); in Uganda, the solidarity of the 'Bantu' peoples of the southern part of the country was less meaningful for most purposes than a 'Ganda', 'Soga', 'Kiga', or 'Gisu' identity; and in Kenya, the dominant Kikuyu group was rent by rivalry between the three Kikuyu districts of Kiambu, Muranga and Nyeri. As Crawford Young explains: 'Most individuals . . . have more than one cultural identity. Which has relevance will depend upon the situational context.' He adds that context will determine 'the saliency and intensity of identities' – thus, in Nigeria ethnic identities flared up as civil war threatened but were more subdued following the federal victory and the policy of reconciliation pursued by General Gowon (the attempted counter-coup of February 1976 revealed, sadly, that they were far from being stilled).[15]

The current, significant alternative to the 'ethnic conflict' model focuses on social class as the prime determinant of political change. This alternative, and predominantly Marxist, model rests on two assumptions: first, that classes exist objectively in Africa, and second that class consciousness is sufficiently developed for political conflict to be explained primarily in class terms.

Class Formation and Class Action

In his paper *Ujamaa*, written in 1962, Julius Nyerere argued that 'the capitalist, or the landed exploiter' was 'unknown to traditional African society'.[16] If this was the reality in some pre-colonial African societies, it was not true of others. In the forest kingdoms of West Africa and the emirates of (what was to become) Northern Nigeria, society was sharply divided between a chiefly strata, often supported by a well-organised bureaucracy, and commoners. Office-holding (especially at the higher levels) and wealth went hand in hand, though some commoners became successful traders.

The advent of colonialism reinforced existing social stratification patterns in some areas, such as Northern Nigeria (the birthplace of indirect rule), but resulted also in the emergence of new, educated élites. Some of the latter became doctors and lawyers; others were employed in the native authorities or the public service (nearly all at the lower levels); and others again became merchants and traders. The class structures generated by colonialism were incipient and uneven in their development; their unevenness depended on the levels of industrialisation and urbanisation reached by the end of the colonial era, as well as on the spread of education. Class formation was distorted in the white settler communities, where Africans competed with whites on very unequal terms.

The resultant class patterns in the newly independent states differed from those to be found in Western settings. The number of Africans in professional occupations was small and, because of the tardiness of Africanisation policies, many senior posts in the public service were still held by expatriates; again, while a mercantile bourgeoisie was present in some states, there were very few African industrial capitalists. The petty-bourgeoisie was of a highly mixed character. Alongside an educated lower-middle class of primary school teachers and clerks, who would be recognisable in Western terms, were a large number of people (many of them women) engaged in private entrepreneurial activity. While a number of them prospered – including some of the West African market women – others scraped together a meagre living as small shopkeepers and traders; most of those engaged in the informal sector had no, or limited, education. Finally, the number of workers in manual employment was small – these workers were also migrant, seeking only seasonal employment; moreover, because of the neglect in most colonies of technical education, there were few craftsmen.

The peasantry at independence was far from constituting a monolithic body, being divided into peasant farmers who grew cash-crops for export, those who produced food for the expanding urban markets, and those – mostly living on marginal land without easy access to the centres of population – who were essentially subsistence farmers. Only those, the smallest category, who were engaged as labourers in plantation agriculture belonged to what might loosely be called a 'rural proletariat'.

There is general agreement that considerable socio-economic differentiation has occurred within the peasantry since independence; this, for example, is what Robert Bates found in Zambia's Luapula Province.[17] However, it is also widely accepted that the peasantry *as a whole* is exploited by urban élites: thus, it is the latter who control the marketing boards which, all too often, fix the price of agricultural produce at a level that bears little relation to the costs of production. Such exploitation is resented and may lead to peasant 'revolt', as in Senegal in 1969–70, when some groundnut-producing peasants expressed their dissatisfaction with government policies by smuggling their harvest across the border to the Gambia (where they both received a higher price and were paid in cash), while others either abandoned or curtailed their cultivation of groundnuts.[18] Though an instance such as this shows that it is not only wage-employees who can develop a common perception of exploitation, it remains true that the peasantry faces substantial problems in organising concerted resistance.

Most African rural economies are not based on plantation

agriculture and the great majority of the people live in scattered homesteads or in small villages, with poor communications linking the various communities. The peasantry is also not a monolithic body: 'Instead of class action in the countryside', wrote Bates of Zambia's Luapula Province, 'we find internal division.'[19] Sandbrook points out that the peasantry is divided by particularistic loyalties to tribe, clan and village, and is 'not so much a "class" as a "society", a distinctive pattern of social and economic life';[20] this is so, though the divisions to which we referred can be horizontal as well as vertical. Again, patron–client networks extend down to the village level and the ability of patrons (such as the Mouride brotherhood of Senegal) to defend peasant interests against governmental economic intrusion reduces the felt need for concerted action; this is particularly the case where there are no visible mechanisms of exploitation such as marketing boards. A further consideration militating against overt resistance is the peasants' ability – shown increasingly in recent years in Tanzania, Uganda and Zambia, among other states – to retreat from production for the market into subsistence farming. These various factors help to account for the lack of a revolutionary consciousness among the peasantry, additional considerations being the absence of a landlord class (except in Ethiopia under Haile Selassie), the remittances received from urban relatives, the habit of deference to superiors (identified by education, public office-holding and wealth), and the lack of peasant self-confidence and requisite leadership to challenge a repressive state apparatus.

While there is broad agreement among scholars of differing ideological persuasion that (in Sandbrook's words) African peasants 'generally exhibit very low "classness"', opinions differ sharply as to whether an identifiable urban proletariat has yet emerged in Africa.[21] In our view, there are several reasons for believing that, over most of the continent, urban workers do not yet show political solidarity as a class. In most states they retain close social ties with their kinsmen in the rural areas and many villagers still migrate to the towns in search of employment; though a settled labour force is now to be found in the towns of Zaire, Zambia and several other states, thus facilitating trade union organisation, seasonal migration is still widespread. The urban workforce, in any case, is not mono-lithic, being divided into skilled, semi-skilled and unskilled workers, the first category being itself subject to many grada-tions. Urban workers in many countries have benefited from state subsidies (often at the expense of the rural population) but in other respects state rewards have most advantaged those who are already well-to-do. Upward mobility, or the prospect of it, dampens class polarisation even when differences of status and wealth are well perceived – Michael Burawoy found that mineworkers on the Zambian Copperbelt saw their own union leaders as part of a new Zambian élite.[22] Moreover, the fact that factional politics has penetrated labour organisations and other modern interest groups also militates against the development of class consciousness.

Though scholars are divided on this issue, they are, for the most part, united in the view that a middle class has emerged, or is emerging, in most African states. This class is made up of political leaders, public servants, businessmen, lawyers, doc-tors and other members of the professions, and military officers – all of whom, in Professor Sklar's terminology, constitute a 'managerial bourgeoisie'.[23] Some scholars are convinced that elements of this bourgeoisie (more commonly termed the 'bureaucratic bourgeoisie'), or the bourgeoisie collectively, consistently act in their own narrow, class interest. Thus Issa Shivji, in his *Class Struggles in Tanzania*, argues that the bureaucratic bourgeoisie in Tanzania sought, through the nationalisation measures which followed in the wake of the Arusha Declaration of 1967, to bring the economy under its control for its own class interests and for the protection of the interests of international capitalism with which this bourgeoisie remains intimately linked. On this view, the Arusha Declaration was not a socialist initiative, but a selfish, class-motivated intervention manipulated into being by the bureaucratic bourgeoisie, whose agent President Nyerere had become. This argument, as Pratt says, brings us 'beyond the credible and into the realm of radical mythology'.[24] If it was valid, Nyerere and his government would not have been so resistant in 1980–2 to the demands of the International Monetary Fund (IMF) that they should moderate the thrust of their socialist policies.

Those Marxists who, after the Arusha Declaration, acclaimed the socialist experiment in Tanzania are now among its severest critics. They allege that Tanzania constitutes a state capitalist system dominated by its bureaucratic bourgeoisie. Their disillusionment stems from a basic misunderstanding of what Julius Nyerere is trying to achieve. Nyerere is, and always has been, a democratic socialist rather than a Marxist. In his introduction to *Freedom and Socialism*, published in 1968, he said that Tanzanian society was groping its way forward toward socialism,

> and we are in danger of being bemused by this new theology, and therefore of trying to solve our problems according to what the priests of Marxism say is what Marx said or meant. If we do this we shall fail. Africa's conditions are very different from those of the Europe in which Marx and Lenin wrote and worked. To talk as if these thinkers provided all the answers to our problems, or as if Marx invented socialism, is to reject both the humanity of Africa and the universality of socialism. Marx did contribute a great deal to socialist thought. But socialism did not begin with him, nor can it end in constant reinterpretations of his writings.[25]

Nyerere's brand of socialism is not therefore of the 'scientific' kind. As Cranford Pratt has pointed out, essential features of Nyerere's transition to socialism are the achievement of a greater measure of equality and an increase in democratic participation in the political institutions of society, the development of a national community that is socialist in its values and in the quality of its life, and the achievement of greater national self-reliance. Important initiatives have been, and continue to be, taken to achieve these objectives. To date, the record is a mixed one of both success and failure. As far as the bureaucratic bourgeoisie is concerned, it is significant that success has been most marked in the very area where it would be least expected if the bourgeoisie was narrowly pursuing its own class interest, that is, in the achievement of a greater equality through the government's policies on income tax, wages and salaries, education and public health. Senior public servants have accepted these policies, though they were initiated by the

politicians and above all by Nyerere himself.[26] Left to themselves, many public servants would no doubt have preferred
that they were not introduced at all – it certainly cannot be
assumed in Tanzania or other African states that the interests
of politicians and bureaucrats will necessarily coincide. Put the
point yet another way: the managerial bourgeoisie comprises
different elements, with often divergent interests, and does not
constitute a monolithic class united in pursuit of its own
aggrandisement. This point can be illustrated briefly from
Zambian experience.

The middle-class has grown markedly in Zambia since
independence. In particular, the economic reforms of 1968–72
resulted in an enormous expansion of the parastatal sector and
therefore of the bureaucracy, and opened up massive new
opportunities for citizen entrepreneurs. All sections of the
middle class subscribe to a materialist ethic, which is strongly
entrenched in Zambian society and which Humanism, Zambia's official ideology, has proved powerless to counter. It is
also true that though the leadership code specifically prohibits
leaders from having private business interests, other than
small-scale enterprises or small-holdings of land, the study of
ownership undertaken by Baylies and Szeftel indicates that an
overlap of public position and private business interests is
characteristic rather than exceptional. Zambian public office-
holders, like their Kenyan counterparts, have either acquired
business interests while still in office or have followed a business
career after leaving office.[27] If such links, reinforced by
connections with multinational companies, warrant Sklar's
description of a managerial bourgeoisie, it is also the case that
the bourgeoisie is subject to internal divisions – divisions which
are reflected in both domestic and foreign policy.

Humanism, which was first elaborated by President Kaunda
in April 1967, favours 'a mixed economy' and combines
capitalist, socialist and populist strands. For Kaunda, socialism has a purely instrumental value; it is 'an instrument for
building a Humanist society'. However, many of the key tenets
of Humanism, such as the commitment to a more egalitarian,
participatory society, are not acceptable to bureaucrats and
businessmen. Mr W. H. Banda, a representative of the latter in
parliament, stated boldly on 5 February 1976 that the party and

government's policy of nationalisation was scaring away foreign investors and endangering the economy. In the next year the indigenous bourgeoisie began to demand that mass welfare programmes and policies should be jettisoned to cope with Zambia's economic crisis, thereby threatening the base of popular support on which the UNIP leadership depends. For the latter, the potential consequences of this trend were serious; as Morris Szeftel has asserted: 'If individuals articulate class interests in their capacities as members of the bourgeoisie, they must nevertheless continue also to articulate geographic interests in their capacities as politicians and leaders of factions.'[28]

That class has not yet become the sole, or even primary, determinant of political behaviour in Tanzania and Zambia is underlined if one considers the position of the urban work-force in the two countries. There is no evidence to substantiate Shivji's contention that the strikes and lock-outs which took place in Dar es Salaam in 1972 were the prelude to a revolutionary struggle for socialism by workers and poor peasants. The latter groups were not out to promote a particular ideology, but wanted to improve the standard of living of themselves and their families. They were, as Hyden suggests, reacting spontaneously to the call made in *Mwongozo*, the TANU Guidelines of 1971, for the assertion of workers' rights.[29] Workers in Tanzania retain close social ties with their rural homes. In Zambia, on the Copperbelt, there is a greater class consciousness among an urban workforce that has become more 'stabilised' since independence. However, mineworkers especially are highly paid and, at least until the downturn of the economy in recent years, have merited the designation of 'labour aristocracy' rather than 'urban proletariat'. To a considerable extent, urban workers do not yet perceive conflict in class terms and political leaders do not seek to win support by exploiting class divisions. The position in Zambia is admirably summarised by Morris Szeftel:

In the urban context, the differential incorporation of various regions has tended to offset the solidarity created by class and interest associations such as trade unions and business groups. The process of labour migration has preserved the links between peasant and proletarian – and indeed combined them within many individuals. In any case, urban groups on their own are generally too small to be attractive as recruiting grounds for political leaders who can more easily and more profitably (in terms of support) continue to use the vertical links based on regionalism. More importantly, uneven development ensures that the most preferred resources and rewards are concentrated in the urban areas. It is there that faction leaders compete for spoils and that many rural people look for the opportunities which might free them from the poverty of the village economy. Thus, within the interest associations of the towns, the regional character of competition for scarce resources is also manifest; allegations of factionalism occur within the arena of trade union or business activities just as they do within the political party itself. In consequence, the articulation of factional interest in the towns takes much the same form as that in rural areas; people compete for a share of the spoils in terms of a faction defined with reference to the region of origin of the individuals concerned.[30]

Evidence from Nigeria also points to the rise of a vigorous and assertive middle class which, since the civil war of 1967–70, has consolidated its class position through the further expansion of the state sector and the indigenisation of capitalist enterprise.[31] However, as the 1979 general elections revealed, Nigerian political leaders still seek, as do their counterparts in Zambia, to win support on the basis of ethnicity and language rather than class. Alhaji Aminu Kano's People's Redemption Party (PRP) hardly constituted an exception to this pattern, despite its appeal to the 'common man'. In any case the party, which is populist socialist rather than Marxist, fared indifferently in the elections as a whole – taking the number of seats which the party won in all types of election and the percentage vote received by its candidate in the presidential election, the PRP attracted on average only 10 per cent support.[32]

It also seems unlikely that class has yet become the main determinant of political behaviour even in the scientific socialist states, such as Angola and Mozambique. Both these states are subject to acute internal divisions, rendering the achievement of national integration an urgent problem; though the ruling party in each case is attempting to raise the level of class consciousness through political education campaigns, patron–client networks, which cut across the party's organisational ties, are often salient in the rural areas. These are, after all, states in transition to socialism rather than socialist states in which the interests of urban workers and poor peasants are already paramount – President Machel of Mozambique, for example, has fulminated against self-seeking state and party bureaucrats.

To summarise this section, it is our contention that, in general, class identifications have not yet emerged sufficiently to structure political conflict in most of sub-Saharan Africa. Pre-capitalist forms of production persist in many up-country areas and the rural people, often operating at little above subsistence level, do not yet see themselves as an obviously or directly exploited class. Urban workers tend to earn high wages by comparison with the rural people, but often retain close social links with them. Despite a relatively high level of cohesion, organised labour has (in the words of Baylies and Szeftel) 'represented a reformist and economistic, rather than radical, voice' in most countries.[33] Class consciousness is most highly developed among the emergent middle class, which is closely associated with the state apparatus; however, this class is internally divided. Even the bureaucracy often lacks unity and cohesion; though an important segment of the middle class, it does not constitute an autonomous centre of power. For its part, the entrepreneurial bourgeoisie can vigorously oppose policies which are detrimental to its interests, but in most countries it is dependent on the state for public subsidies and loans and for creating a climate in which private enterprise can prosper. Of course, the more capitalist the state structure, the greater will be the identity of interest between the state and the indigenous entrepreneurial bourgeoisie; that identity will be reflected, as in Botswana, Gabon, the Ivory Coast, Kenya, Nigeria and Zambia, by a substantial overlap of public position and private business interests.

Moreover, if it is accepted that factionalism is situationally defined, there is on *a priori* grounds no inherent incompatibility between communalism and nationalism since a political leader can be a staunch factionalist in one context and a strong nationalist in another wider context and this can apply to his followers too. While Sandbrook is in general right to argue that 'the study of factionalism *per se* is . . . not particularly edifying', being characterised by 'scheming' and 'manoeuvring', his definition is too negative to fit every situation: 'Factionalism is a form of conflict over access to wealth, power, and status, frequently with only minor ideological and policy implications, in which members of the conflict units are recruited on the basis of mercenary ties.'[34] It can, indeed, be argued that a certain amount of factional competition can be healthy for the body politic, not least in the one-party state. The danger comes when loyalty to faction becomes so all-embracing that it is socially disruptive and functionally disintegrative, as has occurred in Chad throughout much of the post-independence period and in Uganda following the ousting of Idi Amin in 1979.

Communalism and Class

Factional analysis, as a tool for the examination of élite behaviour, applies equally to contexts where ethnic and religious ties are politically salient and to settings where class-based lines of division are uppermost. Many non-Marxists downgrade the class factor. Thus, Ali Mazrui argues that the Marxists are wrong to assume that people of different ethnic and cultural backgrounds have, to a high degree, already been integrated into the nation–state, and adds: 'This is an assumption which cannot be made in analysing integration in, say, African countries. In fact, tribes and races are more total identities than are economic classes. The process of integrating tribes and races tends therefore to be more complex.'[35] On this projection, communalism is at once the prime determinant of political behaviour and the main obstacle to the achievement of national integration. Secondly, at the other extreme, we have the view expressed by some Marxists (though rejected by other Marxists as a crude formulation) that it is above all class which determines political behaviour: 'although traditional rural communities may exist, ethnicity is nothing but an erroneous comprehension of social deprivation which should be understood in class terms.'[36] Such Marxists allege that proponents of the modernisation school, to which Professor Mazrui belongs, are so engrossed with problems of cultural pluralism that they neglect economic-based facts; they themselves see tribalism as 'false consciousness' and peasants as merely the passive victims of the process of change.

To complicate the issues here, we also have a range of intermediate views. There is the argument put forward by Goran Hyden that communal action continues to encapsulate the process of class formation, thereby weakening the social forces set in motion by capitalism. He maintains that this is because capitalism did not destroy existing peasant modes of production and social formations based, for example, on family and kinship units. Though the majority of African producers are small, they have not lost their independence or been marginalised by other social classes in a manner that characterises large parts of Asia and South America. In short, they constitute for Hyden an 'uncaptured peasantry' who share an 'economy of affection', with familial and other communal ties providing the basis for organised activity. They remain outside the control of the state and are thus a barrier to the achievement of both national integration and economic development. This argument may have some validity for those rural dwellers in Tanzania (the focus of Hyden's study) who have not been integrated into the market economy or who, because of depressed prices for their produce, have withdrawn from it and reverted to subsistence farming. However, to several observers Hyden's 'uncaptured peasantry' thesis is more ingenious than convincing.[37]

Another intermediate argument, advanced by Sklar in his 1967 article and by Molteno in 1974, draws upon the currently prevalent Marxist view which denies that class *determines* political behaviour, but asserts instead that class should be the starting-point of political analysis even if one is then obliged to recognise the present importance of communalism as a form of false consciousness. This argument, which has already been referred to, is that traditional attachments may influence political behaviour, but typically not exclusively or primarily – that is, 'tribalism' is a dependent, rather than an independent, variable; it is a vehicle of expression, masking underlying economic divisions, rather than a primordial political force in the nation. The stand which these writers took is consistent with the view subsequently put forward by Morris Szeftel that the pursuit of class interests by members of the (Zambian) bourgeoisie does not prevent them from also articulating ethnic and regional interests as factional leaders. It is also compatible, for that matter, with the view advanced by Crawford Young: 'It is not necessary to deny cultural pluralism in order to assert class.'[38] Young cites the American racial situation to illustrate his argument: the lower-income segment of the Black community is not merely a social class since it is in part Black consciousness which has led to the failure of Blacks and poor Whites to form durable alliances. (This point could equally be illustrated by experience in those parts of colonial Africa where there was substantial European settlement: as Szeftel shows for Zambia, racial divisions prevented any identification of class interests between African and European businessmen or between African and European workers. Instead, it 'created an identity of interest between all classes of a particular race against all classes of the other'.)[39] At times, Young maintains, social stratification may overlap with cultural cleavage, with each reinforcing the other and, in such circumstances, it becomes analytically difficult to demonstrate which factor is primary, which variable independent.

Professor Young's observations merit further elaboration. He points out that competition for power and access to economic resources takes place in most parts of the Third World within a culturally diverse or plural society. It is often expressed in non-economic terms, which correspond with the dominant divisions in society and are easily understandable to the rural people. In this way, the strong rational element in most communal demands may be obscured. The same point may be put another way: since, as Crawford Young maintains, the pattern of cultural pluralism is very different in Africa from that in Asia (and, we may add, different again in Latin America, the Caribbean and the Middle East), factional competition will be expressed in different terms according to the social context; thus, the dominant vehicle of expression is likely to be tribalism or ethnicity in Africa, religion, language or caste in Asia, regionalism in Latin America, and confessionalism in the Lebanon. But basically we are dealing with the same phenomenon – a phenomenon which, incidentally, is not unknown in the industrialised states of the West (including Canada, Belgium and Yugoslavia), though fewer groups are likely to be involved.[40]

These views correspond more closely with those put forward earlier by Sklar and Molteno, each of whom regarded the cultural factor as at most a dependent variable, than with those of Mazrui, who suggested that conflict was rooted primarily in the culture of society itself. Yet it is not difficult to present cases which, on the face of it, substantiate the stand taken by Professor Mazrui. For example, it might be argued that in Botswana the Botswana National Front (BNF) easily won both seats in Kanye, the Ngwaketse tribal capital, in successive general elections (1969, 1974 and 1979) primarily because Mr B. S. Gaseitsiwe, the leader of the BNF, was Chief Bathoen II of the Bangwaketse until 1969, when he resigned his chieftainship to contest the election, being succeeded by his son, Seepapitso, who is still chief.[41] While such an ethnic explanation cannot be lightly dismissed, it obscures the rational element in voting behaviour – in the case of Kanye South constituency, the perception of the people that the ex-chief was the candidate who could best articulate their grievances and demands; he has been both an able and conscientious MP.

There is, in fact, plenty of evidence – for example, from Ghana, Kenya, Nigeria, Uganda and Zambia among Anglophone states – pointing in a different direction from Ali Mazrui and in support of Molteno's argument that sectional groups are merely interest groups competing for scarce economic resources, with the leaders often invoking traditional sentiments to reinforce their appeal. The success of political leaders in winning popular backing depends upon the trust which they inspire and ultimately on their ability to obtain material benefits for their faction, in the shape perhaps of a government job or loan, a clinic or school, a road or a bridge. As we have suggested above and as we show further in the next chapter, we are dealing with a kind of patronage politics, with economic resources used as political currency to enable the leadership to buy support for their policies.[42] Political and bureaucratic leaders may well make their appeal in ethnic, linguistic, religious or regional terms (or a combination of them), thus often obscuring the real causes of group conflict; this pattern, which reflects the present strength of vertical divisions in society, can be expected to change as a national market economy develops further, giving rise to a more nation-wide pattern of social stratification. It should be remembered, however, that the motivational triggers of group conflict, viewed from the popular rather than the élite end, while often rational, can also be both complex and laden with various 'non-rational' and 'non-instrumental' elements, stemming perhaps from what Hyden has called the 'economy of affection'. Further, while the sources of the conflict may ultimately be both economic *and* contemporary, the stereotypes may well be anchored to memories of past (pre-colonial) group hostilities; these stereotypes may acquire a life of their own and affect élite as well as popular attitudes.

Further Reading

Allen, C., and Williams, G. (eds.), *Sociology of Developing Societies: Sub-Saharan Africa* (London: Macmillan, 1982).

Balans, J. L., Coulon, C., and Gastellu, J.-M., *Autonomie Locale et Intégration Nationale au Sénégal* (Paris: Editions A. Pedone, 1975).

Dunn, J., and Robertson, A. F., *Dependence and Opportunity: Political Change in Ahafo* (Cambridge University Press, 1974).

Hyden, G., *Beyond Ujamaa in Tanzania. Underdevelopment and an Uncaptured Peasantry* (London: Heinemann, 1980).

Melson, R., and Wolpe, H., *Nigeria: Modernization and the Politics of Communalism* (East Lansing: Michigan State University Press, 1971).

Molteno, R., 'Cleavage and Conflict in Zambian Politics: A Study in Sectionalism', in Tordoff, W. (ed.), *Politics in Zambia* (Manchester University Press, 1974).

O'Brien, D. B. Cruise, *Saints and Politicians: Essays in the Organisation of a Senegalese Peasant Society* (London: Cambridge University Press, 1975).

Rothchild, D., and Olorunsola, V., *State versus Ethnic Claims: African Policy Dilemmas* (Boulder: Westview, 1982).

Sandbrook, R., 'Patrons, Clients and Factions: New Dimensions of Conflict Analysis in Africa', *Canadian Journal of Political Science*, vol. v, no. 1 (March 1972).

Sandbrook, R., and Cohen, R. (eds.), *The Development of an African Working Class: Studies in Class Formation and Action* (University of Toronto Press, 1975).

Sklar, R. L., 'The Nature of Class Domination in Africa', *Journal of Modern African Studies*, vol. 17, no. 4 (1979).

Young, C., *The Politics of Cultural Pluralism* (Madison: University of Wisconsin Press, 1976).

5

Political Parties

In chapter 3 we examined the contribution made by political parties to the achievement of independence. This chapter asks the question: what was the *raison d'être* of these parties once independence had been achieved? To answer it we identify, at the risk of repeating some of the points made in the introduction, certain political trends.

First, there was the trend towards single-party rule. In 1958 France's African territories (except Guinea which voted 'No' in the Fifth Republican referendum) became autonomous republics within the French Community. Two years later each republic achieved its independence separately under an agreement which guaranteed that close links with France would be retained. The new states inherited the centralising traditions of the French, and most of them quickly became subject to one-party rule. To judge from the high level of support shown in pre-independence elections, most ruling parties in Francophone Africa rested on a broad base of voluntary acceptance – as Ruth Collier shows there were, in general, higher levels of electoral participation in French Africa than in British Africa. However, coercion or electoral fraud was applied in several states (for example, in Cameroon, Chad, Gabon and Togo) where opposition groups did not voluntarily accept a one-party state.[1]

Competitive party politics survived longer in English-speaking Africa, though in the final analysis it continued without interruption only in the Gambia, Botswana, and Mauritius. Between independence in 1960 and the military coup in 1966, Nigeria had no truly national party: the federal government was a coalition of regionally based parties, with the NPC as the dominant partner. In Sierra Leone, competition between the SLPP and the All People's Congress (APC) continued until the military intervened in 1967. In Ghana, the United Party, which had been inaugurated in November 1957 after the CPP Government had proscribed regionally and tribally based parties, survived precariously until the one-party state was officially introduced in 1964. Tanganyika had already become a *de facto* one-party state before independence in 1961; legalisation followed in 1965. In Kenya, the Kenya African Democratic Union, which sought to safeguard the interests of the country's minority communities, dissolved voluntarily at the end of 1964; however, from 1966 another party – the radically-inclined Kenya People's Union – challenged KANU's supremacy until it was banned in October 1969. Thereafter, Kenya settled down as a *de facto* one-party state, though KANU's monopoly of power was eventually legalised in 1982. In Zambia, competitive party politics survived for eight years after independence, until a one-party state was established at the end of 1972.

The political leaders of these various one-party states gave a number of sometimes contradictory reasons for establishing one-party rule; thus, it was said on the one hand that the single party was necessary to end factionalism and to achieve national unity and, on the other, that the single party reflected the basic consensus of African society. Whatever the reason – and selfish motives on the part of the African leaders themselves obviously cannot be excluded – there were often sharp differences between one single party and another. The political monopoly of power by one party might rest on a *de facto* basis and that of another party on a *de jure* basis, while the ideological underpinning of the single party was strong in one case (for example, the PDG in Guinea) and weak or non-existent in another (the PDCI in the Ivory Coast). The mandate for one-party rule was clear in some countries (for example, Tanzania) and uncertain in others (Ghana, Zambia); this was revealed in the pre-independence elections in Tanganyika and the Gold Coast in 1960 and 1956 respectively, and in Zambia in the general election of 1968: whereas TANU won all National Assembly seats except one in Tanganyika, the opposition parties in the

Gold Coast and Zambia did well in terms of both votes and seats. Again, while some parties such as TANU allowed considerable intra-party competition, others, such as the PDG and the CPP increasingly, did not. Such differences between single parties are difficult to plot typologically, though James Coleman and Carl Rosberg made the attempt in 1964, when they distinguished between one-party states of the pragmatic–pluralistic pattern and those of the revolutionary–centralising trend.[2]

A second trend is that many parties, in the post-independence period, rest on a firmer ideological base than they did before independence; this is understandable since party leaders needed to give their followers a new sense of direction and purpose. However, as indicated above, the ideological spectrum has remained wide. Most parties claimed to be socialist, but often it was socialism of a reformist and pragmatic, rather than revolutionary, kind. Rhetorical flourishes notwithstanding, this was true of the CPP and of the Union Soudanaise in Mali, where Modibo Keita's socialism was (in the words of Pierre François) 'always very fluid and imprecise'. Even in Guinea there were deviations from Marxist theory; Sékou Touré concentrated 'on the general political interest, rather than on a more particular class or economic interest', noted Charles Andrain, adding, 'Like Lenin, Touré emphasizes the dominance of the political'.[3] In Tanzania the stress on equality was the vital aspect of Nyerere's brand of non-Marxist socialism, while Zambian Humanism comprised capitalist and populist, as well as socialist, strands. Overall, the ideological base of African political parties was weak in the 1960s. Ideologies were often no more than a cluster of ideas elaborated by the party leader (thus Nasser gave us Nasserism and Nkrumah, Nkrumaism) and lacked systematisation, comprehensiveness and coherence; they therefore served as uncertain blueprints for action. Only in the 1970s did a substantial number of ruling parties comes to rest firmly on Marxist–Leninist doctrine – among them the Movimento Popular de Libertação de Angola (MPLA) in Angola, PAIGC in Guinea-Bissau, and the Frente de Libertação de Moçambique (FRE-LIMO) in Mozambique – giving rise to what Rosberg and Callaghy have described as 'a second wave' of socialist regimes.[4]

A third trend has been not only the move away from political pluralism and towards the concentration of power in the hands of a single, ruling party but also the personalisation of power. In the great majority of cases, the party leader after independence has become the national president, constitutionally vested with the executive power. Though policy-making often remains a complex and composite process, it has increasingly been the president, acting with or without the concurrence of his cabinet, who has taken key policy decisions rather than the leading organs of the party. This feature is to be observed no less in Tanzania and Zambia than in Guinea and Sierra Leone, even though in Tanzania major policy initiatives (such as the Arusha Declaration of 1967) have usually been announced by, or in the name of, the party's national executive committee and, as Jeannette Hartmann shows, in the post-Arusha period party activists have been more assertive in policy-making, with the result that economic considerations have often been neglected. When presidential initiatives fail, either because they have not been critically examined before being promulgated or because the president's interest has shifted elsewhere, the party itself is discredited.

Though an African president might seek, as President Kaunda of Zambia does, to accommodate demands from his party, the state bureaucracy and the business community (both domestic and foreign), among other associations, he is not subject to the constraints imposed upon the head of government in a liberal democratic state by a host of powerful interest groups. This is less because such groups are either rare or weak than because those which do exist tend to lack the resources to command leverage, let alone interact with government on an ongoing basis. What Joel Samoff wrote of Tanzania suggests, further, that the African state itself may function to discourage a climate of 'group enterprise' vis-à-vis government:

In Tanzania, party policy frowns on the formation of interest groups in general, and economic interest groups in particular. Except for trade unions, co-operatives, and social and charitable organizations, it is assumed that the interests of any particular section of the population can be adequately represented by TANU and its auxiliaries, and that adherence to bureaucratic norms assures individuals fair and just treatment without the need for recourse to interest group protection. In other words, it is assumed that the political functions performed by interest groups in other polities – especially interest aggregation, articulation, and communication – are performed by TANU and its auxiliaries, and that interest groups, which could be used to form competing centres of power, are both unnecessary and dangerous. In addition, it is assumed that interest groups with a primarily economic orientation represent anti-socialist elements in the society and therefore should not be tolerated.[5]

The increased limitations on the role of interest groups represent a fourth trend, which can be examined briefly in the light of trade union experience.

There are economic, social and political reasons why the governments of new African states have been inclined to put an end to such trade-union autonomy as existed before independence.[6] In summary form, these are: the position of the state as the chief employer of labour and therefore as the butt of wage demands; the inflationary effect on the economy of conceding such demands, perhaps as a result of strike action, and the consequent widening of the rural–urban gap; and the possible political challenge presented to the government by a well-organised trade union movement, strongly entrenched in the urban areas. The tactics employed by African governments to control the trade unions have included giving recalcitrant labour leaders positive rewards, perhaps in the form of a ministerial or ambassadorial post, as well as invoking negative sanctions such as imprisonment, exile, or the ending of legally protected union privileges (for example, the highly prized check-off system, whereby union dues are automatically deducted by the employer from the workers' wage packets). Other measures used have been to cause a split in the trade union movement by creating a rival union organisation, friendly to the government, and resort to legislation – anti-strike laws have been adopted and a strengthened central trade union body has been helped to control the individual unions compulsorily affiliated to it. However, control over trade unions is not everywhere complete or universally successful in preventing strike action, as the cases of Congo-Brazzaville (now the People's Republic of Congo), Dahomey (now Benin), Ghana, Senegal, Sudan, Tanzania, Tunisia, Upper Volta and Zambia (among others) reveal; in the 1960s the strikes of civil servants, teachers and/or students resulted in the fall of the governments of Abbé Fulbert Youlou in Congo-Brazzaville, General Ibrahim Abboud in the Sudan, and Maurice Yaméogo in Upper Volta. The Tanzanian case is particularly instructive: not only did the National Union of Tanganyika Workers (Establishment) Act, 1964, establish one central union, comprising various industrial sections, it also provided for the general secretary of the union and his deputy to be appointed by the President of the Republic; moreover, as a corollary to the Act, provision was made in the objects of the new union for the latter 'to be affiliated to TANU, to promote the policies of TANU, and to encourage its members to join TANU'. Yet, despite the tightness of the control thereby established over the trade union movement, workers in Dar es Salaam staged a series of strikes and lock-outs in 1972. In pointing to the harmful effects on the economy of such work stoppages, African governments have emphasized the need for government–union dialogue and for wage increases to be linked to improvements in productivity. Some governments, such as those of Mozambique and Tanzania, have also attempted – not yet successfully – to introduce workers' participation in industrial management.

A final trend, closely related to the introduction of the one-party state and the advent of presidential rule, is the subordination of the party to the state. Already at independence the state was the main agent of economic development, and subsequently, through the creation of public enterprises and state marketing boards, it has extended its long arm into most areas of economic life. As the regulation of economic activity has become increasingly technical and scientific, the prime economic activists and advisers have been drawn from government administrators and technical personnel rather than party functionaries. At independence, the party lost a large number of its key personnel to the state and, by contrast with the latter, has been chronically short of well-qualified manpower ever since. In Algeria, as in the great majority of states, the ruling party has been ill-equipped to play a supervisory role. Roberts writes:

> Since independence the FLN has possessed neither the authority nor the technical competence to orient and supervise the activity of the administrative apparatus of the state . . . Neither armed forces nor bureaucracy have been subject to its authority. In a sense, therefore, the Party and its ramifications could be regarded as part of the bureaucracy, performing essentially a public relations function on its behalf . . . Its job was to explain and justify decisions taken elsewhere, not to reason why.[7]

At the sub-national levels of region and district, the various development committees established in many states have tended to be dominated by bureaucrats; this applies even in a country such as Tanzania, where, to a greater extent than in most states, the party has retained some of its former vitality. In sum, the decline of the party and the consequent demoralisation of its personnel has been a fairly universal feature of the post-independence African scene. It remains to be seen whether this trend will also occur in the newer states of Angola and Mozambique; the PAIGC, the party common to both Guinea-Bissau and Cape Verde at independence, survived only on the mainland following the 1980 coup.

Party Roles

The Integrative Function

In the light of these various trends, we can now ask: what role can, and does, a political party still play in the African context? In the first place, the party is expected, as in Nigeria, to fulfil an integrative function. The stress placed on the principle of state equality in the Nigerian constitution of 1979 underlines the perception of its framers that the fabric of national unity is still uncertain in Nigeria. For the purpose of the 1979 elections in that country, a political party could only be registered if it met a number of stringent conditions which were designed to satisfy the Federal Electoral Commission that it was not an association 'confined to a part only of the geographical area of Nigeria'; its headquarters had to be in the federal capital and its executive committee had to reflect Nigeria's 'federal character'.[8] These conditions showed that in Nigeria the constitution-makers looked to the registered political parties to inculcate national values in place of communal or parochial values. This is what FRELIMO in Mozambique is seeking to achieve by means of an intensive political education campaign, especially in those areas which were barely penetrated by pre-independence guerrilla activity. The evidence from certain other states as to how well a political party succeeds in this task is sometimes contradictory: thus, in his *TANU Yajenga Nchi* (1968), Goran Hyden points to the success of TANU in institutionalising new cultural values in the rural communities of mainland Tanzania, but in *Beyond Ujamaa* (1980) he finds that 'familial and other communal ties provide the basis for organized activity' among Tanzanian peasants.[9]

The Legitimising Function

We can also identify what can be termed a legitimising role for the party. In a competitive party situation – such as exists in Botswana, the Gambia, Mauritius and (since 1976) Senegal, and as existed in Ghana between 1969 and 1972 and again between 1979 and 1981, in Nigeria for four years following the restoration of civilian rule in 1979, and in Uganda in 1980 – each party seeks to win maximum support at a general election. However, the winning party will only confer legitimacy on the successor government if the election is widely accepted as being free and fair. This condition was satisfied in Ghana and Nigeria in 1979, but not in Uganda, where the opposition Democratic Party claimed, with some justification, that the 1980 election results were 'doctored' in favour of President Milton Obote's Uganda People's Congress (UPC); Uganda has subsequently suffered from serious outbreaks of political violence. In the one-party context, elections are used by the ruling party in an attempt to demonstrate that it has a mandate for its continuance in office and for its policies. In most of Francophone Africa, and notably in those military regimes, such as that of

Mali, which seek to clothe themselves in civilian garb, the people turn out in large numbers to pledge their support for the ruling party's list of candidates in what are essentially 'plebiscitary' elections. In English-speaking Africa the presidential election, in which electors vote 'Yes' or 'No' for a single candidate put forward by the party, serves the same purpose of reaffirming the government's continued right to rule; parliamentary elections, by contrast, revolve around local rather than national issues. However, while the party makes a major effort to secure a large 'Yes' vote and is able to draw upon government transport and other state resources, the electorate in at least some states is free to register a 'No' vote if it wishes; thus, in Zambia's Southern Province (a former opposition area) 'Yes' votes only narrowly outnumbered 'No' votes in the 1978 presidential election, and in one constituency were under 25 per cent of the votes cast.[10]

The Policy Function

Another potential role for the party is the formulation and execution of policy. For reasons already outlined – including the subordination of the party to the state, the indifferent quality of its personnel, and the increasingly technical nature of economic activity – the party's role in policy-making is often limited to that of ratifying decisions taken elsewhere; this applies, for example, to the drawing up of national development plans. Zambia, under the one-party state, has operated a tandem arrangement, whereby the UNIP central committee supposedly makes policy and the cabinet executes it. In fact, though the central committee stepped in to revoke highly unpopular major price increases of a number of commodities, including bread and cooking oil, in November 1974, this 'bread crisis' affords an isolated instance of the central committee asserting its control over the cabinet, at a time when the President was out of the country. As far as public (as distinct from party-political) policy-making is concerned, the cabinet retains its primacy in advising the President. Morris Szeftel notes: '. . . despite the nominal supremacy of the Central Committee over the Cabinet, real resources and thus real decisions lie with the latter and with the President.'[11]

In most states, too, except perhaps at village level where no or few government officers reside, responsibility for formulating and executing policy has passed increasingly from the party to agents of the state – purposely since independence in Kenya, where President Jomo Kenyatta appointed members of the provincial administration as his agents for development, and in less deliberate but still marked fashion elsewhere. Occasionally, the initiative has been taken by voluntary associations, as in Tanzania's Kilimanjaro Region, of which Samoff records that:

> The local TANU organization plays no direct role in educational decisions, and even though many people seek TANU assistance in a wide range of problems, very few come to the TANU office for school problems. While the TANU regional executive secretary sits on the Moshi Town Council education committee as a nominated councillor, he and other TANU officials subscribe to the prevailing mythology that education is the concern of the technical experts, and do not become directly involved in educational matters.[12]

In fact, it is the Roman Catholic and Lutheran missions – and not the government or TANU – which dominate education decision-making in Kilimanjaro. This picture, underlining the importance of informal mechanisms of decision-making on issues which, like education and liquor licensing, have a high local salience, has probably not changed significantly following the introduction in 1972 of decentralisation measures. The latter have resulted (as have corresponding measures in most other African states) in the deconcentration of administrative authority and the burgeoning of the number of bureaucrats rather than in meaningful political devolution. The chief beneficiaries of this process have been senior civil servants: the regional development director at regional level and the district development director at district level; officials of TANU – rechristened in 1977 as Chama cha Mapinduzi (CCM) following its merger with the Afro-Shirazi Party (ASP) of Zanzibar – have been left to fulfil an ill-defined watching brief over government activity.[13]

Mobilisation and Reconciliation Functions

In some states, the party may retain a limited mobilising role. Indeed, 'mobilisation' (mobilising the people for economic development through self-help) was seen in the early post-independence period as a task for which the party was pre-eminently suited. However, much of this enthusiasm was misdirected or unco-ordinated (thus, a village school might be built without first ascertaining that a teacher would be appointed to it), and could not in any case be sustained over a long period. Even in this sphere, the initiative might be taken by the government, rather than the ruling party, as was the case with Botswana's accelerated rural development programme (ARDP) between 1973 and 1976, or by vote-seeking government ministers, as tends to happen under Kenya's *harambee* programme. If, overall, the party has proved a somewhat weak mobilisation agent, part of the blame must lie with the central government which has usually been reluctant to encourage non-productive participatory activities that increase the demand (for materials and manpower) upon its own resources. Botswana's experience under the ARDP, referred to above, shows however that a policy of devolving responsibility to the local level can pay good dividends, since, as Robert Chambers has noted: 'The ARDP revealed and developed far greater implementation capacity in the districts than was expected. Councils and local contractors did more than many believed they could.'[14] Similarly, the government of Mozambique seeks to tap local energy in order to improve the living standard of the rural people: it places a high value on popular participation and has created new structures to encourage it.

In 1965, David Apter distinguished between political parties which fulfilled mobilisation functions and those which played a reconciliation role.[15] This distinction is not particularly helpful, since accommodating different interests and mediating conflict are functions which any kind of political party might be expected to perform. They were important in Zambia where factionalism within UNIP was rife at the time of, and after, the elections to the party's central committee in 1967. However, in this sphere, too, the initiative in many states has passed to the president and his personal representatives at regional and district levels.

The Patronage Function

Historically, the patronage functions of political parties have been important and in some cases remain so today, especially in multi-party states where a party promises its future patronage in return for electoral support. Take Nigeria, for example. Between 1954 and 1963 the federation was divided into three regions, each region being ruled by a party which was rooted in the region's dominant cultural-linguistic group – Yoruba in the West, Ibo in the East and Hausa-Fulani in the North. Each party (the AG, the NCNC, and the NPC) used its regional power base to confer benefits on its supporters, to strengthen its hold over its own region, and to gain direct access to national resources by capturing power at the centre (in this last respect, the NPC succeeded best because of the numerical preponderance of the Northern population). Events in the Western Region were particularly revealing.[16] In the period before 1962, the AG ruled the region in alliance with leading chiefs and businessmen, and won popular support by providing a wide range of services, including free primary education, medical facilities, tarred roads and water supplies. Moreover, as the Coker Tribunal of Inquiry revealed in 1962, the ruling party siphoned off some £6 million of public money into its own coffers, thus enabling it to strengthen its organisation and further reward its supporters. In 1962, however, the party split into two wings, one led by Chief Awolowo, the federal opposition leader, and the other by Chief S. L. Akintola, Awolowo's former deputy and the Western Region premier. This internal crisis prompted the federal government to replace the elected regional government with an Administrator and to weaken the West and the AG further by carving a new region (the Mid-West) out of the old Western Region in 1963. When Chief Akintola returned in that year as the head of a coalition government, he was dependent on federal support. In order to strengthen his own position and that of the ruling party (the Nigerian National Democratic Party (NNDP), formed as a result of a merger between his own United People's Party and a wing of the Western NCNC) he forged an alliance with the NPC. The NPC-dominated Nigerian National Alliance (NNA) enabled Akintola to tap federal resources for the benefit of the West, but, as world prices for cocoa and other products fell, the region seemed to most voters less prosperous than during the period of AG rule. Convinced that he could not win a 'free and fair' contest, Akintola blatantly rigged the 1965 regional elections and thereby sealed his own fate; in January 1966 he was assassinated by the military, and the NNDP, as well as all other political parties in the country, was proscribed.

The ban on overt political party activity in Nigeria was lifted in September 1978, preparatory to the return to civilian rule in October of the next year. Under the 1979 constitution, the fact that the political parties have to be national in character does not prevent them from exercising a locally-focused patronage function or of conferring maximum benefit on that geographical area of Nigeria where the party is most strongly entrenched – for example, the overwhelmingly Yoruba-speaking states of Ogun, Ondo and Oyo and the Yoruba-dominated Lagos state in the case of Chief Awolowo's Unity Party of Nigeria (UPN), which has inherited the mantle of the former AG. The party all but swept the board in these states in the 1979 elections and formed the government in each of them, thereby underlining the people's trust in Awolowo and their confidence in his party's ability to extract resources from the centre, even though it did not share in the ruling coalition dominated by the National Party of Nigeria (NPN). In 1983, however, the UPN hegemony in the western states was breached in elections which, over the country as a whole, showed a marked trend towards the NPN. The latter retained the presidency, won overall control of both the federal House of Representatives and Senate, and did well in the state gubernatorial and assembly elections. The UPN retained massive support in Lagos and Ogun states, winning in each case the governorship and all the seats in the state assembly, as well as all those in these states for the Senate and House of Representatives. It also won a majority of assembly seats in Ondo state and, following an election petition, its candidate was adjudged by the courts to have been elected governor. In Oyo state, however, the NPN captured the governorship and secured overwhelming control of the assembly. The gubernatorial elections in Ondo and Oyo states were marred by serious outbreaks of violence, and Chief Awolowo alleged that electoral malpractice was widespread. None the less, the overall picture is clear: while a large number of people in the western states, including Lagos, continued to pledge their loyalty to Awolowo and to look to him and his party for benefits, many others perceived that they would fare better by joining the NPN bandwagon.[17]

The Ghana case is no less instructive. In the 1956 general election the majority of the Brongs voted for the ruling CPP in the belief that if the party was returned to power, it would honour the official pledge given in a White Paper published in April 1956 to establish a separate Brong Region, with its own Regional Assembly and House of Chiefs. That this (and the perception that a separate region would lead to the channelling of additional resources to the area) was the real issue and not the fact that the Ashanti, the traditional enemies of the Brongs, strongly supported the rival NLM, was shown in the 1969 election. On that occasion, both the Brongs and the Ashanti voted solidly for the Progress Party (PP) led by Kofi Busia, the former parliamentary leader, as it happened, of the NLM; the PP had assured the Brongs in its election campaign that it would not seek to dismember the Brong–Ahafo Region, which had been legally established in 1959, and had made it clear that the region would benefit more by backing Progress than any of the rival parties.[18]

Zambia affords a third example of the patronage function at work: in this case, as we saw in chapter 4, the predominant pattern is that the various factions which make up UNIP, the ruling coalition, compete with each other for party and government office and therefore for the ability to distribute spoils to their supporters. In the multi-party context (1964–72), this competition was intense. Sometimes a faction operated singly but, most often, linked up with another faction to form a 'super-faction' (in Morris Szeftel's terminology). Thus, in 1967 the Bemba-speaking group combined with the Ila–Tonga speaking group in order to capture key UNIP central committee posts, which at that time guaranteed appointment to a corresponding cabinet office (for example, the party vice-president became national Vice-President and the party treasurer became Minister of Finance). Alliances were determined by a faction's perception of the advantages which it would bring and none proved permanent. Even the solidarity of the Bemba regional-linguistic group, which straddled the Northern, Luapula and Copperbelt Provinces, broke up in 1969 as the Luapulans expressed disillusionment with Northern Province leaders, who had referred to them disparagingly as *batubulu* ('mere fishermen'), and voiced dissatisfaction with their meagre share of the fruits of independence:

> We are now more than convinced that it is because of this attitude against us that our people have not had the benefit of political appointments on the scale enjoyed by those from the Northern Province or other Provinces. In this regard we may mention the appointments to Party leadership on the regional level in the (Copperbelt) Province, politically appointed District Secretaries [civil servants], District Governors, appointments to foreign missions, membership of the statutory bodies and Government Boards, not to mention appointments in the public service.[19]

They asked the President to 'grant political recognition and status to our Province in the same way as other Provinces'. They received some, though in their view inadequate, rewards, and remained loyal – unlike many of the Northern Bemba who broke away from the ruling party when the political pendulum swung against them and in favour above all of the Eastern bloc within UNIP; they joined the United Progressive Party (UPP), which Simon Kapwepwe, a former vice-president of the party and state, had formed in 1971.

Whereas the Luapula Province voted overwhelmingly for Kaunda and UNIP in successive elections, the Southern Province remained a strong opposition area throughout the First Republic. This was due to the Ila–Tonga people's traditional hostility to government – a legacy of the colonial era – and above all to their belief that the African National Congress (ANC) stood for the peasant agrarian interest.[20] Their suspicions of UNIP as a Copperbelt-based, Bemba-dominated party were reinforced in the 1968 election campaign by ANC propaganda that, if UNIP was returned to power, the Bemba would steal their cattle and their wives. During this election, in which UNIP fared badly in both the Southern and Western Provinces, officials of the ruling party revived the slogan, 'It pays to belong to UNIP', which had first been used on the Copperbelt in 1965.

There is evidence, covering the period before as well as after the 1968 elections, to show that this was not an empty slogan. Morris Szeftel cites many examples, ranging from the access to bank overdraft facilities to the appointment of staff to the Lusaka City Council, to show that UNIP membership confer-red material benefits; he concludes that: 'given the relative scarcity of state resources, the monopolization of patronage for UNIP members constituted a major asset for the Party in building and maintaining support.'[21] Instances of discrimina-tion against individual ANC members were numerous, not least in Lusaka and on the Copperbelt; they were often denied trading licences, excluded from the markets, and experienced difficulty in obtaining building plots and planning permission. Nevertheless, the Southern Province received generous alloca-tions of revenue from the centre under the First Republic and has been a major beneficiary of the government's agricultural loan scheme. It would therefore seem, as Bornwell Chikulo suggests, that the UNIP government used economic, rather than political, criteria in making allocations to Zambia's rural provinces – the Southern Province is the country's main cash-crop producing area. It may of course be argued that, in most of the period before 1979 when the Third National Development Plan took effect, the government skewed its pattern of expenditure in favour of the Southern Province in order to demonstrate to the latter's voters that the ruling party could make them prosperous.[22] If this was indeed the govern-ment's tactic it failed dismally: the Ila–Tonga people registered a substantial 'No' vote in the 1978 presidential election.

By the time of that election, the Zambian one-party state had been in existence for six years, having been created in the first place to enable the government to stem factional conflict and concentrate on developing the country. If factional competition has in fact abated since 1972, this has been due not only to the reduction of state resources available for distribution and the increased use of state coercive power, but also to the weakness of party organisation at regional and local levels. Nevertheless, as Dr Szeftel has argued, for many the party was still

> a form of security or insurance – a way of ensuring the continued issuance of trade licences, or an avenue to appeal for loans or other resources when this was necessary. The mass party looked very much like a patronage party in some constituencies in 1973. The link between UNIP activity and the pursuit of patronage was clearly reflected in the registration of Party branches between February and September 1973 as people sought to have a vote in the primary elections and thus a voice in the choice of candidates. It might also have reflected the efforts of those who aspired to stand for Parliament to ensure that branches which might support them were registered.[23]

Moreover, UNIP continued to provide paid employment for politicians at national and regional levels. Though it still did not pay constituency and branch officials (most of the former claimed to work full-time), local officials who are chairmen of ward councils have been made *ex-officio* members of the integrated district councils established – one in each district – under the Local Administration Act of 1980. The local party organisation also aspires to act from time to time as an employment agency by recruiting the labour required for road construction and other purposes.

The operation of patronage in Zambia shows that a faction (aptly described by Dr Szeftel as 'a patronage network organised for conflict') constitutes an informal hierarchy which often disrupts a party's organisational ties. As Richard Sandbrook has written:

> . . . personal alliance networks in many underdeveloped countries, far from being restricted within organizational boundaries, characteristically cut across boundaries to link individuals in different organizational and territorial areas. In many African countries the governing party became after independence merely one more arena within which members of the élite competed for precedence and political resources.[24]

Patrons in the government form linkages which may have little connection with any political party. Sandbrook illustrates his argument by reference to Kenya, where President Kenyatta eschewed an important role for KANU. Instead he elevated clientelism 'into his *modus operandi* of politics by establishing himself as the "Grand Patron" and "Ultimate Arbiter" of factional conflict, whether in central or local political arenas or within organisations,' in a manner reminiscent of King Hassan II of Morocco.[25] Where, as in Kenya, the party machinery is weak, personal political alliances assume added importance and political leaders at the centre 'exacerbate factionalism at the local level and politicize many supposedly apolitical bodies', sometimes including trade unions, co-operative societies and the army. Thus, Sandbrook shows how inter-élite competition in Kenya has penetrated the trade union move-ment, which represents 'a poly-ethnic, territory-wide, organ-izational network invaluable to any politician seeking to extend his influence throughout the country'.[26] Similarly, in his study of *Civil–Military Relations in Sierra Leone*, Thomas Cox reveals how the civilian ruling group cultivated its army connections from about mid-1964, with the result that 'one of the most important elements of Sierra Leone's civil–military relations was the ongoing intimacy, both overt and covert, between officers and important civilians long before the coups of 1967'. The relationship appealed to both sides as mutually beneficial: civilian 'big men' served as patrons to army officers anxious to improve their social standing and further their military careers, while the politicians insured themselves against the time when their legitimacy might decline.[27]

The Political Communication Function

The final party role which we identify is that of political communication. This is a corollary of political competition and it is no accident that, in mainland Tanzania, TANU recognised from the outset the importance of keeping open a two-way channel along which government policies could flow to the people and the people's wishes and reactions to those policies could reach the government. Potentially, communication remains an important party function but many governments

often prefer to use non-party channels – the Tanzanian government, for example, relies substantially on the bureaucracy,
while the government of Senegal, both before and after
independence, has (in O'Brien's words) used 'Muslim leaders
as the effective indirect agents of rural administration'.[28] One
reason for this practice may be that government policies are
sometimes distorted by local party leaders who are reluctant to
communicate unpopular messages. Thus, Judy Molloy's study
of Tanzania's Lushoto District, where land is a scarce and
highly prized commodity, showed that *ujamaa* was misunder-
stood by the people as self-help; the explanation was that
TANU officials were unwilling to press a policy which required
the peasants to give up their individual holdings of land in
favour of communal ownership and production.[29] Similarly,
Rasmussen records that local UNIP officials in the Serenje
District of Zambia were reluctant to denounce the traditional
chitemene form of agriculture which, though condemned by the
Ministry of Agriculture, was still widely practised by farmers in
the district.[30] These findings are reinforced by the results of
Samoff's research in the Kilimanjaro Region of Tanzania.
Samoff found that TANU and other leaders, convinced that
education was 'the key to the good life', not only did not put
over government educational policy, which stressed the need to
divert resources to other, less advantaged areas of the country,
but assisted the missions to thwart government goals and
priorities by establishing new schools. While 'professing support for and adherence to Tanzanian socialism', the political
élite 'confessed that they were able to support the leadership
code in spirit now, and would support it in practice as soon as
their children were educated'.[31]

Conclusion

There is no doubt that, in respect of most of the party
functions which we have discussed, there has been decline since
independence. The general picture is that the party has either
been run down in favour of the burgeoning state machine and,
being less efficient, has been under-utilised, or it has been

dissolved by an incoming military regime (though sometimes the military has subsequently created a new party as a means of strengthening its own legitimacy). An additional reason for party decline is that, decentralisation measures notwithstanding, the government in most African states has imposed central control more than it has encouraged meaningful popular participation. That it is the latter which invigorates and sustains political parties was shown in the pre-independence nationalist period and more recently in those Anglophone states, notably Nigeria and Ghana, where civilian rule and competitive party politics were restored in 1979. In French-speaking Africa, by contrast, 'demilitarisation' has tended to result in the re-establishment of single-party rule, with the leader of the military junta often assuming the civilian garb of an elected president. This is a theme to which we return in chapter 7.

Further Reading

Bienen, H., 'One-Party Systems in Africa', in Huntington, S. P., and Moore, C. H. (eds.), *Authoritarian Politics in Modern Society* (New York: Basic Books, 1970).

Cartwright, J. R., *Politics in Sierra Leone, 1947–67* (University of Toronto Press, 1970).

Coleman, J. S., and Rosberg, C. G., Jr (eds.), *Political Parties and National Integration in Tropical Africa* (Berkeley: University of California Press, 1964).

Dunn, J. (ed.), *West African States: Failure and Promise. A Study in Comparative Politics* (Cambridge University Press, 1978).

Gertzel, C. (ed.), Baylies, C., and Szeftel, M., *The Dynamics of the One-Party State in Zambia* (Manchester University Press, 1984).

Leys, C., and Hyden, G., 'Elections and Politics in Single-Party Systems: The Case of Kenya and Tanzania', *British Journal of Political Science*, vol. 1, no. 2 (1972).

Owusu, M., *The Uses and Abuses of Political Power: A Case Study of Continuity and Change in the Politics of Ghana* (Chicago University Press, 1970).

Pratt, R. C., *The Critical Phase in Tanzania, 1945–68. Nyerere and the Emergence of a Socialist Strategy* (Cambridge University Press, 1976).

Rosberg, C. G., and Callaghy, T. M. (eds.), *Socialism in Sub-Saharan Africa: A New Assessment* (Berkeley: Institute of International Studies, University of California, 1979).

Sklar, R. L., *Nigerian Political Parties: Power in an Emergent African Nation* (Princeton University Press, 1963).

Weiss, H. F., *Political Protest in the Congo: The Parti Solidaire Africain during the Independence Struggle* (Princeton University Press, 1967).

Zolberg, A. R., *Creating Political Order: The Party-States of West Africa* (Chicago: Rand McNally and Co., 1966).

6

Administration

Before examining the basic properties of the adminstrative systems of the African states at independence, it is well to remind ourselves of the colonial legacy. Colonial rule was alien rule, superimposed from outside mainly in the last quarter of the nineteenth century, and established in the midst of ongoing cultures. It was exercised by predominantly European administrators, who were few in number in relation to the population being administered within what was typically a centralised and unitary framework; thus French West Africa, which comprised eight territories, covered a huge area and had a population of some 15 million, was served in 1937 by only 385 colonial administrators, of whom half were posted to offices at headquarters in each colony.[1] These administrators had a political role for, protestations of political neutrality notwithstanding, policy was not only implemented by civil servants but was primarily formulated by them. This role began to change in the terminal stages of colonial rule as government became much more specialised in function and, first in British Africa and then in French Africa, the rudiments of a ministerial system were introduced. Nevertheless, the colonial state was *par excellence* a bureaucratic state. This had its impact on the post-colonial state, which tended to adopt with only slight modifications the inherited civil service structure, rules and procedures, as well as the preferential arrangements for civil servants in relation to salary, housing, and medical services.[2]

While members of the British colonial service could be transferred from one colony to another, most of them spent their whole career in one territory; and, though an African from one British colony was sometimes recruited to serve in another colony (Creoles from Sierra Leone served in the Gold Coast and Nigeria, for example), indigenous members of the service were confined to their own territory. By contrast, the French colonial administrative service tended to be more mobile. Permanent civil servants fell into one of three cadres – the general, the upper, and the local cadres – entry being determined by the standard of education achieved; until 1945 the latter was limited for most Africans, who were French subjects rather than citizens, and enabled them to join only the lower ranks of the civil service.[3] Those in the first category could serve in different colonies within the French empire and those in the second within a group of territories, such as post-war AOF; only those in the local cadres (the majority) served in one territory. In practice, this meant that a non-metropolitan 'Frenchman' – that is, a citizen of the French Union, regardless of race or colour – who was say a Martini-quan in the general cadre could serve equally in Martinique, Chad, or Indo-China, and a Senegalese member of the upper cadre could belong to the administrations of Senegal, the Ivory Coast or Niger. Thus Félix Eboué, who was Guyanese, served as Governor of Chad before the Second World War and as Governor-General of AEF during it, while Gabriel d'Arboussier, who was born in the French Soudan of mixed (French–Soudanese) parentage, served in several AOF territories as a colonial administrator before devoting himself full-time to radical political activity – he was a founder-member of the RDA and became its secretary-general in 1949. This arrangement for senior civil servants made for more uniform patterns of administration in the French empire than the British. Coupled with the fact that many of the indigenous civil servants and politicians in AOF attended the same federal secondary school (the Ecole Normale William Ponty in Dakar), it also no doubt facilitated collaboration between Francophone states after independence. None the less, it was the British rather than the French pattern which prevailed in the post-colonial state. When the French territories in West and Equatorial Africa became independent – mostly in 1960 and as individual states rather than as members of a federal unit – they, like their Anglophone counterparts, proceeded to build up national civil services, recruited from among their own citizenry.

Basic Properties of the Administrative Systems at Independence

In relation to earlier generations of new states – those in Latin America, for example – the post-colonial states of tropical Africa, Asia and the Caribbean were relatively well-off in their administrative endowments; for Africa, this applied especially to the Anglophone states and to some, though not all, of the Francophone states. However, the very sophistication of the inherited administrative machinery, largely modelled on the institutions of the metropolitan countries in the post-1945 period, meant that that machinery was costly to run and difficult to staff without some help from expatriate officers. The bureaucracy constituted a high proportion of the people within a given state who were in wage and salaried occupations, and therefore imposed a substantial drain on the national budget. In Senegal by the late 1960s over half of the national budget was allocated to civil service salaries.[4]

The expansion of state activity, particularly in the economic field, was alleged to be necessary because of the weakness of the indigenous private sector in a majority of African states: neither the colonial power nor intrusive Western economic institutions, such as the commercial banks, had created conditions in which African business enterprise could prosper. The state itself therefore became the main agent of economic development and this in turn stimulated the creation of new public enterprises. Thus in Zambia, which had formed part of the Central African Federation between 1953 and 1963 and had a weaker institutional legacy than many new states, the government at independence in October 1964 had to take account of

the inadequacy of economic and politico-economic institutions inherited from the federal era alike in the government, private and parastatal sectors. Very few civil servants were experienced in the formulation and implementation of policies for rapid economic development. In the private sector, local managers had hitherto been entirely dependent upon policies originating in Rhodesia or South Africa. Almost by definition, the parastatal organisations were federal in character and management. Thus upon independence, parastatal institutions from the Agricultural Rural Marketing Board to the Bank of Zambia had to be created *ex-nihilo* in a very short space of time.[5]

The growth of what in several countries – state capitalist as well as socialist – was to be a vast parastatal sector entailed an expanded role for the bureaucracy.

At independence, heavy demands were also placed on the latter, as well as the political system as a whole, by mass electorates newly enfranchised under pre-independence or independence constitutions. Whereas in the West industrialisation had occurred before fully democratic practices were introduced into the political process, the opposite was true in Africa. Nationalist politicians, only recently installed in office, had scarcely time to formulate economic policies, let alone reap the benefit of them, when universal suffrage was conferred.[6] They could not fulfil their (often rash) electoral promises and some of them found in the bureaucracy a convenient scapegoat, alleging that its members had absorbed colonial values, attitudes and methods. That politicians in English-speaking Africa sought protection behind a bureaucratic smoke-screen was not altogether surprising. Civil servants had largely stood aside from the independence struggle and, as a result, were often distrusted by the politicians (though in Francophone Africa, by contrast, most of the principal post-war leaders had been civil servants by profession and had sought equality rather than independence). Adjustment to the new dispensation was especially difficult for civil servants occupying senior positions in services where indigenisation had taken place at a relatively early date. This was the case in Ghana where, as in many other parts of English-speaking Africa, the traditions of Westminster and Whitehall implied a politician–civil servant relationship that the ruling party was not long willing to sustain.

In most states, the bureaucracy at independence was indeed conditioned by the inherited cultural values of the colonial system. On the other hand, though it was far from being a development-conscious and oriented administration, it was not in most states a stronghold of conservatism, anxious to retain its identification with the former regime. As a result of the impact of indigenisation policies (which we examine below) the change of regime brought also a changeover in personnel in the supporting institutions, the civil service, the police and the army. Most public servants were genuinely committed to the task of socio-economic transformation and, as such, were members of a modernising force. However, they were also pulled in an opposite direction, having been conditioned by the value systems and political cultures of the societies from which they originated. In other words, they were not immune from the communal and particularistic pressures of the society of which they formed such an important part. Hugh Roberts points out that this has been a continuing problem in Algeria, where

> the bureaucracy does not function primarily in accordance with a rational–legal code . . . On the contrary, administrative action is determined in large measure by personal ties and obligations and is characterised by the preferential treatment of friends and relatives.[7]

Bureaucracy and the Post-Colonial State

To those who subscribe to the 'ecological' school of development administration, what Roberts says of Algeria need not be surprising: Fred Riggs, for example, has argued that corruption and inefficiency are naturally endemic to administration in poly-communal and poly-normative societies. Though most of Riggs' field experience was in Asia, where hierarchical social pressures are stronger than in Africa, and though the relevance of his views to Africa has been questioned by a number of writers – most cogently by Nelson Kasfir – they merit examination.[8]

Professor Riggs uses the term 'prismatic society' for the intermediate society which exists at various points of the continuum between the traditional, 'fused' society and the modern, 'diffracted' (and functionally specific) society; it contains elements of each of the other two. He argues that the bureaucracy – the 'sala bureaucracy' as he calls it – is dominant in the prismatic society because there are no political institutions strong enough to control it. The sala is therefore characterised by corruption, nepotism, self-seeking and inefficiency; 'the more powerful officials become', he maintains, 'the less effective they are as administrators'.[9] That there are African bureaucrats with these characteristics is not in question. There is also evidence to suggest that, as bureaucrats seek to maintain their living standards in deteriorating economic circumstances and as opportunities for upward mobility within the public service become progressively reduced, the incidence of corruption in many states has increased – as, for instance, in Tanzania, where corruption was minimal until the late 1970s. Moreover, as was stated above, bureaucrats are subject to social pressures and some of them do accord preferential treatment to their friends and relations, even if not necessarily on the scale suggested by Hugh Roberts. Again, to the extent that the bureaucracy could be held responsible for the dismal economic record of most African states, it has been less than efficient (though 'efficiency' is notoriously difficult to measure). The question is whether such instances of administrative behaviour can be explained satisfactorily in Riggsian terms.

Riggs concedes that the degree to which societies are prismatic may vary. Countries that are more prismatic – that is, where there occurs more substantial overlapping between modern and traditional norms – have bureaucracies approximating to his sala model. However, against this it can be argued that the bureaucracy within a given state is not a monolithic body: some bureaucrats may be corrupt and inefficient and therefore deserve the designation 'sala officials', but not others. Riggs does not distinguish clearly enough between different forms of corruption.[10] The preferential treatment of friends and relations, and the system of rewards in return for services rendered which lies at the heart of patron–client politics, are socially acceptable in African states in a way that theft, fraud and embezzlement are not; the latter forms of corruption are subject to legal prosecution in virtually all states. Nor does Riggs tell us the level that corruption must reach before it ceases to oil the machinery of government and adversely affect government performance. As to efficiency, sala bureaucrats – as Riggs conceives them – would have been incapable of sustaining existing African state machineries for over twenty years and of making them work in adverse conditions, which have included political instability and military takeovers, ill-conceived 'presidential' initiatives and frequently shifting governmental programmes, constant minis- terial reshuffles and organisational changes, as well as exogen- ous events such as natural disasters and world economic depression. If Riggs' theory does not prove helpful in identify- ing *common* strands in the administrative performance of independent African states, it is also not particularly illuminat- ing when employed to examine the experience of individual countries, as can be shown by taking the cases of Ghana and Tanzania.

By most tests, including the quality of its public service, Ghana at independence in 1957 was closer to 'modernity' than Tanzania (then Tanganyika) at independence four years later. Yet in the decade following the independence of each state, there was less corruption among public servants in Tanzania than in Ghana (though it must be emphasised that Ghana had many excellent public servants who maintained the highest standards of integrity); and, to judge by the criterion of economic performance, efficiency was better in poor Tanzania than in the more richly endowed state of Ghana. That Ghana had an indifferent record was not because the 'weight of bureaucratic power' (to use Riggs' terminology) was too great, rendering the bureaucracy uncontrollable, but because it was *too little* – the effectiveness of the bureaucracy was sapped by the political manoeuvring and interference of Nkrumah and the CPP. In Tanzania, by contrast, bureaucrats – especially in the period before 1967 – had a relatively greater say in formulating public policy. Yet as Cranford Pratt's discussion of educational policy shows, in the distribution of secondary-school places the civil service had 'the capacity and the will to serve the public interest rather than narrowly to pursue its own class interest'. Though Africans in public life and in the public service were very well paid in Tanzanian terms, they were 'still responsive to the various influences and pressures which operate to keep public services reasonably efficient and free of corruption.'[11]

Again, as African states have extended the range of their economic and other activities in the post-independence period, structures have become more specific – that is, more institutions (including parastatal bodies) have been created to perform new functions; and at least formally (and often in practice) achievement has counted for more than ascription in bureaucratic recruitment. Universalistic rather than particularistic values have been stressed and the public service, by drawing its members from all parts of the country, has often played a nationally integrative role. Though there is wide variation among African states, it can reasonably be claimed that a number of them have, at least in the above respects, moved towards 'modernity'. According to the view expressed by Riggs in 1964 in *Administration in Developing Countries*, this should mean that the bureaucracy had lost some of its sala characteristics and had become both less corrupt and more efficient; in fact, the evidence points, if anything, in the opposite direction. It is true that Riggs subsequently broadened his concept of prismatic society to include within it a highly differentiated society with a low level of performance. But in this way – and perhaps also by arguing (in 1970) that 'a significant (but not overwhelming) degree of bureaucratic power is functionally requisite for the organisation of a developed system of government' – he modified the meaning which he had earlier attached to his adopted Parsonian variables (functional specificity, universalism and achievement). The utility of the concept 'prismatic society' is reduced the more elusive it becomes.[12]

Nor can Riggs' argument that the bureaucracy in underdeveloped countries is all-powerful be uncritically accepted in its application to Africa. His view on this subject is shared by Joseph La Palombara and several others in the modernisation school, as well as by a number of Marxist scholars, though the latter not only approach the subject from a different perspective but use different arguments and reach different conclusions as to the significance of the *overdeveloped* state concept. In his seminal article on 'The State in Post-Colonial Societies:

Pakistan and Bangladesh', Hamza Alavi argues that the new rulers of the post-colonial society inherited an 'overdeveloped' state apparatus which was designed with metropolitan, rather than their own interests, in mind, thereby conferring on the state apparatus (the army and bureaucracy) a degree of autonomy from the new ruling class; on the other hand, the 'national' character of the post-colonial state bureaucracy and the presence of indigenous political forces provided a counterpoise keeping the civil service 'autonomous' vis-à-vis the formerly dominant metropolitan interests.[13] While not questioning the validity of Alavi's findings for the South Asian states with which he deals, there are grounds for arguing that the extent of the autonomy of the state apparatus in Africa was much more limited; thus, the localisation of the senior levels of the public service and the officer ranks of the army occurred much earlier in the Indian sub-continent than in Africa. In relation to the latter, Colin Leys has correctly argued that the colonial state was not 'very strong in relation to its tasks', which became increasingly economic and technical after independence.[14] With the exception of South Africa and Zimbabwe, his conclusions apply to the colonial state apparatuses inherited by virtually all the ex-colonial African countries. As we show in subsequent sections of this chapter, the new African states were initially short of trained and experienced manpower. Their bureaucracies, weakened on this score, were also subject to internal divisions. Moreover, even though the ruling party in a particular state might itself be incapable of curbing bureaucratic power, effective control over the bureaucracy was often exercised by individual politicians – perhaps the president himself or ministers with administrative ability (of whom there were many in Zambia's first post-independence cabinet). Only in relative terms is the bureaucracy in the African context therefore as powerful as Riggs and a number of other scholars would have us believe.

Finally, it can be said that Riggs was right to argue that to understand 'transitional' societies, a model based on the state systems characteristic of Western societies on the one hand or those typical of traditional, peasant societies on the other was not helpful. Unfortunately, his own model of prismatic society, underpinned as it is by pseudo-scientific theorising, offers an inadequate guide to an understanding of administrative behaviour in underdeveloped countries; however, it must in fairness be added that his ecologically based theory draws our attention, most valuably, to the large number of factors which affect the bureaucracy in such contexts. The paradox in Africa is (in Riggs' terminology) that in the post-independence period state structures have become more diffracted (and the state itself therefore more 'modern'), without a corresponding increase in bureaucratic competence. The bureaucracy has been required to assume tasks, notably that of running a vastly expanded state sector, for which it was not equipped by either training or experience. As Bernard Schaffer has pointed out, the chosen remedy was not to consider alternatives – a change in the inherited administrative model – but to promote institutional administrative training.[15] This was understandable; it is a daunting task for any state to adopt an entirely new pattern of administration. In any case, the political leaders themselves were inexperienced in operating a governmental system on a national scale and were faced with numerous pressing problems. One of these was to Africanise – or 'localise' (since Europeans and Asians took out citizenship in several states) – the public services, both to satisfy political demands and to cope with the problem caused by the exodus of expatriate personnel. It is to a consideration of this issue that we turn in the following section.

Manpower and Africanisation

Undoubtedly, the most serious problem facing new state administrations after independence was thus not so much the value system of the bureaucracy as the shortage of trained and experienced indigenous personnel. More of the latter were available in certain Francophone states, including Dahomey, Senegal, and Madagascar, than in poorer states like Mauritania and Niger, with weaker educational endowments. In general, the manpower situation at independence was healthier in French-speaking West Africa than Equatorial Africa: by 1960 there were only five university graduates in AEF, from which four newly independent states were to emerge later that year. Only in 1955 were hesitant steps taken in AEF to begin training Africans for posts of responsibility, with the result that, as John Ballard records, 'at independence the new governments found it necessary to rely heavily on the continued services of French administrators and technicians in the capitals and regional posts.'[16]

Among the Anglophone states, the problem was more acute in parts of East and Central Africa than in West Africa. In Ghana at independence in March 1957 some 60 per cent of senior posts were Africanised; in mainland Tanzania at independence in December 1961 only 26.1 per cent of senior *and middle* grade posts were filled by citizens. In Zambia, which became independent in October 1964, the position was even worse than in Tanzania. The deliberate withholding of secondary education until the 1940s, and of locally based higher education throughout the colonial period, both retarded the emergence of a nationalist leadership and meant that Zambia entered independence with only a small pool of educated manpower. As late as February 1964 only 38 of 848 administrative and professional posts were filled by Africans, and only 26 per cent of Division I and II posts. The situation was no less dismal at independence in Zaire (July 1960), as a result of Belgium's long neglect of secondary and higher education. However, in some respects the scale of the task was greater in Zambia, where during the colonial period whites had monopolised posts down to very junior levels, such as typists, road and building foremen, and mechanics. As President Kaunda was to observe in 1968: '. . . we entered Independence without a single African technician in one of the most highly industrialised societies on the Continent'.[17] Even Zambia, however, was better-off than the ex-Portuguese colonies of Angola and Mozambique where, at independence in 1975, the desperate shortage of skilled manpower, coupled with the precipitate departure of Portuguese managers and technicians, imposed a formidable constraint on development.

At independence there were insistent demands by politicians and trade unionists that the public service should be Africanised without delay. Though a few leaders, including Houphouet-Boigny in the Ivory Coast and (particularly in relation to the army) Hastings Kamuzu Banda in Malawi, deliberately slowed down the rate of Africanisation, most governments responded to this pressure. They showed little inclination to follow the 'colonial approach', which involved waiting for graduates from school and university to emerge and then to prove themselves within the service. Instead, promising local officers were given intensive training – the 1960s has been described as 'the training decade'[18] – and accelerated promotion, though in some states, there was no alternative to making former chief clerks into permanent secretaries overnight. Sometimes the 'job analysis approach' was also used; this entailed relating the organisation of work and the qualifications required for a post to the local manpower available, even if this meant splitting a job formerly held by a European officer into two. Predictably, it was easier to localise administrative posts than professional and technical ones. Among the earliest posts to be localised were those in field administration – the level at which most people came into contact with the new government; top policy-making posts, such as those of permanent and deputy permanent secretary; sensitive posts, including the offices of chairman of the public service commission and commissioner of police; and the foreign service. At the same time, most government leaders took steps to retain the services of expatriate personnel until local manpower became available, and in many states, Africans newly promoted to very senior positions were initially underpinned by white advisers. When Europeans left more precipitately than the government wished, they were replaced with overseas personnel recruited on contract (as distinct from pensionable) terms, often under technical assistance agreements with the former colonial power.

Administrative Aspects of the Post-Colonial State

The functioning of the administration in the post-colonial state has been vitally affected as a result of the developments identified in the introduction. The creation after independence of authoritarian power structures, which proceeded at a striking pace in Francophone Africa and more slowly in English-speaking Africa, meant that the concept of a neutral, impartial and anonymous civil service was quickly eroded. At the least, new state governments required civil servants to be committed to the achievement of the goals which they laid down. Thus, shortly before Ghana became a Republic in July 1960, *A New Charter for the Civil Service* was issued. This Charter stated:

> . . . the civil servant should appropriately feel a positive and consistent loyalty to the interests of the Government as his employer. This concept will become clearer under a Republican Constitution when the focal point of the civil servant's loyalty becomes the President as both Head of State and Head of Government . . . The control of the Civil Service will . . . in future be vested in the President . . . Where . . . a senior civil servant finds himself out of sympathy with the policies and objectives of the Government it is clearly his duty to retire voluntarily from the Government service . . .[19]

This document, it is true, also stressed that the civil service should be non-political in character and that individual civil servants should avoid identification with a political ideology or party. In practice, such provisions were never very meaningful and disappeared with the creation of the one-party state in 1964. President Nkrumah also weakened the position of administrators outside his own office by creating within it divisions which paralleled existing ministries; thus, the Bureau of the Budget took many of the decisions which would normally have been taken by the Ministry of Finance. In this way ministers became 'little more than presidential secretaries who represent the leader in departments of state',[20] thereby giving rise to acute feelings of frustration on the part of the ministers themselves and the civil servants who worked under them.

In the period before the one-party state was legally created, both Tanzania and Zambia undermined the political neutrality of their civil services by making some senior political and administrative posts interchangeable. In Zambia, the secretary-general to the government was both head of the civil service (replacing the former secretary to the cabinet on 1 February 1969) and a minister of cabinet rank. Nevertheless, party and administration remained broadly distinct in both countries, and merit was retained as the principal criterion for recruitment to the civil service. Even in Guinea where, according to Coleman and Rosberg, the PDG approximated closely to the party state, no symbiosis between the 'parallel party–state hierarchies', which existed at all levels, took place. In an essay published in 1967, Lucy Behrman commented:

> . . . in Guinea, the PDG has grown more, rather than less, powerful since independence. At the same time the position of the administration has been very unclear. It has not fused with the party, as Coleman and Rosberg contend, but remains distinct from it. In fact, the two organizations are continually conflicting with each other, the conflicts being particularly noticeable on the regional level. Throughout the struggles between the party and administrative personnel it has been the party view which has tended to predominate.[21]

Though the PDG was stronger, both ideologically and organisationally, than most other ruling parties, almost everywhere in tropical Africa the uncertain relationship between party and administration led to misunderstanding and conflict. Where, as in Uganda in the 1960s, the governing party and the public service tended to be recruited from different, and indeed politically antagonistic regional backgrounds, the potential for conflict increased. In Tanzania, Hyden noted, the introduction of decentralisation measures in 1972 resulted in 'a certain conflict between TANU and the civil service bureaucracy as each tries to gain the upper hand under the new system. There have been several serious clashes between the political Regional Commissioners and the powerful new civil service Development Directors . . .'. Again, in Kenya, where the government used the administration rather than the party as its main agent of development, as well as its major instrument of control, parliamentarians (writes Okumu) 'publicly attacked the service, often unfairly, either for its neglect of duty or for its corruption in the pursuit of gain'.[22] Political interference, as well as (in most states) poor management, sapped the morale of the civil service. Senior officers were no longer confident that they could count on a career in the civil service, while those below them wondered whether proved political loyalty would be a more important criterion for promotion than administrative or technical efficiency. In the circumstances, it was not surprising that many civil servants resigned from the service to join international organisations or private companies, while others transferred to the parastatal sector.

The lot of the civil servant often eased with the advent of military rule; in Ghana under the National Liberation Council (1966–9), for example, the civil service became (in Dowse's words) the military's 'most important corporate ally'. Again, in states such as the Ivory Coast, the progressive decline of the party after independence was paralleled by the corresponding rise of an extensive state apparatus, of which the civil service was a part.[23] However, it is important to remember the *caveat* entered by Hyden in a different context, when he said of Kenya's ruling party: 'That KANU is weak is no proof that the civil service is powerful.'[24] Paraphrasing Michael Lofchie, we can say of the bureaucracy of most African states that its power is indirect, being exerted on the political leadership; it has no source of legitimacy independent of the political system as a whole; and its internal divisions, principally between a civil service and a parastatal sector, and its fragmentation along functional lines means that it lacks a unified structure.[25] Moreover, as we argued above, authoritarian power structures are inimical to the continuance of a neutral, impartial and anonymous bureaucracy.

In much of tropical Africa the public service has continued to face deep-seated problems, as Zambian experience reveals:

'Such frequent transfers of departments and agencies among Ministries, the general reallocation of subject responsibilities, and the frequent movement of Ministers and civil servants have adversely affected the quality of administration. Chains of command at senior levels have been disrupted, resulting in serious delays; votes have had to be changed; and resources have been wasted both because of the lack of cost-consciousness in the public sector and inadequate financial control inside Ministries, which, like the Ministry of Finance itself, are short of qualified accounting staff. The staff shortage is general and the number of vacant posts in many grades of the civil service is alarmingly high . . .[26]

Zambia is not alone in lacking the indigenous personnel to fill many professional and technical posts, and in having appointments procedures which are cumbersome and time-consuming and facilities for civil service training which are both too limited and too centralised. Moreover, because of the shortage of qualified manpower, so much energy is almost everywhere in tropical Africa absorbed in keeping the state machinery going that fundamental administrative reform is neglected; on the other hand, periodic salary reviews are undertaken and the civil service retains both its hierarchical structure and élite status which were inherited from the colonial era.

This is not to deny, however, that the bureaucracy may be able to reform itself to a limited extent. For this to happen, Professor R. S. Milne argues that bureaucratic procedures – in the form, for example, of general rules and regulations, relating to civil service conduct among other matters – may need to be more closely observed, and elements of the Weberian model of bureaucracy, including the principle of hierarchy, may need to be retained and strengthened. Milne concedes that while particular features of the inherited bureaucracy may have to be modified in developing countries, it should – in the absence of 'clear viable alternatives' – be adapted to the changed circumstances of independence rather than replaced by an entirely new administrative system. These arguments challenge the widely accepted view put forward by Bernard Schaffer that the paramount need in the new state context is for an innovative, non-compartmentalised and change-oriented administration rather than for an administration of the Weberian type. African public services, says Schaffer, have been geared to system maintenance rather than to innovative development administration; this is a valid comment, though we must be careful not to minimise the importance of the law and order, and other non-socio-economic goals pursued by the governments of newly independent countries.[27] To provide innovation in administration, most of these governments have looked to the parastatal sector and in doing so have dodged, rather than solved, the question of administrative reform.

The Parastatal Sector

The rapid growth of this sector, after independence, took place because of the relative weakness of domestic capitalism and because the new state governments wanted to end foreign control over the economy. Such control was extensive: according to Udoji, in Uganda, shortly before President Amin expelled the Asian community in 1972, '4,000 non-Africans controlled 70% of the distributive trade whilst 16,000 Africans were responsible for only 30% of the trade'.[28] Government attempts to change this unhealthy situation took various forms, from the establishment of new public enterprises to the outright nationalisation of foreign-owned companies. In some states, including Botswana, the Ivory Coast, Kenya, Nigeria and Zaire, private enterprise (both domestic and foreign) has been allowed to co-exist with public enterprise, operating either independently or in joint ventures, with the state as majority shareholder wherever practicable. In more radical states, such as Mozambique and Tanzania, the role of private enterprise has been strictly curtailed, though not entirely eliminated. As Hyden points out, the public enterprise has become 'a common phenomenon in all African countries irrespective of political regime',[29] and irrespective of whether that regime has pursued a capitalist or socialist development strategy. It offered government leaders a more flexible instrument of development than the government department, which was subject to the full panoply of parliamentary and treasury control.

Among the parastatal bodies created in the post-independence period were agricultural marketing boards (sometimes to supplement those already existing); national development corporations or corporations split up into sectoral units covering agriculture, industry and mining; state commercial and national banks; and state companies. While the last-named were incorporated like any other private company to pursue a commercial undertaking, many of the other agencies rested on a statutory basis. The growth of these bodies, however established, was rapid. In Mali, in the early 1960s, writes Zolberg:

> The roster of state enterprises had grown longer year by year; it included garages, repair shops, metal works, a printing plant, and a number of processing plants for locally grown produce; also SOMIEX (State Import–Export Organization) and its chain of retail shops, as well as a chain of state pharmacies and another one of book-stores.[30]

The Ivory Coast, less radical than Mali under President Modibo Keita and the Union Soudanaise, followed a strategy which relied on the external infusion of money and manpower; yet here, too, the size and scale of the state apparatus expanded enormously. Campbell comments:

> By 1976 the number of *sociétés d'État* in the Ivory Coast in which the state held more than 50 per cent of the capital had increased to twenty-nine. In all but one of these where public participation represented 82.35 per cent, the corporations were wholly controlled by state capital. These corporations exist in almost every area of the economy whether concerned with regional planning . . . foreign commerce . . . or agricultural production . . . To these must be added a list of eighteen additional *sociétés anonymes* in which the state also represents 50 per cent or more of capital. In addition there are a great many other companies where the Ivorian state is present but represents a minority participation.[31]

Corresponding increases in public enterprise activity have taken place in Anglophone Africa – for example in Tanzania, in the wake of the Arusha Declaration of 1967; in Zambia, from 1968 onwards; and in Nigeria, where domestic increases in both the production and price of oil between 1969 and 1974 precipitated a process which had been underway since independence. Already in Nigeria by 1973, wrote Hyden, 'there were over 250 public enterprises ranging from more conventional forms such as railways, harbours and electricity to such industrial and commercial activities as cement, hotels, newspapers and even soft drinks.' The increase in the number of

Nigeria's constituent states (to 19 in 1976) contributed to further expansion of the public enterprise sector, as the governments of the newly created states joined the federal and existing state governments in forming parastatal organisations committed to the promotion of development.[32]

This burgeoning of new institutions, as well as extensive constitutional change and ministerial reorganisation, began at a time in the early 1960s, when the standard of administration was lowered (albeit temporarily) by the Africanisation of the public service. Not surprisingly, early results were disappointing. In Guinea, the enterprises responsible for basic economic activities, such as railways, roads, air transport, electricity, mining and banking, were relatively successful, but the commercial agencies (*comptoirs*) performed badly. Lucy Behrman observes that this was because

> The Guinean government had neither the personnel nor the experience necessary to move from a mostly private economy to a completely publically-controlled one, and the distribution of imports in Guinea broke down rapidly. Finally on November 1, 1963, the government enterprises which had distributed retail goods were closed.

State enterprises in Nkrumah's Ghana (1957–66), too, were often inefficient and corrupt and saddled with cumbersome administrative procedures; in 1965 only two of fifteen state manufacturing undertakings were making a profit. These enterprises could not compete with the private sector. In Nigeria between 1960 and 1966 the Nigerian Railways alone had thirteen enquiries into its activities, and in 1965 the World Bank described its finances as 'disastrous'.[33]

Experience since the mid-1960s is hardly more encouraging, despite some success in the financial sector – national banks and state commercial banks have performed reasonably well in Tanzania and elsewhere – the relatively better performance of the East African corporations as compared with their West African counterparts, and such valuable spin-offs from public enterprise activity as the rapid training of local staff. Hyden records that by 1973 half of all public enterprises in Ghana and Nigeria had had public enquiries conducted into their operations, while an official review of Kenya's statutory boards in 1979 found the existing enterprises to be over-politicised and inefficient, and recommended that no new parastatal company should be established unless the need was indisputable. In Mali, according to François, the state corporations are responsible for 70 per cent of national economic activity, but have enormous debts, high wage costs (with over 13,000 employees), and are very corrupt; they are used by the bourgeoisie to amass personal wealth. In Zambia a parliamentary select committee, whose report was tabled in August 1978, drew attention to the inefficiency of many parastatal bodies, citing instances of poor management, theft and corruption. Many state-owned companies operated at a loss because they were constantly subject to political pressure and could not be run on businesslike lines; they were also hit by the shortage of qualified and experienced manpower.[34]

Another reason for the disappointing performance of public enterprises, apart from indifferent staffing and poor financial management, is the unsuitability of many of those appointed to the boards of public enterprises: some owe their positions to blatant political patronage – a common practice in both Nkrumah's Ghana and Nigeria under the first Republic – while others are civil servants who, though competent administratively, are completely lacking (through no fault of their own) in business acumen. Some public enterprises have also been choked with bureaucratic regulations issued to check corruption, making the cure sometimes more damaging than the disease. Again, the parastatals have been subject to government direction over both the siting of industries and the pricing of products, resulting – in Zambia, for example – in certain companies incurring heavy losses, thus, in the troubled context of the late 1970s, adding to the pressures forcing governments to have recourse to large-scale external borrowing. The latter may afford international credit organisations a leverage within the domestic economy: in Mali, for example, it is said that the IMF even wants to privatise the country's more profitable state corporations.[35]

It is much easier to identify the problems facing public enterprises than it is for African governments to find solutions to them. One remedy has been reorganisation; thus, in the

1970s Tanzania drastically reformed its inefficient State Trading Corporation and National Milling Corporation, while in 1978–9 the Zambian government overhauled the Zambia Industrial and Mining Corporation, which directly or indirectly controlled over ninety companies, many with substantial foreign minority interests. Another step taken has been for functions previously performed by public enterprises to be transferred to government departments or to private companies. Taking Zambia and Tanzania again as examples, the Zambia Youth Service (a statutory body whose staff was recruited primarily by UNIP regional secretaries) was brought under direct ministerial control as a result of a 1970 report on parastatals, and state-owned butcheries in Tanzania have been restored to private hands. In 1980 the Mozambican government moved in the same direction as Tanzania when it sold to private businessmen most of the small enterprises taken over by the state at independence. In Mali, the Société Malienne de Crédit et d'Aide à l'Equipement Rural has been turned into an agricultural credit bank with private citizens and foreigners as shareholders.

It is unlikely that many states will, and indeed undesirable that they should, follow a policy of full-scale denationalisation; partly for reasons of self-interest but also so that the state can retain some control over its economic affairs, the Malian bureaucracy is resisting demands, said to be made by France as well as the IMF, for the dissolution of some of the state corporations in Mali. At the same time, as Hyden points out, 'the argument that public enterprise should be retained at any price no longer appears very valid'.[36] More African governments may therefore follow Sudan's lead in reducing the size of the parastatal sector by eliminating inefficient public enterprises. They may also make use of the other policy instruments, such as price controls and licensing, which they have at their disposal. Whatever the size of the parastatal sector that is retained, the quality of the manpower responsible for running a country's public enterprises will remain crucial.

In most African states the huge parastatal sector has not yet been subjected to the really critical review which is urgently required. The relations between this sector on the one hand and the civil service on the other continue to be uncertain. Steps taken by a number of states, including Zambia, to bring salaries and conditions of service in the parastatal sector into line with those in the civil service may be justified on the grounds of equity and in order to raise civil service morale; in Ghana early in 1975 salary differentials, as well as revised pension arrangements, were having a serious demoralising effect on the civil service. However, it is also possible that such steps will merely serve to reduce the parastatals' flexibility in recruitment and therefore undermine their operational efficiency. There is still insufficient co-ordination between the civil service and public enterprises, as well as between these agencies and the ruling party, though all of them, in one way or another, are vitally concerned with the implementation of national development plans.

Development Planning

While African leaders have differed over the strategy most likely to promote the development of their countries, they have agreed substantially over methods. 'The instrument of both diagnosis and remedy is the development plan,' comments Martin Minogue. 'The approach comes very close to the equation: development equals planning; without planning, there can be no development.' As he points out, both empirical research and common sense quickly demonstrate that these arguments are either false or inadequate. 'If planning is Everything,' wrote Aaron Wildavsky in 1973, 'maybe it's Nothing.' Professor Hanson had advanced the same argument some years earlier when, in the introduction to his study of planning in India, he observed that there was no general correlation between the extent of economic planning and the rate of economic growth and that the very attempt to plan might actually retard the rate of growth.[37]

Despite many instances of failure, planning has not been abandoned in African states. This is understandable: when resources – material and manpower – are scarce, it is important to assign priorities to the way in which they are allocated. The question facing government leaders has not therefore been whether to plan or not to plan, but what kind of planning to adopt. In general, African states lack the resources and the socio-political structures to undertake Soviet-style centralised, imperative planning. Nevertheless, Guinea, after its break with France in 1958, and Mozambique, following independence in 1975, have both gone a long way in trying to determine centrally what should be produced, in what quantities and at what prices, and to exclude the free play of market forces by the imposition of rigid economic controls. This is not to suggest, however, that Mozambique has allowed its socialist ideology to serve as an economic strait-jacket, as Guinea did in the early 1960s when the bid to maintain socialist purity had an adverse effect on economic planning and organisation.[38]

At the same time, other African states committed to socialist strategies of development and/or with sizeable parastatal sectors have not been content merely to emphasise desirable patterns of economic development and to do little or nothing to enforce them on the private sector. African governments, in other words, have not opted for indicative-type planning, which is better suited to developed, industrialised societies. Given the developmental constraints which they have faced, most African states have chosen a position roughly midway between these extremes. They have adopted controlled planning within a mixed economy, though the mix between the public and private sectors might vary substantially between one state and another, thereby allowing a greater or lesser scope for private enterprise. In this type of planning, the power of the state is invoked to secure the implementation of a 'comprehensive' development plan in order to achieve a given rate of economic growth. In practice, in many African states the targets set for the private sector have proved unrealistic because of the lack of adequate consultation with that sector during plan formulation. Moreover, because of their preference for public over private enterprise, new state leaders have been inclined to over-estimate the potential of the public sector. Thus, here again ideological commitment has tended to work against rational economic decision-making. On the other hand, as Hanson has shrewdly observed, 'If an economically rational decision upsets the political applecart, it is not rational at all in the wider context.' The techniques of planning are inextricably intertwined with the politics of planning.[39]

It may well be that for a professional economist such as Arthur Lewis the techniques of planning are 'not very complicated'.[40] However, in the African context, the economic planner faces the immense difficulty of not only working with inadequate statistical data but also, because of dramatic changes in world trading patterns and prices, among other reasons, of forecasting the size of the national revenue from one year to another. When conditions are adverse and result in an acute shortage of foreign exchange, as had already occurred in several African states by the end of the 1970s, the state concerned may have to seek a loan from the IMF on terms which, if accepted, would seriously distort the whole planning effort. In an attempt to mitigate such problems, planning in most African states has become a continuous process, with built-in mechanisms for the periodic review and adjustment of a 'rolling' plan; there is also a greater emphasis today on setting specific and realistic targets rather than stating long-term objectives, as in the immediate post-independence period. However, even assuming that professional planners can adapt to changing economic circumstances, planning will not be successful without (as Lewis puts it) 'sensible politics and good public administration'.[41] It is to a consideration of these issues that we turn in examining the problems which have arisen in implementing African development plans.

Problems of Implementation

While these problems have been experienced in virtually all African states, their saliency varies according to context. Frequent shifts in the location of the planning unit have proved unsettling. The range of possibilities is wide and different solutions have been adopted in both Anglophone and Francophone Africa. In August 1966 six of the French-speaking countries of tropical Africa had a planning office (*commissariat*) attached to the presidency, four had a Ministry of Planning, and five had a planning division in the Ministry of Finance.[42] There was often also considerable experimentation within particular countries on either side of the linguistic barrier: Tanzania and Zambia, for example, have at various times had separate planning ministries, linked planning with finance or another ministry, and placed the planning agency in the office of president or vice-president in the expectation that it would thereby be given political teeth. It is not possible, on *a priori* grounds, to say which is the best location for the planning unit, since what is best is what produces the best results within a given context.

For underdeveloped countries, Hanson favoured either the Indian system, based on a planning commission containing several government ministers, or the system where the planning agency was attached to the prime minister's or chief executive's own office. However, when the latter location was chosen in Tanzania in 1964–5, the results were disappointing, and led Cranford Pratt to comment: 'Only if the head of state, or possibly a vice-president of unquestioned political authority, is directly and intimately concerned with planning will the necessary discipline be imposed to ensure that priorities are respected and targets vigorously pursued.'[43] On the other hand, a system along these lines worked well in Botswana, where Dr Quett Masire, the Vice-President (and President since 1980), had considerable political weight and enjoyed the respect of civil servants.

In the immediate post-independence period, problems of implementation also arose because planning, in Anglophone Africa especially, tended to be a less open process than in India, with the ruling party and interest groups, parliament and the private sector, and even the cabinet itself insufficiently involved in plan preparation. Sometimes, as in Nigeria in 1960–1, Tanzania in 1964, and Zambia in 1966, the resultant plan was above all 'a planner's plan',[44] to which the politicians did not feel committed and which they subsequently sought to change by introducing major projects not incorporated in the original plan. In parts at least of Francophone Africa, the institutional arrangements for popular involvement in planning in the 1960s surpassed those in English-speaking Africa. As well as the central planning unit (wherever located) and various ministries and local authorities, a number of other bodies were involved in plan formulation. These included high-level consultative bodies (the Conseil National du Plan in Cameroon, for example) representative of government and both management and workers from the public and private sectors of the economy, as well as planning commissions, each dealing with some particular sector of the economy, such as agriculture, or with some particular aspect of planning, such as manpower; 13 commissions, with a total membership of 380, were established in Senegal for the formulation of the Second National Plan.[45] Corresponding, though less elaborate, arrangements for consultation were subsequently introduced into certain of the English-speaking states, as in Zambia in preparation for the Second National Development Plan (1972–6).

There has been a good deal of trial and error in the institutional devices adopted for formulating development plans, but everywhere the same lesson has had to be learned: a plan which is technically sound will stand little chance of general implementation unless it becomes the focus of all government economic activity. However, the commitment of the political leadership to planning is not by itself enough. As Cranford Pratt showed convincingly in the case of Tanzania between 1963 and 1966, the maintenance of political harmony through an exercise in political accommodation – that is, the practice of preserving party unity by accommodating all shades of opinion within the party and government – is an obstacle to the single-minded pursuit of development planning. In these circumstances, which prevailed in Zambia as well as in Tanzania, there will always be, in Pratt's words, 'a tendency to shy away from the hard decisions which will offend an important section of the party or will seriously alienate an important leader within it'.[46]

In other cases, ministries have not been geared structurally for large-scale economic and social development and officials, as well as ministers, have lacked any sense of urgency. Poor personal relations between them and the planning staff have resulted in a failure to co-operate – for example, in supplying the planning office with essential information. This illustrates Lofchie's point that planners 'are, in the last analysis, one group of civil servants among others and as such are politically unequipped to acquire the necessary degree of legitimacy and support to function as an autonomous political force'.[47]

In several states, the planning office itself has been weakened by frequent shifts in its location, by the transfer of key indigenous personnel to posts in other ministries or the parastatal sector, and by the fact that expatriate officers, recruited from different countries, have distinct planning traditions. Such problems, which have been keenly felt in Zambia over much of the post-independence period, have been compounded by over-centralised administrative structures, serious manpower shortages, and a failure to make optimum use of such manpower as is available. The result is that, though many states have launched 'decentralisation' measures, the up-country areas frequently lack the specialist support to make a reality of 'planning from below'. Tanzania is one of the very few Anglophone states which has filled the posts of regional and district planners with university graduates in economics. On the other hand Tanzania, like the great majority of African states, has limited and controlled popular participation in planning, as well as in other aspects of local-level decision-making.

Many state governments have created a plethora of development committees – at regional, district and village levels – but have denied them executive powers and, though often making provision for popular representation, have continued to subject them to tight, central bureaucratic control; Botswana, where sound district planning procedures have been adopted, and the district commissioner and district council secretary are joint plan managers, is to some extent an exception to this pattern.[48] The failure of most states to undertake meaningful local-level planning is fundamental and brings us back to the earlier question of the content of the development plans themselves. Virtually all African countries face the serious problem of producing enough food to feed their growing (and increasingly urbanised) populations, let alone leave enough over for export. Central governments – for example, in Zambia and (prior to the 1983 party congress) Mozambique – are therefore attracted to the quick solutions apparently offered by grandiose measures, such as capital intensive state farms which, however, not only create few jobs but are also beyond the capacity of the state to manage. The experience is now widespread that where peasant farmers are given proper incentives – good prices for their crops, adequate transport and storage facilities, and a plentiful supply of consumer goods to buy – agricultural production will rise, sometimes dramatically. This underlines the fact, already mentioned, that to be successful planning is dependent on 'sensible politics and good public administration'. Centrally conceived policies which – like *ujamaa* in Tanzania, with its emphasis on communal production – are not realistically rooted in the traditions of the people are ultimately doomed to failure. Such failure will have serious repercussions on other sectors of the economy when a country's agricultural and industrial programmes are closely linked – a textile industry dependent on local cotton production, for example. Though industrialisation may understandably remain an important objective, there is no escaping the fact that the first priority of planning in African states, with their predominantly rural populations, must therefore be to provide a sound agricultural base. Unfortunately, the overall record to date has been disappointing.

Conclusion

In this chapter, we have argued that while Riggs was right to stress the importance of the ecological context within which the administration operates – for the new state public servant cannot, like his colonial counterpart, stand outside the society which he helps to rule – he was mistaken in asserting that the buraucracy in underdeveloped countries would inevitably acquire the characteristics of the 'sala'. Our contention is that while the bureaucracy may in some instances be strong in relation to the political institutions of the post-colonial state, it does not therefore constitute an autonomous centre of power, free of political control. Indeed, the effectiveness of the bureaucracy may be reduced because political control, far from being too weak, may be too strong – as a result, for example, of the growth of powerful presidential institutions. Moreover, in our submission, the bureaucracy is likely to lack the organisational capacity to perform the multiple tasks piled upon it by new state governments, including the management of a vast parastatal sector and the drawing up and implementation of development plans. Because it is so often subject to piecemeal attempts at political interference at central and local levels, the bureaucracy may even welcome the advent of military rule. The next chapter focuses on the military and begins by asking why the military intervenes in politics.

Further Reading

Adu, A. L., *The Civil Service in Commonwealth Africa* (London: Allen & Unwin, 1969).

Chambers, R., *Managing Rural Development: Ideas and Experience from East Africa* (Uppsala: Scandinavian Institute of African Studies, 1974).

Finucane, J. R., *Rural Development and Bureaucracy in Tanzania: The Case of Mwanza Region* (Uppsala: Scandinavian Institute of African Studies, 1974).

Hyden, G., Jackson, R., and Okumu, J. (eds.), *Development Administration: The Kenyan Experience* (Nairobi: Oxford University Press, 1970).

Le Vine, V. T., *Political Corruption: The Ghana Case* (Stanford: Hoover Institution Press, 1975).

Mawhood, P. (ed.), *Local Government in the Third World: The Experience of Tropical Africa* (Chichester: John Wiley and Sons, 1983).

Morgan, E. P. (ed.), *The Administration of Change in Africa* (New York: Dunellen, 1974).

Riggs, F. W., *Administration in Developing Countries: The Theory of Prismatic Society* (Boston: Houghton-Mifflin, 1964).

Rweyemamu, A. H., and Hyden, G. (eds.), *A Decade of Public Administration in Africa* (Nairobi: East African Literature Bureau, 1975).

Schaffer, B. B. (ed.), *Administrative Training and Development* (New York: Praeger, 1974).

Seidman, A., *Planning for Development in Sub-Saharan Africa* (Dar es Salaam: Tanzania Publishing House, 1974).

Tordoff, W. (ed.), *Administration in Zambia* (Manchester University Press, 1980).

7
The Military

Military Intervention

In January 1963, disgruntled soldiers assassinated Sylvanus
Olympio, President of the Republic of Togo, and set up a
civilian government under Nicholas Grunitzky. The shock-
wave of this event had not receded before the military
supplanted the civilian government in Congo-Brazzaville in
August 1963 and that in Dahomey two months later. The
governments of Upper Volta, Nigeria and Ghana were toppled
in quick succession by the military in early 1966. Thereafter,
military coups have occurred so frequently in different parts of
Africa that they have lost their capacity to shock, though not to
disturb, African opinion. Thus, since independence in (or
about) 1960, civilian governments have been supplanted by the
military in nearly half of Africa's states, while in many of these
states (especially in Anglophone Africa), one wing of the
military has subsequently been displaced by another – as in
Nigeria in July 1966 and 1975, and Ghana in 1978 and 1979.
Several other states have experienced serious coup attempts,
including Gabon in 1964, Angola in 1977 and Kenya in 1982.
Such statistics underline the basic instability of most African
governments, irrespective of whether the former colonial power
was Britain or France, Belgium, Italy, Portugal or Spain;[1]
whether the state was one-party, like Ghana and Mali, or
multi-party, like Dahomey (in 1963) and Nigeria;[2] whether the
character of the regime was conservative or radical (Niger and
Ahmed Ben Bella's Algeria offer contrasting examples); and

whether the state concerned was prosperous, like oil-rich Libya, or desperately poor, like Upper Volta.

Though opinions differ as to why the military intervenes in the first place, certain facts seem incontrovertible. First, the army can stage a coup because, having control of the weaponry, it has the capacity for organised violence. As the cases of Togo, Burundi, Chad and the Central African Republic illustrated at the time when military intervention occurred, the size of the army, either absolutely or in relation to the civilian population, is not normally a factor; however, the very small number of officers and men engaged in the Nigerian coup of January 1966 proved a major disadvantage in the South, where the coup substantially misfired.[3] The absence of physical obstacles is an advantage for a small force: thus, the fact that Freetown, the capital of Sierra Leone, lay sandwiched between the mountains and the sea made the city particularly vulnerable to an army takeover.[4] Secondly, coups are usually undertaken by those who have operational command, such as battalion commanders. However, more senior officers may soon be brought in both to minimise the disruption to the army's internal command structure and to give respectability to the regime; this happened in Ghana in February 1966 and Nigeria in both January and July 1966, though not in Mali in late 1968 or Liberia in 1980. The Liberian coup, which brought Master Sergeant Samuel Doe to power, and the mutiny of 'other ranks', with the backing of a number of warrant officers, in Sierra Leone in April 1968, substantiates Cox's statement that 'while coup-leaders in black Africa traditionally have been commissioned officers, one can now expect ambitious NCOs and privates to leave their mark on civil–military relations.'[5]

In the third place, African coups are typically army coups: the Ghanaian case of a counter-coup in 1979 and a coup in 1981 led by an airforce officer (Flt-Lieutenant Jerry Rawlings) did not really break this pattern since soldiers were among the armed services' personnel involved; it was the attempted coup by members of Kenya's air force in August 1982 that was atypical. The police alone are unlikely to stage a coup, though a police para-military unit may be capable of doing so. On the other hand, the police, being scattered among the civilian population, may be a useful ally of the military. Fourthly, training has an uncertain role. Officers trained at Sandhurst or Mons, as well as officers trained at St Cyr, the French military academy, have taken part in coups despite the inculcation during training of a tradition of non-military intervention. Indeed, as we shall see below, the Nigerian case showed that Sandhurst training and year of entry into the army served as cohesive factors among the majors who staged the January 1966 coup. On the other hand, training may prove divisive if, as in Ghana in the 1960s, officers of the same army are sent for training in different countries; this was also the experience in mainland Tanzania, where an army mutiny occurred in January 1964. Finally, there is the psychological factor: that is, once the barrier which deters the military from intervening has been broken in one state, it may be broken in a neighbouring state or, the military having intervened once in a state, it may be disposed to intervene again; Dahomey (now the People's Republic of Benin), which experienced six coups in less than ten years, is the prime example of the latter phenomenon.

Though substantial agreement may be reached on points such as these, the basic question remains: why has the military intervened so frequently in African states, as in many other parts of the Third World? There are many theories. The 'Finer' school explains intervention primarily in terms of the social environment in which the military functions; the theory is that Third World states, being of low or minimal political culture, are particularly susceptible to military intervention. The 'Janowitz' school, on the other hand, draws attention to the properties of the military itself – to its hierarchical organisation and its distinctive patterns of recruitment and training, control and discipline. Robin Luckham draws upon both these schools to argue that there is no one variable which is the key to civil–military relations. His own theoretical framework, therefore, puts a number of the different variables together and leads him to make the analytic distinction between the army which, as the custodian of the national interest, fulfils a guardian role and the praetorian-type army which, though retaining distinct group interests of its own, is sucked into politics. Ruth First observes that 'whatever the political background to a coup d'état, when the army acts it generally acts for army reasons, in addition to any other it may espouse'. Samuel Decalo takes up and broadens this observation by asserting, 'Though they may be predominant, secondary, or merely coincidental with civic unrest, corporate and personal motives are invariably present in coup situations and cannot be ignored.'[6]

What none of these theories satisfactorily explains, however, is why the military has intervened in some African states and not in others. For alongside the many African states that have experienced coups and counter-coups are a sizeable number which have retained their civilian governments over a 15–27 year period: among them are Botswana, Lesotho and Swaziland in Southern Africa; Cameroon, Gabon, Malawi and Zambia in Central Africa; Kenya, Mauritius and Tanzania in East Africa; Gambia, Guinea, the Ivory Coast and Senegal in West Africa; and Tunisia and Morocco in North Africa. Moreover, many of these states, including Guinea, the Ivory Coast and Tunisia in Francophone Africa and Malawi, Tanzania and Zambia in Anglophone Africa, are still headed by the nationalist leaders who brought their countries to independence; President Senghor of Senegal and President Ahidjo of Cameroon voluntarily relinquished power in 1981 and 1982 respectively. A further point worth noting is that the political leadership in Africa as a whole has shown significantly greater stability since the early 1960s than that in Latin America, where only General Alfredo Stroessner of Paraguay has been in office for the whole period.

The above list sub-divides into a smallish group of states, including Botswana, Cameroon, the Ivory Coast, Senegal (since Mamadou Dia's attempted coup failed in 1962), Swaziland and Tunisia, which have experienced neither coups nor serious attempts at a coup and a second group of states which have kept their civilian leadership but where there have been significant coup attempts. Among the latter group are Gabon, where only French intervention kept Léon Mba's government in power in 1964; Guinea, where a Portuguese-backed invasion by Guinean dissidents nearly unseated Sékou Touré in 1970 and Sierra Leonean troops were imported to underpin the regime; the Gambia, where a contingent of the Senegalese army carried out a rescue operation on behalf of President Sir Dawda Jawara's government in 1981; and Kenya, where the country's own general service unit put down an air force attempt to overthrow President Daniel Arap Moi's government in 1982. (There were anti-government conspiracies in Zambia in October 1980 and in Tanzania early in 1983, the conspiracy in Tanzania being more serious than the government has been willing to admit.) In short, though the civilian leadership has survived in states such as these, it is not because the military has not tried to topple them. It cannot be convincingly argued that coups have not been attempted, or where attempted have not succeeded, because the states in question have a higher level of political culture than the countries where the armed forces have successfully intervened; as compared with Nigeria, for example, several of them patently have not. It is indeed difficult to validate the argument relating to political culture by comparing one African state with another. The significant fact is that, by comparison with the developed states, virtually all African countries are weak in terms of political culture and are, therefore, susceptible to military intervention; to this extent, Finer's argument is valid. There appears, then, to be an element of chance at work, resulting in some regimes being toppled by coups, but not others. This point needs to be recalled as we consider rational explanations of the survival of civilian regimes.

The argument that the 'non-coup states' are better off economically than the 'coup states' cannot be sustained: true, Kenya and the Ivory Coast have prospered, though the distribution of wealth, both between regions and individuals, is uneven; on the other hand, Lesotho, Malawi and Tanzania remain poor countries, while Zambia (like Tanzania) has been in economic decline throughout the past decade. The army mutiny in Tanzania in early 1964 enabled the government to create, with some help from China, a new-style People's Defence Force. A new army recruiting procedure was devised, which shifted the criterion for selection from physical fitness to loyalty and political affiliation, and all military personnel, as well as members of the police force, could belong to TANU or the ASP of Zanzibar; in fact, they joined in large numbers. Apart from fulfilling its traditional, defensive role, the army was also required to undertake developmental functions, such as road construction and bridge-building. In Zambia, President Kaunda has given the armed forces a privileged position in society: they are well paid, housed and equipped; senior army officers have been brought into the cabinet or given other important government posts (this has also been the practice in Tanzania); and the army has been made directly responsible for running certain units of government, such as the Mechanical Services Branch. Only detailed empirical research can establish whether the 'non-coup states' have, as a group, better preserved the corporate interest of their armed forces than the states where the military has taken over power; on present evidence, this seems unlikely.

Again, without discounting Decalo's reasonable assertion that the personal ambition of military officers may precipitate a coup, as in Uganda in 1971, this factor is in general probably more important in explaining the counter-coup than first-time military intervention. For, otherwise, one would have to advance questionable propositions: that army officers in those states which have not experienced coups or coup attempts had benefited materially and in terms of their career development more than their counterparts in those states where the military has intervened and that they therefore had, as members of their country's 'managerial bourgeoisie', a greater interest in retaining the *status quo* or, alternatively, were more public-spirited and less self-seeking than officers elsewhere.

Alongside the ambitions of military personnel should be set two other factors in explaining why some states have retained civilian governments after independence. The first is the external dimension, which would appear to be of paramount importance in explaining not only why certain of the French-speaking states have avoided coups, but also why Francophone military regimes have, in general, proved more stable than their Anglophone counterparts. All the Francophone states, except Guinea, maintain military assistance agreements with France and seven of them, including (what Robin Luckham has designated) the 'core neo-colonies' and non-coup states of Cameroon, Gabon, the Ivory Coast and Senegal, have entered into defence agreements also. Though France lost her strategically important military bases in Madagascar as a result of an intra-élite struggle that was accelerated when Captain Didier Ratsiraka took over in 1975,[7] she has retained sizeable military bases (sometimes euphemistically called 'facilities' by the host states) in Djibouti and Senegal and smaller ones in Gabon and the Ivory Coast. Otherwise, France has reduced her direct military presence in Africa (to a total of some 6,700 troops in 1981) in favour of maintaining intervention forces stationed in the metropolis. In the 1970s these forces intervened in Chad, Shaba (Zaire), Mauritania, the Central African Republic and (covertly) in Angola; on the other hand, as Dr Luckham has stated:

> In the core Francophone states . . . those in which French investment is more broadly spread and the community of expatriate Frenchmen is large, things were not permitted to degenerate to the point where such intervention was needed. With the current exception of Senegal they all have authoritarian single-party regimes, under-pinned by tightly controlled internal security services. In all, France's military weight has been cast firmly behind the ruling class, a good indicator being its role as their major weapons supplier.[8]

In fact, the bulk of Francophone states still obtain most of their military equipment from France and also look to her for training and other support. Zaire, formerly a Belgian colony, has also established a 'French connection', though, in addition, President Mobutu Sese Seko has cultivated defence links with America (now of diminished importance), Belgium, China, and Israel, which provides the presidential guard and maintains a brigade in Shaba Province.[9] Of the English-speaking states, Kenya comes nearest to the 'neo-colonial' Francophone model: she has provided Britain with training facilities in Kenya and has granted America, from which she now buys most of her defence equipment, the right to use in an emergency the port of Mombasa and two air stations.

The second factor is the political skill shown by leaders such as Habib Bourguiba, Houphouet-Boigny, Nyerere and Kaunda. The converse would also appear to be true: that the lack of political skill may precipitate a coup or encourage a counter-coup.[10] As we shall see, the handling by the Nigerian federal government of the crisis in the Western Region in 1964–5 and General Aguiyi Ironsi's unification decree of early 1966 were cases in point, while the 1967 military takeover in

Sierra Leone was, according to Cartwright, 'to a very large extent . . . the responsibility of one man, Sir Albert Margai', and a handful of advisers.[11] Albert Margai certainly lacked the political skill and conciliatory attitude displayed by his elder brother, Sir Milton Margai, in maintaining the country's political system, but Cartwright's statement over-simplifies a complex situation; this merits our brief attention because of the light which it throws on civil–military relations in Sierra Leone in the pre-coup period.

Albert Margai faced a problem which had not existed under Sir Milton's premiership (when British officers had held most of the army's staff and line commands), namely that of establishing civilian control of a military organisation manned by African officers. Sir Albert did not, like President Nkrumah, seek to establish party control of the military or (when that failed) to build up a countervailing force; instead, as we saw in chapter 5, he encouraged the civilian and military élites, who were predominantly Mende, to join together in defence of their mutual interests. Sir Albert's relationship with Brigadier David Lansana, the army commander, was, according to Cox, 'only the most public of a whole series of army connections with the SLPP'. Faced with electoral defeat at the hands of Siaka Stevens and the APC in March 1967, it was both natural for the Prime Minister and the members of his government to turn for succour to Brigadier Lansana and for the Brigadier to respond by arresting Siaka Stevens and declaring martial law, thus (as he claimed at his trial) averting civil disorder. The coup, then, did represent a failure of leadership, collective as much as individual, but its genesis lay in the development of a kind of symbiotic relationship between the civilian and military élites in the period prior to the initial coup – a coup that was to fail because the army was not united behind its commanding officer.[12]

Following intervention, the military is usually quick to justify its action, and the Sierra Leonean officers who ousted Brigadier Lansana and formed the National Reformation Council on 25 March 1967 were no exception. In Ghana, in February 1966, the army explained that it had intervened to end autocracy and restore democracy; to check corruption and revive a bankrupt economy; to stop interference with the army and police; and to prevent further rash foreign adventures. As Dennis Austin has pointed out, these reasons were largely negative: constitutional integrity was to be restored and the economy revived, but no fundamental reform was proposed.[13] At the end of the day, the dominant motive for intervention in Ghana remains unclear. Evidence of the personalisation and abuse of power, of Nkrumah's absorption with foreign affairs to the neglect of good domestic housekeeping, as well as of economic mismanagement and corruption, had existed for several years. These considerations may have disposed the military to intervene, but if they were the prime cause of the coup, why had the armed forces not intervened sooner? The answer to this question may be military professionalism; the adherence to British standards was well entrenched in the Ghanaian army and its officers may have been unwilling to turn against the country's legally-established government until they were convinced that no other realistic alternative.was open to them. The new factor in 1966 may have been, not so much the creation of the one-party two years earlier, since this changed little politically, but the army's growing perception of the strong threat to its corporate interests represented by several of the President's measures, and above all by his creation of the President's Own Guard Regiment. In the Ghanaian case at least, there is sufficient empirical evidence to substantiate Ruth First's contention that when the military stage a coup d'état, 'army reasons are invariably present', if not necessarily paramount.[14]

There may also have been an ideological motive for military intervention in Ghana. Emmanuel Hansen, writing from a Marxist perspective, points out that the officer corps of the Ghana armed forces 'broadly shared an ideological posture very close to that of the economic nationalists', of whom K. A. Gbedemah, a former Finance Minister under Nkrumah, had been a leading spokesman. The coup-makers may therefore have sought to capture state power in order to create capital for private Ghanaian entrepreneurial activity.[15] Perhaps, too, as Samuel Decalo suggests, Colonel E. K. Kotoka, the leading conspirator, had a personal motive for intervention – he is said to have been on poor terms with Major-General C. M. Barwah, the new army commander, and consequently to have feared for his professional advancement; but this is entirely speculative. While the personal element cannot be dismissed, it probably accounted for less in Ghana in 1966 than in 1972, when Colonel I. K. Acheampong removed Dr Busia's government, and for a great deal less than in General Amin's 1971 Uganda coup. The latter was (in Decalo's words) 'a classic example of a takeover triggered by personal fears and ambitions'[16] – compounded, one might add, by President Obote's serious lack of judgement in leaving such an unstable officer in command of his army at a time when he himself would be out of the country.

The causes of the initial military intervention in Ghana are, then, multiple and complex. Can the same be said of Nigeria, Africa's most populous and, by the late 1960s, richest state? The Nigerian coup of January 1966 and the counter-coup six months later are worth examining in some detail both because of their intrinsic importance and because Robin Luckham's excellent study of the Nigerian military illuminates uniquely civil–military relations in Nigeria between independence in 1960 and the outbreak of civil war in 1967.

The Federal Republic of Nigeria inherited a system of regional power which was wielded by three major political parties: the NPC was the governing party in the North, the NCNC in the East, and the AG in the West, each party being grounded in its main cultural–linguistic group (in turn Hausa–Fulani, Ibo and Yoruba). In the absence at this time of a truly nationalist party with a nation-wide appeal, a coalition government ruled at the centre and, because of the North's numerical (though not technical or educational) superiority, was dominated by the NPC. As the events of 1964–5 made clear, the latter was determined to hold power at all costs.[17] However, it was not only Northerners who abused their power; the impression was widespread that Nigerian politicians generally were self-seeking and corrupt. The politicians failed to agree on methods of resolving conflict; nowhere was conflict more bitter than in the troubled Western Region, which Mackintosh has aptly described as 'the cockpit of Nigerian politics'.[18] The internal split within the ruling Action Group in 1962 (outlined in chapter 5) set in motion a chain of events which, with the controversy over the 1963 national census and the crisis-ridden federal election of December 1964, constituted the backdrop to military intervention in January 1966. The culminating event in the Western Region to reveal the bankruptcy of the old political order was the holding in October 1965 of regional elections; these were rigged by Chief Akintola's NNDP government and resulted in the widespread breakdown of law and order in the region. The federal government, of which the NNDP was now a junior partner, failed to deal with the crisis and therefore shared the discredit of its ally. Maladministration, corruption, electoral abuse and even thuggery had evidently become the coinage of Nigerian politics, and the legitimacy of the civilian authorities was gravely weakened. However, as Richard L. Sklar has pointed out, an enumeration of political sins does not add up to an historical explanation of the military coup of January 1966; other, or at least additional, explanations must be sought.

The explanation which Professor Sklar himself favours is that the coup represented a victory for nationalism over regionalism: 'Typologically, the Ibo junior officers, personified by the young major C. K. Nzeogwu, who killed the Northern Premier, reincarnated the radical Zikists of the later 1940s who had been frustrated by the growth of regionalism and the conditions of bourgeois nationalism.'[19] Robin Luckham's study largely confirms this view.[20] The majors and captains who effected the coup of January 1966 belonged to the professional élite in the officer corps: with one exception, all the majors had university or Sandhurst training and all except one of thè captains were Sandhurst-trained. Though politicisation of the army was not very marked as far as the majority of the officers were concerned until the January coup, the two key figures in the coup (Majors C. K. Nzeogwu and E. A. Ifeajuna, who co-ordinated operations in the North and South respectively) had far-reaching civilian contacts and intellectual interests; Nzeogwu had socialist inclinations and Ifeajuna, a graduate of the University of Ibadan, had close associations with radical intellectuals in the civil service and universities. The core conspirators at least had an explicit set of political objectives – a fact substantiated in books subsequently written by two of the participants;[21] they aimed to destroy the authority of the old, conservative political order and to put an end to the North's political dominance. There was, however, no clear evidence of any link-up with the United Progressive Grand Alliance (UPGA) opposition, which had been defeated in the 1964 federal election.

Luckham also agrees with Sklar that the coup 'did not represent a gigantic Ibo plot', and this despite the fact that almost all the conspirators were Ibos and that their principal victims were the Northern Premier (Sir Ahmadu Bello, the Sardauna of Sokoto), the Northern Federal Prime Minister (Sir Abubakar Tafewa Balewa), and the Western Premier (Chief Akintola), as well as virtually all the Northern and some Yoruba senior officers. Both Ibo regional premiers (of the East and Mid-West) survived, as did the senior officers of Eastern and Mid-Western origin (over two-thirds of whom were Ibo), though this may have been because the coup in the South was largely unsuccessful. Dr Luckham concedes that participation in the January coup was 'associated beyond a chance level with ethnicity.' He thinks it possible that ethnic group interest – sharpened by the interference of Northern Ministers of Defence in army matters, designed (it was believed) to advance Northerners brought into the officer corps through the quota system and to block the promotion of Ibo officers – may have shaped the motivation and objectives of the plotters. However, he argues convincingly that interaction among military colleagues, particularly those of the same rank (major and captain) and belonging to the same entry cohort (1957–61), might be expected 'to cluster around ethnic lines, if only because of unconscious similarities in values and outlook among members of the same ethnic group'. Moreover, organisational requirements – of ease of communication, secrecy, and group cohesion – would all tend to be maximised in a single ethnic group. Luckham points out also that if the old political order was to be destroyed, the Sardauna and Akintola, who were suspected of planning a political putsch in the West, had to be neutralised, while Northern and Western officers, being well represented in key staff and command positions, were natural targets if the coup was to succeed (Ibos dominated the army's middle ranks, though the General Officer Commanding – Major-General Ironsi, who survived – was an Ibo).

An intriguing aspect of the January coup (and, for that matter, of the July counter-coup also) was the way in which military patterns of behaviour and status tended to persist: thus, the responsibilities assumed by the active conspirators coincided with rank; Northern 'other ranks' obeyed their officers' orders, even to the extent of kidnapping the Federal Prime Minister and killing the Sardauna; Major Nzeogwu, anxious to avoid a military conflict, negotiated with, and surrendered to, Major-General Ironsi; and Ironsi, who is unlikely to have had foreknowledge of the coup, assumed power in order to ensure the organisational survival of the army, whose discipline had been seriously dislocated by the coup. Whatever the real motives of the coup-makers, the belief was widespread among Northern soldiers that there had been an Ibo plot and this belief was encouraged both by the failure of the Ironsi regime to prosecute the conspirators and by the advancement of Ibo officers to senior positions in the army hierarchy: the fact that this step could be justified in demographic and seniority terms and did not entail passing over eligible Northern officers, did not assuage the strong sense of grievance on this score. Luckham points out that in the wake of the January coup, and because of the conviction of Northerners that further action, including the dismissal of prominent Northerners in both army and civilian life, was to be taken against them, 'particularistic relations of friendship and clientage, tribe and region tended to develop at the expense of organisational ties'. The strong alienation of Northern rank and file from the Ironsi regime came to be shared by Northern junior officers when, in May 1966, Ironsi, who was personally courageous but politically inept, issued Decree No. 34 with the intention of scrapping the country's federal constitutional structure and establishing Nigeria as a unitary state administered by a single national public service; matters were made worse when Ironsi persisted with this policy even after the outbreak of rioting in several Northern cities later in May.

In July 1966, the junior officers (predominantly Northern but with a sprinkling of Yorubas and Mid-Westerners) and 'other ranks' drawn from all parts of the North, launched a series of poorly co-ordinated operations, as a result of which Ironsi was killed and his regime toppled. In Luckham's assessment, the conspirators probably acted independently of Northern politicians and, though the victims of the coup were mainly Ibos from the Eastern and Mid-Western regions, 'tribal and regional ties never entirely superseded organisational relationships' and neither the Ibos nor the Northerners acted as 'a cohesively structured group'. There were tensions between various levels of the military hierarchy, and the counter-coup represented in part a revolt against authority from below by junior officers and NCOs. Nevertheless, ethnic or regional cleavages were much more explicit in July than they had been in the previous January, and the revolt occurred because these cleavages became linked with organisational strains within an army that was fulfilling the unfamiliar role of government and was therefore directly exposed to pressures from the wider society.

What conclusions can be drawn from this case study? It shows first that the interaction of political and organisational variables differed over time: an army which had been predominantly non-political before the January coup became politicised after it, as army discipline broke down and civil–military boundaries fragmented. Secondly, the coup leaders in January 1966, as distinct from the army officers as a whole, were radically inclined and had clear political objectives: they sought to sweep away the old political order which rested on Northern dominance. Thirdly, the study shows that tribalism and regionalism became more important as vehicles of political expression after the January coup than they had been before it and that the flash-point occurred when these vertical cleavages in society became intertwined with organisational tensions within the army. Finally, it suggests that personal motives, such as the fear that their promotion would be blocked, might have influenced the majors in January 1966, as they did the junior officers and NCOs the following July.

The Nigerian experience, therefore, reinforces the experience of Ghana, and the two cases together suggest that the factors to be taken into account in explaining military intervention in Africa are variable. Besides the level of political culture and the protection of the military's corporate interests and personal ambitions, weight may need to be given to economic conditions, political motivation and ideological persuasion, class interest[22] and factional rivalries, external relations – either with civilian political groups or, on occasion, with foreign powers – and external manipulation (for example, by America's Central Intelligence Agency), the demonstration effect of other coups, and the political skill (or lack of it) shown by the incumbent leadership. The 'mix' between these variables will differ from one state to another: thus, the corporate interests of the army seemed to count for less in Nigeria in January 1966 than they did in Ghana the following month, while the political leanings of the Nigerian coup-makers evidently counted for more. An important lesson of the Nigerian case study is that, while certain generalisations about military intervention in Africa can usefully be made, there is ultimately no alternative than to examine, in relation to a particular state where military intervention has occurred, both the pattern of that state's military organisation and the political and socio-economic context within which it operated.

Military Rule

The first steps taken by the military on assuming power are to suspend the constitution, dissolve the civilian government and parliament, disband the existing political party (or parties), and detain – or, as it is often euphemistically claimed, 'hold in protective custody' – the political leaders of the former regime. The military also establishes a new structure of control, though tending still to rely heavily on the former bureaucracy, and rules by decree. Thereafter, the policies pursued by the military regime will depend on its character and aims.

Martin Dent distinguishes the various types of military government as caretaker, corrective and revolutionary.[23] He believes that in the first case the military intervenes to maintain government and restore constitutional integrity; after cleaning up the mess left behind by the politicians, it will restore civilian rule – as, for instance, the National Liberation Council (NLC) did in Ghana in 1969, only three years after the overthrow of Nkrumah's government. In the second case, the military seeks to correct certain profound deficiencies in the old civilian order, such as the four-state basis of the federal constitution and the regional nature of the political parties in Nigeria. However, while the distinction between these two types of regime may be valid in a few cases – the National Interim Council in Sierra Leone clearly saw itself in April 1968 as a caretaker regime – it is too nice a distinction to fit others, including Ghana's military administration of 1966–9. Both the Nigerian regimes of Generals Yakubu Gowon, Murtala Mohammed and Olusegun Obasanjo, and the Ghanaian regime under General J. A. Ankrah, were essentially corrective: each was pledged to restore stable and democratic government under civilian rule; the main difference between them lay not so much in their aims and character as in the greater scale and complexity of the problems which confronted Nigeria's military rulers. Dent maintains that under Murtala Mohammed (July 1975–February 1976) Nigeria experienced 'genuine corrective government' for the first time; but the difference between the Gowon and Mohammed regimes was more of style than of substance. Gowon, cautious and conciliatory, had earned universal acclaim for the policy of reconciliation, rehabilitation and reconstruction which he had pursued after the Nigerian civil war ended in 1970. However, his authority declined the longer he remained in office; issues which he had neglected, including the status of the disputed 1973 census and the position of corrupt and inefficient state governors, were vigorously tackled by his swashbuckling successor, 'a no-nonsense leader' (as Kirk-Greene has described Murtala Mohammed) from Kano in the far North.[24]

Dent's third category (the revolutionary regime) is valid, though certain *caveats* must be drawn. First, there have been several military regimes whose performance in office has fallen short of their revolutionary promise; these are, therefore, more correctly designated as reformist rather than revolutionary. Thus, in Egypt the revolution of 1952 had a limited impact: it did not transform the structure of society, and the land reforms that were undertaken benefited the middle-level rather than the poorer peasants. Again, the Sudanese government of President Gaafar Numeiri did considerable 'back-tracking' in the wake of an unsuccessful communist-supported counter-coup in 1971, while Decalo maintains that the People's Republic of the Congo has not yet bridged 'the gap between socialist rhetoric and pragmatic reality'.[25] Secondly, a strong sense of nationalism may underlie and distort the regime's

socialist commitment; this has happened in the Somali Democratic Republic, established following the 1969 coup, and has
led to war with Ethiopia for control of the Ogaden, which the
Somalis regard as part of a 'Greater Somalia'.

So great is this gap between pretension and reality – it is
evident also in the People's Republic of Benin – that revolutionary regimes are far outnumbered by non-revolutionary
regimes, whether the latter are designated as reformist, corrective or caretaker. Here we will focus on the non-
revolutionary military regime, which does not seek to alter
substantially the prevailing pattern of élite rule, and will leave
further examination of the revolutionary regime to the next
chapter, although much of the following discussion is relevant
to the latter type of regime also.

Certain conclusions, which command wide acceptance, can
be drawn about military regimes. First, the military organisation and command structure may serve to reduce the effectiveness of the military in office. Habits of discipline and obedience
may incline the armed forces to take a simplistic view of
politics and lead a military government to believe that merely
to issue a command is to have it obeyed. They may also fail to
appreciate that sensitive issues – like those of the census and
revenue allocation in Nigeria – cannot be depoliticised. A
second and related point is that the military lack an organised
popular base and an easy means of communicating with the
people. They may, therefore, forge an alliance with the police
who, as a force scattered among the people, have more sensitive
political antennae than the military; thus, the NLC in Ghana
(1966–9) comprised four senior army officers and four senior
police officers. However, in Nigeria, the fact that Major-
General Ironsi, the head of that country's first military
government (January–July 1966), included a number of police
officers in the narrow circle of bureaucratic advisers (drawn
predominantly from the army and civil service) with which he
surrounded himself did not prevent him from committing
several grave political blunders. His reforms, including Decree
No. 34 referred to above, were largely symbolic but confirmed
Northerners in their worst fears of impending Southern
domination. His myopic view of the North as monolithic – a
view shared by many Southerners – made him neglect to woo

the North's minority politicians and thus to detach the Middle Belt from the far North; this was to prove a costly mistake since it was the impressive unity of the Middle Belt as well as other Northern officers and men which led to Ironsi's ultimate downfall in July 1966.

By contrast with Ironsi, Lt-Colonel Gowon, his successor, displayed a much greater political awareness. In September 1966, he restored the federal constitutional framework by repealing Decree No. 34 and, in a radio broadcast on 30 November, stated that he envisaged a constitutional solution which would include the creation of between eight and fourteen new states or regions. However, the actual creation of new states, which was favoured by the minority areas in the North (to which Gowon himself belonged) and in the East, was delayed as Gowon shied away from a policy of confrontation and tried to achieve consensus among the existing regions (four in number following the establishment of the Mid-West in 1963). Lt-Colonel Odumegwu Ojukwu, the politically-minded Military Governor of the East, held out for some kind of confederation and hoped to carry the East and Mid-West with him. It was only after May 1967, when Eastern secession was imminent, that Gowon decreed the division of Nigeria into twelve states. Though his intention at this time was to undermine Eastern unity (three states were carved out of the old Eastern Region and six out of the North), his action was consistent with his previously expressed views.

Gowon also displayed considerable political acumen by appointing twelve civilians, one from each state, to the federal executive council, then the advisory body to the Supreme Military Council (SMC). What Luckham calls his 'master stroke', which was designed to bind the West to the federal cause, was to make Chief Awolowo the vice-chairman of the executive council and commissioner for finance and, as such, the regime's most powerful civilian adviser. Similarly, his appointment of Chief Anthony Enahoro to the council helped to secure the continued loyalty of the Mid-West, though the critical factor in this respect was the ill-judged invasion of that region by forces from secessionist Biafra.[26]

Politicians had a major impact on policy-making during the civil war and gave the military valuable political help in managing Nigeria's external relations. However, their role diminished thereafter and this may help to account for Gowon's unwise decision, taken on the advice of the SMC but perhaps against his own inclination, to defer the return of civilian rule beyond the promised date (1976). In general, Nigerian experience under Gowon suggests that a military government which is open to political advice is likely to make fewer mistakes than a regime which, like that of Ironsi, cuts itself off from such advice.

A third conclusion that can be drawn about military regimes is that, because of their relative isolation as well as their lack of experience in government, they are prone to look for support from groups not too closely identified with the previous regime. The extent to which they do so may, of course, vary from one regime to another. Thus, in Ghana between 1966 and 1969 the civil service was, in Dowse's words, 'the most important corporate ally' of the NLC;[27] the latter also courted the chiefs and members of the legal profession and the universities, all of whom (together with former opposition leaders) were strongly represented on the various commissions and committees established by the Council. The National Redemption Council under Colonel (later General) Acheampong, however, had a much less marked pro-administration bias than the NLC; moreover, in a populist fashion reminiscent of the CPP, it looked for allies less to the lawyers and other professional and propertied classes than to the ordinary people. In Nigeria, as we have seen, Ironsi put maximum distance between himself and the old politicians; he turned for advice about the North to the Sultan of Sokoto. Gowon worked closely with former politicians, especially during the civil war, though most of them belonged to opposition parties: thus, J. S. Tarka, a federal commissioner, had been leader of the United Middle Belt Congress which joined the UPGA. Murtala Mohammed's government was collegiate in style, but was dominated by the armed forces and police, whose members held 14 of the 25 federal commissioner posts; moreover, the civil commissioners at both federal and state levels tended to be professional and technical experts rather than politicians. Mohammed, himself of aristocratic background, restored the honoured role of chiefs in Nigeria and incorporated them within the reformed local government structure.[28]

A fourth conclusion is that to remedy its lack of a popular base, and to strengthen its claim to rule once the initial euphoria which greeted its (illegal) seizure of power has evaporated, the military may acquire civilian trappings. For example, it may hold presidential elections and seek to build up a national political party linked to, and controlled by itself, as in Egypt, Mali, Somalia, Togo and Zaire. This was never attempted in Nigeria, but in Ghana General Acheampong sought, through the power-sharing device of Union government, to perpetuate military rule by clothing it in civilian dress.

Fifthly, however, 'civilianisation' may merely serve to reinforce a danger which most military governments face: that army officers involved in government may become divorced from the army command structure, giving rise to conflict over policies. This occurred in Nigeria in Gowon's later years in office when the SMC deferred the return to civilian rule beyond the scheduled date (1976), while the army command favoured early withdrawal.[29] On another level, internal jealousies may be created if, for example, the head of the military government should be less senior in rank than serving officers, thereby disrupting the army's hierarchical organisation. However, conflict on this score is not inevitable. To take Nigeria again: it was at the insistence of Northern junior officers and men that Lt Colonel Gowon, the ranking Northern officer, became head of the Nigerian military government in August 1966, even though he was outranked by several Southern officers; the latter accepted this arrangement and only Lt Colonel Ojukwu, who was to lead Biafra's secession, disputed it, claiming that he was himself senior to Gowon. Again, Lieutenant (now General) Moussa Traoré has been in power in Mali since the 1968 coup; he survived an attempt by members of the military government to remove him in 1978. In Liberia Master Sergeant Doe, who swept aside President William R. Tolbert's government in 1980, has not been unseated by the army officer corps.

In the sixth place the military, despite its image of moral integrity and puritanical spirit, may not in fact provide cleaner and more honest government than its civilian predecessor.

Military regimes generally improve the pay and conditions of service of the armed forces, while army officers, like civilian politicians before them, have often enriched themselves at the public expense. In Ghana, the later Acheampong years were marked by massive corruption: thus, cocoa revenues were diverted on a scale never previously experienced.[30] In Nigeria, by 1975, the name of state governor had become a byword for corruption; Murtala Mohammed removed the governors and purged corrupt officers from every branch of government activity, including the army. It was this action, more than any other, which earned for his regime a reputation for clean and energetic administration. While these shock tactics were salutary in many respects, they also had negative consequences – as did Busia's dismissal of 568 Ghanaian public servants early in 1970: many able and upright public servants were caught in the net of those who were compulsorily retired, while public servants who escaped the purge often proved reluctant to take risks or decisions; moreover, corruption in the public service quickly resurfaced.[31] This suggests that 'instant government' is not necessarily 'good government'. Again, most military regimes have not proved to be less authoritarian or repressive than the civilian governments which they supplanted, and some have been a great deal more so, as the regimes under Amin in Uganda, Jean-Bedel Bokassa in the Central African Republic, and Michel Micombero in Burundi bear cruel witness.

Finally, even a military regime which claims, with some justification, to have intervened to restore stable and democratic government may be sucked into politics as the boundaries between the military establishment and its socio-political environment become fragmented; expressed in Luckham's terms, this means that the guardian state then becomes the praetorian state, carrying the danger that factionalism will sap the military's unity of purpose. As Ruth First has pointed out, once in power the military leadership tends to 'soak up social conflicts like a sponge' – that is, in Lamb's words, 'the military organisation immediately becomes vulnerable to social and political pressures from which it was hitherto to some extent protected, and is required to operate under conditions and for purposes for which it was not designed'.[32] We have seen how this happened in Nigeria following the January 1966 coup, leading to moves to regionalise the army and eventually to Biafra's attempted secession. In Ghana, the NLC (1966–9) was subject to ethnic, as well as personal, divisions. Whereas the main ethnic community in Ghana is the Akan-speaking group of peoples, the NLC was dominated numerically by officers from Southern minority communities, namely, the Ga and Ewe. It was widely, though inaccurately, rumoured that the Ewe were over-represented on the advisory bodies established by the NLC, while other events (an attempted counter-coup in April 1967, the Abbott Laboratories controversy in late 1967, and the acrimonious debate in 1968 over Gbedemah's eligibility to stand for parliament) seemed to confirm that the Ewe were politically on the offensive.[33] In fact, despite such divisions, the NLC held together long enough to hold elections and to hand over power to Busia's Progress Party government.

The question whether a military government is better equipped than a civilian government to play a developmental role is more controversial. Again, we take Nigeria and Ghana as our case studies. Viewed overall, military rule in Nigeria, which extended over a period of thirteen years, cannot be judged a resounding success: indeed, in Dr Oyediran's judgement, it was a failure.[34] Tens of thousands of citizens were killed and wounded or rendered homeless in the riots of July and September 1966 and in the civil war which followed. Even Murtala Mohammed's drastic surgery did not purge Nigeria of corruption and maladministration, both of which continued to bedevil the successor civilian regime headed by President Shehu Shagari, leading radical observers to conclude, and the PRP to argue, that moral regeneration in Nigeria is dependent, not upon short-term shock treatment, but upon the fundamental restructuring of society.

Though there is no necessary correlation between political stability and economic development (as the experience of France under the Fourth Republic testified), the outbreak of civil war inevitably resulted in a decline in economic performance. Economic growth was very rapid following the civil war but, given the vastness of Nigeria's oil revenues, the military government can claim little credit for an achievement that was due to geological good fortune; after all, the economic performance of the civilian government was quite encouraging in the 1960–5 period before oil had become the mainstay of the Nigerian economy. Moreover, successive governments were beset with bureaucratic tangles, causing, for example, the gross over-ordering of cement under Gowon, delays in the distribution of cement and other building materials and in the release of foreign exchange (even when available) to pay for essential imports. Economic growth declined in the last years of military rule as the oil boom ended and the government had to resort to large-scale external borrowing in order to meet its heavy import bill. Sectoral performance varied over the period as a whole: it was impressive in the building, construction, manufacturing and oil sectors, while the country's infrastructure, including transport and power, benefited from heavy investment. Performance in the agricultural sector was disappointing, though the sharp fall in the export of certain cash crops (notably groundnuts, groundnut oil, palm oil, cotton and timber) may perhaps be explained by the diversion of production to expanded home markets;[35] food imports increased alarmingly throughout most of the 1970s, partly in response to changing consumer needs. Government attempts to step up agricultural output through changes in the land tenure system (effected by the Land Use Decree of 1978) and through large-scale farming and marketing board reforms were not successful – more might have been achieved by helping the small-scale farmer and by raising the unduly low producer prices; Shagari's civilian administration moved towards this strategy. Thus, stagnating agriculture was one of the major economic problems left unresolved by the military. Other unresolved problems were heavy defence expenditure – this was a continuing burden, though in relative terms, government spending on defence and general administration declined from 1970 while spending on education and social services increased; serious inflation, reflected in the rise of the consumer price index from 150 in 1970 to 423 in 1977; disappointing employment prospects – oil extraction had a small employment effect; and revenue allocation, the military having resorted to a series of *ad hoc* arrangements the cumulative result of which was to channel resources to the centre at the expense of the states, whose financial autonomy was in consequence somewhat impaired.[36]

In industry, the Nigerian Enterprises Promotion Decree of 1972 increased domestic participation (both private and state) in industrial enterprises but at the cost of accentuating existing class divisions within Nigerian society; the decree benefited local merchant capitalists rather than the ordinary people. In the 1970s the Nigerian economy became ever more closely tied to the international capitalist system, though (contrary to what underdevelopment theory would lead us to expect) this did not prevent the military government – particularly the Mohammed and Obasanjo regimes – from pursuing a vigorous and assertive foreign policy which was sometimes, as over Angola and Rhodesia, inimical to the interests of major foreign powers and companies.

On a long-term view, there was no significant difference in the economic performance of the Gowon regime on the one hand and the regimes of Mohammed and Obasanjo on the other, while the military as a whole achieved no better results than might have been expected of a civilian government, similarly blessed with an oil bonanza. Its legacy to the civilian regime in 1979 was a sluggish economy, a worrying level of inflation, a serious balance of payments deficit, and mounting problems in the social sphere. However, by creating a stable political order since 1970 and by shifting the locus of power to the federal centre, the military had also provided President Shagari's government with a favourable context within which to tackle these problems.

In Ghana, the civilian government of Dr Hilla Limann inherited an economy that was in a severely depressed state; much of the blame for this must lie with Ghana's second military regime under General Acheampong (1972–8). Drawing upon cross-national research to assess the performance of this regime, Donald Rothchild finds that 'the Acheampong government had no positive effects different from those of the non-military regime systems, and, if anything, can be described as a disaster'.[37] The level of both cocoa and gold production fell and export earnings declined at a time of high world-market prices and of increasing demand for imported goods; local food production also dropped sharply. On the political front the regime's achievements, measured in terms of political stability, bridging the élite-mass gap, and establishing effective political structures were also poor, while Acheampong's proposed experiment with a non-party representative system of 'Union' (later 'National') government, in which the military would have a role, excited the vigorous opposition of professional bodies, as well as university lecturers and students, and, even according to the official returns, received unenthusiastic endorsement from the electorate in a nationwide referendum held on 30 March 1978. (The referendum result was clearly rigged.)

Performance in relation to such criteria was, therefore, weak, but was more mixed in respect of the regime's ability to achieve its own specified goals of agricultural development and self-reliance, and regional reallocation. The regime, like the preceding civilian government under Dr Busia, placed great stress upon agricultural improvement. In the early years agricultural output, particularly of rice and maize, did expand, though at the cost of increased social inequality; the main beneficiaries were the already advantaged larger-scale farmers, especially the emergent commercial farming community in the Northern areas of Ghana. Of the two major instruments of policy to promote agricultural development – the regional development corporations created in 1973 and the 'operation feed yourself' programme – the first had a positive, if limited impact, while the second served initially, though not permanently, as an incentive to food production; cocoa production, on the other hand, declined steadily. These various agricultural policies were part of the Acheampong regime's attempt to correct inherited regional imbalances in the economy; here again, the regime built upon policies set in motion by the Busia administration. While performance did not match aspirations, the relatively disadvantaged Northern and Upper regions benefited from the northward thrust of the government's agricultural policies, while the highest *per capita* distribution of secondary school expenditure (though not of expenditure on teacher training and technical education) also went to these regions, followed by the underdeveloped Brong-Ahafo region.

Professor Rothchild's article illustrates that the performance of a military regime varies according to whether it is assessed by generalisable criteria or by criteria peculiar to the regime in question: by the first test, the Acheampong regime's performance, alike in the economic and political spheres, was unimpressive; by the second test, the record was mixed. Accurate evaluation of regime performance is therefore both difficult and complex and, given the wide diversity of African states, is likely to remain so even when the tools of social science analysis are further refined.

In the meantime, it seems reasonable to put forward certain general propositions to supplement those presented earlier in this section. First, despite the fact that a military regime might be able to take certain actions which a civilian government would find difficult (for Nigeria, the creation of additional states and the cancellation of the 1973 census came into this category), the record of the military in promoting political development is likely to be no better than that of the civilian regime and, because of the restrictions which it imposes on political party activity and representative institutions at the national and local levels, is likely to be worse. The second proposition is that non-revolutionary regimes made up of officers with predominantly middle-class values tend to reflect the same middle-class bias as non-revolutionary civilian regimes and therefore to promote policies which, though often entailing the redistribution of political and economic power among élites, maintain the socio-economic *status quo*, while a third is that military regimes display no greater capacity in promoting economic development than their civilian predecessors. On the last point Eric Nordlinger, using aggregate data analysis, shows that, if the economy improves, it is often in spite of the military regime in power. His and other empirical studies convince Decalo that, whatever the type of military regime under consideration, 'examples of Ataturk-style socio-economic transformation of new nations are extremely rare'. They also reinforce Ruth First's conclusion that 'the coup as a method of change that changes little has become endemic to Africa's politics'.[38]

Military Withdrawal

In her study of *Regimes in Tropical Africa*, Ruth Collier points out that military withdrawal tends to lead to the resurrection of multi-partyism in Anglophone Africa and to the establishment, under military tutelage, of one-party regimes in Francophone Africa. As a generalisation, this statement is sound, but while generally acceptable for Anglophone Africa, it needs to be qualified in respect of Francophone Africa.

In both Ghana in 1968–9 and again in 1979, and Nigeria in 1978–9, the military governments supervised the drawing up of new democratic constitutions, under which strongly contested multi-party elections were held. Following the declaration of the results, the armed forces handed over power to the newly elected civilian governments – formed in Ghana by Dr Busia (Progress Party) in 1969 and, ten years later, by Dr Limann (People's National Party), and in Nigeria by President Shagari (National Party of Nigeria) in 1979.

In Francophone Africa, on the other hand, the tendency has been for the incumbent military regimes to seek to strengthen their legitimacy by forming single parties and then holding both presidential and parliamentary elections. The latter have been 'plebiscitary' in most cases in the sense that both president and national assembly members have been returned with overwhelming majorities. Thus, in Mali in 1979 the single presidential candidate, General Moussa Traoré, secured 99.89 per cent of the vote, while the 82 single-list candidates of the sole political party, the Union Démocratique du Peuple Malien, were endorsed by 99.85 per cent of the electorate. These elections, therefore, represented only a modest step in the direction of democratic government and resulted in the retention of power by the military leader who had been head of state since the 1968 coup; army officers also held other government ministries. Comparable constitutional changes have taken place in the tiny West African republic of Togo (where in 1979 the electorate overwhelmingly endorsed General Gnassingbe Eyadema as president and the single list of candidates of the ruling Rassemblement Populaire Togolais), as well as in the People's Republic of Benin, the People's Republic of Congo, and Rwanda.[39]

Upper Volta, however, has made important changes to the Francophone pattern that brings it closer to the Anglophone model. In this extremely poor West African state, where General Sangoule Lamizana's administration had a better record in office than most African military governments, an experiment in multi-partyism was conducted in the 1978 general election. As a result of the latter, the hitherto totally dominant Union Démocratique Voltaique (UDV) secured 28 out of the 57 seats contested, as against 13 for the Union Nationale pour la Défense de la Démocratie (UNDD) and 9 for the Union Progressiste Voltaique (UPV). A competitive presidential election was also held: President Lamizana (UDV) failed to secure an absolute majority of votes in the first ballot, but was returned in the second round with 711,736 votes, against 552,619 cast for his opponent, Macaire Quedra-ogo (UNDD). Moreover, there was a large number of abstentions in both the presidential and parliamentary elections, reflecting a further variation from the normal Francophone pattern. Again, whereas in the partial return to civilian rule in Upper Volta in 1971–4 army officers had still held key ministries, in 1978 the army (President Lamizana apart) withdrew completely from political life in favour of an all-civilian government.[40]

Opinions will differ as to whether complete military withdrawal offers the best prospect of stable government. It can be argued that the military, which (in Luckham's view) 'has replaced the party as Africa's most important political institution',[41] should be accommodated in the various organs of government, including the executive and legislature. But in Anglophone Africa, at least, such solutions are likely to be unacceptable – alike to politicians, professional groups, the academic community, and trade unionists. Thus, in Ghana, the proposals put forward in 1977 by General Acheampong for 'Union government' – initially conceived by him as a 'partner-ship of the Military, the police and the Civilians' – provoked a strong public reaction, being rightly seen as a device by the military to surrender some of the form of power, but little of its substance. In the event, Acheampong's proposals – even in the emasculated version recommended by the *Ad Hoc* Committee on Union Government – were never implemented since he himself was removed in a counter-coup in mid-1978. What the head of Ghana's Supreme Military Council wanted, but in the end failed to obtain, has been more easily achieved by military leaders in much of Francophone Africa – a government in civilian guise and embellished with representative institutions, but still under firm military control.

Further Reading

Austin, D., and Luckham, R. (eds.), *Politicians and Soldiers in Ghana* (London: Frank Cass, 1975).

Bienen, H., *Armies and Parties in Africa* (New York: Africana, 1978).

Cox, T. S., *Civil–Military Relations in Sierra Leone: A Case Study of African Soldiers in Politics* (Cambridge, Mass.: Harvard University Press, 1976).

Decalo, S., *Coups and Army Rule in Africa: Studies in Military Style* (New Haven: Yale University Press, 1976).

First, R., *The Barrel of a Gun: Political Power in Africa and the Coup d'Etat* (London: Allen Lane, The Penguin Press, 1970).

Kirk-Greene, A. H. M., and Rimmer, D., *Nigeria since 1970: A Political and Economic Outline* (London: Hodder & Stoughton, 1981).

Luckham, R., *The Nigerian Military: A Sociological Analysis of Authority and Revolt, 1960–67* (Cambridge University Press, 1971).

——, 'A Comparative Typology of Civil–Military Relations', *Government and Opposition*, vol. 6, no. 1 (Winter 1971).

——, 'French Militarism in Africa', *Review of African Political Economy*, no. 24 (May–August 1982).

Oyediran, O. (ed.), *Nigerian Government and Politics under Military Rule, 1966–79* (London: Macmillan, 1979).

Panter-Brick, S. K. (ed.), *Soldiers and Oil: The Political Transformation of Nigeria* (London: Frank Cass, 1978).

Welch, C. E. (ed.), *Soldier and State in Africa: A Comparative Analysis of Military Intervention and Political Change* (Evanston: Northwestern University Press, 1970).

8

Revolution and Revolutionary Regimes

The ideological map of Africa was transformed in the mid-1970s with the advent to independence of the ex-Portuguese colonies of Angola, Cape Verde, Guinea-Bissau, and Mozambique; the leadership was committed in each case to the pursuit of Marxist–Leninist principles. That this commitment was in part a reaction to the oppressive nature of Portuguese rule is evident from Barry Munslow's authoritative study *Mozambique: the Revolution and its Origins*.[1] Portugal's colonies – 'overseas provinces', according to the myth of Lusotropicalism[2] – both provided the cheap raw materials necessary to fuel her nascent industrialisation programme and served as an outlet for poor, and often unskilled or semi-skilled, white immigrants who sought employment opportunities denied them at home. Neutral during the Second World War and not being a member of the United Nations, Portugal did not experience in the post-war period the liberal currents of opinion which influenced most of the other Western imperial powers and she was not subject to strong international, or for that matter, domestic pressure to grant independence to her colonies. Moreover, as opposition began to surface in metropolitan Portugal, the dictatorial regime of Antonio de Oliviera Salazar (who was succeeded by the equally illiberal Marcello Caetano in 1968) was unwilling to enter voluntarily into the power-sharing arrangements inherent in a policy of decolonisation, in the knowledge that these were likely to have serious internal repercussions. There was also, as Dr Munslow has pointed out, the fact that Portugal, a poor state with a weak economy and a sub-metropolitan power dependent upon the more advanced North Atlantic metropolitan powers, could not adopt the neo-colonial option which had existed for Britain, France and Belgium after the Second World War; in his words, 'Portugal did not wish to *decolonise* at the end of the 1950s or in the 1960s because it could not neo-colonise'. Nicos Zafiris has made the same point:

> The benefits of continued possession of the colonies were too great for Portugal to lose, but they could not be guaranteed under conditions of open competition with foreign capitalism. Only direct political domination could ensure the admission of foreign capital on terms advantageous to Portugal.[3]

The Portuguese, therefore, fought to retain their colonies and the MPLA in Angola, like PAIGC in Guinea-Bissau and FRELIMO in Mozambique, had to pursue a protracted armed struggle to win independence. In conducting such a struggle, the movements were not unique: more recently guerrilla warfare has paved the way to independence in Zimbabwe, while the South West African People's Organisation (SWAPO) is still fighting to end South Africa's rule in Namibia. Again, independence in both Algeria in 1962 and Kenya the following year was preceded by several years of bloody conflict. The post-independence government established by Ben Bella in Algeria expressed socialist pretensions, but a pragmatic brand of non-revolutionary socialism was established and maintained until Ben Bella was removed in a military coup in 1965; Zimbabwe, similarly, has not yet attempted to transform the inherited socio-economic structure. In Kenya, where 'Mau Mau' has been described as 'an integral part of an ongoing, rationally conceived nationalist movement',[4] Sessional Paper No. 10 of 1965 on African Socialism did no more than provide a thin socialist veneer to a predominantly capitalist framework. These various examples (from Algeria, Kenya and Zimbabwe) appear to substantiate Munslow's contention that a protracted armed struggle is 'a necessary, but not a sufficient, condition' for the revolutionary transformation of a nationalist movement.[5] In this respect, comparison between the cases of Angola, Guinea-Bissau, Mozambique and Zimbabwe is instructive; we begin with Mozambique.

Mozambique

Dr Munslow has shown how the period 1967–70 was one of internal crisis for FRELIMO, as two sharply opposed conceptions of the nationalist struggle emerged: 'Conflicts centred on the organisation of production and distribution in the liberated zones, the new structures to be created in these areas, the military strategy and tactics to be pursued, the emancipation of women, education, and the very definition of the enemy.'[6] One section of the leadership, represented by the chairmen of Cabo Delgado, saw independence not as a means of accomplishing a social revolution but of establishing themselves in power within a neo-colonial framework; in the meantime, they sought to maintain a private enterprise system based on peasant exploitation in the liberated areas. On the other hand, the revolutionaries in FRELIMO sought to transform the nature of society in the liberated zones, for example, by collectivising production and through co-operatives; they argued that they were not fighting the whites so much as the exploitative system upon which white domination rested, and that women, youths and elders should all participate in the liberation struggle. The views of the revolutionaries prevailed both at the Second Congress of FRELIMO, held at Niassa in July 1968, and subsequently, despite severe setbacks to their cause, including the assassination of Eduardo Mondlane, the party president, in February 1969. With the election of Samora Machel as president and Marcelino dos Santos as vice-president in May 1970, FRELIMO embarked on the final phase of the national liberation struggle: it did so under a leadership convinced that 'in our struggle everything, absolutely everything, depends on the people',[7] and that revolutionary ideology, drawing upon Marxist–Leninist principles, must inform daily practice. Political work was intensified at all levels and increased stress was placed on the primacy of the ideological struggle and the conduct of party cadres in the liberated areas. In this way, writes Munslow, 'Frelimo moved beyond nationalism to adopt a revolutionary programme, and it is this which sets Frelimo apart from most other nationalist movements in Africa'.[8] This programme involved discarding old ideas and structures in favour of new economic and social relationships. The achievement of independence in 1975 provided Samora Machel and his government with the opportunity to carry forward the revolution throughout the new state of Mozambique.

Angola

Angolan nationalism grew apace in the 1950s and by the beginning of 1961 Angola was, in John Marcum's graphic description, 'a black powder keg with a ready fuse';[9] rebellion erupted that year in northern Angola. In a way that was more reminiscent of Rhodesia than Mozambique and Guinea-Bissau, the nationalist movement was subject to deep internal divisions, along primarily ethno-linguistic lines. Under this 'communal tripolarity', as Marcum has called it, the Frente Nacional de Libertação de Angola (FNLA), which resulted in 1962 from the merger of two earlier parties, drew its main support from the Bakongo of the north; the União Nacional para a Independência Total de Angola (UNITA), founded in 1966, from the Ovimbundu and Chokwe of the south; and the MPLA, established in 1956, from the Mbundu of north-central Angola. However, the MPLA especially nurtured wider, national loyalties: it was 'a product of the urban, multiracial Luanda–Mbundu stream of Angolan nationalism' and was strongly entrenched in the major urban centres; it had a well-educated, largely Marxist and mulatto leadership and appealed to the urban intelligentsia of all the country's communities, including the mestiços and the Portuguese.[10] Though the MPLA initially lacked the rural orientation of its rival organisations, it tried to identify with Angola's peasants and established camps, clinics and schools in the liberated areas under its control. Of the three nationalist movements, it was the most active in fighting the liberation struggle and the most assiduous in its attempts to involve the peasants in a variety of participatory structures. It also introduced a politicisation programme in Marxism, though as Lucio Lara, the party's leading theoretician, subsequently admitted on the basis of his experience in eastern Angola in the late 1960s: 'Clearly the ideology had not gone very deep sometimes.'[11] Moreover, no ethno-linguistic region was entirely solid in its support of a particular liberation movement. In the early 1960s the Ovimbundu were linked with the Bakongo in the União das Populações de Angola (UPA) – the dominant element in the 1962 merger which led to the formation of the FNLA – while some of the Bakongo, alienated by the misdeeds of FNLA soldiers and leaders, subsequently came to back the MPLA rather than the FNLA. Nevertheless, the basic 'communal tripolarity' persisted throughout the liberation struggle and Angolan nationalists failed to form a united front.[12]

Apart from these communal differences and the deep mistrust which the leaders of the liberation movements had for each other, the movements varied in their policies and their external alliances. FNLA's chief support came from Zaire (Holden Roberto, its leader, is related to President Mobutu through marriage), and it set up a Governo Revolucionário de Angola no Exilio (GRAE) at Leopoldville in April 1962. The Front was also backed by the OAU (in the early 1960s), as well as by the United States, China, and North Korea. The MPLA's basis of external support was wider and included the OAU (from about 1964), the Soviet bloc, Cuba, Yugoslavia, China, Sweden, solidarity movements in the West, and the left-wing parties in Portugal; it established its headquarters in Congo-Brazzaville. The Soviet Union provided the MPLA with funds and military equipment from late 1968 and, together with Czechoslovakia and Bulgaria, trained MPLA cadets. However, she was not consistent in her support: arms shipments were halted during the 'Chipende crisis' – an internal power struggle within the MPLA in 1972–3 – and afterwards, and were only resumed in mid-1975 (it was the Yugoslavs who, in April 1975, came to MPLA's rescue with a timely shipment of arms). Though the MPLA had established a clear dominance by 1972, this crisis proved a real setback and checked MPLA's penetration into the Huambo-Bie area of central Angola, to the advantage of Jonas Savimbi, the UNITA leader, who was able to gain followers in this important, food-producing region. The result, as Marcum records, was that no movement 'achieved lasting pre-eminence before the collapse of Portuguese rule'.[13]

The coup d'état in Portugal in April 1974 and the preparations for Portuguese withdrawal from her African colonies ushered in a bitter power struggle in Angola. The government of national unity established under the Alvor Agreement of January 1975 collapsed and subsequent attempts by the OAU to revive it through an agreement reached between the MPLA, FNLA and UNITA at Nakuru, Kenya, in June 1975 were unsuccessful. In November 1975 the Portuguese formally recognised Angolan independence, but left open the question which of the two contending governments should inherit power – the People's Republic of Angola founded by the MPLA in Luanda or the Social Democratic Republic of Angola, founded by FNLA and UNITA, linked in an uneasy alliance, in Huambo. The power struggle was internationalised and the decisive factor proved to be the massive Soviet and Cuban intervention on the side of the MPLA. This intervention took place only after South African troops had invaded Angola in October 1975, in support of UNITA and the FNLA. The latter two movements were also helped by clandestine American military aid and the recruitment of mercenaries.[14] Within a few months the MPLA government under Dr Agosthino Neto was widely, if not universally, recognised as the legal government of Angola.

Guinea-Bissau

Of Portuguese Guinea, the smallest and least developed of the Portuguese colonies, Patrick Chabal has observed: 'Unlike Angola and Mozambique, there had been in Guinea no white settlement, no large-scale land alienation, minimal forced labour and no rural displacement, no acute impoverishment of the countryside or rural proletarianisation.'[15] This observation understates the level of Portuguese exploitation which, though not as great as in the other Lusophone territories, was still very real. The colonial state in Guinea was geared to the interests of a large Portuguese firm, the Companhia União Fabril (CUF), which had a near monopoly in the country; forced crop cultivation was widespread and cash crop prices were artificially depressed. Despite the undoubted persistence of strong communal ties in the rural areas of Guinea, the objective conditions of political mobilisation were not therefore absent to the extent that Dr Chabal (in an otherwise valuable article) has suggested.[16]

Created in 1956, the PAIGC combined members of the main ethnic groups of the mainland (Fula, Mandinga, Manjaca and Balante) and the spatially separate and lighter-skinned population of the Cape Verde islands. The party went underground in 1960 and though without weapons, financial resources and international contacts, began the apparently hopeless task of preparing for a war of liberation based in the countryside. Under the leadership of Amilcar Cabral, an agronomist from Cape Verde, it emphasised the importance of the political aspect of the struggle: cadres were trained in Conakry and then sent to the Guinean countryside to win the support of the villagers. Within six years of launching the armed struggle in 1963, the PAIGC controlled over half the country; elected village committees, people's stores and people's courts were established in the liberated areas and the work of socioeconomic reconstruction was begun, emphasis being placed on agricultural production, health care and education. The party's success reflected the effectiveness of both its political mobilisation strategy and its military structure. But this success was not achieved without difficulty. An early tendency towards 'militarism' among some guerrilla leaders, whose abuse of power was alienating the population, was corrected at the Cassaca Congress in 1964. Fighters as well as cadres were reminded by Cabral that they were 'armed militants, not militarists', and the primacy of the political struggle was reasserted. Steps were also taken to reorganise the party and a national army, which was capable of responding to different situations, gradually replaced the original autonomous guerrilla groups. A system of 'dual command' was instituted within the army whereby leadership was exercised at all levels by the military commander and the political commissar, whose positions were interchangeable.[17]

The great strength of the PAIGC was its ability to adapt itself to the conditions imposed by the struggle and, in this respect, it was helped by what Chabal has called its 'pragmatic attitude towards ideology'. Though Cabral drew substantially upon Marxist theory in his own writing, he insisted that the party should avoid doctrinal rigidity. As he told his party cadres, to whose training he gave a great deal of personal attention:

> Always remember that people are not fighting for ideas, nor for what is in men's mind. The people fight and accept the sacrifices demanded by the struggle in order to gain material advantages, to live better and in peace, to benefit from progress, and for the better future of their children. National liberation, the struggle against colonialism, the construction of peace, progress and independence are nothing but hollow words devoid of any significance unless they can be translated into a real improvement of living conditions.[18]

The result of this approach was not only that the party avoided ideological disputes and party splits, but that its cadres spoke in a language which the ordinary villager could understand. Sadly Amilcar Cabral, the architect of the Guinean revolution, was assassinated in January 1973, some nine months before the PAIGC Assembly proclaimed the independence of Guinea-Bissau and the Cape Verde islands (Portugal delayed recognition of independence until 1974 and 1975 respectively).

Zimbabwe

Rhodesia became independent in 1980 as the Republic of Zimbabwe, following a protracted period of armed conflict; the latter culminated in British-supervised elections in February 1980, resulting in a sweeping victory for the ZANU(PF) party led by Robert Mugabe. The conflict took the form of a nationalist struggle rather than (in the words of Samora Machel) 'a revolutionary struggle that implies profound changes in the society'. Despite the claim by a ZANU spokesman that 'ZANU has prevailed in the struggle because of the development of the Party and the masses in revolutionary theory and practice', it is not easy to know how far rural voters were radicalised either by ZANU's guerrilla cadres or by their own war-time experience.[19]

In an article in *Southern Africa* in February 1977, John Saul argued that Joshua Nkomo's Zimbabwe African People's Union (ZAPU) had better credentials for conducting a people's war than ZANU which, under its petty-bourgeois leadership, had broken from the parent body in 1963. Yet both lacked the political clarity essential for effective guerrilla struggle. The main hope, said Saul, lay with the Zimbabwe People's Army (ZIPA), which had been formed in 1976 when disenchanted guerrilla commanders from ZANU and ZAPU agreed, upon the prompting of the front-line presidents, to form a joint military command. This hope was not fulfilled and in the 1978 postscript to his reprinted essay, Saul noted that a resurgent ZANU leadership had reasserted control over those ZANU members who had belonged to ZIPA, though he remained sceptical about the leadership's revolutionary potential.[20]

The writings of Terence Ranger, Lionel Cliffe and others provide a valuable corrective to Saul's essay, without, however, necessarily disagreeing with the scepticism of his conclusion: there can be no guarantee, comments Ranger, 'that Mugabe and his allies will succeed with or even persist in revolutionary transformation'. While Mugabe and the other early nationalist leaders, who were detained inside Rhodesia between 1964 and 1974, lacked direct experience of guerrilla warfare until the mid-1970s and ZANU was wracked by infighting among its various factions, the party changed its methods after 1972; its military wing – the Zimbabwe African National Liberation Army (ZANLA) – improved its guerrilla war tactics, relying heavily on politicising the peasantry.[21] The assassination of Herbert Chitepo, the national chairman, in 1975 and the wholesale detention of leading ZANU members by the Zambian government – events which gave primacy to the young guerrilla commanders in ZIPA – set back the conversion of ZANU into an effective instrument of war. But the setback was only temporary, the existence of ZIPA serving as a spur to train political cadres and build up mass organisations.[22] As a result, though more especially because of the efforts of

Kumbirai Tongogara, who had been elected to the *Dare* (ZANU's war council) in 1973, close links were established between ZANU's political and military wings and the importance of ideology was stressed.

In 1977 top leadership positions in the party were filled by nationalists from the pre-UDI generation, with Mugabe himself now president. Alongside this dominant 'old guard' were other nationalists who had spent long years in exile – some of them were still detained in Zambia; following independence, these two elements were to make up over three-quarters of Mugabe's first cabinet. The third strand in the leadership comprised former ZIPA commanders willing to accept the new dispensation; those who were not willing were disciplined by the party and, together with members of certain other groups, were taken into 'protective custody' by the Mozambican government. New organisational structures, in the form of elected people's committees and a network of *mujibas* (mobilised youth who served as intermediaries between the guerrillas and the people's committees), were also established and some political education was undertaken.[23]

For its part, ZAPU, the older (and increasingly Ndebele-based) nationalist party which became the Patriotic Front Party (PFP) when the Patriotic Front split to contest the 1980 elections, adopted different tactics. The majority of ZAPU troops were not committed to fighting a protracted people's war, of which mass politicisation and mobilisation were essential components, but were held in reserve in their external (mainly Zambian) bases, waiting an opportunity (which never came) to strike against Rhodesia's main economic centres and to seize power in Salisbury and the other cities. Nkomo was confident that the people still supported ZAPU, which relied on organisational structures established in the early 1960s and subsequently maintained underground. The fact was, however, that such residue of countrywide support as remained began to ebb in the second half of the 1970s as the liberation war, spearheaded by ZANU rather than ZAPU, spread and achieved greater impact. While ZAPU retained some support in the operational areas – almost entirely in Matabeleland – through the successes of the Zimbabwe People's Revolutionary Army (ZIPRA), its military wing, it did not assume direct responsibility even here for administering the liberated areas. Its tactics contributed to a marked regional split in the 1980 general election; ZAPU failed to win any seat outside Matabeleland.

Revolutionary Regimes: 1. Ex-Liberation Movements

The context within which the liberation struggle was conducted in each of these countries varied. Initially, conditions for guerrilla warfare were probably least favourable in Guinea-Bissau both because Portuguese exploitation was somewhat less severe in that colony than in Angola and Mozambique, and because of the physical separation between Guinea-Bissau and the Cape Verde islands, as well as the historic and cultural differences between their peoples. On the other hand, the small size of Guinea-Bissau facilitated political penetration and mobilisation. In Mozambique, there were important differences in the levels of political consciousness between the liberated and the non-liberated zones, while in Angola the split within the nationalist movement along communal lines weakened its thrust – as it was to do in Zimbabwe in the wake of the 1980 elections. The achievement of national unity was an urgent priority in each country. Of the four national movements which paved the way to independence, the MPLA probably rested on the firmest ideological base and ZANU(PF) on the weakest. Though Amilcar Cabral was pre-eminent among the leaders of these movements as a Marxist theoretician, the PAIGC's attitude to ideology was pragmatic: the people, Cabral argued, 'are not fighting for ideas' but 'to gain material advantages'. Nevertheless, the PAIGC in Guinea-Bissau, and the MPLA in Angola and FRELIMO in Mozambique tried with varying degrees of success to apply the Marxist method of analysis to their own concrete circumstances, in the conviction that to do otherwise would have been to court disaster.

The challenge facing the new state leaders was whether they would be able to move quickly enough to improve conditions of living in the rural areas before a sense of popular disillusionment set in. It was obviously important that the revolutionary process should not lose its momentum or, through the bureaucratisation of the state and party, become diverted from its original goals. In each state, as Munslow has graphically pointed out, 'The greatest danger was that the state might well be able to transform the revolution before the revolution could transform the state.'[24] In the light of this comment, we review the post-independence experience of these states, beginning with Mozambique.

Mozambique

The credentials of FRELIMO to effect a socio-economic revolution were impeccable. It had conducted a protracted liberation struggle and its leadership, guided by a Marxist–Leninist ideology, knew well (in Munslow's words) 'that the taking of state power is not the end but the beginning of the revolution'. It was 'a party committed to transforming the existing relations of production and to creating a workers' and peasants' state'.[25] Transformation was to proceed by creating communal villages in the rural areas and structures of workers' control in industry. The most urgent task, however, was to extend the high level of political consciousness in the liberated areas to the rest of the country and to this end, FRELIMO in 1975 established *grupos dinamizadores* (dynamising groups) to undertake the work of mobilisation and organisation. The watchwords of these groups were unity, work and vigilance; they afforded FRELIMO a means to spread its message but, according to Middlemas, 'failed almost wholly to galvanise production'. New party schools were also opened to train the top-level cadres essential to provide the people with political education; party cadres were in desperately short supply, causing the gap between party and people to widen alarmingly.[26]

At independence, which was formally achieved on 25 June 1975, the constraints within which President Machel and his government had to operate were formidable. The long years of war had crippled the predominantly agricultural economy (which was also hit by rising oil prices) and weakened the administrative structure, while the country remained intensely dependent on the regional sub-system, centring on South Africa, which it supplied with electricity and labour. The exodus of white shopkeepers and traders in 1975–6 resulted in the breakdown of the transportation system, as well as of marketing and distribution, and adversely affected all sectors of the Mozambican economy. Since Portuguese managers and technicians also left precipitately (90 per cent of whites had left by the end of 1976) trained manpower, which was desperately short at all levels, was not available to sustain the extensive measures of nationalisation that were undertaken, to revive flagging industrial output, and to underpin bold experiments in the communal production of agriculture. At its third congress in February 1977 FRELIMO decided that agriculture should become 'the base and industry the dynamizing factor for development'.

Despite signs of economic recovery by 1978, production in all sectors in 1980 still fell below pre-independence levels, while imports had risen sharply; the result was a growing foreign exchange crisis. Though sugar had once again become the major export crop, food had still to be imported. Distribution problems and the influx of peasants to the urban areas led to food shortages and food rationing in the towns; speculation and black marketeering grew alarmingly. These difficulties were compounded by the sharp reduction in the number of Mozambicans recruited to work in the South African mines, thereby exacerbating an already serious unemployment problem; by the ending in 1978 of the agreement with the South African government whereby Mozambique had sold on the open market and at a substantial profit the gold earned by its migrant workers; by destructive Rhodesian raids against ZANLA guerrilla bases inside Mozambique; by acts of sabotage perpetrated by opposition groups, notably the Mozambique Resistance Movement (MRM), which was directly supported by South Africa; and by a prolonged drought in parts of central Mozambique. The performance of state enterprises, which, said the President, were 'sick with parasites', was also poor.

Beset with mounting problems, though with an impressive record in the spheres of health and education, President Machel's government took tough action against dissidents. It adopted measures which recognised the damage done to the economy and to popular support by the corruption and inefficiency of the state and party bureaucracies. In what has been called an 'experimental shift to the right' in 1980,[27] it made farm and factory managers responsible for looking after workers' interests, authorised the sale of state shops to private traders, invited Western business interests to invest in Mozambique, and gave the army, which had earlier been converted from a guerrilla army into a regular army with ranks, insignia and medals, a more conventional military role than previously. In the external sphere the President, who within a year of independence had closed the frontier with Rhodesia at enormous cost to Mozambique, now put pressure on the Patriotic Front to accept the Lancaster House agreement.

However, President Machel and senior party leaders remained loyal throughout to their commitment to establish a workers' and peasants' state. They quickly realised that the 1980 domestic reform measures had resulted in the abuse of power rather than in increased economic efficiency and therefore launched what Paul Goodison has called 'an almost puritanical cleansing of Mozambican society'.[28] The leadership had helped to create the revolution and the revolution had inherited the state; the danger now was that, as bureaucrats, army officers and private shopkeepers acted in their own rather than the people's interest, the state would undo the revolution. Machel accused managers of adopting capitalist attitudes, shopkeepers of indulging in corrupt practices, and army officers of divorcing the army from the people. Corrective action was therefore taken. Already, in the latter part of 1977, 27,000 deputies had been elected at all levels to serve on people's assemblies, which were to control the state apparatus. Additional measures – in the form, for example, of new laws and methods of work, political study groups and a different class basis for recruitment – were adopted to counteract the problem of bureaucratisation. Greater support was given to private peasant production – peasants, for example, were paid higher prices for their produce and, at its fourth congress in April 1983, FRELIMO shifted the emphasis away from big state farms, whose yields were very low. To help overcome the distribution problems, private trading was still permitted, though made subject to more stringent controls; consumer co-operatives were encouraged to handle the sale of food in the urban areas – the inefficient people's shops were abolished. Managers were allowed to continue to run the factories, but were required to develop socialist methods of directing rather than closeting themselves in their offices and ignoring the opinions of the shop-floor. Workers' committees were revived, made popularly elective, and given a major say in formulating the 1982 state plan; the previous plan, drawn up by managers and professional planners, was found to be unrealistic. Ministries were reorganised and offices of control were introduced within each ministry to improve efficiency. State firms were given a shake-up and the State Housing Corporation, which had been riddled with corruption, was overhauled and the guilty punished. The army, too, though retaining its new command structure, was made to renew its links with the people and help again in producing food. In 1982, as the threat from the MRM – now redesignated the Mozambique National Resistance (MNR) – increased, there was a partial return to the *status quo ante*: former guerrillas were reabsorbed into the army and the formation of popular militias was encouraged. Important steps were also taken to reorganise and revitalise the party so that it could effectively control the state apparatus – this was a long-term task which had been begun in 1977 when the third party congress had decided that FRELIMO should be transformed from a front to a vanguard party; the fourth congress in 1983 doubled the size of the central committee in order to give significantly more say to the provinces. In these various ways President Machel sought to put Mozambique firmly back on the revolutionary socialist path from which, in a bid to improve economic performance and stem mounting discontent, several commentators believe that he and his government had deviated. However, the task of winning popular support and of asserting military control over the whole country remains a daunting one. Mozambique's continued economic dependence on South Africa means that it is no less difficult to make significant shifts in foreign policy. This dependence, which has made it essential to retain for the time being mutually beneficial links, gives point to Munslow's observation that it was easier for Mozambique to remove the colonial yoke of Portugal than it is to disengage from South Africa's economic domination. A first step to end this domination was the establishment in 1979 by nine black African states of a Southern African Development Co-ordination Conference (SADCC), with a transport and communications commission based in Maputo.

Angola

The MPLA was pledged to the radical transformation of Angolan society according to the principles of 'scientific socialism'. However, the leadership insisted that the Angolan revolution would not be 'a carbon copy of any other revolution';[29] because of Angola's lack of an industrial base, it was to be founded on a worker–peasant alliance. Its ideology was eclectic with a predominant Angolan element, and drew substantially upon the thinking of Amilcar Cabral, leader of the PAIGC, and on the Cuban notion of the *nuevo hombre*. The MPLA was also influenced by the Cuban techniques of mass mobilisation and organisation.

The major problems faced by the MPLA government – led by José Eduardo dos Santos following the death in September 1979 of Dr Neto, who is posthumously revered as 'the immortal guide' of the revolution[30] – have been economic, political and administrative. The government has sought to revive an economy shattered by civil war; to end faction-fighting within the MPLA; to extend the MPLA's political control over the entire country; and to provide administrative underpinning for the new state's experiment in socialism. Though potentially a very rich country, with vast mineral deposits and fertile land and under one-tenth of Nigeria's population, post-independence Angola has faced serious economic difficulties alike in production, marketing and distribution. Agricultural output is still low; there is widespread absenteeism and low productivity in industry; and distribution is poor, resulting periodically in acute food shortages in Luanda, the capital, and other urban centres.

The wholesale exodus of Portuguese citizens in 1975 (all except 30,000 out of 335,000 Portuguese left the country) created a shortage of skilled manpower from which the country has not yet recovered; the extraordinary party congress of December 1980 reaffirmed the MPLA's policy of encouraging the entry (or return) of foreign technicians and businessmen. The need for foreign technical assistance (and equipment) was increased as a result of the sweeping nationalisation measures introduced after independence; some 80 per cent of Angola's enterprises are run by the state. The government's ambitious educational programme will eventually ease the manpower problem; in the meantime, indigenous trained personnel are very scarce and a civil service is virtually non-existent.

The 1980 congress also discussed the acute problems facing the agricultural sector. Commercial agriculture suffered a total breakdown during the civil war and cash-crop production is still well below pre-independence levels (Angola used to be the world's fourth largest exporter of coffee), while food imports in 1980 ate heavily into foreign exchange reserves depleted by massive defence expenditure. The congress decided that production should be stepped up by offering higher prices to the peasants. It resolved, too, to revive commercial activity in the countryside by improving the services offered by state shops and by encouraging small private shopkeepers.

Though committed to the creation of 'a revolutionary democratic dictatorship', the MPLA has been pragmatic in pursuit of its socialist goals. It has not nationalised peasants' land or confiscated peasant property and has only taken over foreign-owned estates which have been abandoned by their owners. In general, foreign-owned enterprises are tolerated so long as Angolan interests are respected. In the vital mining sector, the government has renegotiated contracts with America's Gulf Oil Corporation to work the extensive oilfields in the Cabinda enclave (oil provides over 60 per cent of Angola's foreign exchange) and with Diamang (the Angolan Diamond Company) to mine the country's diamonds. Though the state has acquired majority shareholding in both these undertakings, effective control, including day-to-day operations, remains with the foreign companies. Moreover, Angola's trade is still overwhelmingly with the West.

On the political front, following independence the masses were constitutionally guaranteed 'broad and effective participation in the exercise of political power'; neighbourhood committees and workers' discussion groups were introduced. However, legislative and executive authority remained in the hands of the Council of the Revolution, which comprised members of the MPLA political bureau and the general staff of the armed forces. Having overcome two challenges to his leadership in 1974, Neto was confronted three years later with a serious plot to topple him mounted by Nito Alves, a former guerrilla commander and Minister of Internal Administration. Alves and his fellow dissidents, who included respected MPLA militants, disliked the President's policy of non-racialism and resented the influence wielded in post-independence Angola by mestiços and a number of whites. An abortive coup attempt took place in May 1977. The Cubans intervened decisively on Neto's side, leading Brown to suggest that they may have acted as a buffer between the Soviets and Neto who stressed his government's policy of non-alignment and refused to entertain the establishment of Soviet (or any other foreign) military bases on Angolan soil. In order to rid the MPLA of Neto's opponents rather than to institute orthodox Marxism–Leninism, the MPLA announced in December 1977 that the movement would be transformed into a party; the latter was to be 'purged' of opportunistic elements. Power became increasingly central-ised in the President's own hands and the prospects of establishing 'people's power' receded. By 1980, however, the MPLA could afford to relax its centralised control and created predominantly elected bodies – a 223-member National Assembly and assemblies in each of the provinces – dominated by workers and peasants.

While the MPLA has only developed a popularly supported party organisation in certain parts of the countryside, it has been able, with the backing of some 18,000 Cuban troops, to establish *de facto* control of most of Angola. Whereas it seemed to Brown in 1977 that the war with UNITA, which operated from its ethnic home base in the south and was well-supplied with American and South African arms, was 'unwinnable', it now appears that the Ovimbundu are divided in their allegiance and that popular support for UNITA has wavered. However, UNITA guerrilla attacks in the Central Highlands region (the country's maize-producing and cattle-rearing area) impede the government's attempts to achieve self-sufficiency in food production and seriously disrupt the country's transport and distribution system. The government has been plagued by

South African incursions across the Angolan border, allegedly in pursuit of SWAPO guerrillas and, from the middle of 1981, by South Africa's quasi-permanent occupation of the extreme south of the country. The cost to Angola of South African violations of her sovereignty from 1975 to the end of 1982 has been estimated to be $10 billion. Moreover, only when a Namibian settlement has been achieved is the government likely to reduce the present high and costly level of Cuban and Soviet military aid. In the north of the country the problem is less serious since the FNLA, though retaining the residual loyalty of some of the Bakongo, appears moribund. It would be rash however to predict that Angola's 'communal tripolarity' is now a thing of the past and that Angolan socialism has been firmly established under the MPLA government.[31]

Guinea-Bissau

At independence Guinea and Cape Verde, which had been ruled by the Portuguese as separate administrative provinces, became two sovereign republics – Portugal formally recognised Guinea-Bissau in September 1974 and granted independence to the Cape Verde islands in July 1975. However, the two states were linked by a single party – the PAIGC which, from its creation in 1956, constituted a common nationalist movement whose watchwords were 'unity and struggle'; the party's declared policy was to work for an early union of the two states. The assassination in January 1973 of Amilcar Cabral and the ending of the war revived the tensions within the party which Cabral and the demands of the armed struggle had held in check. These tensions resulted from spatial, racial and educational differences. Most Cape Verdeans (numbering today approximately 300,000) are of mixed European–African descent and live in a chain of islands situated some 300 miles off the Senegalese coast. Again, whereas under Portuguese rule less than 0.4 per cent of Guineans were *assimilados* (i.e. Portuguese citizens who were judged to have assimilated Portuguese culture and way of life), the inhabitants of Cape Verde were all considered *assimilados*, a status which gave them much easier access to state education than Guineans; the result was that the number of educated Cape Verdeans (though still small in relation to the country's needs) far exceeded the number of educated Guineans despite the much larger population of the mainland colony – its present population is approximately 800,000. Moreover, many educated Cape Verdeans had served as junior civil servants in other Portuguese colonies and thus, like the Asians in East Africa, were tarred with being colonial auxiliaries.[32]

Following independence, participatory structures were extended in Guinea-Bissau, where they ranged from five-member local committees to regional councils and the People's National Assembly, and were created in the Cape Verde islands where the PAIGC had not formed any liberated zones during the armed struggle. However, the PAIGC on the mainland lost much of its earlier dynamism. The quality of its cadres overall declined and the party was weakened by factional infighting, based on personal and policy differences within the leadership. Hard-line Marxists were said to dislike the government's decentralisation policy and its concentration on agricultural improvements; there was also resentment of the prominence in Guinea-Bissau of Cape Verdeans – Luis Cabral, Amilcar's younger brother, was President of the Council of State (and assistant secretary-general of the party) and Piro Mendes was Prime Minister. Though a network of consultative and co-operative committees, covering the technical, cultural and political fields, was established from 1976 onwards, the prospect of early unification of the two states receded and came to be seen as a long-term goal. A party conference in November 1977 – the first since independence – considered proposals to overhaul the party structure and transform the PAIGC from a mass liberation movement into an ideological vanguard-type party. However, no effective remedial action was taken and, perhaps as a result, the party failed to check the increasing bureaucratisation of the state apparatus and the ostentatious life-style of some of the city-bound officials, whose attitude created widespread resentment. It was also alleged that power was being increasingly personalised in the hands of President Luis Cabral and a small circle of advisers.

Above all, there was mounting dissatisfaction in Guinea-Bissau with the government's handling of the economy, which had been disrupted by the war and badly hit by the increased cost of oil imports and prolonged periods of drought. The economy was heavily dependent on foreign aid, which the government drew from a wide range of donors in order to reduce its reliance on any one source. Following independence, the government nationalised banking, the currency and credit, and ended the monopoly on import–export trade exercised by subsidiaries of the Lisbon-based CUF; it also took steps to improve the country's road network and distribution system, to increase agricultural production and to protect and expand the fishing industry. Comparable measures were taken in Cape Verde, where the government also tackled the recurrent problem of drought by means of water-retaining schemes and a programme of afforestation; financial necessity forced it to allow South African Airways to continue to use the airport on the desert island of Sal. As Basil Davidson suggests, some concrete results were thus achieved on the economic front by the governments of 'these sister republics of the PAIGC'. At the same time, however, there were notable failures. Bad economic management on the mainland meant that a disproportionate amount of resources was swallowed up by the capital and a few large-scale development projects, while the rural areas, particularly in the south, were neglected; rice, the staple diet of many people of Bissau, was frequently unobtainable. Moreover, hoarding and blackmarketeering on the part of urban-based middlemen vitiated the attempts being made to set up state distribution systems.

The *coup d'état* of 14 November 1980 brought to power a revolutionary council composed predominantly of military personnel and led by João Bernardo Vieira, Prime Minister, chairman of the national council of Guinea-Bissau (the country's supreme party organ), and a former guerrilla commander. Its effect was to bring to an abrupt end a unique experiment, whereby a single socialist party (the PAIGC) was in power in two separate countries. The coup-makers alleged that the experiment had been conducted for the benefit of Cape Verdeans; they arrested President Cabral and abolished the existing structures of government. However, they denied that they were staging a counter-revolution and pledged their continued loyalty to the teaching and policies of Amilcar

Cabral and the PAIGC; it is not, therefore, certain that the Vieira regime will be less committed to socialism than its predecessor. Munslow records that 'Anti-Cape Verdian propaganda was widespread and there was much talk of ending their hegemony over the mainland'; the coup, stated Mr Vieira in a radio broadcast, aimed to 'chase off the colonialists that were still in Guinea-Bissau'. The Cape Verdeans, led by President Aristides Pereira, secretary-general of PAIGC, reacted by holding an extraordinary party congress in Cape Verde late in January 1981, when they formed a new party of their own. This is the Partido Africano da Independência da Cabo Verde (PAICV), which inherited the expanded party structure set up by Cape Verdeans who had fought in the PAIGC on the mainland; by early 1981 it was estimated to have 4,500 members.

Zimbabwe

Since coming to power in April 1980 the Zimbabwean government has avoided extreme measures, such as the widespread nationalisation of (predominantly white-owned) private industry. It has also encouraged foreign investment, maintained trade links with South Africa and clamped down on unofficial strikes and work stoppages – all steps designed to revive an economy run down by seven years of war. However, the government is committed to a policy of 'growth with equity' and the latter has been reflected in the provision of free primary schooling and medical care and the racial integration of schools and hospitals, as well as in the introduction of a minimum wage and moves to Africanise the public service. In the last respect, the government was fortunate in the number of qualified black Zimbabweans eligible for appointment and by mid-1981 the percentage of Blacks among public service officers had reached 59 per cent – more than double the percentage in early 1980;[33] on the other hand, not enough Blacks have yet acquired the managerial, technical and artisan skills possessed by Whites who have left the country. The absorption of over 30,000 guerrillas into a new Zimbabwean army proceeded fairly smoothly, though some of the ex-ZIPRA soldiers deserted in

1982 and are said to form the core of dissident elements opposing the government in Matabeleland. That the new army also includes selected former members of the Rhodesian Security Forces is an indication of the government's wish to create racial harmony, but also underlines the continuing influence of the white settler community. The same lessons can be drawn from Mugabe's appointment of two white (Rhodesian Front) MPs to his first 22-member cabinet and the cautious way in which the urgent problem of resettling some half a million rural Africans on the land is being tackled. The land issue faces the government with an acute dilemma. On the one hand, the government needs to satisfy the demand for land of its own black supporters, including those former guerrillas not absorbed into the army and who, possessing few employable skills, eke out a precarious existence in the urban centres; on the other hand, it is anxious to reach again the very high levels of agricultural production achieved in 1980–1 (output has subsequently declined). This last consideration makes the government heavily dependent on the country's 5,000 or so mostly white commercial farmers (some 200 are black) who might well decamp if the pace and scope of land redistribution were to be dramatically increased, resulting in the takeover of some of their own land.[34]

Overall, the record to date suggests a programme of moderate reform attuned to the reality of Zimbabwe's geopolitical situation rather than a fundamental restructuring of the economy and a transformation of relations of production. It remains to be seen whether the present phase of what Mugabe has called 'reconciliation, reconstruction and resettlement' will be followed by a socialist revolutionary phase. This is possible: in January 1982 Mr Mugabe announced a plan to transfer control of selected white-owned mines, farms, factories, and businesses to the black majority (owners would however be compensated). What is more certain is that the government will eventually seek to amend the constitution in order to create a one-party state. The Prime Minister's well-publicised intention to take this step may have been advanced by the discovery early in 1982 of substantial arms hidden on ZAPU farms, the removal of Mr Nkomo from the cabinet, the rooting out of dissidents in Matabeleland (causing much suffering among the civilian population), and Nkomo's flight abroad in March 1983.[35]

Revolutionary Regimes: 2. Civilian (non-guerrilla origin)

Angola, Guinea-Bissau, Mozambique and Zimbabwe are examples of states which, though varying in their commitment to revolution, came into being through protracted guerrilla warfare. Africa has several other socialist states with a different origin or – what may not be the same thing – states which profess to be socialist but whose leadership is committed to maintaining the inherited *status quo* rather than to socio-economic transformation. To use the generic term 'socialist' for all these states is a convenient shorthand, often unsatisfactory but not necessarily devoid of meaning; it may well be, for example, that a particular regime's aspirations to building a socialist state are genuine, but that formidable constraints make any early transition to socialism impossible. Of these various 'states of socialist orientation', some are ruled by civilians and others by soldiers; among states in the first category are Tanzania and Guinea.

Tanzania

Tanzania is not, and indeed has never claimed to be, a Marxist state; it belongs to that category of states which, following Crawford Young, we have subsequently designated 'populist socialist'. Julius Nyerere has argued that while 'Marx did contribute a great deal to socialist thought', Tanzania should not be 'bemused by this new theology' but should adapt Marxism to its own needs. The attempt to do so was made following the issue in January 1967 of the Arusha Declaration, with its three socialist strands: egalitarianism, which was of fundamental importance to Nyerere and was to be attained in part by the application of a leadership code; public ownership and control, a principle that was applied to the banks, commercial houses and existing and new industries; and an emphasis on hard-work and self-reliance, forming the basis of communal socialism. As a result, a non-doctrinaire, pragmatic kind of socialism has emerged under which the state controls nearly all sectors of the economy. The latter remains predominantly agrarian, but a modest industrialisation programme has been initiated, making use, in the textile factory in Dar es Salaam, of locally-produced cotton, though almost entirely dependent on imported raw materials in the case of the fertiliser plant at Tanga. A number of state farms have been established, but the main thrust in agriculture under the Arusha Declaration has been the promotion of communal farming in *ujamaa* villages. In the event, this experiment in rural socialism has not been economically successful and the social rather than the productive aspects of *ujamaa* have come to be emphasized. Though the Tanzanian economy is today in dire straits and the country is heavily dependent on foreign aid, much has been achieved in the provision of educational, health and water facilities in the rural areas and in achieving a greater measure of equality by reducing significantly the gap between the income of the most highly paid and the most lowly paid in Tanzania.[36] Marxist scholars are not impressed by these achievements and, as Cranford Pratt has pointed out, more and more of them 'see Nyerere and his colleagues as members of a bureaucratic bourgeoisie whose ideas on socialism mystify and facilitate the increasing dominance that they as a class have established in Tanzania'. They conclude that Tanzania is no longer in transition to socialism.[37] In this respect, the pretensions of Guinea can be no more readily accepted; it is to a consideration of this West African state that we turn next.

Guinea

The Republic of Guinea can claim to be the longest surviving socialist state in sub-Saharan Africa: the PDG, under its leader Sékou Touré, has been continuously in power since May 1957. The PDG was, and remains, a mass party which drew together trade unionists, peasants and members of the petty-bourgeoisie (from whose ranks Sékou Touré was himself drawn) in radical opposition to the French colonial administration and the chiefs.[38] Touré was, in Johnson's words, 'a reluctant revolutionary' who was trapped by his own rhetoric and a serious misreading of General de Gaulle's character into opting for independence in September 1958. The events of 1958 help to account for the acute sense of insecurity from which the regime has suffered ever since, causing it to launch vigorous attacks upon its enemies, both real and imagined. Between 1958 and 1977 at least six major internal convulsions occurred over plots or alleged plots. The invasion of Conakry in November 1970 by a Portuguese-backed seaborne force of Guinean exiles led to a drastic purge; 16 of the government's 24 ministers were arrested and thereafter Touré, in a manner reminiscent of Nkrumah after the attempt on his life in 1962, has sealed himself off in his presidential palace. He has also come to rely increasingly on those who are related to him directly or by marriage, while members of his own ethnic group (the Malinkés) heavily dominate the national political élite; indeed, this gradual process of Malinké-isation is to be found at all levels of the party and administration and, predictably, has caused resentment among the Foulahs who, like the Malinkés, constitute roughly a third of Guinea's total population.

Following independence the National Assembly quickly became impotent and President Touré ruled through a nine-member Bureau Politique Nationale (BPN). Four great regional ministries were created, but the experiment did not work and was eventually abandoned. The former *commandants des cercles* were replaced by regional governors, who share their power with regional party secretaries; there is a dual structure of control, though the party subsumes the state structure at the lower levels. By the mid-1970s the early party militants had been replaced by members of a younger generation, including graduates of the country's two polytechnics, some of whom serve as directors of major state enterprises. The dominance of this younger generation is also reflected in the activities of the PDG's enlarged youth wing – Jeunesse de la Révolution Démocratique Africaine – whose members (in Johnson's words) constitute the 'shock-troops of the Guinean revolution'. Despite the regime's support for female emancipation, the women's section of the party has lost its former prominence, as has also the trade union movement – strikes are illegal. On the other hand, soldiers were granted full political rights following the Mali coup of 1968 and military leaders have a place in the inner councils of the party. The army is said to be a popular and efficient institution which engages in economic activities, especially road-building.

Despite its considerable economic potential – in rice, cattle and minerals – Guinea was a very poor country at independence, dependent upon its primary exports of bananas, coffee, palm kernels and groundnuts. The new state took over the import–export trade and, progressively, the country's domestic wholesale and retail trade as well; it assumed responsibility for key services such as water and electricity, hitherto run by French capitalist interests; it nationalised some of the smaller mining concerns and established several state farms and a small secondary industrial sector; and it continued to run the railways, ports, airports, airlines and telecommunications. The results of state ownership and control, however, have been disappointing. Johnson notes that 'virtually the whole of this extensive state sector is in a disastrous condition. There is, at every turn, wholesale under-utilisation of capacity, chronic corruption and inefficiency, low quality and low quantity output.' These difficulties, which stem in part from Guinea's shortage of trained manpower, have been compounded by the monetary policy pursued by the government since Guinea left the franc zone in 1960. This policy has involved printing money according to need and has been disastrous economically. The Guinea franc is worthless outside Guinea and there are few goods inside Guinea that it can buy; corruption, blackmarketeering and smuggling – even by PDG-run co-operatives – are rampant.

In view of this dismal record and a disappointing agricultural output (the country has to import rice, the staple diet), Guinea is fortunate in drawing large revenues from her immense bauxite deposits (she also possesses iron ore and some gold and diamond reserves, as yet untapped). While indigenous private enterprise is discouraged – in health and education (both the exclusive concern of the state) no less than in business and trade – foreign private investment has been welcomed. American-dominated multinational companies have worked the huge bauxite deposits at Fria since 1960 and at Boké since the early 1970s; by 1975 bauxite and its semi-processed product, alumina, made up over 95 per cent of all exports and Guinea was mining over 9 million tonnes of bauxite annually.

Without bauxite the country could not have survived economically.

Ladipo Adamolekun has pointed out that for some ten years after independence Sékou Touré resisted attempts by PDG radicals to transform Guinea into a socialist state along orthodox Marxist lines. Touré preferred his own version of African 'communaucracy' and stressed the importance of self-reliance through 'human investment' programmes. In 1967, however, Marxism–Leninism was made the philosophy of the revolution and the President, following Mao's example, initiated the socialist cultural revolution which entailed ending the dominance of a conservative and self-seeking bureaucracy and returning 'power to the people' through the creation of a new unit of the party–state called the Pouvoir Révolutionnaire Locale (PRL). The national leadership supposedly deals directly with the people in their PRLs – there are some 8,000 of these units in the country as a whole, one for every village and urban *quartier* – and the effect is to downgrade the position of both regional governors and 'federal' (i.e. regional) party secretaries. However, to counter the disruptive effects of this move political commissars, responsible to the BPN and therefore to the President, have been appointed to oversee the work of all party sections.

Other major initiatives were taken in 1975, when the government declared private trading a criminal act and launched the full-scale collectivisation of rural production. These were rash moves in view of past experience: the state commercial agencies and shops had been subject to such gross corruption and inefficiency that the services of private (pre-dominantly *dioula*) traders, who were denounced as 'bourgeois traitors to the Guinean revolution', had to be retained, while an earlier experiment in collectivisation between 1960 and 1963 had met with stolid peasant resistance. To a considerable extent, this experience has been repeated: in 1976 the peasants in the Fouta Djalon refused to see their cattle collectivised and peasants elsewhere have shown stubborn opposition to the government scheme. The rural economy has been severely dislocated by these moves.

Without bauxite, the government would not be able to indulge in these disruptive socialist experiments which are sharply at variance with the nature of Guinean society. They are orchestrated, as Johnson observes, by the 'magnetic, awesome figure' of Sékou Touré. Power has come to be increasingly concentrated in his hands; he is 'The Eminent Strategist' who brooks no opposition to his tyrannical rule. While Touré early embraced Leninist ideas of the respective roles of the party and state, he has repeatedly stressed that the PDG is a mass rather than a class party and has checked the growth of class consciousness among the workers and peasants – they belong to 'the people's class'. He also sees no incompatibility between socialism and Islam, and has said that socialism can be reached 'via Islam'. The result, says Adamolekun, is that after more than twenty years of independence Guinea is not yet 'a full-fledged socialist state'. There are certainly contradictions in Guinea's socialist experiment, as witness the recent de-emphasis of the socialist option, the 'opening' of the country to the West and the dominant role which foreign mining companies play in its economy. It can, however, be argued that socialism in Guinea is undermined much more by a cruel authoritarian regime's suppression of individual liberty than it is by the regime's reliance on multinational corporations.

Revolutionary Regimes: 3. Military

Most other surviving African socialist states have emerged as a result of a military *coup d'état*: among them are Somalia and Ethiopia, in the Horn of Africa, on which we concentrate in this section, Benin in West Africa, and the Congo in Central Africa. Of the last two states, Decalo has noted that in Benin socialist rhetoric has been used since 1972 to buttress support for a predominantly northern military leadership, while in the Congo change in a socialist direction has been more symbolical than structural since the military first took over in 1968.[39]

Benin and the Congo

At present these are 'marginal' Marxist–Leninist states;[40] both are members of the franc zone and the EEC is their most important trading partner. However, in the case of Benin at least the reason may be not so much the leadership's lack of socialist commitment as the economic weakness of the state and its geographical position alongside 'the most porous border' in West Africa. – that with Nigeria – across which over three-quarters of Benin's exports are smuggled illegally.[41] Though the economy has been substantially freed from direct foreign private ownership and control, indirect control remains tight and Western economic domination cannnot easily be ended. The Congo story is somewhat different. Modest revenues from offshore oil deposits (discovered in 1969) have enabled the military government to propitiate the left-wing opposition of workers and students by investing in state-controlled enterprises in agriculture and manufacturing; these have proved unprofitable. The government has also struck an independent and radical note in its foreign policy (to a somewhat less extent, the rulers of Benin have done the same). However, key sectors of the economy are still in the hands of foreign capital and the Congo retains – it would seem by choice – many of the features of a neo-colonial state. Heavy foreign indebtedness reduces the manoeuvrability of her government in the economic sphere.

Somalia

In October 1970, one year after overthrowing Somalia's civilian government in a military coup, President Mohamed Siyad Barré and his Supreme Revolutionary Council (SRC) launched a programme of 'scientific socialism' which, claimed the President, was consistent with Islam, the state religion, and with Somali traditional values; the armed forces were said to be a 'vanguard of socialism'.[42] In the early 1970s the regime made provision for increased political participation in local government but was preoccupied with the severe economic problems which beset a poor and backward country, whose principal exports were bananas, livestock and meat, and whose largely rural and illiterate people (of whom over a third were nomadic herdsmen) retained powerful clan ties beneath a strong sense of Somali nationalism. The banks, electricity supplies, transport, shipping and many other economic enterprises were nationalised; state farms were established and land was taken into common ownership; and national agencies for construction materials and foodstuffs were created. Bananas and livestock were allowed to remain under private ownership, but a National Banana Board was made responsible for purchasing and marketing the banana crop; the bulk of livestock trading remained in private hands, less than 10 per cent being handled by the Livestock Development Agency. A number of industrial projects, such as meat and fruit canning, flour milling, and textile and sugar production were included in the 1971–3 and subsequent development programmes, but, in a bid to reduce the urban–rural gap, rural projects received preferential treatment; as David D. Laitin observes, this reflected both 'the high priority given economic development for the nomad' and the regime's commitment to 'political penetration of the bush'.

In 1975 the government sought to turn a severe drought to its own advantage by forcing the pace of 'sedenterisation' – the policy of persuading the country's nomads to become peasant farmers and fishermen. Some 120,000 people moved to new settlements on the north coast and in the Juba region. Students took part in a major mass literacy campaign, made possible by adopting Somali as the official language of the state. The government in fact used language policy to promote social equality – primary school leavers literate in Somali could now be recruited to the bureaucracy – while equal pay for women (for whom better educational provision was made) became part of the Somali labour code. The people's militia ('Victory Pioneers'), formed with Soviet assistance as a revolutionary task force, carried out political indoctrination in 'scientific socialism' and numerous self-help schemes were initiated. In 1976 the SRC was wound up and its powers were transferred to the newly-formed Somali Revolutionary Socialist Party, of which Siyad Barré became secretary-general. Three years later the party nominated all the candidates in the elections to a 171-member People's Assembly and district assemblies, and civilian ministers outnumbered army officers by 16 to 12 in the cabinet formed after the elections. However, the party was disbanded in October 1980 and the Council reinstated.

With aid from China and the West, as well as the Soviet Union, new roads, factories and bridges were built, while heavy rains in 1981 ended a two-year drought and led to a substantial improvement in the rural economy, though not in banana production – exports declined sharply. Subsequently, however, drought conditions have returned and basic foodstuffs have been imported on an increased scale. With the main exception of the production of tinned meats, government claims of economic growth have been exaggerated. 'In terms of economic output', wrote Laitin in 1976, 'there has been little overall difference between Somalia under the socialist regime and under the previous civilian regime.' While he found little that was distinctly socialist in the regime's economic policy, he judged Somalia to have been relatively successful compared with other socialist experiments in the Third World. By the end of the decade, however, this favourable image had been tarnished and, certainly in its external policy, the Somali government had acted in much the same way as a non-socialist military regime might have been expected to do.

To explain what had happened we go back to the earlier period between 1969 and 1976, when Soviet influence had continued to grow (relations with the Soviet Union were already close before the 1969 coup); Clapham notes that in the view of some observers this amounted to 'a process of satellization'. In return for the grant of air and naval facilities at the port of Berbera on the northern coast, the Soviet Union gave Somalia massive assistance, especially in the military sphere, and Somali 'friendship' with the Soviet Union seemed unshakeable. All this changed in 1977, however, when the Soviet Union transferred its support to Marxist Ethiopia. Bowing to the clamours of an impatient nationalism, which had long sought to absorb within the Republic the Somali-inhabited Ogaden region of Ethiopia, the government reacted by breaking its Soviet links and committing its troops and armaments (at first unofficially) to the campaign launched in the Ogaden by guerrillas of the Western Somalia Liberation Front (WSLF). The Ogaden was quickly overrun, but was recaptured the next year by re-equipped Ethiopean forces supported by Cuban troops and Soviet military advisers. The Somali government turned for aid to the West, particularly to the United States, which was able to negotiate port and airfield facilities in return for military credits and budgetary aid, and to

China and Saudi Arabia (Somalia became a member of the Arab League in 1974). The IMF granted stand-by credits of $15 million in 1980 and $50 million in 1981, on conditions which included a 50 per cent devaluation of the Somali shilling.

Thus, Somali irredentism has at least set back President Siyad Barré's attempt to create a socialist state and has made Somalia almost as dependent on America as she had previously been on the Soviet Union. Though in May 1981 the President publicly renounced Somali claims to Kenyan territory occupied by ethnic Somalis, the strong anti-Ethiopian sentiments held by so many Somalis have made it impossible for him to give up Somali claims to the Ogaden; Somali guerrilla groups remain active in this area.

Despite certain positive achievements in the first half of the 1970s, the socialist experiment in Somalia cannot be judged a success. The economy has been crippled by the costly war in the Ogaden, recurrent drought conditions, and the massive influx of refugees from Ethiopia. The regime has lost much of its earlier popularity and several outbreaks of political dissidence have occurred; there was an unsuccessful attempt at a military counter-coup in 1978. The President has relied increasingly on members of his own Marehan clan; however, this narrowing of the base of his regime has led to the formation of a new, Ethiopian-backed organisation known as the Somali Salvation Front which, from its camps in Ethiopia, has launched guerrilla attacks on targets in the Republic.

Ethiopia[43]

As John Markakis has pointed out, the authoritarian and paternalist regime of Emperor Haile Selassie failed to adapt to changing social conditions and thereby limited its capacity to pursue the modernising goals which it had proclaimed; in particular, the landowner class, the main pillar of the regime, blocked any meaningful reform in the vital agricultural sector. The regime's attempt to control social change in order to reduce its political impact incurred the frustration, resentment and finally – as the government proved incapable of handling the crisis caused by drought, famine and rampant inflation – the bitter hostility of the progressive forces initially encouraged by Haile Selassie.[44] However, there were no organised civilian political groups in 1974 to direct the revolutionary process and it was a number of radical junior officers in the armed forces who led the attack on the nobility and ultimately on the Emperor. For several months before the latter's deposition in September 1974 (he died in August of the next year), the effective government of Ethiopia had passed into the hands of a military co-ordinating committee or 'Derg'. This was initially a large body, representative of every branch of the armed forces, though ultimate authority came to rest with its senior radical officer members. In September the Derg announced the formation of a new Provisional Military Administrative Council (PMAC).

As Halliday and Molyneux point out, the military alone did not instigate the revolution, but acted against the background of student and trade union protests in February and March 1974. But only they were capable at this time of toppling the old regime and of filling the vacuum left by its collapse. The armed forces of Ethiopia, compared with those of most other African states, were large, well-trained and well-financed, though not united on the question whether they should themselves permanently assume political power. John W. Harbeson suggests that the new regime turned to socialism (first moderate and then revolutionary) for pragmatic as well as ideological reasons: socialism offered it a way both of stemming urban protest and of meeting peasant demands for land reform, and thus of putting maximum distance between itself and the old discredited order. Paradoxically, he writes, the military regime 'pursued its socialist ideal by promoting change in a manner . . . reminiscent of Ethiopia's former emperors', though, as Halliday and Molyneux point out, PMAC policy was not simply 'a continuation of Amhara chauvinism under a new "Marxist–Leninist" guise'.[45]

Following its assumption of power, the Derg imposed tight control – censorship was re-introduced, strikes were banned and trade union leaders arrested, and the university was closed; university and high school students were sent to the rural areas on a literacy campaign (*zemacha*), designed also to mobilise peasant support for the revolution. In November 1974 two former prime ministers were put to death in a wave of executions whose effect was to increase Ethiopia's international isolation. The next year the Derg extended state control of the economy. Banks, 13 insurance companies and 72 industrial and commercial companies were nationalised, while the government took majority-shareholding in 29 others. The administration of these new acquisitions was vested in some 16 state corporations; however, both at this time and subsequently, many of the government's radical measures for the solution of national problems came to nothing because there was no effective and reliable machinery to implement them. In this respect, Cuban help in rehabilitating the economy was important, particularly in relation to the medical services and sugar plantations.

The Derg also nationalised agricultural and urban land, a significant proportion of which had been granted by Haile Selassie to the nobility. Under these far-reaching reforms – which were undertaken without adequate preparation and therefore proved disruptive – private ownership of rural land was abolished, the size of individual holdings was limited to a maximum of ten hectares and the hiring of agricultural labour was forbidden. Peasant associations, which came into being in 1976 and 1977, were made responsible for implementing land reform and instigating local development efforts. All urban land and all rentable houses and flats were nationalised; the government collected the rent on expensive properties, while rents on cheaper ones (the vast majority) went to urban housing co-operatives (*kebeles*) which were to administer the properties and improve roads, schools and other amenities in their neighbourhoods. Urban workers gained less from the revolution than the peasants and resented the loss of their right to take strike action. Students, trade unionists and professional groups in the urban areas were alienated, even though the military introduced many of the reforms which the civilians were themselves demanding; many students especially belonged to the Ethiopian People's Revolutionary Party (EPRP), a Peking-oriented Marxist group which called for the restoration of civilian rule. The military regime saw the EPRP as a challenge to its own authority and therefore sought to crush it in what Halliday and Molyneux have described as 'a campaign of mobilized terror'. Again, while the rural land reforms won some grass-roots support for the regime, they were bitterly opposed by local and provincial leaders who were treated preferentially in the grant of land-use rights, but did not, like their urban counterparts, receive compensation for their confiscated properties – though urban owners, too, were not compensated for land that was nationalised. Disaffection was widespread in the north, where outbreaks of armed resistance occurred. The government was embarrassed when some urban and rural co-operatives moved further to the left than it desired and attacked small traders who had been exempted from the nationalisation measures.

Government forces were heavily overstretched in the face of widespread internal unrest and the strong challenge posed by the main Eritrean secessionist movements – the Eritrean People's Front and the Eritrean People's Liberation Front[46] – and ethnic Somali guerrilla groups in south-eastern Ethiopia. Some 42 per cent of public expenditure was allocated to national defence and internal security under the 1975–6 budget. In view of the great difficulty which the Derg was experiencing in building political support in both the rural areas and the towns, it promulgated in April 1976 a new programme – the National Democratic Revolution (NDR) – which laid down the guidelines within which the revolution was to develop. The programme aimed at abolishing 'feudalism, imperialism and bureaucratic capitalism from Ethiopia' and called upon the masses to work hard and increase production.[47]

At the end of 1976 the Derg was reorganised on Marx-ist–Leninist lines, but was weakened by an internal struggle for power among its top leadership. This was resolved in early 1977, when Colonel Mengistu Haile-Mariam, the first vice-chairman, emerged (in Clapham's words) as the 'undisputed strong man' and maintained his regime by a 'reign of terror'; the EPRP, which had a military wing and itself resorted to the tactics of urban assassination, was brutally eradicated. Mengistu also reversed Ethiopia's previous dependence on the United States and forged a close alliance with the Soviet Union. By this alliance he obtained the rapid build-up of armaments essential for the survival of his regime – in 1977 only a few urban strongholds remained in government hands in Eritrea; the WSLF, with the backing of the Somali government, attacked and routed the Ethiopian forces in the Ogaden; and there was widespread conflict in all but a few provinces, the main centres of opposition being in the northern provinces of Tigre, Begemder and Wollo, and in the south among the Afar and Oromo groups, as well as among the ethnic Somalis. Various anti-government and secessionist movements emerged, prominent among them being the Tigre People's Liberation Front (TPLF) and the Oromo Liberation Front (OLF). In 1978, with the help of Soviet military advisers and Cuban troops (eventually numbering upwards of 17,000), government forces launched successful offensives in both the Ogaden and Eritrea. By 1979 Ethiopia had achieved a semblance of political stability, though the cost in human suffering was very high. The government tightened its grip on Eritrea the next year and resisted Soviet pressure to negotiate a settlement. The problem of communalism remained serious and the government shelved any decision on the extent of autonomy which, under the NDR, it had promised to grant to the various linguistic–ethnic groups.

On the economic front, the Derg experienced serious problems with the 30,000 or so peasant co-operatives established as a result of its land reform programme. The peasants were reluctant to supply the cities with foodstuffs and Addis Ababa, the capital, became increasingly dependent on imported grains. Land reform remained unpopular in the northern provinces of Tigre and Wollo; the TPLF survived a government drive against it in 1980. The introduction of Amhara, Tigrean and other northern settlers to the agriculturally vital southern provinces offended the Oromos, who constitute by far the largest linguistic–ethnic group in Ethiopia, and resulted both in a growing number of them joining the flow of ethnic Somali refugees to Somalia and increased support for the OLF.[48] The latter stepped up its activities in 1980 when the Amhara ethnic base of the central government was reinforced by the arrest early in the year of several leading Oromo army officers and civilian politicians, including the Minister of Justice. Severe drought has added to the problems facing the military government, which has called for help from the international community.

The final shape of the revolution has not yet been determined. A commission on the establishment of a revolutionary workers' party began sitting in December 1979 (about three-quarters of its approximately 100 members were army officers) but formation of the new party has subsequently been deferred to 1984. Key issues to be decided are the balance of power within the party between military personnel and civilians, and that between what Clapham has called 'the more pragmatic Ethiopian nationalists' (whose position was strengthened as a result of a cabinet reshuffle in January 1980) and 'the ideologically more rigid supporters of Soviet Communism'. A further issue is whether a genuine workers' party can emerge so long as the Ethiopian proletariat lacks a real economic stake in the revolution.

Thus, the Derg still faces the critical question of how to generate political support for the measures which it has taken; their effect has been to stimulate local nationalism. Its increasingly pro-Amhara policies are reminiscent of those pursued by Haile Selassie, as is also its response to the challenges which face it – forcible, indeed brutal, repression is preferred to negotiation and compromise. Perhaps the root of the military regime's difficulties lies in its imposition from above of socio-economic policies which do not correspond with the realities of Ethiopian life. Whether the regime could survive the withdrawal of Soviet and Cuban support is a matter for speculation.

Appraisals of the regime vary widely. Markakis and Ayele believe that it has totally betrayed the revolution, and that 'a brutal and mindless military tyranny' has been established in Ethiopia, screened at first by a 'flimsy politico-ideological facade'. Halliday and Molyneux, however, stress the need for caution in determining whether the country will embark on a transition to socialism or will become dominated by capitalist social relations. 'The revolution itself', they write, 'was not led by an avowedly socialist movement or organization and the new regime's ability and determination to implement its programmes must remain in doubt.'[49] The manner of the revolution promoted bitter rivalry between radical civilian groups and the military, and stimulated the nationalist claims of the country's non-Amharic communities, thereby hampering the Derg's ability to build upon its early reform measures.

While not questioning the commitment to socialism of the group of radical military officers who have captured state power, Halliday and his co-author point to other elements, military as well as civilian, who are opposed to socio-economic transformation. They also raise the possibility that this group, in collaboration with the civilian bureaucracy, will distort the revolution by seeking to entrench themselves as a new ruling class. They point, too, to the disjunction between state and society and to the predominance within an avowedly Marxist–Leninist state framework of 'pre-capitalist, petty commodity and capitalist social relations' and to the inevitability of clashes with the classes benefiting from these relations. This leads them to question the capacity of the state to bring about socio-economic transformation from above and to stress the need for substantial economic aid from abroad if this transformation is to be achieved. If, however, the bulk of this aid comes from the West rather than the Soviet Union and her allies (as is likely), the effect will be to strengthen those forces in Ethiopia who favour a capitalist path of development.[50] For all these reasons, not only is Harbeson right to say that 'it remains unclear whether and how Ethiopian socialism is to gain legitimacy and institutionalization,' but the more fundamental question is raised as to whether what Halliday and Molyneux describe as 'Africa's first major social revolution' will be sustained at all in the long term.[51]

Conclusions

If a feature of the 1970s has been the emergence in Africa of the Marxist state, it must be added that these states vary enormously from one another. They differ, for example, in the party form which they have taken – one-party, multi-party (*de jure* in Zimbabwe and *de facto* in Angola) and, until 1980 in Guinea-Bissau and Cape Verde, single-party/multi-state.[52] There is variation, too, in the leadership's ideological commitment to Marxism and, in relation to the context within which the leadership has to operate, in the way in which it has set about the task of socio-economic transformation. As we have seen, context is extremely important: economic weakness and geographical proximity to South Africa, whose policy is to destabilise the would-be socialist states in Southern Africa, have forced even FRELIMO in Mozambique to be sometimes pragmatic in its approach to socialism; external economic dependence, such as that of the People's Republic of Congo on France, might result in little more than socialist window-dressing; and the persistence of strong nationalist sentiments, as in Somalia, or the eruption of communalism, as in Ethiopia, may weaken the socialist thrust of government policy.

With the sole exception of recently independent Zimbabwe, all the states which we have examined, whether civilian or military, suffer from severe economic weakness, compounded in Angola and Guinea by serious problems of distribution and often also (even in recent years in Tanzania) by blackmar-keteering and corruption – though it should, in fairness, be added that the level of corruption in some of the socialist states, notably Mozambique, is much lower than in capitalist-oriented regimes such as Zaire and Nigeria. Most of the socialist states lack the trained manpower to run the large number of state enterprises established since independence and some, especially Angola and Guinea, rely on the mining activities of multi-national corporations to keep their economies afloat. State and party officials have been guilty of mismanagement as well as of corruption, though, as we saw in the case of Mozambique, remedial action has sometimes been taken to check such abuses, as well as to halt a fairly general process of bureaucratisation. To that end there has almost everywhere been talk of giving 'power to the people' and local institutions such as popular assemblies and neighbourhood committees have indeed been set up; however, residual prob-lems of forging national unity and observance of the Leninist principle of democratic centralism have meant the subjection of these bodies to tight central control. While the creation in Mozambique and Angola of vanguard-type parties may facili-tate the revolutionary penetration of the countryside, their effect will be to exclude a large number of ordinary people from party membership. Given also the down-turn of their economies since independence, it is proving no easy task for either regime to gain countrywide support.

It can be argued, on the one hand, that problems such as

those outlined above are inevitable in states which are, or aspire to be, in transition to socialism and which are seeking to bring about a socio-economic revolution. This claim has some validity; it is also true that Afro-Marxist states operate within a generally hostile international capitalist environment and that significant advances have been made in certain fields, notably in health and education. On the other hand, these regimes do not have indefinite time ahead to effect such a revolution. As Erik Svendsen warned in May 1967: 'The worst enemy of a socialist policy in any African country is bad economic performance. The expectations of the people cannot be removed by a higher political consciousness. Socialism must prove its case in the very short run.'[53] The time factor is linked with the human factor: in order to survive in the midst of mounting economic difficulties, state leaders often seem prepared to sacrifice their socialism on the altar of political expediency. The sad result is that, as in Ethiopia and Guinea, authoritarianism and repression then become the hand-maidens of socialism. Richard L. Sklar pointed out that liberty – 'meaning, at the very least, freedom of speech, freedom of political association, and limited government' – is 'a universal interest', as dear to progressive as to bourgeois movements.[54] The great danger is that under the aegis of an authoritarian regime, socialism will become an empty shell, devoid of meaningful content.

Further Reading

General
Ottaway, D. and M., *Afrocommunism* (New York: Africana, 1981).
Rosberg, C. G., and Callaghy, T. M. (eds), *Socialism in Sub-Saharan Africa: A New Assessment* (Berkeley: Institute of International Studies, University of California, 1979).
Saul, J. S., *The State and Revolution in Eastern Africa* (London: Heinemann, 1979).
Wiles, P. (ed.), *The New Communist Third World* (London: Croom Helm, 1982).
Young, C., *Ideology and Development in Africa* (New Haven: Yale University Press, 1982).

Angola
Davidson, B., *In the Eye of the Storm: Angola's People* (London: Longman, 1972).

Marcum, J., *The Angolan Revolution*, vol. i: *The Anatomy of an Explosion (1950—1962)*, vol. ii: *Exile Politics and Guerrilla Warfare (1962—1976)* (Cambridge, Mass.: Massachusetts Institute of Technology Press, 1969 and 1978).

Wolfers, M., and Bergerol, J., *Angola in the Frontline* (London: Zed Press, 1983).

Benin and Congo

Decalo, S., 'Ideological Rhetoric and Scientific Socialism in Benin and Congo-Brazzaville', in Rosberg and Callaghy (1979) – see above (*General*).

Racine, A. 'The People's Republic of Benin' and 'The People's Republic of Congo', in Wiles (1982) – see above (*General*).

Young (1982) – see above (*General*).

Ethiopia

Halliday, F., and Molyneux, M., *The Ethiopian Revolution* (London: Verso, 1981).

Markakis, J., and Ayele, N., *Class and Revolution in Ethiopia* (Nottingham: Spokesman, 1978).

Ottaway, D. and M., *Ethiopia: Empire in Revolution* (New York: Africana, 1978).

Guinea

Adamolekun, L., *Sékou Touré's Guinea: An Experiment in Nation-Building* (London: Methuen, 1976).

Johnson, R. W., 'Guinea', in Dunn, J. (ed.), *West African States: Failure and Promise. A Study in Comparative Politics* (Cambridge University Press, 1978).

Kaba, L, 'Guinean Politics: A Critical Overview', *Journal of Modern African Studies*, vol. xv, no. 1 (March 1977).

Guinea-Bissau

Cabral, A., *Unity and Struggle* (London: Heinemann, 1980).

Chabal, P., *Amilcar Cabral: Revolutionary Leadership and People's War* (Cambridge University Press, 1983).

Davidson, B., *No Fist is Big Enough to Hide the Sky* (London: Zed Press, 1981).

Mozambique

First, R., *Black Gold. The Mozambican Miner, Proletarian and Peasant* (Brighton: Harvester Press, 1983).

Munslow, B., *Mozambique: The Revolution and its Origins* (London: Longman, 1983).

Vail, L., and White, L., *Capitalism and Colonialism in Mozambique* (London: Heinemann, 1981).

Somalia

Decraene, P., *L'Expérience Socialiste Somalienne* (Paris: Berger-Lerrault, 1977).

Laitin, D. D., 'Somalia's Military Government and Scientific Socialism', in Rosberg and Callaghy (1979) – see above (*General*).

Lynch, B., 'The Somali Democratic Republic. The One that got away', in Wiles (1982) – see above (*General*).

Tanzania

Bryceson, D. F., 'Peasant Commodity Production in Post-Colonial Tanzania', *African Affairs*, vol. 81, no. 325 (October 1982).

Coulson, A. (ed.), *African Socialism in Practice: The Tanzanian Experience* (Nottingham: Spokesman, 1979).

Mwansasu, B. U., and Pratt, C. (eds.), *Towards Socialism in Tanzania* (University of Toronto Press, 1979).

Zimbabwe

Astrow, A., *Zimbabwe: A Revolution that Lost its Way?* (London: Zed Press, 1983).

Martin, D., and Johnson, P., *The Struggle for Zimbabwe: The Chimurenga War* (London: Faber & Faber, 1981).

Stoneman, C. (ed.), *Zimbabwe's Inheritance* (London: Macmillan, 1981).

9

Regional Groupings and the Organisation of African Unity

Following independence most African states had closer ties, especially in the economic field, with outside states than they had with each other, and foreign powers thus exercised considerable leverage within the continent. This applied especially to the former colonial powers since the 'mother country' was normally the new state's principal trading partner; economic, financial and cultural links between France and her former colonies (except Guinea) were particularly tight. To President Nkrumah of Ghana the relationship smacked of neo-colonialism: he charged the metropolitan powers with granting formal political independence while still retaining economic control over their fledglings. He believed that a united Africa, subject to a single government, was the only effective way of terminating this relationship, as well as of ending racist minority rule in Africa. In his view, regional blocs were incompatible with African unity: they not only impeded its achievement, but would sap its strength once it had been achieved.[1] The Organisation of African Unity (OAU), established in 1963, owed much to Nkrumah's statesmanship, but fell well short of his vision. Moreover, regional groupings, more often in the form of functional rather than political unions, continued to proliferate.

Regional Political Unions

Many attempts have been made both before and after 1963 to establish such unions. This is understandable on several grounds. They are a possible means of reducing tensions between states divided by artificial, mostly colonially-imposed boundaries; examples of the latter are the border which separates the Ewe-speaking people of Ghana's Trans-Volta Region from their kinsmen in neighbouring Togo and Somalia's borders with Kenya and Ethiopia, where many ethnic Somalis traditionally reside. The long-standing dispute between Somalia and Ethiopia in particular has meant that money which could otherwise have been used by both states for productive investment has had to be diverted to expanding and equipping their armed forces; it has also opened the gate to intervention by the big powers – the Horn of Africa has become the cockpit of Soviet–American rivalry. A second argument sometimes advanced in favour of regional political union is that the large state can both surmount local crises better than the small one and more easily pursue a policy of non-alignment; union would therefore promote political stability. In the third place, as Richard L. Sklar has pointed out, 'supra-state unity is an historic value of the African nationalist movement. In fact, African leaders do not question the desirability of African unity in principle. The issues are *how* closely unified they should be and *what forms* should their unity take.'[2]

Many attempts have been made, both before and after the establishment of the OAU in 1963, to form regional political unions. The successful cases can be counted on one hand – the union of Ghana and British Togoland in 1957, Italian and British Somaliland in 1960, Southern Cameroons and the Republic of Cameroon in 1961, and Tanganyika and Zanzibar in 1964. It is an interesting fact that in each case one or both of the states coming together was formerly a United Nations trusteeship territory and a significant fact that, with the single exception of Tanganyika and Zanzibar, every successful union took place before the independence of one or more of the states concerned. (Southern Cameroons, which Britain had administered as part of Nigeria, continued under UN trusteeship following Nigeria's attainment of independence in October

1960 and pending the holding of a plebiscite in February 1961.) If the 1981 confederal arrangement between Senegal and the Gambia survives, the case of Senegambia will prove an exception on both counts since each state was independent at the time of union and neither was ever under UN tutelage.

Failures to achieve lasting political union include the Mali federation, the Ghana–Guinea–Mali union, the East African federation, the Greater Maghreb, and the United Arab Republic; the federal aspect of the relationship between Ethiopia and Eritrea disappeared at an early stage because of the centralising policies pursued by the imperial government, though technically the 'union' has continued to exist. Key issues in each case were institutional incompatibility and the perception of incumbent leaders that their political power base was being, or would be, eroded. The short-lived federation between the former French West African colonies of Senegal and Soudan is particularly instructive.

By voting 'Yes' in the referendum of 28 September 1958, seven of the eight states which made up AOF became autonomous republics within the French Community; only Guinea, by voting 'No', severed her links with France. Though the referendum effectively dissolved AOF, it was open to the individual states to form a primary federation, which in turn would have federal links with the metropole. This solution was favoured by the Parti de Regroupement Africain (PRA) and the Union Soudanaise (US), the 'strongly federalist' Soudan-ese section of the RDA, which, like the PRA, was an inter-territorial political party.[3] The federal solution, however, was rejected by the RDA's Ivory Coast section (the PDCI), whose leader – Houphouet-Boigny – preferred direct political links between the individual territories and France; Niger sided with the Ivory Coast, while Mauritania, as a non-Black state, was non-committal. Meeting in Dakar, the Senegalese capital, early in 1959 as the successor of the AOF's grand council, the federal constituent assembly elected Modibo Keita, the Union Soudanaise leader, as its president and promulgated the constitution of a federal union between four states – Senegal, Soudan, Dahomey and Upper Volta. However, internal opposition as well as pressure from the Ivory Coast and the French

Administration quickly led Dahomey and Upper Volta to withdraw from the 'Mali federation', leaving Senegal and Soudan to go it alone. Optimism ran high among the leaders of the latter states, with Mamadou Dia of Senegal claiming that 'The great good fortune of Mali is the complementarity of the Senegalese and Soudanese economies' – Senegal would provide port facilities and, initially at least, the manufacturing base of the federation, while Soudan would supply raw materials and food. It was hoped, too, that other states would be attached to the federation in due course, though the formation of the Conseil de l'Entente between Dahomey, the Ivory Coast, Niger and Upper Volta and of the Ghana–Guinea union reduced this prospect.

Initial difficulties over independence from France were solved when President de Gaulle agreed in December 1959 to transfer full sovereign power from the Community to the Mali federation; independence was achieved in June 1960, with Mali agreeing to remain within the loosened Community and the franc zone. However, the internal problems of the federation could not be solved so easily, its rigid structure making compromise difficult to achieve when disagreements arose – as they did, for example, over economic development. The tendency to personalise political power, especially in Senegal, whose ruling party (the UPS) could not match the Union Soudanaise either in organisational strength or ideological thrust (the US was Marxist-oriented), meant that popular loyalties might be transferred from Léopold Senghor, leader of UPS, to Modibo Keita, the US leader and federal premier. In the absence both of a groundswell of public opinion in favour of federation and significant Senegalese interest groups strongly committed to its continuance, the Senegalese leadership took the initiative in breaking up the federation in August 1960. 'The simplest explanation for Mali's failure', as put forward by William J. Foltz, is no doubt also the correct one: '. . . the Senegalese political leaders felt that the continued existence of the Federation threatened their domestic political base and, therefore, their opportunity to continue to play a significant role in African political life.'[4] Relations between the two states (Soudan changed her name to the Mali Republic) remained poor until September 1963 when, in furtherance of the aims of the newly-established OAU, they patched up their differences: the railway was reopened and trade links resumed.

The perception of the incumbent leadership that political union would curtail a loss or diminution of political power was also a critical factor in the failure of the East African countries of Kenya, Tanganyika and Uganda to federate in 1963; it was reflected, too, in the early experience of the union between Tanganyika and Zanzibar. In East Africa the conditions for union were on the whole propitious. In January 1961 Julius Nyerere, the leader of TANU, surprised his party by announcing that, under certain conditions, he would be willing to delay the date of Tanganyika's independence in order to enable her to join Kenya and Uganda in an independent East African federation. This did not happen: Tanganyika became independent in December 1961 and Uganda in November 1962, while Kenya was to become independent in December 1963. The three states had however been closely linked in the East African High Commission since 1947 and in its successor, the East African Common Services Organisation (EACSO), since 1961, and their leaders (Jomo Kenyatta of Kenya, Julius Nyerere of Tanganyika, and Milton Obote of Uganda) had established a good working relationship cemented, in the case of Nyerere and Obote, by close ties of personal friendship. In 1963 agreement to federate was reached in principle, but in the ensuing negotiations difficulties arose over a number of issues including citizenship, external representation, and defence and security (particularly control over the police); these obstacles were not insuperable and could have been overcome, perhaps by adopting a phased approach to federation. The real stumbling block was the fear on the part of Kenya and Uganda that the political advantages of union would be reaped by Tanganyika which had a secure leadership and an effective, mass-based political party; they were also worried about the institutional incompatibility which resulted from the fact that Tanganyika was already a *de facto* one-party state (Nyerere had deferred legalisation in order to avoid jeopardising the negotiations), whereas both KANU and the UPC faced strong challenges from other parties. The negotiations to establish a federation finally collapsed in 1964.[5]

In April of that year Tanganyika joined with Zanzibar to form a United Republic – redesignated the United Republic of Tanzania in 1965. Officially this move was designed to cement the close historical and cultural links between the two states, but also – on Tanganyika's side – for reasons of security in the wake of the Tanganyikan army mutiny in January 1964 and communist penetration of Zanzibar by East Germany and China following the Zanzibar revolution earlier in January. However, Sheikh Abeid Karume, the President of Zanzibar, was unwilling to forego the substance of power and the Zanzibar revolutionary council of some 32 members, which in practice acted as both the islands' executive and legislature, still retained in its own hands control over certain matters which were constitutionally reserved to the parliament and executive of the United Republic. These included aspects of defence, police, and external borrowing, the public service, immigration, and customs and excise. President Nyerere had to exercise great restraint in order to hold the shaky union together and this situation only began to change after the assumption of power in Zanzibar by Mr Aboud Jumbe following Karume's assassination in 1972. It was only in 1977 that the long-awaited merger between the ruling parties of Tanganyika and Zanzibar took place and the interim constitution of 1965 was replaced by a new constitution for the United Republic, under which Zanzibar, while retaining her separate government, elected representatives to the Union parliament for the first time.[6]

Regional Functional Organisations

These organisations, formed primarily for economic purposes, have fared better than the regional political unions, though they, too, have had a chequered history. Organisations with limited objectives, such as the Conseil de l'Entente, mentioned above, and the Union Douanière et Economique de l'Afrique Centrale (UDEAC), linking Cameroon, the Central African Republic, Gabon and the People's Republic of the Congo, have a long survival record, as does the Organisation Commune Africaine et Mauritienne (OCAM), which has continued, though with a reduced membership (now drawn mainly from the smaller and poorer Francophone states) as the post-1965 successor of the Union Africaine et Malgache (UAM). OCAM survives primarily as a linguistic and cultural organisation, but also serves as an umbrella for a number of specialised agencies, including – until they declared their independence in 1979 – Air Afrique and the African Posts and Telecommunications Union.[7] Among other small regional groupings to have sprung up in the post-independence period, sometimes to collapse and resurface, are the Chad Basin Commission, the Association of West African Rice Growers, the Senegal River Development Organisation, the Mano River Union, the Great Lakes Community, and the French-speaking Communauté Economique de l'Afrique de l'Ouest (CEAO). However, we focus on three major functional groupings in East, West and Southern Africa: the East African Common Services Organisation (EACSO) and its successor, the East African Community (EAC); the Economic Community of West African States (ECOWAS); and the Southern African Development Co-ordination Conference (SADCC).

East African Common Services Organisation (EACSO)/East African Community (EAC)

EACSO was the 1961 successor of the East African High Commission, which officially came into being in January 1948 and was itself the successor of the Conference of East African Governors, instituted in 1926. The Commission comprised the Governors of the three British-ruled territories of East Africa – Kenya, Tanganyika and Uganda – and was supported by an unofficial-dominated central legislative assembly and inter-territorial advisory boards in providing communications and other common services, as well as the basis of a common market. The Governor of Kenya was chairman of the Commission, though most of his functions were exercised by a chief executive, known as the 'Administrator'. The Commission did not have its own source of revenue until 1961 and could only deal with a restricted list of subjects; it was created by, and was responsible to, the British government. The imminence of Tanganyika's independence made it necessary to modify these arrangements and to appoint a local executive responsible to the three governments; this was done in the light of recommendations submitted in 1961 by the Raisman Commission. The latter's report stressed the importance of establishing an organisation which expressed an African point of view and provided for the maintenance of the common market and common services; it noted, however, that the benefits derived by the three states from participating in the common market were unequal and urged that 'there should be some off-setting of these inequalities by means of a redistribution of revenue between the territories'.[8] A distributable pool fund was therefore established, initially under the administration of the High Commission, both to redistribute revenue and to finance some of the common services.

Under the EACSO agreement and constitution of December 1961, the High Commission of Governors was replaced by the East African Common Services Authority, the supreme policy-making body of EACSO comprising the principal ministers of the three territories. Responsibility for the formulation and direction of policy in specified fields, including posts and telegraphs, railways and harbours, airways and currency, was assigned to four ministerial committees (or triumvirates) each consisting of one minister from each territory. Understandably, the demands of their local portfolios reduced the amount of time which ministers could give to EACSO business. They also often failed to take an 'East African' view of the subjects discussed and, as Jane Banfield has pointed out, the committees' decisions tended to be 'based on the lowest common factor of non-disagreement'. The central legislative assembly continued as the legislative arm of EACSO and passed the laws which provided for the administration and running of the services; it comprised nine members elected by, but not necessarily from, each of the territorial parliaments and was a livelier and more critical body than the old assembly. However, the assembly had limited power and responsibility and this fact, as well as the part-time nature of the ministerial committees, meant that the hub of EACSO was the administration headed by a secretary-general in Nairobi. By 1963 there were over 21,000 established officers in the EACSO headquarters and services, of whom more than 17,000 were clerks and artisans; the great majority of the African staff at headquarters were Kenyans, reflecting in part the reluctance of the territorial governments to second able officers to service outside their own countries. While EACSO did valuable work in maintaining the common services, of which three – railways and harbours, posts and telecommunications, and the East African Airways Corporation – were self-contained, it was (as Jane Banfield has argued) 'a temporary and rather makeshift organisation' dominated by its central bureaucracy.

EACSO survived the collapse of the negotiations in 1963–4 to establish an East African federation, but was running into increasing difficulties; it was badly in need of overhaul. At the root of the problem were the unequal benefits which membership of the Organisation conferred on the participant states; Tanganyika, and to a lesser extent Uganda, contended that the advantages went disproportionately to Kenya, which dominated the intra-regional trade in manufactured products. The Raisman formula of fiscal compensation from Kenya to the other two countries did not go far enough if the common market was to survive. The Kampala Agreement of April 1964 therefore outlined five methods of redressing the imbalance of trade between the three states; one was the introduction of a system of quota restrictions on inter-territorial imports. However, remedial action was either not taken (for example, to make the allocation of new industries effective) or failed to have the desired effect, and in 1965 and 1966 the Tanzanian government imposed unilateral import restrictions against Kenya. The end of economic co-operation in East Africa seemed to be in sight. Eventually, however, a compromise was reached on the basis of recommendations submitted by a commission headed by Professor Kjeld Philip, a former Finance Minister of Denmark, and a Treaty for East African Co-operation was signed in Kampala on 6 June 1967.

The treaty established an East African Economic Community and an East African common market, confirming and supplementing the EACSO arrangements.[9] The three heads of state constituted the East African Authority, which was to be assisted by East African ministers appointed by each country and by five councils, replacing the former ministerial triumvirates. The East African legislative assembly was also reconstituted to comprise nine members appointed by each country, together with the East African ministers and certain other members. The headquarters of the common services were decentralised, each country being allocated two headquarters: airways and railways remained in Nairobi, harbours and the Community headquarters were allocated to Tanzania (with the headquarters being located at Arusha in northern Tanzania, near the border with Kenya), and posts and telegraphs and the East African Development Bank (a new institution set up to promote industrial development in the partner states through financial and technical assistance) were assigned to Uganda. Subject to certain exceptions, all trade between the three countries in goods of East African origin was to be free of restrictions. The main exception was that the treaty permitted the imposition of a transfer tax, which (in Robson's words) was 'a euphemistic term for the imposition of limited inter-country tariffs'. In the event, the transfer tax proved an ineffective device for reshaping the distribution of East African industry: 'regional' industries were not attracted to Tanzania and Uganda, and Kenya continued to have the lion's share of smaller-scale industries. Thus, East African experience underlined the validity of Arthur Hazlewood's observation that: 'The integration of states which are at different levels of development tends to concentrate further development in those already most developed, and to result in an unequal distribution of the benefits of cooperation.'[10]

However, the treaty, in an amended form, might have continued to provide the basis for economic co-operation in East Africa given the political will to make it work, though difficulties were bound to arise so long as the unpredictable President Idi Amin remained in charge of Ugandan affairs. A review commission, set up in 1975 under the chairmanship of Mr William Demas, president of the Caribbean Development Bank, reported in November 1976; it recommended, *inter alia*, ways of decentralising the Community corporations which were being starved of finance because of the failure to solve the vexed problem of transferring funds between the partner states. Both Kenya and Uganda blamed Tanzania for the final break-up of the Community in 1977 – unfairly, since the causes of the break-up were multiple and complex. It is true, however, that President Nyerere, who was chairman at that time, refused to convene a meeting of the Authority, the supreme organ of the Community comprising the heads of the three partner states. The Authority had not met since Amin came to power in January 1971 (Nyerere consistently refused to sit at the same table as the Ugandan dictator) yet it was the only body which could have solved the major problems facing the Community.[11] President Nyerere closed his border with Kenya pending agreement on the distribution of the assets (and liabilities) of the Community; agreement was finally reached in November 1983 and the border was reopened.

In view of the sharp ideological differences between Tanzania and Kenya and the personal animosity between Presidents Nyerere and Amin, it can be argued that the East African Community might have stood a better chance of survival if its membership had been expanded to include other states in the East and Central African region. The possibility was mooted from time to time that Ethiopia and Somalia, Burundi and Rwanda, as well as Zambia, would join the Community. Nothing came of these proposals, though the Zambian government did conduct negotiations to join the Community in 1968–9. It eventually decided against this step, realising that, given the high-cost structure of Zambian industry, Zambia's manufactured goods would not be competitive in the East African market without a substantial devaluation. Thus, the Community retained its three-state basis, differing in this respect from both ECOWAS and SADCC.

Economic Community of West African States (ECOWAS)

The negotiations which led to the signing in February 1975 of the Lomé Convention between the European Economic Community (EEC) and 46 African, Caribbean and Pacific (ACP) countries showed that states drawn from different parts of the African continent could reconcile their differences and work together; Lomé, therefore, prepared the way psychologically for the Treaty of Lagos, which was signed in May 1975. The treaty established a 15- (subsequently 16-) nation economic community of predominantly English- and French-speaking West African states; it was not enlarged, as Senegal (suspicious of Nigerian intentions) had wished, to include Zaire and the other Francophone states of Central Africa since the effect would have been to render the union unmanageable and no longer regional. The member states pledged themselves to work towards the free movement of goods and people throughout the community area, with the object of promoting trade between themselves and increasing their independence, as a group, of the rest of the world. Under the treaty, comprehensive trade liberalisation was to be achieved over a period of 15 years by eliminating all the barriers to goods exported from partner countries; a common customs tariff was to be established; and a common commercial policy towards third countries was to be adopted. A fund for co-operation, compensation and development was to be set up, one of its purposes being to compensate states which lost revenue as a result of reducing tariffs (no claim for compensation has yet been made). The headquarters of the fund were located at Lomé and those of the Community at Lagos. Provision was made in the treaty for an annual meeting of heads of state and government, and for a subordinate council of ministers.[12]

Since its effective establishment in 1978, ECOWAS has made progress in certain directions – a common customs nomenclature has been drafted; an energy programme has been formulated and a special energy fund (within the ECOWAS fund) has been set up; an agricultural programme is being devised so that the Community can achieve self-sufficiency in food production within the next few years; work has begun on a permanent headquarters building for the fund in Lomé; and the fund has launched a $25 million communications project. Moreover, relations between the Community secretariat and the fund directorate improved markedly following the decision to establish the fund on a sound financial basis – member states contribute a capital sum and subscribe to an annual budget – and to make the fund's managing director responsible to a board of directors rather than to the Community's executive secretary. President Houphouet-Boigny of the Ivory Coast, though lukewarm towards the OAU, has strongly supported ECOWAS: he serves as an elder statesman of the group and has played a key role in removing misunderstandings between member states.

Nevertheless, the Community has made only halting progress towards the primary aims of customs harmonisation and the free movement of goods and people throughout West Africa; Nigeria's expulsion of some two million aliens in January 1983 was a severe set-back. There are major obstacles to rapid progress, more serious than the linguistic barriers and poor communication links between the treaty signatories. Not only are there differences among the states in the level and structure of the customs duties which they have imposed, but ten of ECOWAS' sixteen member states are also simultaneously members of other West African regional groups, such as the Conseil de l'Entente and CEAO, each of which is made up exclusively of Francophone states, the Mano River Union, and the Cape Verde/Guinea-Bissau Free Trade Area. Trade liberalisation among the six CEAO states is at a relatively advanced stage (a 65-per-cent tariff reduction has been achieved), but CEAO's programme is ultimately incompatible with that of ECOWAS since, unlike the latter, it does not envisage a general free trade area within the customs union. Another serious obstacle to economic co-operation is the proliferation of currencies, and of foreign exchange restrictions and controls, in the West African region; this obstacle will not be easily removed, though monetary union remains the long-term objective. (A monetary union, linking seven West African Francophone states, already exists.)

The work of ECOWAS has been retarded by the persistence in most member states of a strong sense of economic nationalism and by the acute economic difficulties which they face; however, in 1982 poverty-stricken Ghana showed its commitment to the Community by paying off all its arrears to the fund. Political events have also disrupted regional co-operation, though often only temporarily, examples being the military coups in Liberia in April 1980 and in Ghana in December 1981, the ultimately unsuccessful attempt by Gambian dissidents to overthrow the government of President Jawara in August 1981, and Nigeria's expulsion of aliens, referred to above.

Despite all the difficulties and problems which face the Community, its Ivorian executive secretary expressed himself still hopeful – at the meeting of heads of state and government at Cotonou in May 1982 – that a free trade zone would be established by 1989. To further this objective, the summit meeting appointed an *ad hoc* committee of five ministers to review the running of the organisation and, in particular, to investigate why many of the Community's decisions had not been implemented.

Southern African Development Co-ordination Conference (SADCC)

This, the most substantial of the regional groups recently to have emerged, came into being in 1979. On 1 April of the next year the leaders of nine states in Central and Southern Africa – Zambia, Tanzania, Angola, Mozambique, and Botswana (the former 'front-line' states), Malawi, Swaziland, Lesotho and Zimbabwe (due to become independent later that month) – met in Lusaka and approved a declaration on the economic liberation of Southern Africa. The main objectives of the new grouping were to reduce the external economic dependence of member states, especially on South Africa; to secure genuine and equitable regional integration; to mobilise resources to implement national, inter-state and regional policies; and to achieve international co-operation within the strategy of economic liberation.[13] Six areas of co-operation were identified – trade and communications, agriculture, energy, manpower, industrial development and finance. Policy and problems were to be thrashed out at sub-presidential and sub-ministerial level, in order to avoid the kind of high-level confrontations which the EAC had experienced. There was no intention of establishing a free-trade area, while the creation of a regionally integrated and balanced industrial economy was seen as a long-term goal, for which industrial planning on a regional basis was essential if one state, such as Zimbabwe, was not to become regionally dominant.

The emphasis was to be on non-industrial areas of co-operation, with priority given to improving transport and communications as a means of stimulating production and facilitating intra-regional trade – at present, the bulk of the trade of member states, of which six are landlocked, is outside the region. Moreover, progress in this sector affords the best opportunity of loosening South Africa's tight hold over the region – the port of Maputo, as well as most of the railway lines

into Mozambique, are effectively under South African management, and Zimbabwe's rail system is dependent on South
African wagons, engines and technicians, while most of her
trade still goes through South Africa. An immediate start was
therefore made in this sector by establishing a Southern African
regional transport and communications commission, based on
Maputo; Mozambique was given 40 per cent of the $2 billion
allocated to transport projects. A development fund was set up,
finance being supplied mainly by Western countries – SADCC
relies heavily on the West for underwriting its various projects,
including those designed to step up agricultural production. As
Paul Goodison has pointed out, the latter is vitally important,
since food exports to the nine states are 'another weapon in the
South African armoury' and agricultural production must be
expanded rapidly if dependence upon South Africa is to be
reduced.

Potentially, SADCC is an important grouping, but the
constraints within which it has to operate are formidable and
its objectives are unlikely to be achieved quickly. The support
given by South Africa to the dissident groups in Angola and
Mozambique, the two main transit countries in the region,
suggests that South Africa will use its economic and military
strength to maintain the *status quo* in Southern Africa.

There are other obstacles and these are (or have been) faced
by all the regional organisations which we have reviewed.
Among them are the political instability and economic nationalism of individual states; differences in ideology, language and
culture, as well as in ruling-party strength; the difficulty of
achieving an equitable distribution of benefits; lack of manpower and foreign exchange, and the heavy dependence on
external aid, even for co-operative projects; poor inter-state
communications; and the fact that member states tend to have
economies which, not being sufficiently diverse, produce goods
which are competitive with, rather than complementary to,
each other. Most states have difficulty, too, in manufacturing
goods for export at prices which can match those of European
and Japanese companies. In view of these difficulties, the OAU
could play an important role in supporting regional economic
groups; in a loose sense, it may be said to serve already as an
umbrella for them. It is to a consideration of this Africa-wide

organisation that we now turn, focusing first on its origins in the pan-African movement.

The Organisation of African Unity

The Formation of the OAU

The OAU was born, writes Catherine Hoskyns, of a 'strong emotional commitment to unity, based on racial consciousness and the common experience of colonialism'.[14] The sense of racial identity was important and had been nurtured, first in North America and Europe, by a group of West Indians, including Henry Sylvester-Williams and W. E. B. Du Bois, and Afro-American scholars, among whom Booker T. Washington and Marcus Garvey were prominent. Once called the 'ideology of African emancipation', pan-Africanism was more of a dream or vision than a rational political concept: in their writings and speeches, its exponents urged that Africa and people of African descent should be accepted into the modern world on the basis of equality. Ras Makonnen observes that they also used Africa 'to improve the security of their own status in America'. In the period between 1900 and 1945, they organised a series of conferences – in London, Paris, New York and Manchester; a recurrent early theme was the need to establish a homeland for Africans in Africa. But by 1945, when the fifth and most famous of these conferences was held at Manchester, pan-Africanism had become a good deal more than the 'back to Africa movement' championed by Marcus Garvey and was now linked with African nationalism. This conference, which was attended by Kwame Nkrumah of Ghana and other Africans, worked out a strategy of 'positive action' and issued the threat of revolution if the colonial authorities did not themselves initiate constitutional reform. Thereafter, pan-Africanism took root in African soil, its strength deriving from the common experience of colonialism and the drive to achieve African independence. Its prime mover was Nkrumah, advised by the West Indian George Padmore.[15]

Having led his country to independence in March 1957, Nkrumah convened two conferences in Accra, the Ghanaian capital. The first, in April 1958, was attended by representatives of the eight African states, excluding South Africa, which were then independent – Egypt, Libya, Morocco, Tunisia, Sudan, Ethiopia, Ghana and Liberia. It resulted in the formation of the Conference of Independent African States (CIAS), whose members agreed to work more closely together and to promote the independence of the rest of Africa. Julius Nyerere and other nationalist leaders from East Africa attended this conference as observers and in September 1958 formed the Pan-African Freedom Movement of East and Central Africa (PAFMECA); the latter embraced Kenya, Nyasaland, Tanganyika, Uganda and Zanzibar. In December 1958, Nkrumah convened a second and more ambitious conference, to which he invited representatives from the political parties and trade unions of both independent and still dependent African countries. The aim of the All-African People's Conference (AAPC) which thus emerged was to support and co-ordinate the nationalist struggle in the various parts of the continent; a secretariat was established in Accra.

A second conference was held by the AAPC at Tunis in January 1960 and by the CIAS (now expanded to include independent Guinea and Cameroon) at Addis Ababa the following June. However, with the accession to independence in 1960 of some twenty new states (mainly French-speaking but also including Nigeria in October) and the emergence of deep divisions between the African states over what policies should be followed in the Congo, over the war in Algeria, and over Morocco's claim to Mauritania, these organisations became moribund. In their place a number of new groupings were formed, the most important being the Casablanca bloc which was created in January 1961 and comprised the most radical of the African states – Ghana and Guinea, which had announced their political unification in November 1958, Mali, which subsequently joined their short-lived union, Algeria, the United Arab Republic, and Morocco – and the Brazzaville bloc. The latter, which subsequently became known as the Union Africaine et Malgache, was made up exclusively of French-speaking states and valued the retention of its relations with France. Whereas most members of the Casablanca group leaned towards socialism, the Brazzaville group sought to

assert an African cultural identity through *négritude*; President
Senghor of Senegal, who was himself a poet, was the group's
most articulate advocate of this concept. (There was also an
intermediate, predominantly English-speaking Monrovia
group which included Nigeria and Liberia). PAFMECA, in
the meantime, continued to prosper and extended its activities
to include Northern and Southern Rhodesia, Congo-Léopoldville, Ruanda–Urundi (the Belgian-administered trust territory which attained independence as two separate states in
1960), Ethiopia and the Somali Republic. At a conference in
Addis Ababa in February 1962 the organisation revised its
constitution and structure and adopted a new title – the
Pan-African Freedom Movement of East, Central and Southern Africa (PAFMECSA). This expanded grouping was reluctant to become the captive of either the Casablanca or the
Brazzaville bloc; other states, including Nigeria, Tunisia and
Liberia, similarly took a neutral stand.[16]

By 1962 the tensions over the Congo, Algeria and
Mauritania had diminished and attempts to reconcile the
differences between the two blocs were made at conferences
held at Lagos and Monrovia. These proved unsuccessful, but,
with all the various groups favouring some form of African
unity, it was decided to try again by convening a new
conference at Addis Ababa in May 1963. This conference was
attended by thirty independent African states, which agreed to
form the Organisation of African Unity; Morocco and Togo
were not present, but signed the OAU Charter later in 1963.
Both the Casablanca and UAM blocs were then disbanded as
'partial' organisations whose aims and objectives were incompatible with membership of a 'universal' organisation. As
Catherine Hoskyns has pointed out, each could claim certain
achievements – notably, the UAM had helped to preserve the
federal economic links in former French West Africa, while the
Casablanca states had exerted a strong influence on the way in
which the UN handled the Congo crisis. Though PAFMECSA
was not formally wound up, most of its activities were taken
over by the OAU. It is not easy to say precisely why this
particular conference succeeded. Perhaps African leaders were
determined not to repeat the failures at Lagos and Monrovia;
certainly, they refused to be diverted by secondary issues and

showed a willingness to compromise. There was also an acute awareness among some African leaders that the division of Africa into rival groups was playing into the hands of outside powers which, as events in the Congo and Algeria had shown, could exploit these differences to their own advantage.

The OAU Charter was essentially a compromise document which could accommodate the divergent views of the Casablanca and Brazzaville groups; it fell far short of Nkrumah's vision of a united Africa, subject to a single government. As Catherine Hoskyns has written:

> The Casablanca states would only accept the defensive aspects of the OAU Charter (respect for sovereignty, condemnation of subversion and non-interference in internal affairs) if their own more outward-looking concerns (non-alignment, anti-colonialism) were also included. The Casablanca states also demanded that absolute priority must be given to assisting the liberation movements in Southern Africa. The result was a curious hotch-potch of principles and purposes, which combined rather conservative statements designed to protect the *status quo* in inter-African relations with radical commitments towards the outside world.

Agreement on structure, revolving round four principal institutions, was more readily obtained. The supreme organ was the assembly of heads of state and government, which was to meet once a year in ordinary session. Preparation for these annual summit conferences was to be undertaken by the council of (foreign) ministers, which was also to prepare the OAU budget and be responsible for implementing the assembly decisions. It was to meet twice a year in ordinary session, but (like the assembly) could also hold extraordinary sessions – as it did, for example, at Dar es Salaam in April 1975 to discuss the Southern African, and particularly the Rhodesian, problem. The third organ was the general secretariat, which was based in Addis Ababa and headed by an administrative secretary-general elected for a four-year term – Diallo Telli of Guinea was the first to hold this post. The secretariat was responsible to the council of ministers for providing central administrative services for the various OAU organs. The fourth principal institution intended to be established was the commission of mediation, conciliation and arbitration; this was to have twenty-one members and was to attempt to settle disputes between member states. Provision was also made in the Charter for specialised commissions to deal with technical aspects of co-operation; these were: the economic and social commission; the commission on education, science and culture; and the defence commission (the conference of African trade ministers was made a specialised commission of the OAU at the 1976 summit). A co-ordination committee for African liberation (popularly known as the African Liberation Committee – ALC) was also established, with headquarters in Dar es Salaam; however, this committee, which normally met twice a year and had an initial membership of nine (subsequently increased), was not based on the Charter but on a resolution passed by the assembly at Addis Ababa in 1963.[17]

The OAU has now existed for twenty years and has had a mixed record of success and failure. Given the diverse, and often divergent, interests of its member states, the Organisation's survival against the odds has itself been a considerable achievement, though it remains to be seen whether it can surmount its present (1982–3) crisis. Annual summit conferences have been held. However, the nineteenth summit was postponed twice in 1982, first over the Western Sahara dispute and then over the Chad issue; it was eventually held at Addis Ababa in June 1983 and produced a peace plan for Western Sahara as its main achievement. Meetings at below heads of government level have in any case tended to be more effective; at least until 1982, such meetings helped to remove misunderstandings and reduced the possibility of conflict between the various states. The OAU has served as a continental forum for African leaders and its voice has probably counted for more – if still not a great deal – in world affairs than member states could have achieved separately. As we shall see, it has acted as an umbrella for regional organisations and UN agencies, such as the Economic Commission for Africa (ECA); its underlying principle of unity has been invoked to settle inter-state disputes; and its liberation committee has helped several countries to throw off the colonial yoke.

On the other hand, there have been significant failures and the OAU has faced, and continues to face, a host of problems.[18] Structural defects account for some of these. The organisation is cumbersome – it has proved difficult to assemble annually all the heads of state and government. Understandably, some of the latter are preoccupied with pressing domestic issues and cannot easily leave their capitals, but others choose not to do so either because they are less than enthusiastic about the Organisation (President Houphouet-Boigny of the Ivory Coast, for example) or because of animosity to the current OAU chairman – Nyerere, Kaunda, and Sir Seretse Khama of Botswana all refused to attend the 1975 summit in Kampala chaired by President Amin. Sometimes attendance is poor – only 10 out of 41 attended the annual summit meeting at Addis Ababa in 1971 and only 6 out of 45 that held in Port Louis, Mauritius, in 1976 – and the sad fact is that the annual Franco-African conferences of heads of state, instituted in 1973, often attract more participants than the OAU summits. These conferences have not only been used to strengthen France's links with her former colonies, but also to establish new relations outside France's traditional sphere of influence; recent meetings have been attended by former Belgian colonies (Zaire, Burundi and Rwanda), as well as by some of the smaller Lusophone and Anglophone countries (Guinea-Bissau, Cape Verde, Sierra Leone and Mauritius).[19] It would therefore seem that the growing strength of the Franco-African conferences has redounded to the disadvantage of the OAU.

When only a minority of states are represented at OAU summits, the decisions taken carry diminished weight. With the benefit of hindsight, it was a mistake to have kept decision-making so firmly in the hands of the assembly and to have restricted the secretary-general to an administrative role. This last fact, that the secretariat has strictly limited executive authority, means that the OAU is not geared to swift decision-making. The secretary-general can take few initiatives, yet the office is strongly contested; it took twenty ballots before Mr Eteki Mboumoua of Cameroun was elected in 1974, while even more ballots failed to produce a majority for any of the three candidates contesting the election in 1983 (an acting secretary-general was appointed to hold office until the 1984 summit in Conakry, Guinea).[20] The secretariat, based in Addis Ababa, has not been reconstructed on the lines suggested in January 1972 by Mr A. L. Adu, a former deputy secretary-general of the Commonwealth secretariat in London – his report favoured two secretaries-general and pointed to weaknesses in personnel administration. The OAU does not keep or publish any official record of its discussions, reflecting its limited concern for public involvement and debate. Moreover, the secretariat lacks the expertise that it really needs, especially in the technical field, with the result that its specialised agencies count for much less than UN agencies, notably the ECA. Another structural defect of the OAU is its insecure financial base. Member states are required to contribute according to the UN scale of assessment and contributions may have been pitched too high for the smaller and poorer states; delays in payment are frequent. In 1975 significant arrears of payments were due from ten states to the regular budget of the OAU in respect of the 1965–75 period.[21]

Other problems facing the OAU have stemmed from the underlying principles of the Charter, including those on which the UAM states insisted. The clause which laid down that each independent African state had the right to join the Organisation has been faithfully applied, but has been the cause of some difficulty. Mauritania was admitted at the outset despite Morocco's claim to suzerainty over it and the three former High Commission territories (Lesotho, Botswana and Swaziland) were admitted despite their economic dependence on South Africa. Representation is the right of sovereign states, irrespective of who is head of state or government at any particular time, but difficulties arose when Mr Moise Tshombe threatened to attend the July 1964 Cairo summit conference shortly after becoming Prime Minister of Congo-Léopoldville, while the objections of Libya and a number of other states to seating a delegation from the new pro-Western government of Chad, headed by President Hissene Habré, caused the postponement of the (August) 1982 summit. States which were made subject to military rule have retained their places, though some military leaders were more readily accommodated than others – President Mobutu of Zaire more readily than General Ankrah of Ghana, General Gowon of Nigeria, and President

Amin of Uganda. The question whether Transkei should be admitted upon her achievement of 'independence' from South Africa in October 1976 did not prove contentious since there was general agreement that Transkei was still a dependent territory within the Republic of South Africa; successor Bantustans have been treated in the same way. However, the OAU was deeply divided over the application in 1980 of the Saharan Arab Democratic Republic (SADR) to become a member of the Organisation. The republic, which had been declared by the Polisario Front (PF) – the movement fighting to wrest control of the former Spanish Sahara from Morocco – was recognised by twenty-six member states and admission therefore seemed certain if a formal vote should be taken, despite the strong opposition of Morocco and some ten other states; a compromise was reached on this occasion and the issue deferred. Subsequently, however, the secretary-general announced that he had admitted the SADR as the OAU's fifty-first member state on the grounds that technically a majority of member states had recognised the Polisario regime, and the dispute flared up again; as a result, the ministerial session at Tripoli in July 1982 was inquorate and the summit, which should have followed, had to be postponed. The foreign ministers met at Tripoli in November, the SADR having agreed to withdraw temporarily from the session. It was the refusal of President Habré's Chadian delegation to do the same that scuttled both the ministerial meeting and the ensuing summit.[22]

Another principle adopted at Addis Ababa in 1963 was that of non-interference in internal affairs. Eight Francophone states (which were members of OCAM – the post-1965 successor to the UAM) showed the importance which they attached to this principle when they boycotted the 1965 summit in Accra on the ground that President Nkrumah had violated this clause in the Charter. Another and clearer instance that this principle was not strictly applied occurred in 1968 when four member states – Tanzania, Zambia, the Ivory Coast and Gabon – recognised 'Biafra' as a republic independent of Nigeria; the OAU, as a body, was pledged to maintain Nigeria's territorial integrity. The Nigerian government countered in 1979 by accusing President Nyerere of interfering in

Uganda's internal affairs – Tanzanian troops, in conjunction with a Ugandan guerrilla force, had fought their way to Kampala and ousted Amin. Nyerere's view was that the OAU was discredited when, under pretext of upholding the principle of non-interference, it failed to condemn atrocities perpetrated by African leaders and to take remedial action.

Again, the clause stating that each sovereign state should be non-aligned has not been strictly applied. Many French-speaking states, both individually and collectively (as members of OCAM), have retained close economic and other links with France; Siyad Barré's Somalia allied itself with the Soviet Union between 1969 and 1974 and with the United States thereafter, while Ethiopia, following the 1974 coup, turned her back on America and looked for help from Moscow and Havana; and since 1976 the MPLA government in Angola has been dependent for its survival on Soviet and Cuban support. No doubt, some of these alliances have been tactical: the Marxist-oriented government of Angola, for example, can reasonably claim that the Soviet and Cuban presence is essential so long as South Africa continues to send troops across Angola's borders and back its UNITA opponents; and, as an earnest of its non-alignment, it can point to the fact that its oil-fields at Cabinda are being worked by Gulf Oil, an American-based company. Nevertheless, there is no doubt that the principle of non-alignment has been eroded in several of Africa's post-1970 revolutionary regimes, as it has been also in a country such as Kenya which, in June 1980, consolidated her existing close economic and political ties with the West by agreeing to allow the United States to use in an international crisis the port of Mombasa and two air stations. These external alignments, the domestic tensions which they sometimes reflect, and foreign lobbying (for example, over Angola in 1976 and the SADR in 1982) have affected, and still affect adversely performance in the three major areas of activity established by the Charter – the liberation of the remaining dependent territories, the settlement of disputes within the continent, and the promotion of economic co-operation. It is to a consideration of these issues that we now turn.

The African Liberation Committee (ALC)

The formation of the ALC in 1963 gave a boost to the morale of the liberation movements by showing that Africa's independent states were committed to ending colonial rule in Africa. The committee, which has its own secretariat, has been an extremely active institution; nevertheless, it has encountered serious difficulties in fulfilling this commitment. One recurring difficulty has been financial; the ALC has its own budget, distinct from the general budget of the OAU, but, after the first year, many member states failed consistently to pay their contributions to the special fund for liberation. (These contributions were at first voluntary but, following the Cairo summit in July 1964, were subsequently levied in accordance with the UN scale of contributions.) A number of reasons can be suggested for this failure to contribute. There was dissatisfaction with the working of the committee on the part of those who were not members of it – the ALC began with nine members, but the membership was increased to 11 in 1965 and to 21 in 1972. Distance from the areas – mostly in Southern Africa – where the liberation struggle was being fought was another factor. Again, there was disagreement both within the ALC and among African states generally as to which of a country's various liberation movements deserved support. The latter problem – probably the most serious which the committee has encountered – had been foreseen at the 1963 summit by Mr Cyrille Adoula, then Prime Minister of Congo-Léopoldville, who observed that the nationalists were 'more and more divided for the purpose of obtaining aid'. He believed that:

> We must determine here, if possible, to whom we will give our aid as I know that in one and the same country, three, four or even five liberation movements confront each other. They confront each other and even create difficulties for those who wish to aid them.[23]

It was not easy for the ALC to decide between the competing claims of the liberation movements and the committee, and therefore the OAU, sometimes brought itself into political controversy by its decisions – as with its early recommendation on Angola, adopted by the council of ministers in August 1963, to accord exclusive and full diplomatic recognition to Holden Roberto's government in exile. The committee revised this decision in November 1964 and granted aid to both the GRAE and the rival MPLA; from 1965 the bulk of its aid went to the latter. Mozambique posed no such problem since FRELIMO, with its headquarters in Dar es Salaam and strongly backed by Tanzania, was almost universally recognised as the dominant nationalist movement to which all aid should be channelled; today, similarly, SWAPO is accepted by the ALC as the sole representative of the Namibian independence struggle. The situation in Portuguese Guinea was rather more complicated since Senegal, a member of the ALC, objected to the exclusive recognition of the PAIGC and was able to insist (in 1964–5) that a portion of the committee's aid should go to the Frente para a Libertação e Independência da Guiné Portuguesa (FLING).[24] Rhodesia proved an even greater headache for the ALC than Angola. The committee was endlessly frustrated in its attempts to persuade the two main nationalist movements (ZANU and ZAPU) to settle their differences. In 1976 it gave its full support to ZIPA, the newly-formed guerrilla army based on Mozambique, but once ZANU had reorganised and reasserted itself, the ALC was again faced with the problem of supporting two rival nationalist movements. To some extent, this problem persisted even after ZANU and ZAPU formed the Patriotic Front in 1976.

In promoting the liberation of Southern Africa, the OAU mainly worked through the ALC, though never exclusively. In Southern Africa – always its main area of concern – it also relied on the initiatives taken by groups of states with a primary interest in the area. Thus, in April 1975 the OAU council of ministers, meeting in Dar es Salaam, authorised four of its member states – Botswana, Mozambique, Tanzania and Zambia (which subsequently, with Angola, formed the 'front-line states') – to explore 'ways whereby the objectives of the OAU, namely the transfer of power to the African majorities in Rhodesia and Namibia, and the ending of apartheid in South Africa, could be achieved peacefully rather than by the use of violence'.[25] The hopes for this policy of 'détente', as far as Rhodesia was concerned, rested on contact between the heads of these states (particularly President Kaunda) and the South African and Rhodesian Prime Ministers. But the negotiations proved abortive and the armed struggle went on. The ultimate failure of the Geneva conference convened in October 1976 confirmed the OAU in its view that Rhodesia would only be liberated by military means and its liberation committee therefore continued to channel aid to the Zimbabwean nationalist movements, now united in the Patriotic Front. The OAU could reasonably claim to have played a significant part in the achievement of Zimbabwe's independence in April 1980, as it had done earlier in relation to Portugal's African colonies. However, its moral backing was probably more important than its financial support – according to James Mayall, the liberation movements received the bulk of their assistance from outside sources; his conclusion, as of the early 1970s, that the ALC at no time provided more than 10 per cent of their financial requirements most likely remained broadly true.[26]

The Settlement of Disputes

From the outset the OAU faced the problem of artificial, colonial-imposed boundaries. The problem was particularly acute where, as in Somalia, these boundaries divided people belonging to the same ethnic group. President Aden Abdullah Osman presented the Somali case at the OAU inaugural summit conference in May 1963:

> Briefly the Somali problem is this: unlike any other border problem in Africa, the entire length of the existing boundaries, as imposed by the colonialists, cut across the traditional pastures of our nomadic population. The problem becomes unique when it is realised that no other nation in Africa finds itself totally divided along the whole length of its borders from its own people.[27]

Though boundary revision had been favoured by the All-African People's Conference, at both its first and second meetings, and a resolution specifically supporting the Somali case had been adopted at the second, the OAU member states shelved the sensitive border issue in 1963. They did, however, incorporate the principles of sovereignty and territorial integrity in the Charter and made provision for the establishment of a separate commission of mediation, conciliation and arbitration to handle inter-state disputes. By July 1964, when the second summit was held in Cairo, it was essential that the OAU member states should take a stand on the boundary issue. Fighting had broken out between Morocco and Algeria in October 1963 and, in the months which followed, border clashes became more frequent between Somalia and the neighbouring states of Ethiopia and Kenya. At Cairo therefore the OAU assembly adopted a general resolution on border disputes, whereby the member states pledged themselves 'to respect the borders existing on their achievement of national independence'.[28]

As James Mayall has pointed out in a valuable article, the disputes in both the above cases were settled through the mediation of individual African heads of state. It was, he believes, 'the appeal to OAU principles (particularly to the incompatibility of armed conflict and Unity) rather than the mediatory efforts of the institution itself, that contributed to a settlement.' The latter part of this statement is not in question since the mediation commission was never formed, partly because the heads of state were unwilling to create a strong bureaucracy at OAU headquarters, with powers of initiative. As to the first part, it is doubtful whether the two irredentist states, Morocco and Somalia, would have responded to the appeal to OAU principles if they had not been diplomatically isolated in their stand, both within and outside Africa. It can also be argued that the reason why the Somali government did not press its case for the reunification of the Somali territories for some years after the 1967 agreement had much less to do with its acceptance of OAU principles and resolutions than with the preoccupation of the President – Major-General Siyad Barré, who had seized power in a military coup in October 1969 – in establishing a socialist state. Somalia had not relinquished her claims, particularly to the Ogaden region of Ethiopia, and the attack on the Ogaden by the Western Somalia Liberation Front in July 1977 precipitated war between the two states.[29] Once again, the Somali government's perception of national self-interest ultimately proved stronger than its adherence to OAU principles.

Substantially, the same lessons can be drawn from East African experience. Neither President Nyerere nor President Amin observed the OAU principle of non-interference in the affairs of a sovereign state. In September 1972 Nyerere condoned the invasion of Uganda from Tanzanian soil by armed supporters of ex-President Obote. A major war between the two East African states was averted through the mediation of President Siyad Barré of Somalia and a five-point peace agreement was concluded at Mogadishu, the Somali capital. In October 1978 regular forces of the Ugandan army occupied some 700 square miles of Tanzanian territory on the north-west border, north of the Kagera river. Though Amin withdrew his forces the next month under pressure from a number of OAU states, the strong feelings of animosity between the two heads of state overrode observance of OAU principles. This was confirmed early the next year when some 45,000 Tanzanian troops, accompanied by a 2,000-strong Uganda National Liberation Army, entered south-western Uganda, captured Kampala, and ousted Amin.[30] Nyerere was criticised by Sudan and Nigeria for interfering in Uganda's internal affairs. However, Nyerere's view – first given in 1967 when he vainly urged the OAU to recognise Biafra – was that African states lost all moral credibility in their condemnation of South Africa's minority, racist regime if they failed to criticise instances of injustice within black-ruled Africa. Though Nyerere underrated the complexity of the Nigerian conflict, the general principle which he enunciated was sound. There is little doubt that the OAU, under cover of the principle of non-interference, did the African cause a disservice by failing at least to condemn the massacre in Burundi of thousands of Bahutu by the ruling Tutsi minority in 1972 and the atrocities committed by Francisco Macias Nguema in Equatorial Guinea and Bokassa in the Central African Empire, as well as by Amin in Uganda. James Mayall has argued cogently that:

> . . . it is internal rather than external conflicts which pose the greatest threat not only to the states concerned but to African stability generally. It is this paradox which confronts the

OAU with the dilemma of justice against order in its starkest form: for if Unity is held to be inconsistent with racial oppression and minority rule – as the emphasis in the Charter on confrontation with the white South indicates – should it not also be inconsistent with the forceful coercion of African minorities [and, remembering Burundi, majorities] by their own governments?

However, it would be wrong to assume that the OAU has consistently upheld the principle of non-interference in the domestic affairs of other states. As the Congo-Léopoldville experience showed, it depends on issue and circumstance. The memory of Katanga's secession from the Congo following Belgium's precipitate grant of independence in 1960 was not forgotten and when civil war broke out after Tshombe's appointment as Prime Minister in 1964, 'the legacy of the past proved stronger than the OAU Charter'. Mayall adds that 'the radical States were still too firmly committed to the Lumumbist cause to accept the OAU prohibition on interference in the domestic affairs of other States'.[31]

Again, the OAU and its committees have been slow to act over a number of explosive, or potentially explosive, issues. Instances in the 1970s included the invasion of Zaire's Shaba (formerly Katanga) Province by Zairean dissidents based in Angola; the protracted struggle for control of the former Spanish Sahara; and the civil war in Chad. At the OAU summit conference held at Khartoum in July 1978 – two months after Belgian and French troops had been dispatched to Zaire – African opinion was deeply divided over the relative threats posed by Soviet–Cuban and Western interventions in Africa. A compromise resolution was adopted which stated that Africans alone should be responsible for defending the security and stability of the continent, but that every state had the right to seek assistance from any other state when its security and independence were threatened. It was also resolved to consider further the formation of a pan-African force and to 'co-ordinate' the committee of mediation to enable it 'to contain and solve all our conflicts and problems in a peaceful manner and in an African spirit'.[32]

Upon withdrawing from her north-west African colony in

1976, Spain handed over the phosphate-rich territory to joint Moroccan–Mauritanian control – Mauritania eventually withdrew her claim in 1979. This transfer was challenged by the Polisario Front (PF), a liberation movement; the Front, which was strongly supported by Algeria, proclaimed the SADR. The OAU gave little attention to this potentially dangerous confrontation at a time when, in the mid-1970s, a settlement might have been possible. In 1977 a special summit to discuss the Saharan question was agreed upon, but never held. A 'committee of wise men', drawn from five states, was set up the next year to find a solution compatible with the principle of self-determination; the committee got off to a slow start but eventually produced a report recommending that a referendum should be held. The PF, with sophisticated weapons probably supplied by Libya, stepped up its campaign in 1979, while King Hassan of Morocco lost diplomatic ground – only the threat of withdrawal by himself and the leaders of some ten other states prevented the OAU summit conference at Freetown in July 1980 from admitting the SADR to membership. In a surprise move at the Nairobi summit in June of the next year King Hassan disarmed some of his critics by undertaking to test the wishes of the Saharan people in a referendum; however, he did not commit himself to a cease-fire as recommended by the OAU committee on the Western Sahara.[33]

Similarly, the OAU was slow to act on Chad, a vast, land-locked and mostly arid country, whose northern region has been racked by bitter communal strife since the mid-1960s and which in recent years has been torn apart by civil war, rendering it a 'broken-back' state. In these circumstances, the main initiative in finding a solution was taken by Nigeria which was instrumental in convening OAU-sponsored conferences in Kano and Lagos, and subsequently in assembling the OAU peace-keeping force, referred to below. Other initiatives were taken by the Sudan, whose President had successfully reconciled the conflicting interests within his own country and mediated in a number of African conflicts, and Libya, as well as by France, the former colonial power. A precarious government of national unity was installed at Ndjamena, the capital, in November 1979, but fell apart after four months when fighting broke out between the rival armies of the President, Goukouni Oueddei, and his Defence Minister and the former rebel leader, Hissene Habré. Colonel Muammar Qaddafi of Libya, whose troops occupied a strip of territory in northern Chad, stepped up his support for the provisional government when France withdrew her garrison in April 1980 and the OAU failed to establish a peace-keeping force. In November 1981, however, Qaddafi withdrew his troops at the request of the Chad government and the next month (after Habré had launched a vigorous offensive in eastern Chad) the OAU did manage to assemble in Chad a force, under Nigerian command, of 3,800 Nigerian, Zairean and Senegalese troops (Togo, Benin and Guinea could not afford to send their promised contingents). Goukouni was dissatisfied that the OAU force saw its mission as holding the ring between Chad's warring factions, preliminary to peace negotiations, rather than to attack Habré's forces, as the Libyans had done. Following a two-day meeting of the OAU Chad committee at Nairobi in February 1982, President Goukouni rejected OAU plans for a ceasefire and for fresh elections, to be held by the end of June, under the threat of withdrawing its troops. The fact was that the OAU, which had received initial financial and/or other support from France, the United States and Britain (all these states were anxious, as were many African governments, to get the Libyans out of Chad) could not afford to maintain its force there beyond that date – President Moi of Kenya, the OAU chairman, sought financial help from the UN. In the event, the issue was settled by the superiority of Mr Habré's forces: they over-ran the capital in June and Habré was installed as the new President; withdrawal of the OAU force was completed by 1 July. The ousted President, Mr Goukouni, fled to Cameroon and then went into exile in Algeria. He turned again to Colonel Qaddafi for help and, with Libyan backing, set up a rival government in northern Chad. Both governments sent delegations to the abortive OAU summit meeting at Tripoli in August and again to the foreign ministers' meeting (also in Tripoli) in November, thus precipitating the crisis referred to above.[34]

In the large number of inter-African disputes, of varying seriousness, which have occurred in the post-independence period, more effective mediation has been provided by individual heads of state, *ad hoc* commissions, and even regional functional groups than by the OAU itself. Thus, as Mayall notes: 'it was within the OERS [Organisation of Senegal River States], not the OAU, that a working relationship was temporarily achieved between Mali and Guinea after a military *coup* had overthrown President Keita in 1967 [1968].'[35] The OAU's armed intervention in Chad – accepted by President Goukouni's government reluctantly and under pressure – was the first occasion on which the Organisation had actually assembled a multinational peace-keeping force, though this proposal, in one form or another, had been mooted ever since the inception of the OAU in 1963. However, the importance of this particular intervention must not be exaggerated: only three African states were represented in the peace-keeping force and the latter could not have been launched without financial and logistical assistance from the United States and France; Britain provided the Nigerian contingent with Land-Rovers. Moreover, there was no opportunity for the Chad action to be reported to, or reviewed by the heads of state and the question whether the OAU as such could have exercised effective control over the participating governments was therefore never tested, but must remain doubtful. What is certain is that the Organisation's expensive and unrewarding experience in Chad means that this type of experiment will not be repeated in the near future.

That the OAU has often been slow to respond to crisis is in part due to its cumbersome machinery, but it also results from the understandable difficulty of getting the member states, with their often divergent interests, to agree on a common policy. Agreement is most likely to be forthcoming when an issue arises which threatens African interests generally. This occurred eventually over Angola: the heads of state, meeting (for the first time) in emergency session at Addis Ababa in January 1976, were evenly divided (by 22 votes to 22) over the question whether to recognise the MPLA government or to continue working for a government of national unity; however, many wavering states swung behind the MPLA when South Africa intervened against it. Thus, only the activities of a country external to the OAU had enabled an 'African' policy to emerge.

The Promotion of Economic Co-operation

In the 1970s the OAU showed an increasing concern with economic afairs; economic issues were on the agenda of several of the annual summit conferences. At the 1973 summit in Addis Ababa an economic charter for Africa's second decade was approved; this charter stressed the need for economic independence and inter-African co-operation as the surest basis for lasting unity, thereby complementing the original (1963) charter which had laid down fundamental political principles. Three years later at Port Louis, Mauritius, the heads of state approved a proposal from Zaire for the establishment of an economic co-ordinating committee covering the entire continent; the OAU economic ministers referred this question, and a proposal to form an African common market, to the ECA. On the initiative of the OAU secretary-general a symposium on African economic development in the 1980s was held at Monrovia in February 1979 and, as a result, a strategy on economic policy was formulated and adopted by that year's summit conference. In April 1980 an African economic summit was convened at Lagos and adopted a 'plan of action', which aimed to create an African common market by the year 2000. The plan was to be based on existing regional economic committees in Africa – notably ECOWAS and SADCC – and was to be implemented in two ten-year stages. Emphasis was placed on food production – it was envisaged that the continent would be self-sufficient in food, as well as building materials, clothing and energy, by 1990; the importance of transport and communications was also stressed.[36]

The prospect of the OAU implementing these economic resolutions was, however, remote. From the outset the Organisation has faced serious financial problems and has had to give prior attention to urgent, and often divisive, political issues, as at the Lagos economic summit in April 1980 when decisions had to be taken on Chad and the Western Sahara and a successor as current OAU chairman had to be found to President Tolbert of Liberia who had been killed shortly before in a military coup. At an individual level, many OAU member states were having to import grain on a substantial scale, thereby adding to their existing balance of payments difficul-

ties. The latter were due above all to the huge increase after
1973 in the cost of imports – oil especially, but also capital and
manufactured goods – without any corresponding rise in
commodity export prices; in fact, these prices declined sharply
from about 1977 and the poorer countries, such as Somalia and
Tanzania, were particularly hard hit.

In these straitened economic circumstances facing the OAU
and its member states, the Organisation continued what had
become normal practice in the 1970s of referring economic
development questions to the ECA. It was predictable, too,
that the OAU would turn for economic assistance (as well as
support in the liberation struggle in Southern Africa) to the
oil-rich Arab states. The 1974 summit conference at
Mogadishu discussed the effects of the oil crisis on OAU
member states and set up a special body within the Organisation to strengthen Afro-Arab co-operation and development.
After considerable delay the first ever Afro-Arab summit was
held at Cairo, Egypt (an OAU member state from the outset) in
March 1977; it was sponsored jointly by the OAU and the Arab
League and attended by representatives of sixty countries and
the Palestine Liberation Organisation. A charter of political
and economic co-operation, known as the Cairo declaration,
was signed, pledging the signatories to promote Afro-Arab
co-operation in finance, mining, trade, industry, agriculture,
transport, energy and communications. It was also agreed that
preferential tariff agreements should be negotiated and that the
capital of both the Arab Bank for Development in Africa and
the African Development Bank should be increased. A concrete
result of the conference was the commitment of further Arab
aid to Africa – $1,500 million was pledged (two-thirds by Saudi
Arabia) and of this sum nearly one-third was to go immediately
to the two banks.[37] However, the other commitments entered
into at the conference have not yet been fulfilled and, with the
fall in the revenue of the oil-producing states in the early 1980s
as a result of the world economic recession, it is clear that Africa
cannot rely on the Arab states to solve her problems.

The OAU has been involved in other efforts to promote
economic development in Africa. As Wallerstein records, in its
early years it invested much energy in presenting Africa's case at
meetings of UNCTAD, but to little avail – the 'persistent

tendency towards external imbalance associated with the development process', referred to by the UNCTAD secretary-general in his report to the conference held in Geneva from March to June 1964, remained uncorrected. The 1973 OAU summit conference passed resolutions on relations with the EEC, and negotiations for 46 ACP countries to join the Community were initially conducted under OAU auspices. However, prime responsibility for the negotiations in 1973–4, as well as for the renegotiations in 1978–9 leading to Lomé II, rested with the Council of African Ministers (subsequently expanded to become the Council of ACP Ministers) and its secretariat. The OAU gave its blessing to the Sixth Pan-African Congress – and the first on African soil – held at Dar es Salaam in 1974, when the struggle against 'economic imperialism' was discussed.[38] The OAU also continued to act as an 'umbrella' for regional organisations, such as ECOWAS, and UN agencies; the latter, and notably the ECA, whose headquarters were also in Addis Ababa, were more effective than its own specialised agencies. In general the OAU, through the resolutions tabled for debate at its various conferences, provided a forum at which African economic issues could be discussed. However, the main initiative in promoting economic development remained with individual member states, as well as the regional functional groups which they had formed, and with the ECA.

Conclusion

The OAU has had a chequered history, now extending over a period of twenty years. Its record is one of success and failure: success above all in providing a forum in which issues of concern to member states can be discussed and disputes arising between them sometimes resolved; failure in that its members have frequently flouted the principles enshrined in its original Charter. The Organisation's weakness is that it is not underpinned by a groundswell of popular support and that, in the unstable political conditions which have prevailed over much of the continent since its inception, the governments of its member states have, necessarily, often been preoccupied with their own domestic problems. Yet the existence of such problems can only be part of the explanation for the lukewarm support given by many heads of state to the OAU, since a number of those who never attend summit meetings – such as Houphouet-Boigny of the Ivory Coast – are active participants in such regional organisations as ECOWAS and in the annual Franco-African conferences. In the perception of these leaders, the latter meetings deal with concrete issues, such as collective security arrangements and economic co-operation agreements, which promise to be of greater benefit to their states than the matters raised, and often discussed acrimoniously, at OAU summit conferences. There is no doubt that the 'French connection' and the member states' other external linkages – financial, commercial and sometimes military – have detracted from that continental solidarity which Kwame Nkrumah, the champion of African unity, believed that the OAU should express.

Further Reading

Andemicael, B., *The OAU and the UN: Relations between the Organization of African Unity and the United Nations* (New York: Africana, 1976).

Cervenka, Z., *The Unfinished Quest for Unity: Africa and the OAU* (New York: Africana, 1977).

Foltz, W. J., *From French West Africa to the Mali Federation* (New Haven: Yale University Press, 1965).

Geiss, I., *The Pan-African Movement* (London: Methuen, 1974).

Hazlewood, A. (ed.), *African Integration and Disintegration: Case Studies in Economic and Political Union* (London: Oxford University Press, 1967).

Hazlewood, A., 'The End of the East African Community: What are the Lessons for Regional Integration Schemes?', *Journal of Common Market Studies*, vol. xviii, no. 1 (September 1979).

Leys, R., and Tostensen, A., 'Regional Co-operation in Southern Africa: the Southern African Development Co-ordination Conference', *Review of African Political Economy*, no. 23 (January–April 1982).

Mayall, J., 'African Unity and the OAU: The Place of a Political Myth in African Diplomacy', *The Handbook of World Affairs*, vol. 27 (1973).

Ravenhill, J., 'Regional Integration and Development in Africa', *Journal of Commonwealth and Comparative Politics*, vol. xvii, no. 3 (November 1979).

Rothchild, D. (ed.), *Politics of Integration. An East African Documentary* (Nairobi: East African Publishing House, 1968).

Wallerstein, I., *Africa: The Politics of Unity* (New York: Random House, 1967).

Wolfers, M., *Politics in the Organisation of African Unity* (London: Methuen, 1976).

10

Conclusions: Ideology, the Post-Colonial State and Development

In his book *Ideology and Development in Africa* (1982), Crawford Young argues that in two decades of independence, African political economies have become widely differentiated along two axes, one defined by ideology and the other by performance. Though, as he points out, there are difficulties in evaluating regime performance and in relating performance to ideological preference, his own book shows the attempt to be worthwhile. He concludes firstly that ideology *does* matter – it is not merely froth on the African beer, paling to insignificance beside the almost universal dependence of African states on the Western-dominated international economy; and secondly, that it has some bearing on performance.

There is, however, a prior difficulty – to reach agreement on the meaning of the concepts 'ideology' and 'development'. As Clifford Geertz has said, 'the term "ideology" has itself become thoroughly ideologized', being on one view a cloak for interests and on another a response to deep-rooted social strains.[1] According to Edward Shils,

> An ideology differs ... from a prevailing outlook and its creeds through its greater *explicitness*, its greater *internal integration* or *systemization*, its greater *comprehensiveness*, the greater *urgency* of its application, and its much higher *intensity of concentration* focused on certain central propositions or evaluations.[2]

By this test, states such as Botswana, the Ivory Coast, Kenya and Nigeria can hardly be said to possess an ideology at all, while Algeria, Tanzania and most of the other 'first wave' of African socialist states have weak ideologies. We prefer, therefore, to take the looser definition of John Plamenatz, for whom ideology was 'any system of ideas which acts to support or subvert accepted modes of thought and behaviour'.[3] Not only does this definition accommodate the great majority of African states, it also has the advantage of laying equal stress on the supportive and subversive roles of ideology – Shils, by contrast, saw ideologies as the main preserve of opposition groups excluded from power.

In classifying polities, Professor Young relies primarily upon the self-ascription of a regime's leadership and this leads him to distinguish three major streams: Afro-Marxism, populist-socialism, and African capitalism. The first category comprises states such as Mozambique and Ethiopia which have officially espoused Marxism–Leninism; the second is made up of states like Algeria and Tanzania which embrace their own brand of socialism; and the third type of regime, of which the Ivory Coast, Kenya and Nigeria are leading examples, rests upon an ideological base which has often to be inferred from the market-economy policies pursued. This is an acceptable typology but the method of arriving at it, while having the merit of consistency, does not take sufficient account of the fact that the actions of political leaders may be at variance with the ideas which they express. The most serious discrepancy in Young's classification is his placing of Guinea-Bissau in the populist-socialist bracket rather than in the category of Marxist states, to which (both before and after the coup of 1980) it rightfully belongs; the PAIGC has always been closer to its sister movements in Angola and Mozambique than to African populist-socialism and has recently declared itself to be a vanguard party with a Marxist–Leninist ideology. Moreover, though Guinea has deviated from Marxist orthodoxy, it, too (taking the post-independence period as a whole), has more of the character of an Afro-Marxist than of a populist-socialist regime.

To define 'development' is even more difficult. The concept is Western and was originally expressed in economic terms: in the 1950s it spelt industrialisation, which was seen as an essential and inevitable stage of economic growth. However, the stages of growth outlined by Rostow and others were not fulfilled and the importance of factors other than the economic came to be realised; economists were not agreed on what economic growth entailed or how it might best be measured: if industrialisation alone was not a satisfactory measure, neither was Gross National Product (GNP). Lucian Pye's study of Burma, published in 1962, showed that development was a more complex process than had previously been assumed, and it came to be realised that it was not appropriate to take the West (or the Soviet Union for that matter) as a precise blueprint for development; though the developed world 'still furnished the raw material for the meaning of modernity', wrote Nettl, 'the means of reaching it were now seen as much more varied than before'.[4] Third World countries had values and goals which were often very different from those of a modern, industrialised society, and in seeking to achieve development they might discard the Western democratic process in favour of a much more authoritarian approach. Some analysts, including Samuel Huntington, even welcomed this possibility in the belief that such an approach might promote order and stability on which a high valuation was placed in the United States of the 1960s, with civil rights movements and anti-Vietnam war protests.

Peter Nettl said that in empirical terms, the Third World and the developed world interacted, with the latter controlling the former, and he dismissed the model and history of the existing developed world as 'only marginally relevant' to the Third World in terms of any general theory of development. While arguing that theories of development helped greatly 'to over-come the parochialism of individual studies of societies', he saw development as 'a highly differential process according to par-ticular societies and their goals'.[5] This formulation is a useful reminder of the pitfalls to be encountered in trying to measure the 'development' achieved by one Third-World state against that achieved by another. It is particularly pertinent to a comparative study of African states which, as we have seen, differ widely in their colonial experience, in the strength of their inherited political institutions, and in their socio-economic structure. It reinforces the argument of Fred Riggs, outlined in chapter 6, that developing countries should be studied within their entire ecological context; though their interaction with the 'developed' world is important, it is not enough to see these countries (as early dependency theorists were inclined to do) as mere pawns on an international chess-board controlled and exploited by more powerful 'kings' and 'queens'. Nettl's definition also raises the question whether state performance should be judged by external canons (how far, for example, has a state such as Tanzania 'progressed' according to the criteria indicated by the Marxist model), or in the light of the goals which the political leadership has set itself. While there may be disagreement on this last point, Nettl's argument that it is not helpful to produce a rank-ordering of states based on superficial 'standard of living' indices, such as the number of motor cars and radios, will find wide acceptance.

Crawford Young is aware of pitfalls such as these and stresses that his appraisal of ideology and performance is preliminary; it is offered as a contribution to an ongoing debate, rather than as a final verdict.[6] The six criteria which he takes to evaluate performance are growth, equality of distribution, autonomy and self-reliance, human dignity, participation, and the expansion of state capacity. From this we can reasonably conclude that the more a state satisfies these criteria, the more 'developed' it becomes. Our method in what follows is to summarise and elaborate on Professor Young's helpful findings, and to indicate their relevance to this study.

Growth

As one might expect, Young's conclusions are firmest in relation to growth and equality. He finds that to date, rapid growth has eluded the Afro-Marxist states; that the growth results of the populist–socialist group of states has varied from 'respectable' in the case of Algeria, Egypt and Tanzania to mediocre in the case of Ghana, Guinea and Mali; and that while the capitalist camp has had its disasters, like Zaire, the potential of 'the statist model of nurture capitalism' for high growth has been demonstrated by the Ivory Coast, Kenya and mineral-rich Gabon especially, but also by Malawi (like the first two a predominantly agrarian economy) and Botswana, where the extraction of minerals (copper, nickel and diamonds) has supplemented the cattle industry (see Table 10.1). One cannot quarrel with these overall findings, though a number of points need to be made (some of which are, in fact, made by Young himself).

First, to compare performance on the basis of GNP growth rates is often misleading because of the different baselines from which growth proceeds. Thus, GNP figures for Tanzania, Ghana and Guinea in the 1970s might obscure the stark reality, namely that economic performance in Tanzania has been poor and in Ghana abysmal, while rich bauxite deposits have alone saved Guinea from bankruptcy. It cannot be said that oil has had a similar effect on the Nigerian economy, which was quite buoyant in the pre-oil period, if at a lower level of development resources, but there is no question that oil has given a tremendous boost to that economy.

Secondly, therefore, the geological factor can reduce the validity of comparisons between one regime and another. It can be said with confidence that the high growth rates achieved by Nigeria after the civil war were due to the oil bonanza rather than to the prowess of the military government; thus Nigeria provides no exception to the caution noted in chapter 7 that military regimes do not possess any special formula for achieving economic development. While one can therefore exclude (as Crawford Young has done) oil-producing states such as Nigeria and Libya from comparison, it is less easy to weigh the performance, in GNP terms, of a country like copper-rich Zambia against that of the agrarian-based economies of the Ivory Coast, Kenya, Malawi, Somalia, Tanzania and Upper Volta. The experience of Nigeria and Zambia suggests that there may be an inverse ratio between the possession of extensive mineral resources and agricultural output, making such states particularly subject to economic reversal when the price of their mineral product drops sharply on the world market.

Thirdly, the time-span is still too short to test with any degree of certainty the economic performance of the 'second wave' of socialist states which came to independence in the

TABLE 10.1   *Non-mineral-exporting capitalist countries in Africa*

	Population 1979 (in millions)	Average annual growth rate of GDP (per cent)		Life expectancy at birth (years)		Industry as per cent of GDP		Manufacturing as per cent of GDP	
		1960–70	1970–9	1960	1979	1960	1979	1960	1979
Sahel									
Chad	4.4	0.5	−0.2	35	41	12	11	4	8
Senegal	5.5	2.5	2.5	37	43	17	24	12	19
Sudan	17.9	1.3	4.3	39	47	15	13	5	6
Mali	6.8	3.3	5.0	37	43	10	11	5	6
Upper Volta	5.6	3.0	−0.1	37	43	14	20	8	14
Other									
Ghana	11.3	2.1	−0.1	40	49		21	10	8
Benin	3.4	2.6	3.3	37	47	8	12	3	8
Sierra Leone	3.4	4.3	1.6	37	47		23		5
Uganda	12.8	5.9	−0.4	44	54	13	7	9	6
Rwanda	4.9	2.7	4.1	37	47	7	21	1	15
Burundi	4.0	4.4	3.0	37	42		15		10
Kenya	15.3	6.0	6.5	41	55	18	21	9	13
Ivory Coast	8.2	8.0	6.7	37	47	14	23	7	12
Cameroon	8.2	3.7	5.4	37	47		16		9
Malawi	5.8	4.9	6.3	37	47	11	20	6	12
Lesotho	1.3	4.6	7.0	42	51		15		2

Source: *Accelerated Development in Sub-Saharan Africa*, World Bank (Washington, D.C.: 1981); and *World Development Report*, 1981.
Note: This table has been reproduced from C. Leys, 'African Economic Development in Theory and Practice', *Dedalus*, vol. iii, no. 2 (Spring 1982), p. 109.

1970s. The auguries, however, are not good: Angola, for example, has only been kept afloat by her oil exports, while Mozambique has, as yet, barely achieved pre-independence levels of agricultural and manufacturing output. Several explanations are to hand for what does seem at present to be a disappointing record of economic growth in these states: an acute shortage of skilled manpower, exacerbated by the exodus at independence of most of the Portuguese population; civil war in Angola and, until 1980, the spillover effects on Mozambique of the Rhodesian conflict; South African support for UNITA forces in Angola and for the MNR in Mozambique; the incursions by South African troops across Angola's southern border, allegedly in pursuit of SWAPO guerrillas, and South Africa's tight grip on the Mozambican economy. Possibly these states have made the mistake (in Hanson's graphic phraseology) of attempting 'to hit Soviet-type targets by un-Soviet type methods',[7] though, given the circumstances in which they have to operate, it is doubtful whether the governments of Angola and Mozambique have sufficient power, let alone inclination, to enforce ruthless Stalinist policies. In any event where, as in Ethiopia, what Young calls 'the soft-option version' of Marxism–Leninism has not been adopted and a reign of terror has sometimes prevailed, the results, on both the economic and political fronts, have been no more encouraging.

There is a final point of great significance and one to which we shall return in discussing state capacity: it is that a state organised on Marxist lines and which assumes prime responsibility for production, distribution and exchange, places a heavier demand on trained and experienced manpower than any other. As we noted above, Angola and Mozambique are critically vulnerable in this sphere; in post-independence Angola, as in Guinea in the early 1960s, there was an almost complete collapse of the country's distribution network. Guinea's experience at that time, as analysed by Elliot Berg,[8] showed the danger of allowing ideology to become an economic strait-jacket, making changes in direction difficult. The 'second wave' of Afro-Marxist states have avoided this mistake: President Machel of Mozambique, for example, has bowed to economic necessity and modified his socialism with pragmatism, without however losing sight of his long-term socialist objectives.

Though the sharp fall in export commodity prices in recent years has adversely affected the economies of Kenya and the Ivory Coast, causing mounting foreign exchange problems, even their severest critics concede that these two states (together with Gabon) stand out among black African states for the high rates of growth which they have achieved in the post-independence period; some critics believe, however, that the growth of their economies cannot be sustained. While Kenya cannot easily be compared with neighbouring Tanzania, given its much stronger administrative and economic base at independence, the Ivory Coast and Ghana do bear comparison: in 1957, when Ghana became independent, the two countries were similar in resource endowment, size, and level of development.[9] When Nkrumah fell from power in 1966, Ghana was on the verge of bankruptcy, while the Ivory Coast was already performing what seemed to some observers to be an 'economic miracle'. The state-capitalist model pursued by the Ivory Coast with French assistance had evidently triumphed over Nkrumah's aberrant brand of socialism. There were, of course, other factors involved besides ideology – such as the quality of the political leadership – yet the economic strategies based on that ideology (explicit in Ghana especially after 1961, implicit in the Ivory Coast) were significantly different both in their content and results. These and other examples (Malawi and Botswana among them) raise at least the possibility that states which adopt a capitalist system and retain close ties with the West may attain more rapid economic growth than other types of regime, though it must be added at once that there can be no guarantee that the market-economy formula will produce growth results – the economy of Zaire, for example, is in a mess, while that of Nigeria is under increasing strain due to the fall in oil revenues and the decline in agricultural production. If valid, this conclusion is important: true, economic growth alone does not equal development; yet it is an *essential* part of development – as much for the socialist regime as any other.

Equality

Critics of the capitalist-type strategies pursued by Gabon, Kenya and the Ivory Coast are quick to point out that the high rates of growth achieved by these states have been at the cost of increased dependency and increased inequality. These regimes have, it is said, emphasised 'external infusion' rather than 'internal mobilisation' and forged close ties with the West at the expense of economic integration within each state; the resultant pattern of growth has accentuated inherited regional and social imbalances. Certain sections of the urban workforce and the peasantry – usually those peasants living nearest the coast or the capital city or farming the best land – have benefited, but at the cost (it is maintained) of the people living in less advantaged and remote areas, which are neglected by government agricultural extension officers; many of these 'marginalised' peasants migrate to the towns or other parts of the country in search of work. Attention to the social consequences of a fundamental imbalance in the economy has been drawn by Richard E. Stryker and Bonnie Campbell, writing on the Ivory Coast, by the 1972 ILO mission on unemployment in Kenya, and by Crawford Young, who characterises Gabon as a 'perverted capitalist state', in which the foreign-operated mineral economy booms, but the rural economy stagnates.[10]

The fact that such criticims do have substance leads to what *may* be a wrong conclusion: that growth and redistribution are incompatible. Chenery and his co-authors argue that the two are compatible and point out that fiscal policy can be used for redistribution purposes.[11] However, as Crawford Young observes, in many African states, irrespective of ideology, fiscal policy has the opposite effect and is 'a veritable suction pump drawing resources out of the peasant sector'. Of the states which he examines, only Kenya has imposed relatively low levels of rural taxation (using that term to embrace pricing policies, as well as direct and indirect fiscal levies). He goes on to state:

More generally, policies that bring about stagnation of rural marketed production are probably by nature inegalitarian. Conversely, rising rural output – if it is not merely expanded plantation production – does raise the incomes of the poorest segment of the populace. Viewed from this angle, the effective agricultural policies in Ivory Coast and Kenya partly mitigate the high degrees of inequality visible at the top of the social scale. In the Ivory Coast, Ivorian farmers in the perennial crop zones of the south have experienced major gains. The northern savanna has much less potential, but the remarkable increase in cotton production suggests some benefits here as well. The lowest end of the social scale tends to be occupied by foreign migrants – those who truly are the victims of inequality.[12]

This is not to suggest that in ideological terms capitalist regimes like those of Kenya and the Ivory Coast match the commitment of socialist regimes, whether Marxist or populist–socialist, to the egalitarian principle: rather it is to argue that as a result of the pricing, marketing and other policies which they pursue, some of these regimes may enhance the living standards of their rural population more than the socialist regimes have yet shown themselves to be capable of doing. For economic growth is the essential corollary of equality and, despite the underlying imbalances of Gabon's economy and the limited number of Gabonese employed in her foreign-controlled mining industry, there is little doubt that some of the benefits of the spectacular growth rate achieved by Gabon in the 1970s have trickled down to many sections of the one-and-a-half million or so population – Gabon has extensive educational, health and other social services.[13] Conceivably, equality without growth will satisfy the ethical values of a country's leadership, but it will bring little comfort to the ordinary villager, on whose behalf Amilcar Cabral spoke when he addressed PAIGC cadres: 'National liberation, the struggle against colonialism, the construction of peace, progress and independence are nothing but hollow words devoid of any significance unless they can be translated into a real improvement of living conditions.'[14]

In fairness, it must be said that a number of African socialist states, including the Marxist states of Mozambique and Somalia and the populist–socialist states of Algeria and Tanzania, have made commendable progress (often with limited resources at their disposal) in extending educational and health facilities to the rural people; many of the Afro-Marxist regimes have also made serious attempts to move towards women's equality – progress is slow because of deep-rooted social prejudices. Yet it remains true that such gains can only be sustained and consolidated if the economy is buoyant. In many ways, Tanzania provides an object lesson in the promotion of egalitarian measures and in their erosion through economic decline from the mid-1970s. For Nyerere, equality is fundamental: he has said that 'its acceptance as a basic assumption of life in society is the core and essence of socialism'. It has been reflected not only in educational and public health policies but also in the adoption of a tough leadership code and of income tax, wage and salary policies which have, in Cranford Pratt's assessment, succeeded in narrowing 'very significantly' the differential between the income of the most highly paid and the most lowly paid in Tanzania.[15] That Tanzanians, of whom the great majority live in the rural areas, are now experiencing great economic hardship and that the government is hard-stretched to maintain the existing level of social services is partly due to circumstances, such as the increased cost of imports and the decline in export earnings, outside the government's control. On the other hand, the government is itself directly responsible for the failure of several policy initiatives, such as the *ujamaa* village policy, which was based on the incorrect assumption that it was possible to adapt traditional work methods to the needs of modern production systems. It can also be argued, as Suzanne Mueller has done, that Nyerere paid too much attention to checking the process of class formation in Tanzania and that more material advantages might have been gained for the rural people by 'letting the kulaks run'.[16]

While the pursuit of equality by African socialist states may provide a moral climate which checks the large-scale corruption to be found in some African capitalist regimes (Zaire is the prime offender, with Nigeria possibly the runner-up), equality is likely to prove an elusive goal. As a result of his investigations, Professor Young reaches this sobering conclusion:

Performance on egalitarianism . . . draws an ambiguous

evaluation. African capitalist states permit very high returns to a relatively narrow segment of African political figures, top functionaries, and businessmen, as well as to expatriate managerial and technical personnel. Afro-Marxist and populist socialist states are likely to inhibit wealth accumulation at the top stratum. For wage earners and smallholders, however, it is much less clear that sluggish growth is compensated for by efficacious redistribution, as appears to have been the case in Cuba. The rural-based economic growth achievements in Ivory Coast and Kenya make at least arguable the proposition that these states have brought an improvement in the well-being of farmers that is not matched by most of the other cases considered.[17]

Autonomy

Contrary to what development theory would lead us to expect, Young finds that there is no close correlation between degree of autonomy and self-reliance and ideology. The difference between the two extremes – the African capitalist state and the Afro-Marxist state – is not that the former is more externally dependent than the latter, but that close co-operation with the West is the basis of the state's development strategy in the first case, while external support is often a matter of necessity rather than choice in the second. The evidence also suggests that there is no automatic correlation between external linkages and domestic policy, but that all regimes, including even those of the market-economy type, may pursue policies which are antithetical to the interests of their international backers.

This was demonstrated a few years after independence in Zambia where the starkness of the state capitalist economy is moderated by socialist and populist strands. At independence, international capitalism was firmly entrenched within the Zambian economy, which was overwhelmingly dependent upon the copper produced by two multinational copper-mining companies – the giant Anglo-American Corporation and Roan Selection Trust. Yet this dependence did not prevent the state acquiring, in 1969–70, majority control of the copper industry against the wishes and immediate (though not long-term) interests of the mining companies.[18] Again, in the 1970s, Zambia's policy of confrontation with the white minority regimes of Southern Africa was often at variance with the wishes of Britain and the United States, as well as of domestic opponents of the Zambian government. Members of Zambia's 'managerial bourgeoisie' were not, therefore, merely puppets on strings pulled by external forces. Moreover, while that segment of the bourgeoisie made up of indigenous businessmen has accepted links with foreign companies willing to invest in Zambia, it has also continued to display a strong sense of economic nationalism[19]

These comments are, *mutatis mutandis*, substantially valid for Nigeria also. Here, too, alike under military and civilian rule, there is a predominantly state-capitalist economy, with an increasing share of the market being cornered by the private sector as a result of the indigenisation policy pursued by successive governments after the end of the civil war in 1970. State power has been exercised (as increasingly in Zambia from 1968) in the interests of indigenous businessmen, with whom the holders of state power (military officers, civilian politicians and public servants) have forged important links. While major aspects of economic organisation remain subject to foreign control and capitalist development is dependent upon public and foreign investment, the ruling élite is not subservient to a foreign class in the way that Samir Amin and certain other Marxist scholars have alleged. Though fundamentally Nigeria is still an economically dependent state, nationalisation measures and industrial growth have (as Sklar points out) undermined traditional forms of foreign economic domination;[20] the latter, in Nigeria as indeed in the great majority of African states, is strongest in the financial sphere where increasing external debts give foreign capital considerable leverage over debtor states. In the 1970s, with the confidence born of mounting oil revenues, the Nigerian military government pursued an assertive foreign policy, especially over Southern Africa, to the extent that in 1979 it seized BP holdings as a punishment for the company's dealings with that part of the continent. What Professor Sklar, himself a radical scholar, has written is relevant to Nigeria and a large number of African states:

The idea of foreign domination by proxy, through the medium of a clientele or puppetised upper class, is controverted by a large body of evidence. In many post-colonial and newly developing countries, governments, businessmen and leaders of thought regularly defy the demands and frustrate the desires of their counterparts in the industrial countries. The diplomatic independence of states that are formally non-aligned in the conflict of superpowers is a leading feature of contemporary international relations. In the economic sphere, it is now commonplace for countries that welcome foreign investment to nationalise, or 'indigenise', foreign-owned enterprises, in whole or in part. Furthermore, the evidence of sustained industrial growth in agrarian countries that have adopted capitalist strategies of economic development is unmistakable.[21]

In the case of the Afro-Marxist states also, 'the boundaries of autonomy', writes Young, 'do not seem so rigidly determined as the dependency school would suggest'. Despite its heavy dependence on the oil pumped from the Cabinda enclave by Gulf Oil, an American-based multinational company, the Angolan regime has continued to espouse, and substantially to base its internal policies on, Marxist–Leninist doctrine, and it has resisted American pressure to order the withdrawal of Soviet and Cuban military personnel. The presence in Guinea of American and other multinationals to extract the rich bauxite deposits has not changed the nature of that country's capricious, revolutionary regime, which has long been a thorn in the side of France and Guinea's Francophone neighbours.[22] Again, though the Ethiopian regime of Colonel Mengistu Haile Mariam relies heavily on Soviet and Cuban support and is said to owe the Soviet bloc at least £1,250 million for arms and other supplies,[23] it is not a puppet regime: Mengistu dallied for a fortnight before endorsing the Soviet Union's intervention in Afghanistan, while Soviet pressure has not persuaded the regime to reach a settlement with the Eritrean secessionists or, as yet, to create the vanguard-type workers' party projected more than three years earlier – a decision on this issue has been deferred until 1984. Of Africa's other revolutionary regimes, Mozambique has moderated neither her internal nor external policies as a result of her dependence on South Africa and has paid dearly for her support of first Rhodesian and more recently of South African liberation movements.

Similar arguments apply to the populist–socialist states, of which Tanzania may be taken as an example. Following independence in December 1961, mainland Tanzania diversified her trade and aid partners but preferred to forego aid rather than be tied to the apron-strings of an external power: in 1964, following the union with Zanzibar, she refused to allow West Germany to dictate the pattern of diplomatic representation and in December 1965 she broke off diplomatic relations with Britain over the latter's Rhodesian policy. On the other hand, while seeking to be as self-reliant as his country's weak economic position allowed, Nyerere never pursued a policy of autarchy and Tanzania has in fact become one of the main recipients of foreign aid in Africa. However, such aid has been given on Tanzanian terms; even after 1980, when the country was in dire straits as a result of the war with Uganda, adverse weather conditions, and the sharp fall in export commodity earnings, Nyerere refused to accept the stringent conditions, which included a heavy devaluation of the currency and a sharp cut in spending on the social services, imposed by the IMF in return for a further loan.[24]

There are, of course, exceptions to the picture painted above. In negotiations with the IMF, African capitalist regimes tend to be less assertive of their autonomy than regimes of a socialist orientation, while most of the Francophone states show solidarity with France in voting at the UN General Assembly. Again, in June 1980, the Kenyan government agreed to allow America to use in international crises the port of Mombasa and two air stations. Nevertheless, a strong sense of nationalism, both political and economic, leads regimes of all ideological types to display substantial autonomy in the conduct of their international relations. It would, moreover, be rash to conclude that even a Francophone state such as the Ivory Coast, which retains particularly close economic and military links with France, shapes her foreign policy (which led to recognition of Biafra and dialogue with South Africa) solely at France's bidding.

Human Dignity

We turn next to the criterion of human dignity to assess regime performance. Among the post-independence trends identified in earlier chapters were those leading to the creation of the one-party state and the personalisation of power in the hands of the party and national president. These moves took place more quickly in Francophone than in Anglophone Africa but were well-nigh universal and occurred irrespective of the type of regime. Opposition parties were banned, while interest groups, such as trade unions, lost much, if not all, of their former autonomy. Though a few states, such as Tanzania, fostered 'democracy' within the one-party system and rulers like Nyerere were alive to the problem of reconciling liberty and state security, most regimes, which often faced acute problems of achieving national integration, adopted authoritarian measures. (As the experience of Ghana showed between 1957 and 1964, and Zimbabwe in early 1983, multi-party states might also adopt such measures, especially where the ruling party occupies a dominant position.)

Despite this fairly uniform pattern of one-party states and presidential rule, one would expect on *a priori* grounds that African capitalist and populist–socialist regimes would have a better record in observing human rights than the Afro-Marxist regimes. This is firstly because the latter alone have transcendental goals – the achievement of socio-economic transformation – and may need to apply coercion in order to achieve them, and secondly because, where independence was gained through a protracted liberation struggle (as in Angola and Mozambique), certain areas of the country will not have been politicised by guerrilla activity and are likely to resist fundamental social change. Cases can be quoted to substantiate this proposition.[25] Among the populist-socialist states, Algeria has a mostly good record, especially under President Chadli Bendjedid, while mainland Tanzania (as distinct from Zanzibar under Sheikh Abeid Karume) has a moderate one, its image being somewhat tarnished by the practice of political detention over most of the 22-year post-independence period. Of the African capitalist states, Botswana, the Ivory Coast and Senegal have upheld human dignity. Though the Nigerian military regimes of 1966–79 proscribed all political party activity until the eve of military withdrawal, Nigeria, too, had a good record, but this was sullied by the abrupt expulsion of some two million aliens in January 1983. In Kenya, the overall human rights record was fairly good prior to 1982 – the air force revolt which occurred in August of that year was immediately preceded by a spate of illiberal government acts, and the revolt itself was harshly suppressed. However, even in the period before 1982 the weapon of preventive detention was used against opposition leaders such as Oginga Odinga and out-spoken parliamentary critics of the regime such as George Anyona, while another vigorous critic of the government, as well as a champion of the poor – Josiah M. Kariuki, MP – was murdered in March 1975 in circumstances which led a parliamentary select committee to accuse the police of staging a massive cover-up operation and to point an accusing finger at certain senior figures in the Administration.[26] The government of Zambia, which was a multi-party state until 1972 and which exhibits features both of populist socialism and African capital-ism, dealt severely with the Lumpa Church followers of Alice Lenshina just before independence and detained most of the UPP's leading members in 1971–2. Nevertheless, it generally respected human rights in the period before the abortive coup of October 1980; the press was not muzzled and, as in Kenya, the judiciary remained independent of the executive. On the other hand, both Guinea and Ethiopia have appalling human rights records, the worst periods being after the Portuguese-inspired invasion of Guinea in November 1970 and between December 1977 and April 1978 in Ethiopia when, ironically, the main victims of the 'red terror' were members of the revolutionary urban intelligentsia.

However, to quote cases selectively in this way is to distort the picture unfairly against the revolutionary regime as a regime-type. The Afro-Marxist states appear in a more favour-able light if we take different examples: Cape Verde has a good human rights record overall; Guinea-Bissau has, too, though after the 1980 coup President Luis Cabral's regime was alleged to have murdered dissidents; and Somalia respected human rights substantially prior to the 1978 coup attempt, following which (in typical fashion) an increasingly 'security conscious' regime imprisoned many of its opponents. Mozambique's record is uneven: the number of political detainees is alleged to be considerable and extensive use is made of 're-education' camps for offenders, but Samora Machel's regime has not carried out mass executions of its political opponents or used state terror in other ways as an instrument of policy. Arbitrary arrests have been reported from Angola, where a civil war situation still prevails. The African capitalist group, in turn, appears in a less favourable light if we take Burundi, where the Batutsi-dominated military regime killed thousands of the Bahutu majority in 1972; Malawi, where President Banda has dealt harshly with his opponents; Mauritania, where 'chattel slavery' (the complete ownership of one person by another) existed until 1983; Uganda, which experienced a reign of terror under Idi Amin (and which has fared little better under President Obote following his return to power in 1980); and Zaire, where Amnesty International has reported 'flagrant and gross' infringements of human rights.

Overall, the evidence supports the conclusion reached by Crawford Young:

> What stands out above all is that massive and systematic assaults upon human dignity are a function not of ideological strategy but of insecure and paranoid rulers [such as Amin (Uganda), Bokassa (Central African Republic) and Nguema (Equatorial Guinea)]. The quite insignificant role of repression in a number of Afro-Marxist states demonstrates that this option – perhaps because of the 'soft', non-Stalinist form of Marxism–Leninism in Africa – does not require *gulag archipelagoes* or the unlimited terror of a Pol Pot. Nor is there support for the O'Donnell argument in the Latin American context that capitalism – international and domestic – can survive only through the creation of a powerful bureaucratic-authoritarian, national-security state strong enough to contain and depoliticize the 'popular sectors'.[27]

It is important to avoid a narrow moral stand that takes insufficient account of the very real threat posed by dissident elements to the national security of states, such as Mozambique, which are grappling with the problem of social reconstruction amidst formidable economic obstacles, or for that matter does not recognise the immense sacrifices made by certain of the socialist states, notably Angola and Mozambique, in support of the liberation movements in Rhodesia and Namibia, as compared with the more ambiguous position taken by a state such as Zambia. Nevertheless, we believe that many Marxist scholars give insufficient attention to the human rights performance of Afro-Marxist regimes and that they are guilty of casuistry in sometimes equating human rights with bourgeois values. Nor is it enough to argue that where, as in Ethiopia and Guinea, human rights performance is abysmal and results in a massive outflow of refugees, such regimes are not yet socialist, but are said to be either in transition to socialism or preparing to embark upon such a transition. For in circumstances such as those described in Ethiopia and Guinea in chapter 8, socialism is debased and discredited. We end this section with a further quotation from Professor Sklar, for whom 'liberal Marxism' is not a contradiction in terms:

> In newly developing countries, as elsewhere, the founda-
> tions of class domination include political factors that are
> basic to the structure of society. Of them, the most important
> is the presence or absence of liberty – meaning, at the very
> least, freedom of speech, freedom of political association, and
> limited government. In the absence of liberty, democracy
> will collapse upon an insubstantial foundation, and attempts
> to build socialism will be retarded, if not foiled, by
> dominant-class practices. This conclusion is supported by
> the decline of socialist thought and practice under various
> authoritarian regimes that were, at first, dedicated to the
> elimination of class privilege and the prevention of bourgeois
> rule ... there should be a working (or subject) class
> struggle for liberty as well as equality in Africa.[28]

In somewhat tardy recognition of the need to uphold human rights in Africa, the OAU established a human rights commission in 1979.

Participation

Crawford Young argues that 'participation . . . is not a measure that clearly distinguishes the three pathways'. That this is, substantially, a valid comment will be seen from an examination of the structures which exist for popular participation.

One of the post-independence trends to which we have earlier drawn attention was the progressive decline of the party as the centre of power and decision-making and the corresponding rise of the bureaucracy. In Republican Ghana, the CPP at its end 'was struggling to survive . . . by imprisoning its opponents', according to Dennis Austin, while Aristide Zolberg, writing in 1966, anticipated that Ghana, Guinea, the Ivory Coast, Mali and Senegal would soon be 'composed of a senescent party and of a young, vigorous governmental bureaucracy'.[29] The phenomenon of party decline was widespread: it was also to be found, for example, in Zambia where, following the creation of the one-party state in 1972, UNIP's up-country organisation crumbled and its officials became demoralised; in Algeria and Nasser's Egypt, where the FLN and the Arab Socialist Union respectively were moribund; and in Guinea-Bissau, where the PAIGC tended to atrophy. Not surprisingly, in states such as these the party was ill-equipped to mobilise the population for economic development through self-help; in Kenya, President Kenyatta purposely made the provincial administration rather than KANU his 'agent of development'.

Tanzania was one of the few states which achieved independence around 1960 to take active steps to check this party decline, as well as to broaden the opportunities for popular participation; it devised, for example, a new parliamentary electoral system which combined both a party ballot and a popular vote. Variants of this system, which was first introduced in Tanzania in 1965, have been followed by several other non-Marxist states, including the Ivory Coast, Kenya and Zambia. Though such elections do not allow voters to change the direction of government policy (let alone unseat the government itself) – the issues are local and personal and all candidates belong to the ruling party – they have frequently resulted in the defeat of government ministers; these elections are more meaningful than the plebiscitary type of election typical of most of Francophone Africa. We have also noted earlier that in parts of Anglophone Africa, presidential elections allow the electors to vote 'Yes' or 'No' for a single presidential candidate and that a high 'No' vote is tantamount to a vote of 'no confidence' in the government – the 'No' vote in Zambia's Southern Province, a former opposition area, was substantial (though less than 50 per cent) in 1978. Nevertheless, as far as real voter choice is concerned, one-party state elections, whether parliamentary or presidential, are a poor substitute for multi-party elections of the kind that were held following the restoration of civilian rule in Ghana in 1969 and 1979 and in Nigeria in 1979, as well as at the end of the liberation struggle in Zimbabwe in 1980. In Senegal, too, voters in recent years have been able to exercise a more meaningful choice than is possible in one-party states, however enlightened. This is because a constitutional revision of 1976 allowed two political parties other than the governing party, the PSS, to register and compete in the legislative and presidential elections of February 1978. While electoral conflict in Senegal remains subject to tight governmental control and the regime remains presidential in essentials, President Abdou Diouf has now removed virtually all the restrictions on political party registration and a plethora of parties has emerged.[30]

The experience of political parties which, like FRELIMO in Mozambique and the MPLA in Angola, engaged in protracted guerrilla warfare to win independence, was very different from parties like the CPP and the PDCI. For FRELIMO, it was said: 'in our struggle everything, absolutely everything, depends on the people', and regimes established by such parties placed a higher premium on grass-roots popular participation than on representative democracy of, say, the Nigerian type; in Portuguese Africa especially there was no tradition of democratic rule. In Mozambique, as we saw in chapter 8, FRELIMO early set up 'dynamising groups' to undertake the work of mobilisation and organisation and, in the latter part of 1977, 27,000 deputies were elected at all levels to serve on people's assemblies, which were, *inter alia*, to control the state apparatus. Not all the regime's experiments were successful, however – the early attempt to establish workers' control of industry ran into difficulties, though workers' committees have subsequently been revived and made popularly elective; they were given a major say in formulating the 1982 state plan. It has, moreover, not been easy for FRELIMO to replace the experienced party personnel who, following independence, became absorbed in affairs of state and, like one-party states of a different origin, Mozambique has had to grapple with the problem of mounting bureaucratisation. Potentially, the latter is a serious problem: under the Leninist principle of democratic centralism, key decisions are taken centrally and it is therefore vitally important for party and state bureaucrats to be in close touch with the people. President Machel is aware of this need and the conversion of FRELIMO into a vanguard-type party in 1977 was taken to revitalise the party and control the state apparatus.

However, this step – the creation of a vanguard party – carries its own danger of narrowing the base of party recruitment. This was recognised by Tanzania's Presidential Commission on the One Party State in 1965, which decisively rejected the argument that the party should see itself as an élite group – 'a minority ideologically dedicated who provide from above the leadership necessary to activate the inert mass of the community'.[31] Crawford Young takes up this point and argues that Leninist vanguard movements based on democratic centralism will become 'weapons for control rather than instruments of participation'. This is a valid argument though, as the following discussion of decentralisation shows, the same danger is present in all one-party states, including those which have retained a mass-type structure.

The decentralisation measures introduced (often with loud fanfare) in many states, including Tanzania and Zambia, have had precisely the opposite effect from that publicly stated to be intended; they have increased central control and (except perhaps at village level in Tanzania) reduced opportunities for citizen participation. In Anglophone Africa, representative rural local authorities have been variously abolished (Tanzania, though steps to revive them are now being taken), indefinitely suspended (Sierra Leone), stripped of their major functions (Kenya), or replaced by non-popularly elected district councils, dominated by party office-holders (Zambia).

With French-speaking African states tending to retain a variant of the French prefectoral system which they inherited at independence, the emphasis throughout most of Anglophone and Francophone Africa has been on the deconcentration of administrative authority rather than on political devolution. (Kenya is a prime example of this pattern and federal Nigeria the most important exception to it.) The reasons – apart from the obvious ones of the paranoiac ruler who is reluctant to share his power with anyone and the government which is too uncertain of its own legitimacy to test its popularity at the polls – are varied. An early post-independence consideration was the political risk, in view of the country's often fragile national unity, attached to the creation of strong regional assemblies intermediate between the centre and the locality (where, in Anglophone Africa especially, inadequately staffed and under-financed local authorities were sometimes retained). This risk has diminished considerably in most states, though by no means all – certainly not in 'broken-back' states such as Chad and Uganda. In any case, economic considerations have almost everywhere remained. Central governments, with limited resources at their disposal, fear that these resources will be entirely used by locally elected representatives for social welfare measures – schools and clinics, roads and bridges – rather than for productive investment. In the event, the retention of tight central control and the denial of meaningful popular participation have proved a doubtful strategy. Zambia's experience is not atypical: on the one hand, the rural people have lacked the incentive to grow sufficient food to meet local needs, let alone to provide a surplus for export; on the other hand, ill-conceived central government policies (or policies embarked upon but not sustained) have been largely responsible for the failure of successive plans to reduce the rural–urban gap and to provide employment opportunities.

The overall picture is therefore clear: in the post-independence period, African governments have placed much more emphasis on political control than on political participation. Even if we accept Henry Bienen's argument, based on his study of Kenya, that the administration itself can become 'a vehicle' for citizen access to the state, the general trend in Africa (though not, according to Bienen, in Kenya) has been towards a shrinking of the political arena and a consequent reduction in the levels of popular participation.[32] Though it is rather too early to assess the record of some of the 'second wave' of Afro-Marxist states, and notably Mozambique, this same trend towards increased state control is already discernible; this is certainly the case in Ethiopia, despite the existence of some participatory structures, such as the peasant associations formed to administer the land reforms. Crawford Young identifies Nigeria, Kenya, Tanzania and Mozambique as countries with 'a somewhat stronger participation record than the continental norm', but reminds us of the significant fact that all ideological camps are represented on this list.

State Capacity

By the term 'state capacity', we mean the capacity of the institutions of state to fulfil the development goals which that state's leadership, whether civilian or military, has set itself. Since leaders of the Afro-Marxist state aim at the total transformation of society, Crawford Young is right to assert that 'the demands on state capacity are highest for the Afro-Marxist state, with its aspiration for a command economy, comprehensive central planning, and an extensive public sector.'[33] Yet it is precisely the Marxist state which often (though not invariably) has the weakest legacy of public institutions. This is obviously true of the ex-Portuguese states of Angola, Mozambique and Guinea-Bissau, where colonial educational provision for Africans was sparse and Africanisation policies were, in consequence, virtually non-existent. At independence in these states, an indigenous public service had to be created virtually from scratch and a guerrilla force had to be converted into a regular army. The state had to take over enterprises abandoned by departing Portuguese settlers and to revive an economy depleted by long years of war. In desperation, Angola turned for technical (as well as military) help to the Soviet bloc and Cuba, while Mozambique recruited some 5,000 young professionals, sympathetic to the regime's aspirations, from both East and West.

It is not easy to think of any African capitalist or populist–socialist state which has faced such formidable problems; perhaps Zaire, which was catapulted into independence by Belgium within a brief six months, comes closest, though she had the benefit of a large number of primary-school leavers, including many with technical skills. As compared with neighbouring Angola and Mozambique, the inherited man-power situation of Zimbabwe (which can, perhaps, be more accurately characterised as a populist–socialist rather than Marxist state) was very favourable and has enabled her government to embark on a quite rapid programme of African-isation. Again, by contrast with the ex-Portuguese Afro-Marxist states, African capitalist states such as Gabon, Kenya and the Ivory Coast and other populist–socialist states such as Algeria and Ghana under Nkrumah inherited both a stronger administrative machinery (largely modelled on the institutions of the metropolitan countries) and less ambitious goals. The breadth of goals in relation to state capacity is important and, in this regard, there is cause to question Nyerere's assertion that 'no under-developed country can afford to be anything but socialist'.

Though the leaders of African capitalist states were not lacking in nationalist sentiment, and we have argued earlier that it is wrong to regard them merely as imperialist stooges, they saw no threat to state autonomy by entering into technical assistance agreements with the former colonial power and other Western governments; the Ivory Coast stands out for its reliance on French personnel and the slow rate at which it Africanised the public service, police and army. However, it would be mistaken to assert that non-Afro-Marxist regimes invariably inherited strong administrations – the latter only *appear* strong in relation to the weakness of the Portuguese legacy. Of course, the picture across Africa varies considerably: the institutional inheritance was (again, in comparative terms) enviable in a few states such as Kenya and the Sudan, and generally better in West African states, with their longer colonial association and absence of settler politics, than in East, Central and most of Southern Africa. However, it remains true that 'underdeveloped countries tend to have underdeveloped administrations', and the fact that the ruling party often proved weak within a few years of independence did not mean that the administration was therefore strong – though, by contrast, it sometimes was and came to be relied upon heavily by successor military regimes.

This relative administrative incapacity would have mattered less if the new African states had been able to rely on an extensive indigenous private sector to develop their economies. Indigenous entrepreneurial activity, however, was generally limited (though, as Nicola Swainson has shown for Kenya, not necessarily non-existent),[34] and the state had itself to assume many of the tasks which in more developed market-economy-type states are left to the private sector. Moreover where, as in Zambia, the latter was extensive, it was dominated by expatriates – employed, in the Zambian case, predominantly by South African companies – and nationalist-minded politicians were anxious to wrest control of the economy from foreign hands. As a result, in virtually all African states, irrespective of ideological commitment, a vast expansion of public enterprise activity has taken place in the post-independence period. Unfortunately, as we saw in chapter 6, the record of performance of most of the newly-created 'parastatal' bodies – both statutory boards and state companies – has been disappointing, though the fault has often been less that of the staff manning these bodies than government interference with their operation; many governments have appointed ineffective management boards and dictated industrial location, pricing and investment policies. While it is true that state (and, for that matter, party) bureaucrats have done well for themselves as members of their country's 'managerial bourgeoisie', it is also fair to add that public servants in many states have a good record of performance given the adverse conditions under which they so often have to operate; these conditions have included political instability, ill-considered presidential policies and frequent shifts in public policy, almost constant ministerial reorganisation, and the frequent transfer of ministers and personnel. So much energy has been absorbed in keeping the state machinery going that fundamental administrative reform has been neglected, so that in most states the civil service (for example) has retained both the rigid hierarchical structure and the élite status inherited from the colonial era.

Crawford Young therefore correctly points out that, while

the Afro-Marxist state makes the highest demands on state capacity, 'The scope of state action in all three development models places a high premium on the effectiveness and capacity of public institutions.'[35] He goes on to substantiate with examples his argument that there is not 'an extensive overlap of patterns of state capacity expansion and ideology'. Of the African capitalist group, Gabon, the Ivory Coast and Kenya have relatively effective state apparatuses; Nigeria's record is uneven, revealing a high capacity in certain spheres, such as administering the 1979 elections, but lower standards of performance in terms of probity and rural development. Among the populist–socialist states, Algeria has (Young maintains) constructed 'a reasonably competent government' which manages a large segment of the economy, while Tanzania draws mixed appraisals – some highly critical, others much less so. Of the Afro-Marxist states, Benin under Colonel Mathieu Kérékou has demonstrated 'reasonable capacity', while the prospects of developing a similar capacity in Mozambique are judged to be fairly good.

Professor Young finds the gap between regime objectives and state capacity to be most evident in Ethiopia, which lacks an effective rural administration and has had to rely on peasant associations to execute the revolutionary land reforms of 1975. Other examples which might be quoted are capitalist Zaire, where public institutions are mostly weak and the government has sometimes had to turn to private corporations or even missionary societies to undertake road work and to manage social programmes;[36] Nkrumah's Ghana, where a potentially capable administrative service suffered disruption due to the President's political excesses and the creation within his office of divisions paralleling existing ministries; and Angola, where no more than the rudiments of a civil service yet exist.

As Young says, the competence of the state is indeed 'fundamental to all developmental designs'. It is, however, extremely difficult to compare one type of regime's achievements in *enlarging* state capacity with that of another. For in measuring performance by this criterion above all, many factors must be weighed, including the colonial legacy, the strength or weakness of the inherited institutions and manpower, arrangements for training the latter, and the breadth of the goals set by the political leadership. What can be said is that on all these counts, a number of the 'second wave' of socialist states face an up-hill task in trying to improve their state capacity; this is a vitally important task since the failure to accomplish it will react adversely on economic performance.

Does Ideology Matter?

Ideology does matter in the sense that it determines the development strategy which a particular state adopts; the contrast between the strategies pursued by a Marxist regime such as Ethiopia and a capitalist regime such as neighbouring Kenya is very sharp. However, it is not easy to say on the basis of Crawford Young's six criteria that regime performance is determined by ideological commitment; other factors, such as resource endowment and the quality of a states's political leadership, must obviously be taken into account. Taking the post-independence period as a whole and excluding the oil-rich states, capitalist Ivory Coast and Kenya have achieved high rates of growth, though some observers believe that this growth cannot be sustained. We have suggested that their performance, like that of Botswana and Malawi, leads to the speculation that the market-economy formula, which entails close links with the West, may be most conducive to rapid growth; however, we also pointed out, by quoting the notorious case of Zaire, that such growth can by no means be guaranteed. The socialist regimes – both Afro-Marxist and populist–socialist – have, with one or two partial exceptions such as Benin, performed indifferently. Even 'when all allowances are made', writes Colin Leys (whose category of 'socialist' is broader than that adopted here),

> the general economic record of the African socialist countries has also disappointed sympathetic observers. Several of them have succumbed to antisocialist coups (Mali, Ghana, and perhaps Guinea-Bissau). In others, socialism has reduced itself largely to the nationalization of major foreign assets, combined with redistributive, welfarist, and normally agrarian rhetoric, more or less imperfectly matched by

performance on the part of the single party or military leadership (e.g. Zambian 'humanism'). Others have not yet really emerged from the trauma of the liberation struggle. In the socialist camp, Tanzania stands out, like the Ivory Coast and Kenya in the capitalist camp, as the focus of debate, because of its persisting socialist initiative and a relatively well-sustained growth rate unfavoured by natural resource endowment.[37]

The socialist regimes (both Marxist and populist) attach considerable importance to the achievement of equality and citizen participation; they avoid the grossest forms of inequality – the wide gap between the very rich and the very poor to be found in the Ivory Coast, Kenya and Nigeria – but do not otherwise perform significantly better on this count than the capitalist regimes. Nor can they match Nigeria (when under civilian rule) in the extent of citizen participation, though, to be fair, their emphasis on grass-roots participatory democracy rather than on representative democracy makes comparison difficult. While the capitalist states operate voluntarily within the international capitalist framework and the external dependence of the socialist states is enforced, it is not easy to say that, in practical terms, one type of regime is more autonomous than another. There is also little to choose between the various regimes in respect of human dignity and the expansion of state capacity.

An important conclusion is that because of their limited state capacity at independence, the economic constraints within which they often have to work, and their ambitious goal of socio-economic transformation, many of the 'second wave' of socialist states, and especially the ex-Portuguese colonies, have a long up-hill struggle to achieve high rates of economic growth. If our earlier argument is accepted that growth is essential for *all* states – for the reason, noted by Amilcar Cabral, that 'people are not fighting for ideas' but expect to gain material advantages and because, as Erik Svendsen pointed out, 'the expectations of the people cannot be removed by a higher political consciousness'[38] – the legitimacy of regimes which fail to improve the people's standard of living will eventually be undermined. In these circumstances, the political leadership may be tempted to increase the level of state coercion, thereby curtailing liberty, and to limit popular participation. The scarcity of economic resources will also make equality less meaningful and may lead the regime to rely increasingly on external support, thus threatening state autonomy. These are not fanciful, but very real dangers: given the present international economic climate and barring geological good fortune, such as the finding of rich deposits of oil or uranium, significant growth will be even more difficult for *all* African states to achieve than it has been over the past two 'development decades'. Again, we quote Professor Leys:

> More than four fifths of the sub-Saharan African countries still fall in the low-income category of developing countries (with annual per capita incomes of less than $360 in 1978), and their average rate of growth per capita of 0.9 percent over the two decades was the lowest of all the regions of the Third World. Worse, the World Bank's most optimistic forecast is that the African countries will experience only a one percent average annual per capita growth rate in the 1980s; more likely they will on balance experience a slight decline, with a growing number of people in absolute poverty.[39]

Leys also points out that most African countries have high population growth rates (closer to 3 than to 2 per cent per annum), and this means that economic growth will need to be very high, by world standards, if Africans are to be better off.

African states, like the great majority of states in the Third World, are dependent on a world capitalist system, with its tendency to periodic crises which – as in the early 1930s and over the past decade – always hit the periphery the hardest. The general, stark picture in recent years has been that Third World states receive low prices for their produce on the world market, yet have to pay inflated prices for their imports. President Nyerere of Tanzania illustrated this point vividly in his address to the nation on 9 December 1981:

> In 1973 we suddenly began to have to pay more than four times as much for our oil as we had paid before that. Since

then the price of oil has gone up many times . . . for the amount of money with which we used to buy thirteen barrels of oil, we now only get one.

Other prices of the goods we have to buy from abroad have also increased greatly. We have to give about four times as much cotton to buy a 7-ton lorry as we had to give in 1972, or ten times as much tobacco or three times as much cashew. This means that the amount of tobacco which used to be sufficient for ten lorries is now only enough to buy one lorry.[40]

The result for African states is acute foreign-exchange problems and heavy foreign indebtedness. The cost of servicing Zambia's debts accounted for about half the nation's falling foreign-exchange earnings in 1982, while the World Bank predicts that by 1990 repaying and servicing old debts will use up over 80 per cent of all new borrowing by the African countries.[41] While the African states can as of *right* (as retribution for past exploitation) press the industrialised states of the 'North' to release them from this 'debt-trap' and increase the proportion of aid which is given in the form of outright grants, it would be foolhardy to be over-optimistic. Little that is of concrete benefit to the Third World has yet emerged from the 1980 Brandt Report or from the more positive follow-up report of 1983. U.S. aid fell from 0.53 per cent of U.S. GNP in 1960 to 0.18 per cent in 1980, compared with the target for the Second Development Decade of 0.7 per cent.[42] Nor can much be expected of the initiatives for a New International Economic Order, which only France and the Nordic countries among the developed states have consistently supported.

What matters above all is that the African states should secure more favourable terms of trade and that they should be assisted to help themselves. Self-reliant strategies, which place emphasis on the internal mobilisation rather than the external infusion of resources, are important. On the other hand, to achieve autarchy is impossible in an inter-dependent world; like it or not, African economies are dependent economies and there is no easy way out of their present or future difficulties. As Colin Leys has written:

The most important shortcoming of dependency theory is

that it *implies* that there is an alternative, and preferable, kind of development of which the dependent economies are capable, but which their dependency prevents them from achieving – when this alternative does not in fact exist as an available historical option.[43]

Sadly, the options open to African states within their chosen development strategy are strictly limited. They include the pursuit of goals which are realistically related to existing institutional capacity and the attempt, at the same time, to expand that capacity and thus make possible the attainment of more ambitious goals. There is an obvious and urgent need for African states to step up food production to levels adequate to national needs, and thus cut out costly imports of foodstuffs; this will entail a policy of maximum support for the peasant sector of the economy. They can also attempt to improve their bargaining position in relation to the industrialised states in the Northern hemisphere. Given the sharp internal divisions to which it is subject, the OAU is a weak vessel for this purpose, while past attempts to form regional political unions, such as the Mali federation, have mostly foundered. Perhaps the best immediate hope for concerted action by African states lies in regional functional unions such as ECOWAS and SADCC, as well as in continued membership of the ACP group of states which, in 1978–9, displayed remarkable unanimity in negotiating 'Lomé II' with the EEC.

   Samir Amin has rightly argued that Third World countries cannot afford 'to ignore the real, and even great, diversity of conditions that exist among themselves. On the contrary, this diversity should be brought out into the open, objectively analysed, and practical measures of active cooperation evolved and implemented which take full account of them.'[44] The importance of this statement is borne out by experience within SADCC since its foundation in 1979. As Paul Goodison shows, SADCC is subject to internal contradictions which stem in part from conflicts of national interest; there are also conflicts between different socio-economic groupings, some within and some straddling national borders. These internal contradictions must be resolved if the Southern African region is to avoid creating new forms of dependence through the indiscriminate search for foreign aid and investment. At present, the interests of SADCC and the West converge, but they may cease to do so when the priority within SADCC eventually shifts from improving transport and communication links between member states to that of creating a regionally integrated and balanced industrial economy.[45] So long as SADCC, ECOWAS and most other functional groupings in Africa remain dependent on external backing for their programmes, they must, through active co-operation, try to ensure that foreign aid and investment are channelled into projects which are of their own choosing and which are compatible with their long-term objectives.

*   *   *

In this concluding chapter, and throughout this book, we have followed Crawford Young in distinguishing between African capitalist, populist–socialist and Afro-Marxist regimes. A more fully elaborated and sophisticated typology could undoubtedly have been utilised. However, we have not tried to construct such a typology because the more refined and specific the categories, the more precise must be the judgements concerning individual cases. Unfortunately, the data is too frequently incomplete so that the record adds up to a very mixed (and uncertain) picture. Moreover, a particular state may straddle a number of categories due to changes of regime, among other causes. We have also not considered it worthwhile to enter the current debate as to how Africa's radical regimes should most appropriately be designated – as states embarking on the transition to socialism; as states in transition to socialism; as socialist states; or as new communist/Afro-communist states.[46] Stronger arguments can be advanced in favour of each of the first three descriptions than of the last. Since all the radical states claim attachment to Marxist–Leninist principles, even though not all ruling parties have yet become vanguard-type parties, the designation 'Afro-Marxist states' seems to us as good as any other.

In concluding this study, it is necessary to stress that the primary solutions to Africa's development problems are of a long-term nature and that none of the available development options will make a decisive difference in the short-term. The severe pressures to which African states have been subjected since the mid-1970s have not simply arrested development, but for many states have entailed a burdensome legacy with which they will have to cope in the years to come. Even if the international economic climate was to become more favourable in the foreseeable future, the damage to the administrative and physical infrastructure which many states have experienced since the mid-1970s, as well as the heavy burden of debt which their governments must manage, mean that African states would require an extended recuperation before they could benefit from even markedly improved conditions.

Further Reading

Geertz, C., 'Ideology as a Cultural System', in Apter, D. E. (ed.), *Ideology and Discontent* (New York: The Free Press, 1964).

IDS Sussex Bulletin, vol. 12, no. 2 (April 1981) – 'Britain on Brandt'.

International Journal, vol. xxxv (Autumn 1980): special issue on 'Africa's Prospects'.

Kirkpatrick, C., and Nixson, F., 'Transnational Corporations and Economic Development', *Journal of Modern African Studies*, vol. 19, no. 3 (September 1981).

Legum, C., *et al.*, *Africa in the 1980s: A Continent in Crisis* (New York: McGraw-Hill, 1979).

Leys, C., 'African Economic Development in Theory and Practice', *Dædalus*, vol. iii, no. 2 (Spring 1982).

Lofchie, M. F. (ed.), *The State of the Nations: Constraints on Development in Independent Africa* (Berkeley:University of California Press, 1971).

North-South: A Programme for Survival, and *Common Crisis* – Reports of the Independent Commission on International Development Issues under the Chairmanship of Willy Brandt (London: Pan Books, 1980, 1983).

Rosberg, C. G., and Callaghy, T. M. (eds.), *Socialism in Sub-Saharan Africa:A New Assessment* (Berkeley: Institute of International Studies, University of California, 1979).

Rothchild, D., and Curry, R. L., Jr., *Scarcity, Choice and Public Policy in Middle Africa* (Berkeley: University of California Press, 1978).

Sklar, R. L., *Democracy in Africa* – presidential address to the 25th annual meeting of the African Studies Association, Washington D.C., 5

November 1982 (Los Angeles: African Studies Center, University of California, Los Angeles).

Young, C., *Ideology and Development in Africa* (New Haven: Yale University Press, 1982).

Notes and References

All references are given in full at the first mention and are limited thereafter to the name of the author and the year of publication. The bibliography lists all the documents cited in the text.

Chapter 1: Introduction: African Politics since Independence

1. M. F. Lofchie (ed.), *The State of the Nations: Constraints on Development in Independent Africa* (Berkeley: University of California Press, 1971), pp. 12–13.
2. W. H. Morris-Jones, 'Dominance and Dissent: Their inter-relations in the Indian party system', *Government and Opposition*, vol. 1, no. 4 (July–September 1966), p. 452.
3. See W. H. Friedland, 'For a Sociological Concept of Charisma', New York State School of Industrial and Labor Relations, Reprint Series No. 160 (New York, 1964), pp. 20–1.
4. Quoted in I. Wallerstein, 'Elites in French-Speaking West Africa', *Journal of Modern African Studies*, vol. 3, no. 1 (May 1965), p. 24.
5. J. K. Nyerere, *Freedom and Socialism: A Selection from Writings and Speeches, 1965–67* (Dar es Salaam: Oxford University Press, 1968), p. 15.
6. W. H. Friedland, 'Basic Social Trends', in W. H. Friedland and C. G. Rosberg, Jr (eds.), *African Socialism* (Stanford University Press, 1964), ch. 1.
7. A. R. Zolberg, *Creating Political Order: The Party-States of West Africa* (Chicago: Rand McNally, 1966), p. 125.
8. R. W. Johnson, 'Guinea', in J. Dunn (ed.), *West African States: Failure and Promise. A Study in Comparative Politics* (Cambridge University Press, 1978), p. 53; R. E. Stryker, 'A Local Perspective on Development Strategy in the Ivory Coast', in Lofchie (1971), p. 137; I. Wallerstein, 'Decline of the Party in Single-Party African States', in J. La Palombara and M. Weiner (eds.), *Political Parties and Political Development* (Princeton University Press, 1966), p. 208; D. B. Cruise O'Brien, 'Senegal', in Dunn (1978), pp. 186–7.
9. B. Munslow, 'A Critique of Theories of Socialist Transition on the Periphery: Some Preliminary Comments', paper presented to the 1981 annual conference of the Development Studies Association, University of Oxford, fn. 17; O'Brien, 'Senegal', p. 186.
10. Stryker in Lofchie (1971), p. 136.

11. R. L. Sklar, 'The Nature of Class Domination in Africa', *Journal of Modern African Studies*, vol. 17, no. 4 (1979), p. 540.

12. *Ibid.*, pp. 535, 539–40.

13. P. François, 'Class Struggles in Mali', *Review of African Political Economy*, no. 24 (May–August 1982), p. 35.

14. Sklar (1979), p. 531.

15. For a good summary, see J. S. Barker, 'Political Economy and Political Management', in *The African Review*, vol. 1, no. 3 (January 1972), pp. 148–9.

16. C. E. Welch, Jr (ed.), *Political Modernization: A Reader in Comparative Political Change* (Belmont, California: Wadsworth, 1967), pp. 2, 4.

17. L. W. Pye, *Politics, Personality, and Nation Building: Burma's Search for Identity* (New Haven, Yale University Press, 1962); W. W. Rostow, *Stages of Economic Growth: A Non-Communist Manifesto* (Cambridge University Press, 1960).

18. S. P. Huntington, 'Political Development and Political Decay', *World Politics*, vol. xvii, no. 3 (1965), and *Political Order in Changing Societies* (New Haven: Yale University Press, 1968).

19. See P. R. Brass, 'Political Participation, Institutionalisation and Stability in India', *Government and Opposition*, vol. 4, no. 1 (1969).

20. S. N. Eisenstadt, 'Initial Institutional Patterns of Political Modernization', in Welch (1967), p. 247.

21. E. Shils, 'The Concept and Function of Ideology', *A Reprint from the International Encyclopedia of the Social Sciences*, vol. 7 (New York: Macmillan and the Free Press, 1968), p. 67. C. S. Whitaker, Jr, has challenged the thesis that the impact of modernisation is always to erode and destroy tradition. See his book, *The Politics of Tradition, Continuity and Change in Northern Nigeria, 1946–1966* (Princeton University Press, 1970).

22. F. W. Riggs, *Administration in Developing Countries: The Theory of Prismatic Society* (Boston: Houghton-Mifflin, 1964); D. Cruise O'Brien, 'Modernization, Order, and the Erosion of a Democratic Ideal: American Political Science, 1960–70', *Journal of Development Studies*, vol. 8, no. 4 (July 1972), pp. 359, 361.

23. R. L. Sklar, *Nigerian Political Parties: Power in an Emergent African Nation* (Princeton University Press, 1963); J. S. Coleman, *Nigeria: Background to Nationalism* (Berkeley: University of California Press, 1958); C. Pratt, *The Critical Phase in Tanzania, 1945–1968: Nyerere and the Emergence of a Socialist Strategy* (Cambridge University Press, 1976); I. G. Shivji *et al.*, *The Silent Class Struggle* (Dar es Salaam: Tanzania Publishing House, 1973) and I. G. Shivji, *Class Struggles in Tanzania* (London: Heinemann, 1976); J. Saul, 'African Socialism in One Country: Tanzania', in G. Arrighi and J. Saul (eds.), *Essays on the Political Economy of Africa* (New York: Monthly Review Press, 1973); Barker (1972), pp. 150–4; W. F. Ilchman and N. T. Uphoff, *The Political Economy of Change* (Berkeley: University of California Press, 1971).

24. C. Leys, *Underdevelopment in Kenya: The Political Economy of Neo-Colonialism* (London: Heinemann, 1975), p. 7. I have followed closely in this section Professor Leys' account in chapter 1 of his book. For a good, recent

survey of the literature, see P. Limqueco and B. McFarlane (eds.), *Neo-Marxist Theories of Development* (London: Croom Helm, 1983).

25. Leys, (1975), p. 14.

26. *Ibid.*, p. 10.

27. I. G. Shivji, 'The Class Struggle Continues' (Dar es Salaam, 1973) and Shivji (1976); T. M. Shaw, 'Zambia's Foreign Policy', in O. Aluko (ed.), *The Foreign Policies of African States* (London: Hodder and Stoughton, 1977), and T. M. Shaw and A. T. Mugomba, 'The Political Economy of Regional Détente: Zambia and Southern Africa', *Journal of African Studies*, 4 (Winter, 1977). Shaw's views are further elaborated in D. G. Anglin and T. .M. Shaw, *Zambia's Foreign Policy: Studies in Diplomacy and Dependence* (Boulder, Colorado: Westview Press, 1979).

28. R. L. Sklar, *Corporate Power in an African State: The Political Impact of Multinational Mining Companies in Zambia* (Berkeley: University of California Press, 1975), p. 201.

29. B. Warren, *Imperialism: Pioneer of Capitalism* (London: Verso, 1980); C. Leys, 'Capital Accumulation, Class Formation and Dependency' in R. Miliband and J. Saville (eds.), *The Socialist Register, 1978* (London: Merlin Press, 1978); N. Swainson, *The Development of Corporate Capitalism in Kenya, 1918–1977* (London: Heinemann, 1980), p. 288. Leys provides a list of Cowen's papers at p. 265, n. 22, of his article.

30. See the debate on Kenya between R. Kaplinsky, J. S. Henley and C. Leys in *Review of African Political Economy*, no. 17 (January–April 1980), pp. 83–113, and compare this debate with, for example, R. Jenkins, *Dependent Industrialization in Latin America* (New York: Praeger, 1977) and *Transnational Corporations and Latin American Industry* (London: Macmillan, 1983) and P. Evans, *Dependent Development: The Alliance of Multinational, State and Local Capital in Brazil* (Princeton University Press, 1979).

31. G. Hyden, *Beyond Ujamaa in Tanzania: Underdevelopment and an Uncaptured Peasantry* (London: Heinemann, 1980), p. 18 (the 'economy of affection') and *passim*; C. Young, *The Politics of Cultural Pluralism* (Madison: University of Wisconsin Press, 1976), especially ch. 2.

32. J. Lonsdale, 'States and Social Processes in Africa: A Historiographical Survey', *African Studies Review*, vol. xxiv, nos. 2/3 (June/September 1981), p. 140.

33. I. Wallerstein, *The Capitalist World Economy* (Cambridge University Press, 1979); A. Callinicos and J. Rogers, *Southern Africa after Soweto* (London: Pluto Press, 1977), p. 203, quoted in Munslow's 'A Critique of Theories of Socialist Transition' (1981). I have found Dr Munslow's paper helpful in preparing this section.

34. S. D. Mueller, 'Retarded Capitalism in Tanzania', in *The Socialist Register, 1980*; see especially B. Beckman, 'Imperialism and Capitalist Transformation: Critique of a Kenyan Debate', *Review of African Political Economy*, no. 19 (September–December 1980), pp. 48–62.

35. Munslow, 'A Critique of Theories of Socialist Transition' (1981), pp. 4–6.

36. P. Goodison, 'The Construction of Socialism in Mozambique' (B.A. Econ, dissertation, University of Manchester, April 1982), pp. 44, 78.

37. Young (1976), p. 40.
38. See p. 188.
39. Goodison (1982), pp. 22, 85; Munslow, 'A Critique of Theories of Socialist Transition' (1981), p. 4.
40. Sklar (1979), p. 537.

Chapter 2: Colonialism and the Colonial Impact

1. Quoted in R. Oliver and J. D. Fage, *A Short History of Africa* (Harmondsworth: Penguin, 1962), pp.106–7. I have drawn substantially on Oliver and Fage in this chapter. See also H. Seton-Watson, *Nations and States: An Enquiry into the Origins of Nations and the Politics of Nationalism* (London: Methuen, 1977), ch. 8.
2. J. Iliffe, *A Modern History of Tanganyika* (Cambridge University Press, 1979), p. 9, ch. 2 and *passim*.
3. E. A. Brett, *Colonialism and Underdevelopment in East Africa: The Politics of Economic Change, 1919–1939* (London: Heinemann, 1973), p. 51.
4. R. Robinson and J. Gallagher, with A. Denny, *Africa and the Victorians: The Official Mind of Imperialism* (London: Macmillan, 1961), pp. 393, 397–8.
5. Quoted in W. Rodney, *How Europe Underdeveloped Africa* (Dar es Salaam: Tanzania Publishing House, 1972, and London: Bogle-L'Ouverture, 1972), p. 162.
6. *Ibid*.
7. This section on French Africa is based substantially upon K. E. Robinson, 'Political Development in French West Africa', in C. W. Stillman (ed.), *Africa in the Modern World* (University of Chicago Press, 1955), pp. 140–81, supplemented by M. Crowder, 'Indirect Rule – French and British Style', in M. Crowder (ed.), *Colonial West Africa: Collected Essays* (London: Frank Cass, 1978), ch. 9. Professor Crowder's essay also proved helpful in preparing the first part of the subsequent section on (British) indirect rule.
8. T. Hodgkin, *Nationalism in Colonial Africa* (London: Frederick Muller, 1956), pp. 33–40.
9. W. Tordoff, *Ashanti under the Prempehs, 1888–1935* (London: Oxford University Press, 1965), pp. 301–9 and 322ff.
10. B. B. Schaffer, 'The Concept of Preparation: Some Questions about the Transfer of Systems of Government', *World Politics*, vol. xviii, no. 1 (October 1965), p. 59.
11. Hodgkin (1956), pp. 48–55. See also R. Slade, *The Belgian Congo* (London: Oxford University Press, 2nd edn, 1961).
12. G. J. Bender, *Angola under the Portuguese: The Myth and the Reality* (London: Heinemann, 1978), ch. 1; B. Munslow, *Mozambique: the Revolution and its Origins* (London: Longman, 1983), p. 8.
13. Munslow, *ibid* (1983), part 1.
14. Oliver and Fage (1962), chs. 17 and 19, provide a good and succinct account of these various phases.
15. B. Munslow, *FRELIMO and the Mozambican Revolution* (PhD

thesis, University of Manchester, April 1980), pp. 76–93, 415; Munslow, *op. cit.* (1983), part 1.

16. Quoted by A. H. M. Kirk-Greene, 'The Thin White Line: The Size of the British Colonial Service in Africa', *African Affairs*, vol. 79, no. 314 (January 1980), p. 26.
17. Oliver and Fage (1962), p. 200, and ch. 17, *passim*.
18. For the hold-up of palm-oil 'for several months' by local traders in the Eastern Palm Belt of Southern Nigeria, see D. Forde and R. Scott, *The Native Economies of Nigeria*, ed. M. Perham (London: Faber & Faber, 1946), ch. 2, especially p. 54, n. 1. On Senegal, see D. B. Cruise O'Brien, *Saints and Politicians: Essays in the Organisation of a Senegalese Peasant Society* (London: Cambridge University Press, 1975), p. 138.
19. Oliver and Fage (1962), p. 218.
20. *Ibid.*, ch. 19; Hodgkin (1956), *passim*.
21. Oliver and Fage (1962), pp. 221, 245; Rodney (1972), ch. 5.
22. Quoted in D. Austin, *Politics in Ghana, 1946–60* (London: Oxford University Press, 1964), p. 275.
23. See R. H. Bates, *Unions, Parties and Political Development – A Study of Mineworkers in Zambia* (New Haven: Yale University Press, 1971), pp. 198–200, and *passim*.

Chapter 3: Nationalism and the Transfer of Power

1. Seton-Watson, *Nations and States* (1977), p. 332.
2. Ernest Gellner stresses the importance of a homogeneous educational system for a modern society: *Contemporary Thought and Politics*, ed. J. C. Jarvie and J. Agassi (London: Routledge & Kegan Paul, 1974), p. 147. For his earlier and subsequent reflections on nationalism, see his *Thought and Change* (London: Weidenfeld & Nicolson, 1964), ch. 7, and *Nationalism and Nations* (Oxford: Blackwell, 1982).
3. See D. O. Mannoni, *Prospero and Caliban: The Psychology of Colonization* (London: Methuen, 1956).
4. Cf. Gellner (1974), pp. 154–6.
5. Tordoff (1965), p. 190; R. Young and H. A. Fosbrooke, *Smoke in the Hills. Political Tension in the Morogoro District of Tanganyika* (Evanston: Northwestern University Press, 1960), *passim*.
6. Hodgkin (1956), p. 94. This section draws substantially upon chapter 3 ('Prophets and Priests') of Hodgkin's book.
7. Coleman (1958), p. 108.
8. Quoted in *ibid*.
9. Coleman (1958), pp. 175–7; Hodgkin (1956), p. 104.
10. Hodgkin (1956), p. 99. See also B. Sundkler, *Bantu Prophets in South Africa* (London: Oxford University Press, 1961, 2nd edn).
11. See Tordoff (1965), p. 197.
12. Quoted in Hodgkin (1956), p. 111.
    Jesus, Saviour of the elect and Saviour of us all.
    We shall be the conquerors sent by You.

The Kingdom is ours. We have it.
They, the Whites, have it no longer.

13. Quoted in I. Wallerstein, 'Voluntary Associations', ch. 8 in J. S. Coleman and C. G. Rosberg, Jr. (eds.), *Political Parties and National Integration in Tropical Africa* (Berkeley: University of California Press, 1964), p. 331. I have drawn substantially upon Wallerstein's chapter in the first part of this section.

14. *Ibid.*, pp. 326–7; Hodgkin (1956), pp. 88–9.

15. See S. Low, 'The Role of Trade Unions in the Newly Independent Countries of Africa', in E. M. Kassalow (ed.), *National Labor Movements in the Post-war World* (Evanston: Northwestern University Press, 1968), pp. 215–6; G. Fischer, 'Syndicats et Décolonisation', *Présence Africaine*, no. 34–35 (October 1960–January 1961), especially pp. 23ff.; and E. J. Berg and J. Butler, 'Trade Unions', in Coleman and Rosberg (1964), p. 341.

16. V. D. Du Bois, 'Guinea', in Coleman and Rosberg (1964), p. 208.

17. Berg and Butler in Coleman and Rosberg (1964), pp. 347, 351–2.

18. *Ibid.*, p. 344.

19. *Ibid.*, pp. 348–51. The most authoritative account of trade union developments in Ghana is R. Jeffries, *Class, Power and Ideology in Ghana: The Railwaymen of Sekondi* (Cambridge University Press, 1978).

20. A. H. Amsden, 'Trade Unions and Politics: Kenya', in collected seminar papers on *Labour Unions and Political Organisations* (Institute of Commonwealth Studies, University of London, January–May 1967), no. 3, p. 122.

21. See W. H. Friedland, *VUTA KAMBA: The Development of Trade Unions in Tanganyika* (Stanford: Hoover Institution Press, 1969), and W. Tordoff, *Government and Politics in Tanzania* (Nairobi: East African Publishing House, 1967), ch. 5.

22. Jeffries (1978), p. 207 and *passim*; R. Sandbrook and R. Cohen (eds.), *The Development of an African Working Class: Studies in Class Formation and Action* (University of Toronto Press, 1975), pp. 18–19 and 313–4 (by the editors) and pp. 117–25 (by C. H. Allen on Francophone West Africa).

23. Quoted in R. Emerson and M. Kilson (eds.), *The Political Awakening of Africa* (Englewood Cliffs, N.J.: Prentice-Hall, 1965), pp. 9–10.

24. Hodgkin (1956), ch. 5, *passim*; Emerson and Kilson (1965), p. 13.

25. Quoted in Hodgkin (1956), p. 146.

26. See Austin (1964), especially ch. 2.

27. Coleman (1958), chs. 15–16; K. Ezera, *Constitutional Developments in Nigeria* (Cambridge University Press, 1960), chs. 5 and 8.

28. Hodgkin (1956), pp. 151, 164; R. S. Morgenthau, *Political Parties in French-Speaking West Africa* (Oxford: Clarendon Press, 1964), *passim*.

29. Hodgkin (1956), pp. 152–6.

30. Morgenthau (1964), p. 72.

31. See T. Hodgkin, *African Political Parties* (Harmondsworth: Penguin, 1961).

32. W. J. M. Mackenzie and K. E. Robinson (eds.), *Five Elections in Africa* (Oxford: Clarendon Press, 1960), p. 478.

33. In *One-Party Government in the Ivory Coast* (Princeton University Press, 1964), Aristide R. Zolberg notes that the PDCI 'emerged as an

organization for the masses rather than as a mass organization' (p. 185) and that it 'had created a sort of confederation of ethnic associations' (p. 129). More recently, Bonnie Campbell has drawn attention to 'the continuing importance of ethnicity as an organizational principle of the single party' in the Ivory Coast. B. Campbell, 'Ivory Coast', in Dunn (1978), p. 90.

34. See Friedland, 'For a Sociological Concept of Charisma' (see ch. 1, note 3). The quotation from Chinoy is taken from this paper.

35. Austin (1964), pp. 347, 347 n. 35, 354 (*Note* – the figures for adults aged 21 and over, and the registered electorate do not include those for five uncontested constituencies).

36. D. Austin, 'The British Point of No Return?', ch. 9 in P. Gifford and W. R. Louis (eds.), *The Transfer of Power in Africa. Decolonization, 1940–1960* (New Haven: Yale University Press, 1982), p. 234.

37. Hodgkin (1956), p. 36.

38. Morgenthau (1964), pp. 70, 72.

39. R. B. Collier, *Regimes in Tropical Africa: Changing Forms of Supremacy, 1945–75* (Berkeley: University of California Press, 1982), chs. 2 and 3, *passim*. I have drawn substantially on these chapters in this final section.

40. *Ibid.*, p. 47; see also H. F. Weiss, *Political Protest in the Congo: The Parti Solidaire Africain during the Independence Struggle* (Princeton University Press, 1967), part 1.

41. Zolberg (1966), p. 25.

42. Collier (1982), pp. 78–9. As Collier recognises, the picture was distorted because voters were allowed to cast their ballots in uncontested constituencies in French Africa and did so on a substantial scale; no voting took place in uncontested constituencies in British Africa. See *ibid.*, pp. 78 and 88.

43. *Ibid.*, p. 91. 'The bandwagon effect is a description of a process in which a dominant party is successful in mobilizing and attracting supporters', *ibid.*, p. 90.

44. Morgenthau (1964), p. 73.

45. *Ibid.*, pp. 73–4.

46. R. Luckham, 'French Militarism in Africa', *Review of African Political Economy*, no. 24 (May–August 1982), pp. 58–9; S. K. Panter-Brick, 'French African Administration', University of Zambia lecture, 1969, P.A. 320/430.

47. Austin in Gifford and Louis (1982), p. 233.

48. Seton-Watson (1977), p. 353.

49. R. H. Jackson and C. G. Rosberg distinguish between empirical statehood and juridical statehood and argue that the latter is more important than the former 'in accounting for the persistence of states in Black Africa'; indeed, 'the survival of Africa's existing states is largely an international achievement'. See their article: 'Why Africa's Weak States Persist: The Empirical and the Juridical in Statehood', *World Politics*, vol. xxxv, no. 1 (October 1982), pp. 21–2 and *passim*.

Chapter 4: State and Society

1. C. Leys, 'The Political Climate for Economic Development', *African Affairs*, vol. 65, no. 258 (1966), p. 55.
2. Quoted in C. Geertz, 'The Integrative Revolution: Primordial Sentiments and Civil Politics in the New States', in C. Geertz (ed.), *Old Societies and New States* (New York: Free Press, 1963), p. 106.
3. *The Autobiography of Kwame Nkrumah* (Edinburgh: Nelson, 1957), p. x.
4. R. Molteno, 'Cleavage and Conflict in Zambian Politics: A Study in Sectionalism', in W. Tordoff (ed.), *Politics in Zambia* (Manchester University Press, 1974), ch. 3. All subsequent references to Molteno in this chapter refer to this essay.
5. R. L. Sklar, 'Political Science and National Integration – A Radical Approach', *Journal of Modern African Studies*, vol. 5, no. 1 (1967), p. 6.
6. R. Melson and H. Wolpe, *Nigeria: Modernization and the Politics of Communalism* (Michigan State University Press, 1971), p. 6.
7. See G. de Lusignan, *French-Speaking Africa since Independence* (London: Pall Mall, 1969), pp. 159–69.
8. R. Sandbrook, 'Patrons, Clients, and Factions: New Dimensions of Conflict Analysis in Africa', *Canadian Journal of Political Science*, vol. v, no. 1 (March 1972), pp. 105–6.
9. M. Szeftel, *Conflict, Spoils and Class Formation in Zambia* (PhD thesis, University of Manchester, 1978), especially ch. 6.
10. Apart from Szeftel, the main sources of the Zambian material used in this chapter are Molteno in Tordoff (1974) and W. Tordoff (ed.), *Administration in Zambia* (Manchester University Press, 1980), especially introduction.
11. A. Kirk-Greene in A. Kirk-Greene and D. Rimmer, *Nigeria since 1970: A Political and Economic Outline* (London: Hodder & Stoughton, 1981), p. 30.
12. A. L. Epstein, *Politics in an Urban African Community* (Manchester University Press, 1958); R. Sandbrook, *Proletarians and African Capitalism: The Kenyan Case, 1962–70* (London: Cambridge University Press, 1975); A. M. Elhussein, *Decentralization and Participation in Rural Development: The Sudanese Experience* (PhD thesis, University of Manchester, February 1983), especially part 3; O'Brien, *Saints and Politicians* (1975), especially ch. 5.
13. O'Brien, *ibid.*, pp. 164–5 and ch. 5, *passim*, and D. B. Cruise O'Brien, 'Ruling Class and Peasantry in Senegal, 1960–1976: The Politics of a Monocrop Economy', in R. Cruise O'Brien (ed.), *The Political Economy of Underdevelopment: Dependence in Senegal* (Beverly Hills, California: Sage, 1979), pp. 223–5.
14. Szeftel (1978), p. 332.
15. Melson and Wolpe (1971), p. 9; C. Young, 'Patterns of Social Conflict: State, Class and Ethnicity', *Dædalus*, vol. iii, no. 2 (Spring 1982), p. 91; C. Gertzel, *The Politics of Independent Kenya* (London: Heinemann, 1970), p. 17; Kirk-Greene and Rimmer (1981), p. 16.
16. J. K. Nyerere, *Freedom and Unity: A Selection from Writings and Speeches, 1952–65* (Dar es Salaam: Oxford University Press, 1966), p. 165.

17. R. .H. Bates, *Rural Responses to Industrialisation: A Study of Village Zambia* (New Haven: Yale University Press, 1976), pp. 133–6.
18. O'Brien (1975), p. 138 and in R. C. O'Brien (1979), ch. 7.
19. Bates (1976), p. 259.
20. Sandbrook (1972), p. 107.
21. For an informed discussion, see Sandbrook and Cohen (1975).
22. M. Burawoy, 'Another Look at the Mineworker', *African Social Research*, no. 14 (December 1972), pp. 261–7, 276ff.
23. Sklar (1975), pp. 198ff.
24. Shivji (1976), pp. 76–9; Pratt (1976), pp. 241–2.
25. Nyerere (1968), p. 15.
26. See C. Pratt, 'Tanzania's Transition to Socialism', and R. H. Green, 'Tanzanian Political Economy Goals, Strategies and Results, 1967–74', in B. U. Mwansasu and C. Pratt (eds.), *Towards Socialism in Tanzania* (University of Toronto Press, 1979). In a new interpretation, Jeannette Hartmann argues that policy-making in Tanzania is a tripartite process involving the President, the government and the party. See J. Hartmann, *Development Policy-Making in Tanzania, 1962–1982: A Critique of Sociological Interpretations* (PhD thesis, University of Hull, April 1983).
27. Szeftel (1978), ch. 7; C. L. Baylies and M. Szeftel, 'The Rise of a Zambian Capitalist Class in the 1970s', *Journal of Southern African Studies*, vol. 8, no. 2 (April 1982); Swainson (1980), p. 203.
28. Szeftel (1978), p. 455.
29. Shivji (1976), p. 145; Hyden (1980), ch. 6.
30. Szeftel (1978), pp. 330–1.
31. Sklar (1979); in this article (p. 537), Sklar advances the controversial proposition that 'class relations, at bottom, are determined by relations of power, not production'.
32. See B. .J. Dudley, 'Political Parties and the 1979 Elections', in M. Dent *et al.* (eds.), *Nigeria: The First Year of Civilian Rule. The Operation of the Constitution* (Keele, N. Staffs.: The University of Keele Conference Papers (mimeo.), September 1980); Kirk-Greene and Rimmer (1981), pp. 35–41.
33. Baylies and Szeftel (1982), p. 212. Their observation is limited to Zambia, but has a wider application.
34. Sandbrook (1972), p. 115.
35. A. A. Mazrui, 'Pluralism and National Integration', in L. Kuper and M. G. Smith (eds.), *Pluralism in Africa* (Berkeley: University of California Press, 1969), p. 339.
36. Young (1976), p. 40. Young, himself a non-Marxist scholar, summarises what he believes to be the Marxist stand, as put forward by Archie Mafeje.
37. Hyden (1980), p. 18 and *passim*; Young in *Dædalus* (1982), p. 96, n. 23. For an informed discussion which bears directly on Hyden's thesis, see D. F. Bryceson, 'Peasant Commodity Production in Post-Colonial Tanzania', *African Affairs*, vol. 81, no. 325 (October 1982), p. 561, where the author argues, *inter alia*, that: 'The decline in peasants' terms of trade constitutes a very serious disincentive for peasant commodity produc-

tion, resulting in the tendency for peasants to revert to subsistence production.'
38. Young (1976), p. 40.
39. Szeftel (1978), p. 86.
40. Young (1976), ch. 2, p. 47 and *passim*.
41. See J. A. Wiseman, 'The Opposition Parties of Botswana', *Collected Papers*, vol. 4 (Centre for Southern African Studies, University of York, 1979), especially pp. 189–90.
42. This point is made by Hyden (1980), p. 30.

Chapter 5: Political Parties

1. Collier (1982), ch. 3.
2. Coleman and Rosberg (1964), especially p. 5.
3. C. F. Andrain, 'Guinea and Senegal: Contrasting Types of African Socialism', in Friedland and Rosberg (1964), pp. 165–6; François (1982), p. 27.
4. C. G. Rosberg and T. M. Callaghy (eds.), *Socialism in Sub-Saharan Africa: A New Assessment* (Berkeley: Institute of International Studies, University of California, 1979), p. 1.
5. J. Samoff, *Tanzania: Local Politics and the Structure of Power* (Madison: University of Wisconsin Press, 1974), p. 69.
6. On trade unionism in the pre-independence period, see Berg and Butler in Coleman and Rosberg (1964), ch. 9, and for a corrective of their view of union–party relationships, Jeffries (1978), p. 207 and *passim*, and Sandbrook and Cohen (1975). On Tanzania, see Friedland (1969), Tordoff (1967), ch. 5 and Shivji (1976), ch. 13.
7. H. Roberts, 'The Algerian Bureaucracy', *Review of African Political Economy*, no. 24 (May–August 1982), p. 53.
8. See Kirk-Greene and Rimmer (1981), ch. 3.
9. G. Hyden, *TANU Yajenga Nchi: Political Development in Rural Tanzania* (Lund: Scandinavian University Books, 1968), p. 241 and (1980), p. 18.
10. Collier (1982), ch. 5; G. Hyden and C. Leys, 'Elections and Politics in Single-Party Systems: The Case of Kenya and Tanzania', *British Journal of Political Science*, vol. 1, no. 2 (1972); B. Chikulo, *Rural Administration in Zambia: Organisation and Performance in Former Opposition Areas* (PhD thesis, University of Manchester, 1983), pp. 180–1.
11. Szeftel (1978), p. 395; Tordoff (1980), p. 18.
12. Samoff (1974), p. 52.
13. See J. R. Finucane, *Rural Development and Bureaucracy in Tanzania: The Case of Mwanza Region* (Uppsala: Scandinavian Institute of African Studies, 1974), ch. 6.
14. R. Chambers, *Botswana's Accelerated Rural Development Programme 1973–6: Experience and Lessons* (Gaborone: Government Printer, February 1977), p. 37.
15. D. E. Apter, *The Politics of Modernization* (University of Chicago Press, 1965), pp. 397ff.

16. The account which follows is based on J. P. Mackintosh, 'The Action Group, the Crisis of 1962 and its Aftermath', in J. P. Mackintosh *et al.*, *Nigerian Government and Politics* (London: Allen & Unwin, 1966), ch. 10.
17. See R. L. Sklar, 'Nigerian Politics in Perspective' and 'Contradictions in the Nigerian Political System', in Melson and Wolpe (1971), chs. 2 and 19; Kirk-Greene and Rimmer (1981), p. 43, table 5, on the 1979 elections; and the weekly magazine *West Africa* (London), issues for August and September 1983, on the 1983 elections. Electoral malpractices were one reason given by the military for seizing power on 31 December 1983.
18. W. Tordoff, 'The Brong–Ahafo Region', *The Economic Bulletin* (Accra), vol. 3, no. 5 (May 1959); D. Austin, *Ghana Observed: Essays on the Politics of a West African Republic* (Manchester University Press, 1976), ch. 9.
19. Quoted in Szeftel (1978), p. 335; see also Tordoff (1974), chs. 3 and 4.
20. Chikulo (1983), pp. 278–80.
21. Szeftel (1978), p. 282.
22. Chikulo (1983), pp. 228–36.
23. Szeftel (1978), p. 396.
24. Sandbrook (1972), p. 109; also p. 111.
25. *Ibid.*, p. 117. Sandbrook also quotes from John Waterbury's study of Moroccan politics: 'The entire political elite is the field of action for the alliance-building of the King, and he maintains a number of clientele groups of which he is the patron.'
26. *Ibid.*, pp. 113–5.
27. T. S. Cox, *Civil–Military Relations in Sierra Leone: A Case Study of African Soldiers in Politics* (Cambridge, Mass.: Harvard University Press, 1976), p. 135.
28. O'Brien (1975), p. 156.
29. J. Molloy, *Political Communication in Lushoto District, Tanzania* (PhD thesis, University of Kent at Canterbury, November 1971), *passim*.
30. T. Rasmussen, 'The Popular Basis of Anti-Colonial Protest', in Tordoff (1974), p. 58.
31. Samoff (1974), p. 55 and n. 37.

Chapter 6: Administration

1. R. Delavignette, *Freedom and Authority in French West Africa* (London: Oxford University Press, 1950), p. 71.
2. F. G. Burke, 'Public Administration in Africa: The Legacy of Inherited Colonial Institutions', paper presented at the World Congress of the International Political Science Association, Brussels, 18–23 September 1967, pp. 38–44 and *passim*.
3. Morgenthau (1964), p. 13.
4. O'Brien in Dunn (1978), pp. 179–80.
5. C. .M. Elliott, 'The Zambian Economy' (Lusaka, 1968, mimeo.), quoted in Tordoff (1980), pp. 6–7.
6. M. F. Lofchie, 'Representative Government, Bureaucracy, and Political Development: The African Case', *Journal of Developing Areas*, vol. II, no. 1 (October 1967), pp. 41–2.

7. Roberts (1982), p. 47. See also G. Hyden, 'Social Structure, Bureaucracy and Development Administration in Kenya', *The African Review*, vol. 1, no. 3 (January 1972), pp. 123–4.
8. See Riggs (1964), especially ch. 8; N. Kasfir, 'Prismatic Theory and African Administration', *World Politics*, vol. 21, no. 2 (January 1969).
9. Riggs (1964), p. 227.
10. The upsurge of modern academic concern with the question of corruption dates from the early 1960s. Riggs' own analysis of corruption represented an early and important contribution. Other significant contributions to this growing literature include M. McMullan, 'A Theory of Corruption', *Sociological Review*, vol. 9, no. 2 (June 1961); C. Leys, 'What is the Problem about Corruption?', *Journal of Modern African Studies*, vol. 3, no. 2 (1965); J. S. Nye, 'Corruption and Political Development: A Cost-Benefit Analysis', *American Political Science Review*, vol. LXI, no. 2 (June 1967); J. C. Scott, *Comparative Political Corruption* (Englewood Cliffs, N. J.: Prentice-Hall, 1972); V. T. Le Vine, *Political Corruption: The Ghana Case* (Stanford: Hoover Institution Press, 1975); and D. J. Gould, *Bureaucratic Corruption and Underdevelopment in the Third World: The Zaire Case* (Oxford: Pergamon Press, 1980).
11. Pratt (1976), pp. 224–5.
12. See F. W. Riggs, 'Administrative Development: An Elusive Concept', in J. D. Montgomery and W. J. Siffin (eds.), *Approaches to Development: Politics, Administration and Change* (New York: McGraw-Hill, 1966), pp. 237–44, and 'The Context of Development Administration', in F. W. Riggs (ed.), *Frontiers of Development* (Durham, N.C.: Duke University Press, 1970), p. 79.
13. H. Alavi, 'The State in Post-Colonial Societies: Pakistan and Bangladesh', *New Left Review*, no. 74 (July–August 1972).
14. C. Leys, 'The "Overdeveloped" Post Colonial State: A Re-evaluation', *Review of African Political Economy*, no. 5 (January–April 1976), p. 42.
15. B. B. Schaffer, 'Introduction: The Ideas and Institutions of Training', in B. B. Schaffer (ed.), *Administrative Training and Development* (New York: Praeger, 1974), p. 31.
16. J. A. Ballard, 'Four Equatorial States', in G. M. Carter (ed.), *National Unity and Regionalism in Eight African States* (Ithaca, N.Y.: Cornell University Press, 1966), p. 236.
17. K. G. Younger, *The Public Service in New States: A Study in Some Trained Manpower Problems* (London: Oxford University Press, 1960), p. 53; Austin (1964), p. 8, n. 10; Tordoff (1967), p. 202, (1974), p. 242 and (1980), p. 6; D. L. Dresang and R. A. Young, 'The Public Service', in Tordoff (1980), ch. 3.
18. B. Schaffer, 'Administrative Legacies and Links in the Post-Colonial State: Preparation, Training and Administrative Reform', *Development and Change*, vol. 9, no. 2 (April 1978), p. 183.
19. *Ghana: A New Charter for the Civil Service* (Accra: Government Printer, 1960), pp. 1–3.
20. J. M. Lee, 'Parliament in Republican Ghana', *Parliamentary Affairs*, vol. XVI, no. 4 (1963), p. 382.

21. Tordoff (1967), pp. 86, 103–4, (1974), ch. 7, especially p. 259, and (1980), ch. 3; Coleman and Rosberg (1964), p. 678; and L. Behrman, 'Party and State Relations in Guinea', in J. Butler and A. A. Castagno (eds.), *Boston University Papers on Africa: Transition in African Politics* (New York: Praeger, 1967), p. 335.

22. G. Hyden, 'Decentralisation in Tanzania': Summary of a lecture delivered at the University of Zambia, Lusaka, March 1973 (mimeo.), pp. 2–3; J. J. Okumu, 'The Socio-Political Setting', ch. 2 in G. Hyden, R. Jackson and J. Okumu (eds.), *Development Administration: The Kenyan Experience* (Nairobi: Oxford University Press, 1970), p. 31.

23. R. Dowse, 'Military and Police Rule', ch. 1 in D. Austin and R. Luckham (eds.), *Politicians and Soldiers in Ghana* (London: Frank Cass, 1975), p. 21; Zolberg (1966), p. 125.

24. Hyden (January 1972), p. 124.

25. Lofchie (1967), *passim*.

26. Tordoff (1980), p. 21.

27. R. S. Milne, 'Bureaucracy and Development Administration', *Public Administration*, vol. 51 (Winter 1973), pp. 413–15 and *passim*. Robert Chambers stresses the importance of procedures in rural development administration and area-based planning: see 'Planning for Rural Areas in East Africa: Experience and Prescriptions', in D. K. Leonard (ed.), *Rural Administration in Kenya* (Nairobi: East African Literature Bureau, 1973), pp. 14–38. See also B. B. Schaffer, 'The Deadlock in Development Administration', in C. Leys (ed.), *Politics and Change in Developing Countries: Studies in the Theory and Practice of Development* (London: Cambridge University Press, 1969), p. 199 and *passim*.

28. J. O. Udoji, 'Some Measures for Improving Performance and Management of the Public Enterprises', in A. H. Rweyemamu and G. Hyden (eds.), *A Decade of Public Administration in Africa* (Nairobi: East African Literature Bureau, 1975), p. 238.

29. G. Hyden, 'Economic Development through Public Enterprises: Lessons from Past Experience' (mimeo., 1981), p. 4, forthcoming in a book edited by A. H. Rweyemamu.

30. A. R. Zolberg, 'The Political Use of Economic Planning in Mali', in H. G. Johnson (ed.), *Economic Nationalism in Old and New States* (London: Allen & Unwin, 1968), p. 117, quoted in Hyden (1981), p. 2.

31. Campbell in Dunn (1978), p. 88.

32. Hyden (1981), p. 2; G. Williams and T. Turner, 'Nigeria', ch. 6 in Dunn (1978), p. 153.

33. Behrman in Butler and Castagno (1967), p. 325; B. Callaway and E. Card, 'Political Constraints on Economic Development in Ghana', ch. 4 in Lofchie (1971), p. 83; and Udoji in Rweyemamu and Hyden (1975), p. 241.

34. Hyden (1981), p. 5; *Review of Statutory Boards* (Nairobi: Government Printer, 1979), pp. 18–19; François (1982), p. 32; and *Report of the Committee on Parastatal Bodies* (Lusaka: Government Printer, 1978).

35. See G. K. Simwinga, 'Corporate Autonomy and Government Control of

State Enterprises', in Tordoff (1980), ch. 5; Callaway and Card in Lofchie (1971), p. 85; and François (1982), p. 32.

36. François (1982); Hyden (1981), p. 10.

37. M. M. Minogue, 'The Politics of Development Planning': lecture for the core course 'Perspectives on Development' (M.A. Econ. programme in Development Studies, University of Manchester, 1979); A. Wildavsky, 'If planning is Everything, maybe it's Nothing', *Policy Sciences*, vol. 4, no. 2 (June 1973); A. H. Hanson, *The Process of Planning: A Study of India's Five-Year Plans, 1950–1964* (London: Oxford University Press, 1966), p. 1.

38. See E. J. Berg, 'Socialism and Economic Development in Tropical Africa', *Quarterly Journal of Economics*, vol. LXXVIII, no. 4 (November 1964), pp. 558–60.

39. Hanson (1966), p. 474.

40. W. A. Lewis, *Development Planning. The Essentials of Economic Policy* (London: Allen & Unwin, 1966), preface, p. 7.

41. *Ibid.*

42. Panter-Brick, 'French African Administration', 1969.

43. A. H. Hanson, *Planning and the Politicians and Other Essays* (London: Routledge & Kegan Paul, 1969), p. 198; R. C. Pratt, 'The Administration of Economic Planning in a Newly Independent State: The Tanzanian Experience, 1963–66', *Journal of Commonwealth Political Studies*, vol. v, no. 1 (March, 1967), p. 57.

44. See R. H. Green, 'Four African Development Plans', *Journal of Modern African Studies*, vol. 3, no. 2 (1965), pp. 253–4.

45. Panter-Brick, 'French African Administration', 1969.

46. Pratt (1967), p. 55; Tordoff (1974), chs. 4 and 7.

47. Lofchie (1967), p. 54.

48. See W. Reilly, 'District Development Planning in Botswana', in M. Minogue (ed.), *Manchester Papers on Development. Studies in Decentralisation: Papua New Guinea, Botswana, Sri Lanka*, issue no. 3 (Manchester: Administrative Studies, December 1981), p. 35 and *passim*.

Chapter 7: The Military

1. General Joseph-Désiré Mobutu seized power in Congo-Léopoldville in 1965 and Colonel Muammar Qaddafi in Libya in 1970, while President Luis Cabral was arrested and his government removed in Guinea-Bissau in 1980. In Equatorial Guinea, the tyrannical rule of President Francisco Macias Nguema was ended with his overthrow in 1979.

2. Ruth Collier (1982) criticises Professor Finer for introducing a blanket single-party concept and for his finding that one-party and multi-party regimes are equally likely to experience military intervention. She makes a valid distinction within the one-party category and argues that multi-party regimes above all, but also one-party regimes formed by coercion rather than as a result of electoral victory or merger, are likely to prove unstable. There may be something in this argument, but it cannot be pushed too far: Botswana, the Gambia and Mauritius are examples of

multi-party states which retain civilian governments, as did Zambia between 1964 and 1972. On the other hand, the single-party mobilising regime of Modibo Keita in Mali was toppled by a military coup in 1968.

3. Only about 30 officers and 100–150 men were involved out of an army of over 500 officers and more than 10,000 men. R. Luckham, *The Nigerian Military: A Sociological Analysis of Authority and Revolt, 1960–67* (Cambridge University Press, 1971), p. 33.

4. Cox (1976), p. 114.

5. *Ibid.*, p. 220.

6. S. E. Finer, *The Man on Horseback: The Role of the Military in Politics* (London: Pall Mall Press, 1962); M. Janowitz, *The Military in the Political Development of New Nations: An Essay in Comparative Analysis* (University of Chicago Press, 1964); A. R. Luckham, 'A Comparative Typology of Civil–Military Relations', *Government and Opposition*, vol. 6, no. 1 (Winter 1971); R. First, *The Barrel of a Gun: Political Power in Africa and the Coup d'Etat* (London: Allen Lane, 1970), p. 20; S. Decalo, *Coups and Army Rule in Africa: Studies in Military Style* (New Haven and London: Yale University Press, 1976), p. 19.

7. S. K. Panter-Brick, 'A Different Model? Some Aspects of Francophone Educational Ties', postgraduate seminar paper, Institute of Commonwealth Studies, University of London, 16 November 1982.

8. Luckham, 'French Militarism in Africa' (1982), p. 70. This paragraph as a whole is based on Luckham's article. For a discussion of the international dimension generally, see his 'Armaments, Underdevelopment, and Demilitarisation in Africa', in *Alternatives: A Journal of World Policy*, vol. vi, no. 2 (July 1980), in which he argues that the process of militarisation in Africa includes not only the actual acquisition of weapons, but also the extension of military values into political and social structures.

9. Information supplied by Robin Luckham.

10. Ruth Collier shows, very reasonably, that regime manipulation in general and manipulation of elections in particular contributed to the context of crisis in which civilian sectors intensified their opposition to government and the military ultimately intervened. Such manipulation is a substitute for the exercise of political skill.

11. J. R. Cartwright, *Politics in Sierra Leone, 1947–67* (University of Toronto Press, 1970), p. 255.

12. Cox (1976), p. 135, and *passim*.

13. D. G. Austin, 'The Ghana Case', in *The Politics of Demilitarisation* (Collected Seminar Papers, Institute of Commonwealth Studies, University of London, April–May 1966).

14. First (1970), p. 20.

15. E. Hansen, 'The Military and Revolution in Ghana', *Journal of African Marxists*, issue 2 (August 1982), pp. 10–11.

16. Decalo (1976), p. 18.

17. See R. L. Sklar, 'Nigerian Politics in Perspective' and 'Contradictions in the Nigerian Political System', in Melson and Wolpe (1971), ch. 2, pp. 46–7, and ch. 19.

18. Mackintosh (1966), p. 550. Mackintosh referred particularly to 1963, but his description applies to the 1962–66 period as a whole.

19. Sklar in Melson and Wolpe (1971), p. 49.

20. The account which follows draws heavily on Luckham (1971), especially chs. 1 and 2; all the quotations are from the same source.

21. A. Ademoyega, *Why We Struck: The Story of the First Nigerian Coup* (Ibadan: Evans, 1981); B. Gbulie, *Nigeria's Five Majors* (Onitsha: Africana Educational Publishers, 1981).

22. Michael F. Lofchie concluded that 'antagonistic social forces within Uganda society' led to the coup of January 1971. See his article 'The Uganda Coup – Class Action by the Military', *Journal of Modern African Studies*, vol. 10, no. 1 (1972). However, this view was challenged in a subsequent issue of the same journal (vol. 10, no. 4) by J. D. Chick and I. Gershenberg.

23. M. J. Dent, 'Corrective Government: Military Rule in Perspective', in S. K. Panter-Brick (ed.), *Soldiers and Oil: The Political Transformation of Nigeria* (London: Frank Cass, 1978), ch. 4.

24. Kirk-Greene in Kirk-Greene and Rimmer (1981), p. 11.

25. S. Decalo, 'Ideological Rhetoric and Scientific Socialism in Benin and Congo-Brazzaville', in Rosberg and Callaghy (1979), p. 255.

26. Luckham (1971), pp. 310–25.

27. Dowse in Austin and Luckham (1975), p. 21.

28. A. D. Yahaya, 'The Struggle for Power in Nigeria, 1966–79', in O. Oyediran (ed.), *Nigerian Government and Politics under Military Rule, 1966–79* (London: Macmillan, 1979), ch. 13; Dent in Panter-Brick (1978), pp. 113ff.

29. See M. Berry, 'Factional Conflict in the Nigerian Army: the July 1975 Coup and the Decision to Demilitarise', *Huddersfield Papers in Politics*, 3 (mimeo., Autumn 1981).

30. See C. Young, *Ideology and Development in Africa* (New Haven: Yale University Press, 1982), p. 164.

31. O. Oyediran, 'Civilian Rule for How Long?', in Oyediran (1979), ch. 14, especially p. 279.

32. First (1970), p. 436; G. Lamb, 'The Military and Development in Eastern Africa', in *Military Regimes*, Bulletin of the Institute of Development Studies, University of Sussex, vol. 4, no. 4 (September 1972), p. 22.

33. Dowse in Austin and Luckham (1975), pp. 25ff.

34. Oyediran (1979), p. 280.

35. As suggested by Rimmer in Kirk-Greene and Rimmer (1981), p. 76. The preponderant view, however, is that agriculture 'consistently stagnated during the military era': see A. Iwayemi, 'The Military and the Economy', in Oyediran (1979), p. 56.

36. In this section on the economy, I have drawn on Kirk-Greene and Rimmer (1981), part 2; Iwayemi in Oyediran (1979), ch. 3; O. Oyediran and O. Olagunju, 'The Military and the Politics of Revenue Allocation', in Oyediran (1979), ch. 10; and Sklar (1979).

37. D. Rothchild, 'Military Regime Performance: An Appraisal of the Ghana Experience, 1972–78', *Comparative Politics*, vol. 12, no. 4 (July 1980), p.

460. Unless otherwise stated, the section which follows is based on this article.

38. Decalo (1976), pp. 26–7; E. Nordlinger, quoted by Decalo, p. 26; and First (1970), p. 22.

39. O. E. Wilton-Marshall, 'Mali', 'Ivory Coast, Upper Volta, Niger, Benin, Togo', and 'People's Republic of the Congo', and R. Hallett, 'Rwanda and Burundi', in H. V. Hodson (ed.), *The Annual Register: A Record of World Events*, 1979 (London: Longman, 1980), pp. 235, 236, 239 and 245 (hereafter *The Annual Register*).

40. Wilton-Marshall, 'Upper Volta', *The Annual Register*, 1978, pp. 227–8.

41. Luckham (1980), p. 217.

Chapter 8: Revolution and Revolutionary Regimes

1. B. Munslow, *Mozambique* (1983): an amended version of Dr Munslow's PhD thesis, *FRELIMO and the Mozambican Revolution* (April 1980).

2. See Bender, *Angola under the Portuguese* (1978), part 1.

3. Munslow (1983), p. 12; N. Zafiris, 'The People's Republic of Mozambique: Pragmatic Socialism', in P. Wiles (ed.), *The New Communist Third World* (London: Croom Helm, 1982), pp. 116–7.

4. C. G. Rosberg, Jr and J. Nottingham, *The Myth of Mau Mau: Nationalism in Kenya* (New York: Praeger, 1966), p. xvii.

5. Munslow (April 1980), p. 410.

6. Munslow (1983), p. 104. The small, anti-FRELIMO Comité Revolucionário de Moçambique (COREMO), based in Lusaka, had only a limited impact on the liberation struggle and is not discussed in this section.

7. *Mozambique Revolution*, no. 56, June–September 1973, quoted in Munslow (April 1980), p. 380.

8. Munslow (April 1980), p. 384.

9. J. Marcum, *The Angolan Revolution*, vol. I: *The Anatomy of an Explosion (1950–1962)* (Cambridge, Mass.: Massachusetts Institute of Technology Press, 1969), p. 123. As well as this excellent study (in two volumes), I have drawn in this section on C. Legum and T. Hodges, *After Angola: The War over Southern Africa* (London: Rex Collings, 1976). See also the study prepared by the Research Department of the Institute for the Study of Conflict, London: 'Angola after Independence: Struggle for Supremacy', *Conflict Studies*, no. 64 (November 1975) and B. Davidson, *In the Eye of the Storm: Angola's People* (London: Longman, 1972).

10. Marcum (1969), pp. 10 and 318.

11. Quoted by J. Steele, 'Social Upheaval', *The Guardian* (London and Manchester): special issue on Angola, 2 March 1981 (hereafter *The Guardian*).

12. J. Marcum, *The Angolan Revolution*, vol. II: *Exile Politics and Guerrilla Warfare (1962–1976)* (Cambridge, Mass.: Massachusetts Institute of Technology Press, 1978), p. 206.

13. Information supplied by B. Munslow; Legum (1976), pp. 10–11; Marcum (1978).
14. J. Stockwell, *In Search of Enemies: A CIA Story* (New York: Norton, 1978).
15. P. Chabal, 'National Liberation in Portuguese Guinea, 1956–1974', *African Affairs*, vol. 80, no. 318 (January 1981), pp. 79–80. I have drawn substantially in this section upon this article, which is extracted from Dr Chabal's Cambridge University thesis and book: *Amilcar Cabral: Revolutionary Leadership and People's War* (Cambridge University Press, 1983). For an alternative interpretation, see B. Davidson, *No Fist is Big Enough to Hide the Sky* (London: Zed Press, 1981).
16. Based on discussions with Dr B. Munslow.
17. A. Cabral, *Unity and Struggle* (London: Heinemann, 1980); Chabal (1981), pp. 92–8. The small, anti-PAIGC Frente para a Libertação e Independencia da Guiné Portuguesa (FLING), based in Dakar and supported by the Senegalese government, had a minimal impact on the liberation struggle and is not discussed in this section.
18. Statement by Cabral, quoted in Chabal (1981), p. 88, n.60.
19. J. S. Saul, *The State and Revolution in Eastern Africa* (London: Heinemann, 1979): Machel quoted, p. 116; T. Ranger, 'The Changing of the Old Guard: Robert Mugabe and the Revival of ZANU', *Journal of Southern African Studies*, vol. 7, no. 1 (October 1980): ZANU spokesman quoted, p. 87.
20. Saul (1979), pp. 112, 117, and 120–1. The original essay is published in substantially the same form in Saul's book (ch. 5), from which all references are taken.
21. L. Cliffe, 'Towards an Evaluation of the Zimbabwe Nationalist Movement', paper presented to the Political Studies Association, University of Exeter, 31 March–2 April 1980, p. 8. See also D. Martin and P. Johnson, *The Struggle for Zimbabwe: The Chimurenga War* (London: Faber & Faber, 1981).
22. *Ikwezi*, 10, December 1978, quoted in Ranger (1980), p. 87.
23. A valuable account of ZANU(PF) structures is to be found in L. Cliffe, J. Mpofu and B. Munslow, 'Nationalist Politics in Zimbabwe: The 1980 Elections and Beyond', *Review of African Political Economy*, no. 18: special issue on Zimbabwe (May–August 1980), pp. 49–54.
24. Munslow (1983), p. 150.
25. B. Munslow, 'The Liberation Struggle in Mozambique and the Origins of Post-Independence Political and Economic Policy', in *Mozambique* (University of Edinburgh: Seminar Proceedings, Centre of African Studies, 1979), pp. 86–99. This section is based on this and other works by Dr Munslow, notably *Mozambique: the Revolution and its Origins* (1983), part 4 and 'Disengagement from a Regional Sub-System: Problems and Prospects', *Journal of Area Studies*, no. 4 (Autumn 1981). Unless otherwise stated, all quotations are from Munslow. Supplementary information is drawn from the accounts by D. H. Jones (1975–78) and by R. Hallett (1979–81) in *The Annual Register*; J. Hanlon, 'Machel back-pedals on private enterprise', *The Guardian*, 15 July 1981; and Zafiris in Wiles (1982), ch. 4.

26. K. Middlemas, 'Mozambique: Two Years of Independence', in *Mozambique* (1979), p. 104 (see n. 25 above); L. Vail and L. White, *Capitalism and Colonialism in Mozambique* (London: Heinemann, 1981).
27. Hanlon in *The Guardian*, 15 July 1981, p. 8.
28. P. Goodison, 'The Construction of Socialism in Mozambique' (BA Econ. dissertation, University of Manchester, April 1982), p. 77.
29. An MPLA pamphlet quoted by K. Brown, 'Angolan Socialism', in Rosberg and Callaghy (1979), p. 299. The rest of this paragraph is based on Brown's essay, pp. 298–304.
30. J. Steele, 'Party Leaders', *The Guardian*, 2 March 1981. The various articles in this special issue on Angola, notably those by Jonathan Steele, provide information which usefully supplements Brown's earlier (1977) account. I have drawn upon both sources in this section. On the Angolan economy, see N. Zafiris, 'The People's Republic of Angola: Soviet-Type Economy in the Making', in Wiles (1982), ch. 2.
31. Brown (1979), pp. 310, 321 and *passim*, supplemented by information supplied by B. Munslow.
32. Chabal (1981), pp. 76–9; B. Munslow, 'The 1980 Coup in Guinea-Bissau', *Review of African Political Economy*, no. 21 (May–September 1981), p. 110. The remainder of this section is based on the latter article, supplemented by B. Davidson, 'No fist is big enough to hide the sky: building Guinea-Bissau and Cape Verde', *Race and Class*, vol. XXIII, no. 1 (Summer 1981), pp. 43–64, extracted from Davidson (1981).
33. S. K. Panter-Brick, 'Africanisation in Zimbabwe', in P. Lyon and J. Manor (eds.), *Transfer and Transformation: Political Institutions in the New Commonwealth* (Leicester University Press, 1983).
34. 'Focus on Zimbabwe', *The Times* (London), 10 February 1982, especially the articles by Stephen Taylor.
35. Nkomo returned to Zimbabwe five months later.
    R. W. Baldock, 'Zimbabwe', in *The Annual Register*, 1980, pp. 255–60; C. Nyawo and T. Rich, 'Zimbabwe after Independence', and 'Peter Yates', 'The Prospects for Socialist Transition in Zimbabwe', *Review of African Political Economy*, no. 18 (May–August 1980); *The Guardian*, 18 January, 18 February 1982 and 19 August 1983.
36. Nyerere (1968), introduction, chs. 26, 27 and 37; A. Coulson, 'Tanzania's Fertilizer Factory', in A. Coulson (ed.), *African Socialism in Practice: The Tanzanian Experience* (Nottingham: Spokesman, 1979), ch. 14; Hyden (1980), *passim*; Mueller (1980); and Bryceson (1982).
37. Pratt in Mwansasu and Pratt (1979), p. 203.
38. In this section I have drawn heavily on R. W. Johnson's chapter on 'Guinea' in Dunn (1978). Supplementary material has been taken from Ladipo Adamolekun, 'The Socialist Experience in Guinea', in Rosberg and Callaghy (1979). Except as otherwise indicated, all quotations are from Johnson.
39. See Decalo in Rosberg and Callaghy (1979), pp. 231–64.
40. This designation is adopted by Andrew Racine on whose essays I have drawn in this section: see his 'The People's Republic of Benin' and 'The

People's Republic of Congo', in Wiles (1982), chs. 6 and 7. Wiles also includes Madagascar and Somalia in the category of 'marginals'.

41. *West Africa* (London), 24 May 1982, pp. 1379–80.

42. In this section I have drawn substantially upon the articles on 'Somalia' contributed annually by Christopher Clapham to *The Annual Register* from 1969 to 1981, and David D. Laitin's chapter on 'Somalia's Military Government and Scientific Socialism', in Rosberg and Callaghy (1979). Additional points have been drawn from B. Lynch, 'The Somali Democratic Republic. The one that got away', in Wiles (1982), ch. 9.

43. This section is based on Christopher Clapham's annual articles on 'Ethiopia' for *The Annual Register*, 1974–81; J. W. Harbeson's essay on 'Socialist Politics in Revolutionary Ethiopia' in Rosberg and Callaghy (1979), pp. 345–72; and F. Halliday and M. Molyneux, *The Ethiopian Revolution* (London: Verso, 1981).

44. J. Markakis, *Ethiopia: Anatomy of a Traditional Polity* (Oxford: Clarendon Press, 1974), p. 394 and conclusion, *passim*.

45. Harbeson in Rosberg and Callaghy (1979), p. 353; Halliday and Molyneux (1981), p. 165.

46. For an informed account of Eritrean guerrilla movements, see D. Pool, *Eritrea: Africa's Longest War* (London: Anti-Slavery Society, 1979).

47. The text is reproduced in D. and M. Ottaway, *Ethiopia: Empire in Revolution* (New York: Africana, 1978), appendix A.

48. An additional grievance among the Oromos was 'the regime's desire to extract the surplus from the countryside and carry through the "second" land reform against the interests of richer peasants': Halliday and Molyneux (1981), p. 197. Dr P. T. W. Baxter of the Department of Social Anthropology, University of Manchester, questions whether the land reform was regarded as beneficial throughout the southern region and maintains that some of the settlements in the south only appeared to work well because northern peoples had been imported. The indigenous inhabitants were strongly opposed to the presence of these immigrants. For the significance of the Oromo, see his article: 'Ethiopia's Unacknowledged Problem: The Oromo', *African Affairs*, vol. 77, no. 308 (July 1978).

49. J. Markakis and N. Ayele, *Class and Revolution in Ethiopia* (Nottingham: Spokesman, 1978), p. 176; Halliday and Molyneux (1981), p. 269.

50. Halliday and Molyneux (1981), ch. 7: conclusions, p. 271 and *passim*.

51. Harbeson in Rosberg and Callaghy (1979), p. 371; Halliday and Molyneux (1981), p. 283.

52. I am indebted to Dr Barry Munslow for this formulation.

53. K. E. Svendsen, 'Socialist Problems after the Arusha Declaration', *East Africa Journal*, vol. IV, no. 2 (May 1967), p. 12.

54. Sklar (1979), pp. 551–2.

Chapter 9: Regional Groupings and the OAU

1. K. Nkrumah, *Neo-Colonialism: The Last Stage of Imperialism* (New York:

International Publishers, 1965); *Africa Must Unite* (London: Heinemann, 1963).

2. R. L. Sklar, 'Political Aspects of Regional Organization in Africa', synopsis of a lecture in the 'Africa and the World' series, University of Zambia, 1966 (mimeo.). The first two points are also made by Professor Sklar in this paper.

3. W. J. Foltz, *From French West Africa to the Mali Federation* (New Haven: Yale University Press, 1965), p. 97. This account of the Mali federation is based substantially on Foltz's study.

4. *Ibid.*, p. 187.

5. J. S. Nye, Jr., *Pan-Africanism and East African Integration* (Cambridge, Mass.: Harvard University Press, 1966), supplemented by my personal recollections as a result of attending a University of East Africa conference on federation in Nairobi in 1963.

6. See W. Tordoff (1967), pp. 171–3, and 'Tanzania', in *The Annual Register*, 1977, p. 217.

7. O. E. Wilton-Marshall, 'African Conferences and Institutions', in *The Annual Register*, 1979, p. 368.

8. Quoted in E. N. Gladden, 'The East African Common Services Organisation' (mimeo., 1963), p. 3. The early part of this section is based on this account, and especially on that of J. Banfield, 'The Structure and Admnistration of the East Africa High Commission and the East African Common Services Organisation', University of East Africa Conference on East African Federation, Nairobi, 26–30 November 1963.

9. The section which follows is based on 'The Reshaping of East African Economic Co-operation', part 1 by P. Robson, and part 2 by A. R. Roe, in *East Africa Journal*, vol. IV, no. 5 (August 1967), pp. 3–16.

10. A. Hazlewood, 'The End of the East African Community: What are the Lessons for Regional Integration Schemes?', *Journal of Common Market Studies*, vol. XVIII, no. 1 (September 1979), p. 44.

11. See my contributions on 'The East African Community' in *The Annual Register* in 1971, 1973 and 1975–7, those from 1975 onwards being subsumed within the section on 'African Conferences and Institutions' by O. E. Wilton-Marshall.

12. This section is based on Wilton-Marshall, *op. cit.* in *The Annual Register*, 1976–80, and on articles in *West Africa* (London), 24 May and 7 June 1982 – the article by S. K. B. Asante on 'Trade problems and prospects' in the 24 May issue was particularly helpful.

13. This section is based on P. Goodison, 'SADCC: Prospects and Problems until the Year 2000' (mimeo., 1982), p. 3 and *passim*. See also R. Leys and A. Tostensen, 'Regional Co-operation in Southern Africa: the Southern African Development Co-ordination Conference', *Review of African Political Economy*, no. 23 (January–April 1982).

14. C. Hoskyns, 'The Organisation of African Unity and Eastern Africa' (University of Dar es Salaam, mimeo., December 1966), p. 1, subsequently published in an amended form as 'Pan-Africanism and Integration' in A. Hazlewood (ed.), *African Integration and Disintegration: Case Studies in Economic and Political Union* (London: Oxford University Press,

1967). I have found this paper helpful in preparing this section; quotations are taken from the original version.

15. Ras Makonnen, *Pan-Africanism from Within*, as recorded and edited by K. King (Nairobi: Oxford University Press, 1973), p. 67; other studies of Pan-Africanism include C. Legum, *Pan-Africanism: A Short Political Guide* (London: Pall Mall, 1962) and I. Geiss, *The Pan-African Movement* (London: Methuen, 1974).

16. The story of PAFMECSA is told by R. H. F. Cox in *Pan-Africanism in Practice: An East African Study, PAFMECSA, 1958–64* (London: Oxford University Press, 1964). For the background to the formation of the OAU, see I. Wallerstein, *Africa: The Politics of Unity* (New York: Random House, 1967).

17. Hoskyns (1966); Z. Cervenka, *The Organisation of African Unity and its Charter* (New York: Praeger, 1968).

18. *Ibid., passim*; D. Austin and R. Nagel, 'The Organization of African Unity', *The World Today*, vol. 22 (December 1966); and R. Nagel and R. Rathbone, 'The OAU at Kinshasa', *The World Today*, vol. 23 (November 1967).

19. Luckham (1982), p. 77. For an account of the Franco-African conferences, see J. L. Dagut, 'Les Sommets Franco-Africains: Un Instrument de la Présence Française en Afrique', *Année Africaine*, part II, ch. 2 (Paris: Editions A. Pedone, 1980).

20. *The Guardian*, 13 June 1983.

21. See M. Wolfers, *Politics in the Organisation of African Unity* (London: Methuen, 1976), pp. 88–9 and 201.

22. Wilton-Marshall, 'African Conferences . . .', *The Annual Register*, 1980, p. 366; *The Guardian*, 18, 23 and 24 November 1982.

23. Quoted in Wolfers (1976), pp. 168–9.

24. T. H. Henriksen, 'People's War in Angola, Mozambique and Guinea-Bissau', *Journal of Modern African Studies*, vol. 14, no. 3 (1976), p. 395 and *passim*.

25. Quoted in Z. Cervenka, 'The Organisation of African Unity and the Crisis in Southern Africa,' *Interstate*, no. 1 (1976–77).

26. J. Mayall, 'African Unity and the OAU: The Place of a Political Myth in African Diplomacy', *The Handbook of World Affairs*, vol. 27 (1973), p. 121.

27. Quoted in C. Hoskyns (ed.), *Case Studies in African Diplomacy, No. 2: The Ethiopia–Somali–Kenya Dispute, 1960–67* (Dar es Salaam: Oxford University Press, 1969), p. 32.

28. *Ibid.*, p. 68.

29. Mayall (1973), p. 128; Clapham, 'Ethiopia' and 'Somalia', *The Annual Register*, 1977, p. 214.

30. See my articles on Tanzania and Uganda in *The Annual Register*, 1972, 1978 and 1979.

31. Mayall (1973), pp. 130–1. Some of the radical states gave extensive aid to the Congolese rebels on a bi-lateral basis, but this came too late seriously to affect the issue and by mid-1965 the rebellion had been more or less crushed. Hoskyns (1966), p. 5.

32. Quoted in Wilton-Marshall, *The Annual Register*, 1978, p. 352.

33. *Ibid.*, and 1980, p. 366; *The Guardian*, 27 June 1981.
34. Wilton-Marshall, 'Chad', in *The Annual Register*, 1979, pp. 237–8 and 1980, pp. 240–1; *The Guardian*, 21 January, 12 February and 18 November 1982, and 13 June 1983.
35. Mayall (1973), p. 119. See also Z. Cervenka, *The Unfinished Quest for Unity: Africa and the OAU* (New York: Africana, 1977).
36. K. Whiteman, 'African Conferences and Institutions', *The Annual Register*, 1973; Wilton-Marshall, *ibid.*, 1974–80.
37. *Ibid.*
38. Wallerstein (1967), pp. 147–8; Whiteman, 'African Conferences,' *The Annual Register*, 1973, and Wilton-Marshall, *ibid.*, 1974 and 1979; and Tordoff, 'Tanzania', in *The Annual Register*, 1974.

Chapter 10: Conclusions: Ideology, the Post-Colonial State and Development

1. C. Geertz, 'Ideology as a Cultural System', in D. E. Apter (ed.), *Ideology and Discontent* (New York: The Free Press, 1964), pp. 47 and 52ff.
2. Shils (1968), p. 68.
3. Paper on 'Ideology' presented to the Political Theory seminar, Department of Government, University of Manchester, 1972. In his book *Ideology* (London: Pall Mall, 1970), p. 15, Plamenatz provided the following minimal definition of ideology: 'a set of closely related beliefs or ideas, or even attitudes, characteristic of a group or community'.
4. J. P. Nettl, 'Strategies in the Study of Political Development', in Leys (1969), p. 18. This section is based on Nettl's account.
5. *Ibid.*, pp. 21, 22, 31.
6. Young (1982), p. 298. I have drawn especially upon Young's ch. 6: 'By way of Conclusion: A Preliminary Appraisal of Ideology and Performance', pp. 297–326. Page references are given only for longer quotations or where Professor Young's authorship would otherwise be unclear.
7. Hanson (1966), p. 535.
8. Berg, 'Socialism and Economic Development in Tropical Africa' (November 1964).
9. Young (1982), p. 1.
10. Stryker in Lofchie (1971), pp. 124ff.; Campbell in Dunn (1978), pp. 100ff.; *Employment, Incomes and Equality* (Geneva: ILO, 1972), *passim*; Young (1982), p. 242.
11. H. Chenery *et al.*, *Redistribution with Growth* (London: Oxford University Press, 1974), p. xv and *passim*.
12. Young (1982), pp. 304–5.
13. *Ibid.*, pp. 241–2; information supplied by Keith Panter-Brick.
14. Cabral, quoted in Chabal (1981), p. 88, n. 60.
15. Nyerere (1968), p. 4; Pratt in Mwansasu and Pratt (1979), p. 216.
16. D. Feldman, 'The Economics of Ideology: Some Problems of Achieving Rural Socialism in Tanzania', in Leys (1969), p. 105; Mueller (1980).

17. Young, (1982), pp. 307–8. For supporting evidence on Kenya, see H. Bienen, *Kenya: The Politics of Participation and Control* (Princeton University Press, 1974), pp. 183ff.

18. It is to be noted, however, that the mining companies were able to safeguard their long-term interests by management and sales contracts which left control of the copper industry in their own hands. Even after 1973, when the Zambian government terminated these contracts, it did not necessarily establish firm 'national' control over the industry since key technical-production positions were still held by non-Zambians in both mining groups. The Zambian case reveals how, after as before nationalisation, foreign-based multinational companies (MNCs) press hard to uphold their own interests; they appear to succeed to a surprising extent by using a variety of devices, including transfer pricing, patents, management agreements and the control of marketing. Thus, the management and sale contracts referred to above might be taken to typify the changing patterns of penetration and domination which MNCs have been prepared to use. For an informed study, see C. Kirkpatrick and F. Nixson, 'Transnational Corporations and Economic Development', *Journal of Modern African Studies*, vol. 19, no. 3 (September 1981), pp. 367–99.

19. Tordoff (1974) and (1980), *passim*.

20. Sklar (1979), pp. 532, 539, and *passim*.

21. *Ibid.*, pp. 531–2.

22. Johnson in Dunn (1978), p. 45.

23. *The Observer* (London), 2 January 1983.

24. See Tordoff (1967), ch. 6, and my contributions on Tanzania to *The Annual Register*, 1980–82.

25. The following section draws substantially upon Young (1982), pp. 313–9.

26. See Tordoff, 'Kenya', *The Annual Register*, 1975–82.

27. Young (1982), p. 316.

28. Sklar (1979), pp. 551–2.

29. Austin (1976), p. 159; Zolberg (1966), p. 125.

30. O'Brien in R. C. O'Brien (1979), pp. 216–7; J. Mende, 'Senegal: Diouf's New Directions', *Africa Report*, vol. 27, no. 6 (November–December 1982); information supplied by Keith Panter-Brick.

31. *Report of the Presidential Commission on the Establishment of a Democratic One Party State* (Dar es Salaam: Government Printer, 1965), p. 15.

32. Bienen (1974), pp. 64 and 195; N. Kasfir, *The Shrinking Political Arena* (Berkeley: University of California Press, 1976).

33. Young (1982), p. 321.

34. Swainson (1980), p. 288.

35. Young (1982), p. 321.

36. *Ibid.*, p. 322.

37. C. Leys, 'African Economic Development in Theory and Practice', *Dædalus*, vol. III, no. 2 (Spring 1982), p. 116.

38. Svendsen (1967), p. 12.

39. Leys (1982), p. 100.

40. Address on the Occasion of Mainland Tanzania's Twentieth Anniversary of Independence (Dar es Salaam, mimeo., December 1981).
41. *The Guardian*, 8 January 1983 on Zambia; Leys (1982), p. 100.
42. Leys (1982).
43. *Ibid.*, p. 104.
44. S. Amin, 'New World Economic Order. Reactions of the developed world and strategy of use of the financial surpluses of certain developing countries' (Dakar: United Nations African Institute for Economic Development and Planning, R/2903), p. 9.
45. P. Goodison, 'Does SADCC need a new dimension?', Conference on Research in Progress in Southern Africa, 21–23 March 1983 (Centre for Southern African Studies, University of York, mimeo.), pp. 1–12. See also Leys and Tostensen (1982), *passim*.
46. Halliday and Molyneux (1981), ch. 7; Wiles (1982), chs. 1, 14 and 15; D. and M. Ottaway, *Afrocommunism* (New York: Africana, 1981), *passim*; and B. Munslow, 'Afrocommunism?', paper presented at the Political Studies Association Annual Conference, University of Newcastle, April 1983.

Bibliography

The Bibliography is limited to documents cited in the text.

1. Books, Monographs and Articles

Adamolekun, L., 'The Socialist Experience in Guinea', in Rosberg and Callaghy (1979), below.

Ademoyega, A., *Why We Struck: The Story of the First Nigerian Coup* (Ibadan: Evans Bros., 1981).

Alavi, H., 'The State in Post-Colonial Societies: Pakistan and Bangladesh', *New Left Review*, no. 74 (July–August 1972).

Allen, C. H., 'Union–Party Relationships in Francophone West Africa: A Critique of "Tèlèguidage" Interpretations', in Sandbrook and Cohen (1975), below.

Aluko, O. (ed.), *The Foreign Policies of African States* (London: Hodder & Stoughton, 1977).

Amin, S., 'New World Economic Order. Reactions of the developed world and strategy of use of the financial surpluses of certain developing countries' (Dakar: United Nations African Institute for Economic Development and Planning, R/2903).

Andrain, C. F., 'Guinea and Senegal: Contrasting Types of African Socialism', in Friedland and Rosberg (1964), below.

Anglin, D. G., and Shaw, T. M., *Zambia's Foreign Policy: Studies in Diplomacy and Dependence* (Boulder: Westview Press, 1979).

Apter, D. E. *The Politics of Modernization*, (University of Chicago Press, 1965).
—— (ed.), *Ideology and Discontent* (New York: The Free Press, 1964).

Arrighi, G., and Saul, J. (eds.), *Essays on the Political Economy of Africa* (New York: Monthly Review Press, 1973).

Austin, D., *Politics in Ghana, 1946–60* (London: Oxford University Press, 1964).
——, *Ghana Observed: Essays on the Politics of a West African Republic* (Manchester University Press, 1976).
——, *Politics in Africa* (Manchester University Press, 1978).

——, 'The British Point of No Return?', in Gifford and Louis (1982), below.

——, and Nagel, R., 'The Organization of African Unity', *The World Today*, vol. 22 (December 1966).

——, and Luckham, R. (eds.), *Politicians and Soldiers in Ghana* (London: Frank Cass, 1975).

Ballard, J. A., 'Four Equatorial States', in Carter, G. M. (1966), below.

Barker, J. S., 'Political Economy and Political Management', *The African Review*, vol. 1, no. 3 (January 1972).

Bates, R. H., *Unions, Parties and Political Development – A Study of Mineworkers in Zambia* (New Haven: Yale University Press, 1971).

——, *Rural Responses to Industrialization: A Study of Village Zambia* (New Haven: Yale University Press, 1976).

Baxter, P. T. W., 'Ethiopia's Unacknowledged Problem: The Oromo', *African Affairs*, vol. 77, no. 308 (July 1978).

Baylies, C. L., and Szeftel, M., 'The Rise of a Zambian Capitalist Class in the 1970s', *Journal of Southern African Studies*, vol. 8, no. 2 (April 1982).

Beckman, B., 'Imperialism and Capitalist Transformation: Critique of a Kenyan Debate', *Review of African Political Economy*, no. 19 (September–December 1980).

Behrman, L., 'Party and State Relations in Guinea', in Butler and Castagno (1967), below.

Bender, G. J., *Angola under the Portuguese: The Myth and the Reality* (London: Heinemann, 1978).

Berg, E. J., 'Socialism and Economic Development in Tropical Africa', *Quarterly Journal of Economics*, vol. LXXVIII, no. 4 (November 1964).

——, and Butler, J., 'Trade Unions', in Coleman and Rosberg (1964), below.

Bienen, H., *Kenya: The Politics of Participation and Control* (Princeton University Press, 1974).

Brass, P. R., 'Political Participation, Institutionalisation and Stability in India', *Government and Opposition*, vol. 4, no. 1 (1969).

Brett, E. A., *Colonialism and Underdevelopment in East Africa: The Politics of Economic Change, 1919–1939* (London: Heinemann, 1973).

Brown, K., 'Angolan Socialism', in Rosberg and Callaghy (1979), below.

Bryceson, D. F., 'Peasant Commodity Production in Post-Colonial Tanzania', *African Affairs*, vol. 81, no. 325 (October 1982).

Burawoy, M., 'Another Look at the Mineworker', *African Social Research*, no. 14 (December 1972).

Butler, J., and Castagno, A. A. (eds.), *Boston University Papers on Africa: Transition in African Politics* (New York: Praeger, 1967).

Cabral, A., *Unity and Struggle* (London: Heinemann, 1980).

Callaway, B., and Card, E., 'Political Constraints on Economic Development in Ghana,' in Lofchie (1971), below.

Callinicos, A., and Rogers, J., *Southern Africa after Soweto* (London: Pluto Press, 1977).

Campbell, B., 'Ivory Coast', in Dunn (1978), below.

Carter, G. M. (ed.), *National Unity and Regionalism in Eight African States* (Ithaca, New York: Cornell University Press, 1966).

Cartwright, J. R., *Politics in Sierra Leone, 1947–67* (University of Toronto Press, 1970).

Cervenka, Z., *The Organization of African Unity and its Charter* (New York: Praeger, 1968).

——, 'The Organization of African Unity and the Crisis in Southern Africa', *Interstate*, no. 1 (1976–77).

——, *The Unfinished Quest for Unity: Africa and the OAU* (New York: Africana, 1977).

Chabal, P., 'National Liberation in Portuguese Guinea, 1956–1974', *African Affairs*, vol. 80, no. 318 (January 1981).

——, *Amilcar Cabral: Revolutionary Leadership and People's War* (Cambridge University Press, 1983).

Chambers, R., 'Planning for Rural Areas in East Africa: Experience and Prescriptions', in Leonard (1973), below.

——, *Botswana's Accelerated Rural Development Programme, 1973–76: Experience and Lessons* (Gaborone: Government Printer, February 1977).

Chenery, H., *et al.*, *Redistribution with Growth* (Oxford University Press, 1974).

Chick, J. D., 'Class Conflict and Military Intervention in Uganda', *Journal of Modern African Studies*, vol. 10, no. 4 (December 1972).

Cliffe, L., Mpofu, J., and Munslow, B., 'Nationalist Politics in Zimbabwe: The 1980 Elections and Beyond', *Review of African Political Economy*, no. 18: special issue on Zimbabwe (May–August 1980).

Coleman, J. S., *Nigeria: Background to Nationalism* (Berkeley: University of California Press, 1958).

——, and Rosberg, C. G., Jr (eds.), *Political Parties and National Integration in Tropical Africa* (Berkeley: University of California Press, 1964).

Collier, R. B., *Regimes in Tropical Africa: Changing Forms of Supremacy, 1945–75* (Berkeley: University of California Press, 1982).

Coulson, A. (ed.), *African Socialism in Practice: The Tanzanian Experience* (Nottingham: Spokesman, 1979).

Cox, R. H. F., *Pan-Africanism in Practice: An East African Study, PAFMECSA, 1958–64* (Oxford University Press, 1964).

Cox, T. S., *Civil–Military Relations in Sierra Leone: A Case Study of African Soldiers in Politics* (Cambridge, Mass.: Harvard University Press, 1976).

Crowder, M. (ed.), *Colonial West Africa: Collected Essays* (London: Frank Cass, 1978).

Dædalus, vol. iii, no. 2 (Spring 1982): 'Black Africa: A Generation after Independence'.

Dagut, J. L., 'Les Sommets Franco-Africains: Un Instrument de la Présence Française en Afrique', *Année Africaine*, part ii, ch. 2 (Paris: Editions A. Pedone, 1980).

Davidson, B., *In the Eye of the Storm: Angola's People* (London: Longman, 1972).

——, *No Fist is Big Enough to Hide the Sky* (London: Zed Press, 1981).

——, 'No fist is big enough to hide the sky: building Guinea-Bissau and Cape Verde', *Race and Class*, vol. xxiii, no. 1 (Summer 1981).

Decalo, S., *Coups and Army Rule in Africa: Studies in Military Style* (New Haven: Yale University Press, 1976).

——, 'Ideological Rhetoric and Scientific Socialism in Benin and Congo-Brazzaville', in Rosberg and Callaghy (1979), below.

Delavignette, R., *Freedom and Authority in French West Africa* (Oxford University Press, 1950).

Dent, M. J., 'Corrective Government: Military Rule in Perspective' in Panter-Brick (1978), below.

Dowse, R., 'Military and Police Rule', in Austin and Luckham (1975), above.

Dresang, D. L., and Young, R. A., 'The Public Service', in Tordoff (1980), below.

Du Bois, V. D., 'Guinea', in Coleman and Rosberg (1964), above.

Dunn, J. (ed.), *West African States: Failure and Promise. A Study in Comparative Politics* (Cambridge University Press, 1978).

Eisenstadt, S. N., 'Initial Institutional Patterns of Political Modernization', in Welch (1967), below.

Elliott, C. M., 'The Zambian Economy' (Lusaka, 1968, mimeo.).

Emerson, R., and Kilson, M. (eds.), *The Political Awakening of Africa* (Englewood Cliffs, N.J.: Prentice-Hall, 1965).

Epstein, A. L., *Politics in an Urban African Community* (Manchester University Press, 1958).

Evans, P., *Dependent Development: The Alliance of Multinational, State and Local Capital in Brazil* (Princeton University Press, 1979).

Ezera, K., *Constitutional Developments in Nigeria* (Cambridge University Press, 1960).

Feldman, D., 'The Economics of Ideology: Some Problems of Achieving Rural Socialism in Tanzania', in Leys (1969), below.

Finer, S. E., *The Man on Horseback: The Role of the Military in Politics* (London: Pall Mall Press, 1962).

Finucane, J. R., *Rural Development and Bureaucracy in Tanzania: The Case of Mwanza Region* (Uppsala: Scandinavian Institute of African Studies, 1974).

First, R., *The Barrel of a Gun: Political Power in Africa and the Coup d'Etat* (London: Allen Lane, The Penguin Press, 1970).

Fischer, G., 'Syndicats et Décolonisation', *Présence Africaine*, no. 34–35 (October 1960–January 1961).

Foltz, W. J., *From French West Africa to the Mali Federation* (New Haven: Yale University Press, 1965).

Forde, D., and Scott, R., *The Native Economies of Nigeria*, ed., Perham, M. (London: Faber & Faber, 1946).

François, P., 'Class Struggles in Mali', *Review of African Political Economy*, no. 24 (May–August 1982).

Friedland, W. H., 'For a Sociological Concept of Charisma', New York State School of Industrial and Labor Relations, Reprint Series No. 160 (New York, 1964).

——, *VUTA KAMBA: The Development of Trade Unions in Tanganyika* (Stanford: Hoover Institution Press, 1969).

——, and Rosberg, C. G., Jr (eds.), *African Socialism* (Stanford University Press, 1964).

Gbulie, B., *Nigeria's Five Majors* (Onitsha: Africana Educational Publishers, 1981).

Geertz, C., 'The Integrative Revolution: Primordial Sentiments and Civil Politics in the New States', in Geertz, C. (ed.), *Old Societies and New States* (New York: Free Press, 1963).

——, 'Ideology as a Cultural System', in Apter (1964), above.

Geiss, I., *The Pan-African Movement* (London: Methuen, 1974).

Gellner, E., *Thought and Change* (London: Weidenfeld & Nicolson, 1964).

——, *Contemporary Thought and Politics*, ed. Jarvie, J. C., and Agassi, J. (London: Routledge & Kegan Paul, 1974).

——, *Nationalism and Nations* (Oxford: Blackwell, 1982).

Gershenberg, I., 'A Further Comment on the 1971 Uganda Coup', *Journal of Modern African Studies*, vol. 10, no. 4 (December 1972).

Gertzel, G., *The Politics of Independent Kenya* (London: Heinemann, 1970).

Gifford, P., and Louis, W. R. (eds.), *The Transfer of Power in Africa. Decolonization, 1940–1960* (New Haven: Yale University Press, 1982).

Gladden, E. N., 'The East African Common Services Organisation' (mimeo., 1963).

Goodison, P., 'SADCC: Prospects and Problems until the Year 2000' (Manchester, mimeo., 1982).

Gould, D. J., *Bureaucratic Corruption and Underdevelopment in the Third World: The Zaire Case* (Oxford: Pergamon Press, 1980).

Green, R. H., 'Four African Development Plans', *Journal of Modern African Studies*, vol. 3, no. 2 (1965).

——, 'Tanzanian Political Economy Goals, Strategies and Results, 1967–74', in Mwansasu and Pratt (1979), below.

Halliday, F., and Molyneux, M., *The Ethiopian Revolution* (London: Verso, 1981).

Hansen, E., 'The Military and Revolution in Ghana', *Journal of African Marxists*, issue 2 (August 1982).

Hanson, A. H., *The Process of Planning: A Study of India's Five Year Plans, 1950–1964* (Oxford University Press, 1966).

——, *Planning and the Politicians and Other Essays*, (London: Routledge & Kegan Paul, 1969).

Harbeson, J. W., 'Socialist Politics in Revolutionary Ethiopia', in Rosberg and Callaghy (1979), below.

Hazlewood, A., 'The End of the East African Community: What are the Lessons for Regional Integration Schemes?', *Journal of Common Market Studies*, vol. xviii, no. 1 (September 1979).

——, (ed.), *African Integration and Disintegration: Case Studies in Economic and Political Union* (Oxford University Press, 1967).

Henriksen, T. H., 'People's War in Angola, Mozambique and Guinea-Bissau,' *Journal of Modern African Studies*, vol. 14, no. 3 (1976).

Hodgkin, T., *Nationalism in Colonial Africa* (London: Frederick Muller, 1956).

——, *African Political Parties* (Harmondsworth: Penguin, 1961).

Hoskyns, C., 'The Organisation of African Unity and Eastern Africa' (Dar es Salaam, mimeo., December 1966).

——, 'Pan-Africanism and Integration', in Hazlewood (1967), above.

——, (ed.), *Case Studies in African Diplomacy, no. 2: The Ethiopia – Somali – Kenya Dispute, 1960–67* (Dar es Salaam: Oxford University Press, 1969).

Huntington, S. P., 'Political Development and Political Decay', *World Politics*, vol. xvii, no. 3 (1965).
——, *Political Order in Changing Societies* (New Haven: Yale University Press, 1968).
Hyden, G., *TANU Yajenga Nchi: Political Development in Rural Tanzania* (Lund: Scandinavian University Books, 1968).
——, 'Social Structure, Bureaucracy and Development Administration in Kenya', *The African Review*, vol. 1, no. 3 (January 1972).
——, *Beyond Ujamaa in Tanzania. Underdevelopment and an Uncaptured Peasantry* (London: Heinemann, 1980).
——, 'Economic Development through Public Enterprises: Lessons from Past Experience' (mimeo., 1981).
——, Jackson, R., and Okumu, J. (eds.), *Development Administration: The Kenyan Experience* (Nairobi: Oxford University Press, 1970).
——, and Leys, C., 'Elections and Politics in Single-Party Systems: The Case of Kenya and Tanzania', *British Journal of Political Science*, vol. 1, no. 2 (1972).
Ilchman, W. F., and Uphoff, N. T., *The Political Economy of Change* (Berkeley: University of California Press, 1971).
Iliffe, J., *A Modern History of Tanganyika* (Cambridge University Press, 1979).
Iwayemi, A., 'The Military and the Economy', in Oyediran (1979), below.
Jackson, R. H., and Rosberg, C. G., 'Why Àfrica's Weak States Persist: The Empirical and the Juridical in Statehood', *World Politics*, vol. xxxv, no. 1 (October 1982).
Janowitz, M., *The Military in the Political Development of New Nations: An Essay in Comparative Analysis* (University of Chicago Press, 1964).
Jeffries, R., *Class, Power and Ideology in Ghana: The Railwaymen of Sekondi* (Cambridge University Press, 1978).
Jenkins, R., *Dependent Industrialization in Latin America*, (New York: Praeger, 1977).
——, *Transnational Corporations and Latin American Industry* (London: Macmillan 1983).
Johnson, H. G. (ed.), *Economic Nationalism in Old and New States* (London: Allen & Unwin, 1968).
Johnson, R. W., 'Guinea', in Dunn (1978), above.
Kaplinsky, R., Henley, J. S., and Leys, C., 'Debate on "Dependency" in Kenya', *Review of African Political Economy*, no. 17 (January–April 1980).
Kasfir, N., 'Prismatic Theory and African Administration', *World Politics*, vol. 21, no. 2 (January 1969).
——, *The Shrinking Political Arena* (Berkeley: University of California Press, 1976).
Kassalow, E. M. (ed.), *National Labor Movements in the Post-war World* (Evanston: Northwestern University Press, 1968).
Kirk-Greene, A. H. M., 'The Thin White Line: The Size of the British Colonial Service in Africa', *African Affairs*, vol. 79, no. 314 (January 1980).
——, and Rimmer, D., *Nigeria since 1970: A Political and Economic Outline* (London: Hodder & Stoughton, 1981).

Kirkpatrick, C., and Nixson, F., 'Transnational Corporations and Economic Development', *Journal of Modern African Studies*, vol. 19, no. 3 (September 1981).

Kuper, L., and Smith, M. G. (eds.), *Pluralism in Africa* (Berkeley: University of California Press, 1969).

Laitin, D. D., 'Somalia's Military Government and Scientific Socialism', in Rosberg and Callaghy (1979), below.

Lamb, G., 'The Military and Development in Eastern Africa', in *Military Regimes*, Bulletin of the Institute of Development Studies, University of Sussex, vol. 4, no. 4 (September 1972).

La Palombara, J., and Weiner, M. (eds.), *Political Parties and Political Development* (Princeton University Press, 1966).

Lee, J. M., 'Parliament in Republican Ghana', *Parliamentary Affairs*, vol. xvi, no. 4 (1963).

Legum, C., *Pan Africanism: A Short Political Guide* (London: Pall Mall, 1962).

——, and Hodges, T., *After Angola: The War over Southern Africa* (London: Rex Collings, 1976).

Leonard, D. K. (ed.), *Rural Administration in Kenya* (Nairobi: East African Literature Bureau, 1973).

Le Vine, V. T., *Political Corruption: The Ghana Case* (Stanford: Hoover Institution Press, 1975).

Lewis, W. A., *Development Planning. The Essentials of Economic Policy* (London: Allen & Unwin, 1966).

Leys, C., 'What is the Problem about Corruption?', *Journal of Modern African Studies*, vol. 3, no. 2 (1965).

——, 'The Political Climate for Economic Development', *African Affairs*, vol. 65, no. 258 (1966).

——, *Underdevelopment in Kenya: The Political Economy of Neo-Colonialism, 1964–1971* (London: Heinemann, 1975).

——, 'The "Overdeveloped" Post Colonial State: A Re-evaluation', *Review of African Political Economy*, no. 5 (January–April 1976).

——, 'Capital Accumulation, Class Formation and Dependency', in *The Socialist Register, 1978* – see Miliband and Saville, below.

——, 'African Economic Development in Theory and Practice', *Dædalus*, vol. iii, no. 2 (Spring 1982).

——, (ed.), *Politics and Change in Developing Countries: Studies in the Theory and Practice of Development* (Cambridge University Press, 1969).

Leys, R., and Tostensen, A., 'Regional Co-operation in Southern Africa: the Southern African Development Co-ordination Conference', *Review of African Political Economy*, no. 23 (January–April 1982).

Limqueco, P., and McFarlane, B. (eds.), *Neo-Marxist Theories of Development* (London: Croom Helm, 1983).

Lofchie, M. F., 'Representative Government, Bureaucracy, and Political Development: The African Case', *Journal of Developing Areas*, vol. ii, no. 1 (October 1967).

——, 'The Uganda Coup – Class Action by the Military', *Journal of Modern African Studies*, vol. 10, no. 1 (1972).

——, (ed.), *The State of the Nations: Constraints on Development in Independent Africa* (Berkeley: University of California Press, 1971).

Lonsdale, J., 'States and Social Processes in Africa: A Historiographical Survey', *African Studies Review*, vol. xxiv, nos. 2/3 (June/September 1981).

Low, S., 'The Role of Trade Unions in the Newly Independent Countries of Africa', in Kassalow (1968), above.

Luckham, R., *The Nigerian Military: A Sociological Analysis of Authority and Revolt, 1960–67* (Cambridge University Press, 1971).

——, 'A Comparative Typology of Civil–Military Relations', *Government and Opposition*, vol. 6, no. 1 (Winter 1971).

——, 'Armaments, Underdevelopment, and Demilitarisation in Africa', in *Alternatives: A Journal of World Policy*, vol. vi, no. 2 (July 1980).

——, 'French Militarism in Africa', *Review of African Political Economy*, no. 24 (May–August 1982).

Lusignan, G. de, *French-Speaking Africa since Independence* (London: Pall Mall, 1969).

Lynch, B., 'The Somali Democratic Republic. The one that got away', in Wiles (1982), below.

Lyon, P., and Manor, J. (eds.), *Transfer and Transformation: Political Institutions in the New Commonwealth* (Leicester University Press, 1983).

Mackenzie, W. J. M., and Robinson, K. E. (eds.), *Five Elections in Africa* (Oxford: Clarendon Press, 1960).

Mackintosh, J. P., *et al.*, *Nigerian Government and Politics* (London: Allen & Unwin, 1966).

Makonnen, Ras, *Pan-Africanism from Within*, as recorded and edited by King, K. (Nairobi: Oxford University Press, 1973).

Mannoni, D. O., *Prospero and Caliban: The Psychology of Colonization* (London: Methuen, 1956).

Marcum, J., *The Angolan Revolution*, vol. i: *The Anatomy of an Explosion (1950–1962)*, vol. ii: *Exile Politics and Guerrilla Warfare (1962–1976)* (Cambridge, Mass.: Massachusetts Institute of Technology Press, 1969 and 1978).

Markakis, J., *Ethiopia: Anatomy of a Traditional Polity* (Oxford: Clarendon Press, 1974).

——, and Ayele, N., *Class and Revolution in Ethiopia* (Nottingham: Spokesman, 1978).

Martin, D., and Johnson, P., *The Struggle for Zimbabwe: The Chimurenga War* (London: Faber & Faber, 1981).

Mayall, J., 'African Unity and the OAU: The Place of a Political Myth in African Diplomacy', *The Handbook of World Affairs*, vol. 27 (1973).

Mazrui, A. A., 'Pluralism and National Integration', in Kuper and Smith (1969), above.

McMullan, M., 'A Theory of Corruption', *Sociological Review*, vol. 9, no. 2 (June 1961).

Melson, R., and Wolpe, H., *Nigeria: Modernization and the Politics of Communalism* (East Lansing: Michigan State University Press, 1971).

Mende, J., 'Senegal: Diouf's New Directions', *Africa Report*, vol. 27, no. 6 (November–December 1982).

Miliband, R., and Saville, J. (eds.), *The Socialist Register, 1978* and *1980* (London: Merlin Press, 1978 and 1980).

Milne, R. S., 'Bureaucracy and Development Administration', *Public Administration*, vol. 51 (Winter 1973).

Minogue, M. (ed.), *Manchester Papers on Development. Studies in Decentralisation: Papua New Guinea, Botswana, Sri Lanka*, issue no. 3 (Manchester: Administrative Studies, December 1981).

Molteno, R., 'Cleavage and Conflict in Zambian Politics: A Study in Sectionalism', in Tordoff (1974), below.

Montgomery, J. D., and Siffin, W. J. (eds.), *Approaches to Development: Politics, Administration and Change* (New York: McGraw-Hill, 1966).

Morgenthau, R. S., *Political Parties in French-Speaking West Africa* (Oxford: Clarendon Press, 1964).

Morris-Jones, W. H., 'Dominance and Dissent: Their Inter-relations in the Indian Party System', *Government and Opposition*, vol. 1, no. 4 (July–September 1966).

Mueller, S. D., 'Retarded Capitalism in Tanzania', in *The Socialist Register, 1980* – see Miliband and Saville, above.

Munslow, B., 'The 1980 Coup in Guinea-Bissau', *Review of African Political Economy*, no. 21 (May–September 1981).

——, 'Disengagement from a Regional Sub-System: Problems and Prospects', *Journal of Area Studies*, no. 4 (Autumn 1981).

——, *Mozambique: The Revolution and its Origins* (London: Longman, 1983).

Mwansasu, B. U., and Pratt, C. (eds.), *Towards Socialism in Tanzania* (University of Toronto Press, 1979).

Nagel, R., and Rathbone, R., 'The OAU at Kinshasa', *The World Today*, vol. 23 (November 1967).

Nettl, J. P., 'Strategies in the Study of Political Development', in Leys (1969), above.

Nkrumah, K., *The Autobiography of Kwame Nkrumah* (Edinburgh: Nelson, 1957).

——, *Africa Must Unite* (London: Heinemann, 1963).

——, *Neo-Colonialism: The Last Stage of Imperialism* (New York: International Publishers, 1965).

Nyawo, C., and Rich, T., 'Zimbabwe after Independence', *Review of African Political Economy*, no. 18 (May–August 1980).

Nye, J. S., Jr., *Pan-Africanism and East African Integration* (Cambridge, Mass.: Harvard University Press, 1966).

——, 'Corruption and Political Development: A Cost-Benefit Analysis', *American Political Science Review*, vol. LXI, no. 2 (June 1967).

Nyerere, J. K., *Freedom and Unity: A Selection from Writings and Speeches, 1952–65* (Dar es Salaam: Oxford University Press, 1966).

——, *Freedom and Socialism: A Selection from Writings and Speeches, 1965–67* (Dar es Salaam: Oxford University Press, 1968).

O'Brien, D. B. Cruise, 'Modernisation, Order and the Erosion of the Democratic Ideal', *Journal of Development Studies*, vol. 8, no. 4 (July 1972).

——, *Saints and Politicans: Essays in the Organisation of a Senegalese Peasant Society* (London: Cambridge University Press, 1975).

——, 'Senegal', in Dunn (1978), above.

——, 'Ruling Class and Peasantry in Senegal, 1960–1976: The Politics of a Monocrop Economy', in O'Brien, R. Cruise (1979), below.

O'Brien, R. Cruise, (ed.), *The Political Economy of Underdevelopment: Dependence in Senegal* (Beverly Hills: Sage, 1979).

Okumu, J. J., 'The Socio-Political Setting', in Hyden, Jackson and Okumu (1970), above.

Oliver, R., and Fage, J. D., *A Short History of Africa* (Harmondsworth: Penguin, 1962).

Ottaway, D., and M., *Ethiopia: Empire in Revolution* (New York: Africana, 1978).

——, *Afrocommunism* (New York: Africana, 1981).

Oyediran, O., and Olagunju, O., 'The Military and the Politics of Revenue Allocation', in Oyediran (1979), below.

Oyediran, O. (ed.), *Nigerian Government and Politics under Military Rule, 1966–79* (London: Macmillan, 1979).

Panter-Brick, S. K. (ed.), *Soldiers and Oil: The Political Transformation of Nigeria* (London: Frank Cass, 1978).

——, 'Africanisation in Zimbabwe', in Lyon and Manor (1983), above.

Plamenatz, J., *Ideology* (London: Pall Mall, 1970).

Pool, D., *Eritrea: Africa's Longest War* (London: Anti-Slavery Society, 1979).

Pratt, R. C., 'The Administration of Economic Planning in a Newly Independent State: The Tanzanian Experience, 1963–66', *Journal of Commonwealth Political Studies*, vol. v, no. 1 (March 1967).

——, *The Critical Phase in Tanzania, 1945–68. Nyerere and the Emergence of a Socialist Strategy* (Cambridge University Press, 1976).

——, 'Tanzania's Transition to Socialism', in Mwansasu and Pratt (1979), above.

Pye, L. W., *Politics, Personality, and Nation Building: Burma's Search for Identity* (New Haven: Yale University Press, 1962).

Racine, A., 'The People's Republic of Benin' and 'The People's Republic of Congo', in Wiles (1982), below.

Ranger, T., 'The Changing of the Old Guard: Robert Mugabe and the Revival of ZANU', *Journal of Southern African Studies*, vol. 7, no. 1 (October 1980).

Rasmussen, T., 'The Popular Basis of Anti-Colonial Protest', in Tordoff (1974), below.

Reilly, W., 'District Development Planning in Botswana', in Minogue (1981), above.

Riggs, F. W., *Administration in Developing Countries: The Theory of Prismatic Society* (Boston: Houghton-Mifflin, 1964).

——, 'Administrative Development: An Elusive Concept', in Montgomery and Siffin (1966), above.

——, (ed.), *Frontiers of Development* (Durham, N.C.: Duke University Press, 1970).

Roberts, H., 'The Algerian Bureaucracy', *Review of African Political Economy*, no. 24 (May–August 1982).

Robinson, K. E., 'Political Development in French West Africa', in Stillman (1955), below.

Robinson, R., and Gallagher, J., with Denny, A., *Africa and the Victorians: The Official Mind of Imperialism* (London: Macmillan, 1961).

Robson, P., and Roe, A. R., 'The Reshaping of East African Economic Co-operation', parts 1 and 2, *East Africa Journal*. vol. IV, no. 5 (August 1967).

Rodney, W., *How Europe Underdeveloped Africa* (Dar es Salaam: Tanzania Publishing House, 1972, and London: Bogle L'Ouverture, 1972).

Rosberg, C. G., Jr and Nottingham, J., *The Myth of Mau Mau: Nationalism in Kenya* (New York: Praeger, 1966).

Rosberg, C. G., and Callaghy, T. M. (eds.), *Socialism in Sub-Saharan Africa: A New Assessment* (Berkeley: Institute of International Studies, University of California, 1979).

Rostow, W. W., *Stages of Economic Growth: A Non-Communist Manifesto* (Cambridge University Press, 1960).

Rothchild, D., 'Military Regime Performance: An Appraisal of the Ghana Experience, 1972–78', *Comparative Politics*, vol. 12, no. 4 (July 1980).

Rweyemamu, A. H., and Hyden, G. (eds.), *A Decade of Public Administration in Africa* (Nairobi: East African Literature Bureau, 1975).

Samoff, J., *Tanzania: Local Politics and the Structure of Power* (Madison: University of Wisconsin Press, 1974).

Sandbrook, R., 'Patrons, Clients and Factions: New Dimensions of Conflict Analysis in Africa', *Canadian Journal of Political Science*, vol. V, no. 1 (March 1972).

——, *Proletarians and African Capitalism: The Kenyan Case, 1962–70* (Cambridge University Press, 1975).

——, and Cohen, R. (eds.), *The Development of an African Working Class: Studies in Class Formation and Action* (University of Toronto Press, 1975).

Saul, J. S., 'African Socialism in One Country: Tanzania', in Arrighi and Saul (1973), above.

——, *The State and Revolution in Eastern Africa* (London: Heinemann, 1979).

Schaffer, B. B., 'The Concept of Preparation: Some Questions about the Transfer of Systems of Government', *World Politics*, vol. XVIII, no. 1 (October 1965).

——, 'The Deadlock in Development Administration', in Leys (1969), above.

——, 'Administrative Legacies and Links in the Post-Colonial State: Preparation, Training and Administrative Reform', *Development and Change*, vol. 9, no. 2 (April 1978).

——, (ed.), *Administrative Training and Development* (New York: Praeger, 1974).

Scott, J. C., *Comparative Political Corruption* (Englewood Cliffs, N.J.: Prentice-Hall, 1972).

Seton-Watson, H., *Nations and States: An Enquiry into the Origins of Nations and the Politics of Nationalism* (London: Methuen, 1977).

Shaw, T. M., 'Zambia's Foreign Policy', in Aluko (1977), above.

——, and Mugomba, A. T., 'The Political Economy of Regional Détente: Zambia and Southern Africa', *Journal of African Studies*, 4 (Winter 1977).

Shils, E., 'The Concept and Function of Ideology', *A Reprint from the International Encyclopedia of the Social Sciences*, vol. 7 (New York: Macmillan and the Free Press, 1968).

Shivji, I. G., 'The Class Struggle Continues' (Dar es Salaam, mimeo., 1973).

——, *Class Struggles in Tanzania* (London: Heinemann, 1976).

——, *et al.*, *The Silent Class Struggle* (Dar es Salaam: Tanzania Publishing House, 1973).

Simwinga, G. K., 'Corporate Autonomy and Government Control of State Enterprises', in Tordoff (1980), below.

Sklar, R. L., *Nigerian Political Parties: Power in an Emergent African Nation* (Princeton University Press, 1963).

——, 'Political Science and National Integration – A Radical Approach', *Journal of Modern African Studies*, vol. 5, no.1 (1967).

——, 'Nigerian Politics in Perspective', and 'Contradictions in the Nigerian Political System', in Melson and Wolpe (1971), above.

——, *Corporate Power in an African State: The Political Impact of Multinational Mining Companies in Zambia* (Berkeley: University of California Press, 1975).

——, 'The Nature of Class Domination in Africa', *Journal of Modern African Studies*, vol. 17, no. 4 (1979).

Slade, R., *The Belgian Congo* (London: Oxford University Press, 2nd edn, 1961).

Stillman, C. W. (ed.), *Africa in the Modern World* (University of Chicago Press, 1955).

Stockwell, J., *In Search of Enemies: A CIA Story* (New York: Norton, 1978).

Stryker, R. E., 'A Local Perspective on Development Strategy in the Ivory Coast', in Lofchie (1971), above.

Sundkler, B., *Bantu Prophets in South Africa* (Oxford University Press, 2nd edn, 1961).

Svendsen, K. E., 'Socialist Problems after the Arusha Declaration', *East Africa Journal*, vol. iv, no. 2 (May 1967).

Swainson, N., *The Development of Corporate Capitalism in Kenya, 1918–1977* (London: Heinemann, 1980).

Tordoff, W., 'The Brong-Ahafo Region', *The Economic Bulletin* (Accra), vol. 3, no. 5 (May 1959).

——, *Ashanti under the Prempehs, 1888–1935* (Oxford University Press, 1965).

——, *Government and Politics in Tanzania* (Nairobi: East African Publishing House, 1967).

——, (ed.), *Politics in Zambia* (Manchester University Press, 1974).

——, (ed.), *Administration in Zambia* (Manchester University Press, 1980).

Udoji, J. O., 'Some Measures for Improving Performance and Management of the Public Enterprises', in Rweyemamu and Hyden (1975), above.

Vail, L., and White, L., *Capitalism and Colonialism in Mozambique* (London: Heinemann, 1981).

Wallerstein, I., 'Voluntary Associations', in Coleman and Rosberg (1964), above.

——, 'Elites in French-Speaking West Africa', *Journal of Modern African Studies*, vol. 3, No. 1 (May 1965).

——, 'Decline of the Party in Single-Party African States', in La Palombara and Weiner (1966), above.

——, *Africa: The Politics of Unity* (New York: Random House, 1967).

——, *The Capitalist World Economy* (Cambridge University Press, 1979).

Warren, B., *Imperialism: Pioneer of Capitalism* (London: Verso, 1980).

Weiss, H. F., *Political Protest in the Congo: The Parti Solidaire Africain during the Independence Struggle* (Princeton University Press, 1967).

Welch, C. E., Jr (ed.), *Political Modernization: A Reader in Comparative Political Change* (Belmont, California: Wadsworth, 1967).

Whitaker, C. S., *The Politics of Tradition, Continuity and Change in Northern Nigeria, 1946–1966* (Princeton University Press, 1970).

Wildavsky, A., 'If planning is Everything, maybe it's Nothing', *Policy Sciences*, vol. 4, no. 2 (June 1973).

Wiles, P. (ed.), *The New Communist Third World* (London: Croom Helm, 1982).

Williams, G., and Turner, T., 'Nigeria', in Dunn (1978), above.

Wolfers, M., *Politics in the Organisation of African Unity* (London: Methuen, 1976).

Yahaya, A. D., 'The Struggle for Power in Nigeria, 1966–79', in Oyediran (1979), above.

'Yates, P.', 'The Prospects for Socialist Transition in Zimbabwe', *Review of African Political Economy*, no. 18 (May–August 1980).

Young, C., *The Politics of Cultural Pluralism* (Madison: University of Wisconsin Press, 1976).

——, *Ideology and Development in Africa* (New Haven: Yale University Press, 1982).

——, 'Patterns of Social Conflict: State, Class and Ethnicity', *Dædalus*, vol. III, no. 2 (Spring 1982).

Young, R., and Fosbrooke, H. A., *Smoke in the Hills. Political Tension in the Morogoro District of Tanganyika* (Evanston: Northwestern University Press, 1960).

Younger, K. G., *The Public Service in New States: A Study in Some Trained Manpower Problems* (Oxford University Press, 1960).

Zafiris, N., 'The People's Republic of Angola: Soviet-Type Economy in the Making', and 'The People's Republic of Mozambique: Pragmatic Socialism', in Wiles (1982), above.

Zolberg, A. R., *One-Party Government in the Ivory Coast* (Princeton University Press, 1964).

——, *Creating Political Order: The Party-States of West Africa* (Chicago: Rand McNally and Co., 1966).

——, 'The Political Use of Economic Planning in Mali', in Johnson (1968), above.

2. Conference and Seminar Papers

Amsden, A. H., 'Trade Unions and Politics: Kenya', in collected seminar papers on *Labour Unions and Political Organizations* (Institute of Commonwealth Studies, University of London, January–May 1967), no. 3.

Austin, D. G., 'The Ghana Case', in collected seminar papers on *The Politics of Demilitarisation* (Institute of Commonwealth Studies, University of London, April–May 1966).

Banfield, J., 'The Structure and Administration of the East Africa High Commission and the East African Common Services Organisation', paper presented at the University of East Africa Conference on East African Federation, Nairobi, 26–30 November 1963.

Berry, M., 'Factional Conflict in the Nigerian Army: the July 1975 Coup and the Decision to Demilitarise', *Huddersfield Papers in Politics*, 3 (Autumn 1981).

Burke, F. G., 'Public Administration in Africa: The Legacy of Inherited Colonial Institutions', paper presented at the World Congress of the International Political Science Association, Brussels, 18–23 September 1967.

Cliffe, L., 'Towards an Evaluation of the Zimbabwe Nationalist Movement', paper presented at the Political Studies Association, University of Exeter, 31 March–2 April 1980.

Dudley, B. J., 'Political Parties and the 1979 Elections', in Dent, M., Yahaya, A., and Austin, D. (eds.), *Nigeria: The First Year of Civilian Rule. The Operation of the Constitution* (University of Keele: Conference Papers, mimeo., September 1980).

Goodison, P., 'Does SADCC need a new dimension?', paper presented at the Conference on Research in Progress in Southern Africa, 21–23 March 1983 (Centre for Southern African Studies, University of York).

Middlemas, K., 'Mozambique: Two Years of Independence', in *Mozambique* (University of Edinburgh: Seminar Proceedings, Centre of African Studies, mimeo., 1979).

Munslow, B., 'The Liberation Struggle in Mozambique and the Origins of Post-Independence Political and Economic Policy', in *Mozambique* (1979), above.

——, 'A Critique of Theories of Socialist Transition on the Periphery: Some Preliminary Comments', paper presented at the Conference of the Development Studies Association (University of Oxford, 1981).

——, 'Afrocommunism?', paper presented at the Conference of the Political Studies Association (University of Newcastle, April 1983).

Panter-Brick, S. K., 'A Different Model? Some Aspects of Francophone Educational Ties', postgraduate seminar paper (Institute of Commonwealth Studies, University of London, November 1982).

Plamenatz, J., 'Ideology', paper presented to the Senior Political Theory seminar (Department of Government, University of Manchester, 1972).

Wiseman, J. A., 'The Opposition Parties of Botswana', *Collected Papers*, vol. 4 (Centre for Southern African Studies, University of York, mimeo., 1979).

3. Government Reports

Ghana: A New Charter for the Civil Service (Accra: Government Printer, 1960).

Republic of Kenya: Review of Statutory Boards (Nairobi: Government Printer, 1979).

Republic of Zambia: Report of the Committee on Parastatal Bodies (Lusaka: Government Printer, 1978).

The United Republic of Tanzania: Report of the Presidential Commission on the Establishment of a Democratic One Party State (Dar es Salaam: Government Printer, 1965).

4. Lectures and Addresses

Hyden, G., 'Decentralisation in Tanzania': summary of a lecture delivered at the University of Zambia, Lusaka, March 1973.

Minogue, M. M., 'The Politics of Development Planning': lecture for the core course 'Perspectives on Development', M.A. Econ. programme in Development Studies, University of Manchester, 1979.

Nyerere, J. K.: Address on the Occasion of Mainland Tanzania's Twentieth Anniversary of Independence (Dar es Salaam, December 1981, mimeo.).

Panter-Brick, S. K., 'French African Administration', lecture for course P.A. 320/430, University of Zambia, Lusaka, 1969.

Sklar, R. L., 'Political Aspects of Regional Organization in Africa', synopsis of lecture in the 'Africa and the World Series', University of Zambia, Lusaka, 1966.

——, *Democracy in Africa*: presidential address to the 25th annual meeting of the African Studies Association, Washington D.C., 5 November 1982 (reproduced by the African Studies Center, University of California, Los Angeles).

5. Newspapers and Magazines

The Guardian (London and Manchester), 1981–83, especially the special issue on Angola, 2 March 1981, including articles on 'Social Upheaval' and 'Party Leaders' by J. Steele, and the article on Mozambique – 'Machel back-pedals on private enterprise' – by J. Hanlon, 15 July 1981.

The Observer (London), 2 January 1983, on Ethiopia's relations with the Soviet Union and Cuba.

The Times (London), 10 February 1982: 'Focus on Zimbabwe', especially the articles by S. Taylor.

West Africa (London), 24 May and 7 June 1982 on ECOWAS (especially the article on 'Trade problems and prospects', by S. K. B. Asante) and the issues for August and September 1983 covering the Nigerian elections.

6. Theses and Dissertations

Chikulo, B., *Rural Administration in Zambia: Organisation and Performance in Former Opposition Areas* (PhD thesis, University of Manchester, 1983).

Elhussein, A. M., *Decentralization and Participation in Rural Development: The Sudanese Experience* (PhD thesis, University of Manchester, 1983).

Goodison, P., *The Construction of Socialism in Mozambique* (BA Econ. dissertation, University of Manchester, 1982).

Hartmann,, J., *Development Policy-Making in Tanzania, 1962–1982: A Critique of Sociological Interpretations* (PhD thesis, University of Hull, 1983).

Molloy, J., *Political Communication in Lushoto District, Tanzania* (PhD thesis, University of Kent at Canterbury, 1971).

Munslow, B., *FRELIMO and the Mozambican Revolution* (PhD thesis, University of Manchester, 1980).

Szeftel, M., *Conflicts, Spoils and Class Formation in Zambia* (PhD thesis, University of Manchester, 1978).

7. Miscellaneous

'Angola after Independence: Struggle for Supremacy', *Conflict Studies* (London, November 1975), prepared by the Research Department of the Institute for the Study of Conflict.

Employment, Incomes and Equality (Geneva: ILO, 1972).

Ikwezi, 10, December 1978: 'ZANU and the Advancement of the Zimbabwean Revolution' (Nottingham – A Black Liberation Journal).

Mozambique Revolution, no. 56, June–September 1973 (Dar es Salaam – the organ of FRELIMO).

North-South: A Programme for Survival, and *Common Crisis* – Reports of the Independent Commission on International Development Issues under the Chairmanship of Willy Brandt (London: Pan Books, 1980, 1983).

The Annual Register. World Events, 1969–72 (ed. I. Macadam), 1973–82 (ed. H. V. Hodson), each volume published in London by Longman in the year following the events recorded:

    Baldock, R. W., 'Zimbabwe', 1980.

    Clapham, C., 'Ethiopia', 1974–81.

    ——, 'Somalia', 1969–81.

    Hallett, R., 'Mozambique', 1979–81.

    ——, 'Rwanda and Burundi', 1979.

    Jones, D. H., 'Mozambique', 1975–78.

    Tordoff, W., 'Kenya, Tanzania and Uganda', 1971–82.

    ——, 'The East African Community', 1971, 1973 and 1975–77, the articles from 1975 being subsumed within the section on 'African Conferences and Institutions'.

    Whiteman, K., 'African Conferences and Institutions', 1973, 1981.

    Wilton-Marshall, O. E., 'African Conferences and Institutions', 1974–80.

——, 'Chad', 1979–80.
——, 'Mali', 'Ivory Coast, Upper Volta, Niger, Benin, Togo' and 'People's Republic of the Congo', 1979.

Index

AAPC, *see* All-African People's Conference
Aborigines' Rights Protection Society (ARPS), 62
Accelerated Rural Development Programme (ARDP) (Botswana), 112
Action Group (AG) (Nigeria), 64, 161; origins, 65–6; seeks electoral allies, 83; use of regional power base, 113
Adamolekun, Ladipo, 208
Administration, 125–31; Africanisation, 132–4, in Zimbabwe, 202; Belgian colonies, 38–9; British colonies, 36–7; characteristics at independence, 125–7; civil service relations with military regimes, 137; decentralisation, 9–10; degree of autonomy, 131; Ethiopia, 214; French colonies, 34–5, 123; Guinea, 206; Guinea-Bissau, 200; inter-war years, 41–2; parastatal sector, 139–44; Portuguese colonies, 39–40; post-colonial, effect on development, 134–9; colonial legacy, 4, 123, 125; shortage of skilled local staff, 79, 132, 138; *see also* Bureaucracy; Institutions
AEF (Afrique Equatoriale Française), *see* French Equatorial Africa
African Liberation Committee (ALC), 243, 248–50
African Mineworkers' Union (AMU), 60, 84
African National Congress (ANC) (Zambia), 116–17
Afrique Occidentale Française (AOF), *see* French West Africa
Afro-Shirazi Party (ASP) (Zanzibar), 111

AG, *see* Action Group (AG) (Nigeria)
Agriculture, development corporations, 139; functional specialists, 43; in Angola, 197; in Ghana, 176; in Guinea, 207; in Mozambique, 193, 194; in Tanzania, 205; in Zimbabwe, 203; investment in inter-war years, 43; marketing boards, 139, 210, 211; planning measures, 149–50; Somalia, 211, 212; subsistence farming, 89; use of indigenous labour, 41, 88; *see also* Cash crops
Ahidjo, Ahmadou, 59
Akintola, S. L., 113–14, 162, 163
Akoto, Bafuor Osei, 65
Alavi, Hamza, 131
ALC, *see* African Liberation Committee (ALC)
Algeria, 44, 107–8; human rights record, 276
All-African People's Conference, 240
All People's Congress (APC) (Sierra Leone), 103
Alves, Nito, 198
Amin, Idi, 160, 161, 172, 233
Amin, Samir, 15, 292
AMU, *see* African Mineworkers' Union (AMU)
Andrain, Charles, 104
Anglo-American Corporation, 23, 42, 272
Anglo-Nigerian Defence Pact (1960), 75
Angola, class not yet political determinant, 94–5; Cuban intervention, 198; degree of autonomy, 274; early trade with Europeans, 30; educational standards, 3; human rights record, 278; independence, 186;

legislative and executive authority, 198; liberation struggle, 191; Marxist-Leninist ideology, 181; military coup attempt, 152; power struggle, 186; problems following independence, 196–7; revolutionary regimes, 7, 184–6, 196–9; South African incursions, 186, 199; trading links, 13; *see also* Portuguese colonies

Ankrah, J. A., 167

AOF (Afrique Occidentale Française), *see* French West Africa

Apter, David, 15, 112

Arboussier, Gabriel d', 63, 124

ARDP, *see* Accelerated Rural Development Programme (ARDP) (Botswana)

ARPS, *see* Aborigines' Rights Protection Society (ARPS)

Arusha Declaration (1967), 5–6, 16–17, 22, 90, 105, 204

Ashanti, 29; backing NLM, 65; cocoa hold-ups (1930s), 42; sub-nationalism, 80; support for NLM, 115

Ashanti Confederacy, 36, 37

Austin, Dennis, 70, 160, 280

Awolowo, Obafemi, 83, 113, 114, 115, 169

Azikiwe, Nnamdi, 45

Balewa, Sir Abubakar Tafewa, 163

Banfield, Jane, 231, 232

Banks, 139; performance, 141; public ownership, 7

Baran, Paul, 15

Barker, Jonathan, 20

Barotseland, 80

Barré, Mohamed Siyad, 210

Barwah, C. M., 160

Bates, Robert, 88

Bauxite, 47

Bechuanaland, pre-independence elections, 71; *see also* Botswana

Behrmann, Lucy, 141

Belgian colonies, 30, 38–9, 44

Belgian Congo, 31, 38, 72; *see also* Zaire

Bello, Sir Ahmadu, 163

Benin, 81; military regime, 10–11; revolutionary regimes, 7, 209–10; single-party election held by military regime, 178

Benin City, 29–30

Berg, Elliot, 58, 61

Berlin Conference (1884–5), 30, 34

Biafra, 81, 169, 173

Bloc Démocratique Sénégalais, 65

BNF, *see* Botswana National Front (BNF)

Boigny, Félix Houphouet, 6–7

Bokassa, Jean-Bedel, 172

Botswana, Accelerated Rural Development Programme (ARDP), 112; competition in party politics, 102; education, 12; exclusively civilian government, 155; human rights record, 276; position of private enterprise, 139; republic, 71; youth unemployment, 12; *see also* Bechuanaland

Botswana National Front (BNF), 99

Bowdich, Thomas, 29

Brass, Paul, 18

Brazzaville Conference (1944), 35, 41

British colonies, 30, 40; administration, 36, 123–4; competitive party politics, 102; decolonisation, 44; increasing nationalism, 51; indirect rule, 36–7; preparation for self-rule, 38; route to independence, 76; transfer of power, 69–75; union/party links, 58

British Petroleum, Nigerian holdings, nationalised, 13

British West Africa, congress-type organisations, 63; National Congress of, 62

Buganda, 50; constitutional position, 70, 80; Kabaka removed, 80; move away from federalism, 9

Burawoy, Michael, 90

Bureaucracy, additional demands at independence, 126; as communication channel, 120; colonial pattern, 126–7; corruption, 128; dominating sub-national levels of government, 108; growth in Zambia, 92; in post-colonial states, 127–32; limits of competence and power, 95, 132, 137; nationalism, 23, 52; power, 3; power-seeking, 90; pre-colonial kingdoms, 29; reforms, 138; relationship with politicians, 126; supplanting political parties, 7

Burundi, 153; human rights record, 252, 278

Busia, K. A., 65

Butler, Jeffrey, 58, 61

Cabral, Amilcar, 27, 187, 188, 191, 199;

Cabral, Amilcar – continued
  influence on MPLA, 196
Cabral, Luis, 200
Caetano, Marcello, 181
Callaghy, T. M., 104
Callinicos, A., 25
Cameroon, electoral coercion, 102;
  exclusively civilian government, 155;
  planning, 147–8; presidential power, 5;
  see also French Cameroons
Campbell, Bonnie, 269
Cape Verde Islands, human rights
  record, 277; independence, 188;
  Marxist-Leninist ideology, 181;
  population, 199; *see also* Portuguese
  colonies
Capitalism, European, propped up by
  colonisation, 33; exploitation of Third
  World, 21; in traditional African
  society, 87; peasant production modes
  not destroyed by, 97; policy models
  adopted, 7; progressive elements, 23;
  restrained to prevent imbalances, 12
Cardoso, Fernando Henrique, 15, 25
Cash crops, 41; associations of farmers
  formed, 52; dependence on, 2; impact
  on rural life, 46–7; increased prices, 43;
  socio-economic impact, 52; *see also*
  Agriculture
CCM, *see* Chama cha Mapinduzi (CCM)
Central African Federation, 70
Central African Republic, 153
CFAO, *see* Compagnie Française de
  l'Afrique Occidentale (CFAO)
Chabal, Patrick, 186
Chad, 254–5; decolonisation, 44;
  electoral coercion, 102; military coup,
  153
Chama cha Mapinduzi (CCM), 111; *see
  also* Tanganyika African National
  Union (TANU)
Chamberlain, Joseph, 32, 33
Chambers, Robert, 112
Chiefs, attitudes to nationalist
  movements, 51; in social stratification,
  87; resentment towards, 37
Chikulo, Bornwell, 117
Chitepo, Herbert, 189
Christian nationalists, 54
Christianity, cultural implications, 53–4;
  United Native African Church, 54; *see
  also* Religious associations
CIAS, *see* Conference of Independent

African States (CIAS)
Class, *see* Socio-economic aspects
Cliffe, Lionel, 189
Coastal trading, 29–30
Cocoa, 2; Ghana, production during
  military rule, 175; hold-ups in trade
  (1930s), 42; increased prices, 43;
  influence on Ghana's development,
  46–7; socio-economic impact in
  Ghana, 52
Cohen, Robin, 61
Coleman, James, 15, 20, 53, 104, 136
Collier, Ruth, 72, 73–4, 102, 178
Colonialism, 1–2; beneficial effects, 34;
  characteristics, 41, of administration,
  123; condemnation, 51; during
  Depression, 42; influencing social
  stratification, 87; inter-war
  administration, 41–2; phases, 40;
  post-war discontent, 43–4; surviving
  legacies, 3–4, 45–8; to protect trade,
  21; *see also* Pre-colonial history
Colonisation, 30; aims, 31–2; arbitrary
  boundaries, 30, 250
Communalism, 79–87; relationship with
  class, 96–100
Compagnie Française de l'Afrique
  Occidentale (CFAO), 43
Conference of Independent African
  States (CIAS), 240
Congo, decolonisation, 44; elections, 73,
  178; Katangese secession, 253; limited
  impact of revolution, 167; military
  coup, 152; revolutionary regime, 7,
  209–10
Congo Free State, *see* Belgian Congo
Congress-type organisations, 63
Constitutions, power-sharing
  arrangements, 37
Convention People's Party (CPP)
  (Ghana), 4; competition with United
  Party, 103; foundation, 64; general
  election results (1956), 70; patronage
  of Brongs, 115; 'positive action'
  campaign, 59; proscription, 8; type of
  party, 67
Copper, 2, 47; increased exports, 43;
  Zambian nationalisation, 13, 23
Corruption, 220; combative measures in
  Mozambique, 193–4; in bureaucracy,
  128; in miltary regimes, 171–2
Coups d'états, *see* Military coups
Cowen, Michael P., 24

Cox, Thomas, 119
CPP, *see* Convention People's Party (CPP) (Ghana)
Craft organisations, 57
Crowder, Michael, 35
Cuba, intervention in Angola, 198
Cultures, authority and behaviour patterns, 17; disrupted by western-style institutions, 51; importance in development, 27; increasing self-awareness, 51; pluralism, 98; shaping administrative style, 19; variety, 1, 50, 78, 98

Dahomey, effects of communalism, 82; elections, 73; military coup, 152, 154; *see also* Benin
Davidson, Basil, 201
Decalo, Samuel, 154–5, 157, 160, 167, 177, 209
Decolonisation, 44
Defence agreements, 75, 157
Delano, Isaac, 54
Demas, William, 233
Demographic aspects, variety, 1
Dent, Martin, 166
Development, convergence of theories, 25; importance of ideology, 288–93; long-term solutions, 293–4; mobilisation role of political parties, 112; modernisation theory, 15, 16–20, 97, western basis, 18–19; national development corporations, 139; planning, 144–6, problems of implementation, 146–50; problems of definition, 262–3; related to capacity of state institutions, 284–8; schemes in 1950s, 43; state as main agent, 125; strategy limitations, 292; Third World interaction with developed world, 263; underdevelopment theory, 15, 20–6
Diplomacy, low status, 3
Doe, Samuel, 153
Du Bois, W. E. B., 239
Dupuis, Joseph, 29

EAC, *see* East African Community (EAC)
EACSO, *see* East African Common Services Organisation (EACSO)
East African, degree of poverty, 3; European colonisation, 30; proposed federation, 228

East African Common Services Organisation (EACSO), 230–4
East African Community (EAC), 230–4; demise, 14
East African Development Bank, 233
Eboué, Félix, 124
Economic Commission for Africa, 243
Economic Community of West African States (ECOWAS), 14, 234–7
Economic co-operation, promoted by OAU, 257–9; *see also* Economic organisations
Economic organisations, 229–39; smaller regional groupings, 230
Economies, at independence, 2; development, 2; effects of military regimes, 173–4; external imbalance, 258–9; growth, 264–8, comparisons, 265–6, 268, effect on equality, 269–72; ideological and performance differences, 261; in inter-war years, 42; indebtedness, 291; regional imbalances, 4; remaining dependent, 45, 47; weaknesses, 220; *see also* Development
ECOWAS, *see* Economic Community of West African States (ECOWAS)
Education, 12; affecting Africanisation of administration, 132–3; as aim of nationalist movement, 53; benefit to minority, 78; comparison between states, 3; cut-backs in Depression, 42; decision making, 111; forming élites, 87; functional specialists, 43; in Congo Free State, 38; mission schools, 54
Egypt, limited impact of revolution, 167
Eisenstadt, S. N., 18, 19
Elections, British and French systems compared, 73; coercion, 102; following withdrawal of military regimes, 11, 178; in French colonies, 72; pre-independence, 69; to legitimise president, 110; *see also* Ideologies; One-party system
Élites, attitudes to nationalist movements, 51; cause of political instability, 18; comparison of British and French policy effects, 73; conflict in Zambia, 82–3; distanced from mass, 3; exploitation of peasantry, 88; factions as technique of competition, 84
Enahoro, Anthony, 169

Entrepreneurship, indigenous, 45–6, 88, 125, political situation, 95
EPRP, *see* Ethiopian People's Revolutionary Party (EPRP)
Equality, effect of economic growth on, 269–72, 289
Eritrea, secessionist movements, 216
Ethiopia, administration, 214; economic reforms, 215; Eritrean secessionist movements, 216; human rights record, 277; Marxist-Leninist administration, 216; military regime, 11; problems facing regime, 218; Provisional Military Administrative Council, 214; revolutionary regime, 7, 213–19; sphere for US–Soviet rivalry, 225; war with Somalia, 14
Ethiopian churches, 54
Ethiopian People's Revolutionary Party (EPRP), 215
Ethnic aspects, conflict and cooperation, 82; cross-ethnic patron-client links, 83–4; disaffection of minorities, 79; intra-ethnic conflict, 85; pluralism, 78
Europe, first contacts with Africa, 30
Executive councils, creation, 38
Exploitation, 33; by colonisation, 51; in Portuguese colonies, 39; of peasants by urban elites, 88
Explorers, 30

Factionalism, *see* Communalism
Fanon, Frantz, 15
Farms, public ownership, 7; *see also* Agriculture; Cash crops
Federal government, demands in Ghana, 80; moves away from, 9; pressures for, 79; *see also* Nigeria
First, Ruth, 154, 160, 172, 177
Fischer, Georges, 58
FNLA, *see* Frente Nacional de Libertação de Angola (FNLA)
Forced labour, 35, 39, 41
Foreign aid, 12–13; to Somalia, 211
Foreign policies, 12–13
France, military presence, 157–8; reaction against nationalism, 66
Franchise, 2; aim of nationalist movements, 52; in French colonies, 72, 74
Frank, André Gunder, 15, 20, 25
FRELIMO, *see* Frente de Libertação de Moçambique (FRELIMO)

French Cameroons, party/union links, 58–9; United Native Church, 54; *see also* Cameroon
French colonies, 30; administration of, 34–5, 123, organisation of service, 124; changes in policy, 35–6; decolonisation, 44; economic and social phases, 40; elections, 72–4; forced labour, 35, 41; increasing nationalism, 51; military assistance and defence agreements, 75; transfer of power, 69–75; type of franchise, 74; union/party links, 58; vote to become autonomous republics, 102
French Equatorial Africa, administration, 34; autonomous republic, 74–5
French West Africa, administration, 34, 123–4; autonomous republic, 74–5; federal union proposal, 226; vote to become autonomous republic, 226
Frente de Libertação de Moçambique (FRELIMO), 191, 220; aims and tactics, 192; conflicts within, 183; Marxist-Leninist basis, 104; role, 109; transformed into vanguard party, 195
Frente Nacional de Libertação de Angola (FNLA), ethnic support, 184; external support, 186
Front de Libération Nationale (FLN) (Algeria), 108
Furtado, Celso, 15

Gabon, attempted military coup, 152, 155; decolonisation, 44; electoral coercion, 102; exclusively civilian government, 155
Gallagher, John, 32
Gambia, attempted military coup, 155; competition in party politics, 102; delays before independence, 69; exclusively civilian government, 155; groundnuts, 2; union with Senegal, 226
Garvey, Marcus, 239
Gaseitsiwe, B. S., 99
Geertz, Clifford, 79, 261.
Germany, break up of African empire, 41; colonisation by, 30
Ghana, Charter for the Civil Service, 135; cocoa, 2, socio-economic impact, 52; constitutional amendment, 9; degree of corruption, 129; democratic constitutions to follow military regime,

178; executive presidency, 71; factions
disrupting military regime, 173;
federal elements, 37; general election
results (1956), 70; increasing
bureaucratic power, 7–8; influence of
cocoa, 46–7; military coup, 152,
ideological basis, 160; military regime,
10, economic effects, 175–7, role of civil
service, 137; move away from
federalism, 9; National Liberation
Council, 11; one-party system, 4, 103;
patronage of political parties, 115;
performance of public enterprise, 141;
presidential power, 5; restoration of
multi-party politics, 4; restoration of
power to civilians, 166; transition to
independence, 66–7; *see also* Gold
Coast
Ghana Congress Party, 65
Gold Coast, 30; cocoa hold-ups (1930s),
42; decolonisation, 44; independence,
69; National Liberation Movement,
37; nationalism, clash with Ashanti,
80; progress to self-government, 69;
representative government, 38, 43;
riots (1948), 44, 64, 69, 76; unions'
political activism, 59; *see also* Ghana
Gold mining, 47, 175
Gold trade, 30
Goodison, Paul, 26, 27, 194, 238, 292
Gowon, Yakubu, 167, 169, 170
Groundnuts, 2, 84; *see also* Senegal
Grunitzky, Nicholas, 152
Gueye, Lamine, 65
Guinea, 74; administration, 206,
relations with party, 136; attempted
military coup, 155; development
planning, 145; dominance of rising
generation, 206; economy, 207;
exclusively civilian government, 155;
human rights record, 209,
277; ideology, 208; increasing
bureaucratic power, 7–8; one-party
system, 4; performance of public
enterprise, 141, 207; political
insecurity, 206; private trading, 208;
revolutionary regime, 205–9;
union-party links, 58
Guinea-Bissau, administration, 200;
economic problems, 201; human rights
record, 277; independence, 188;
internal conflict, 200–1; liberation
struggle, 191; Marxist-Leninist

ideology, 181; military coup, 201;
revolutionary regime, 7, 186–8,
199–202; weakness of political party, 9;
see also Portuguese colonies

Haile Selassie, Emperor of Ethiopia,
213–14
Hansen, Emmanuel, 160
Hanson, A. H., 144, 147
Harbeson, John W., 214
Harbours, *see* Infrastructural
development
Harris, William Wade, 55
Hartmann, Jeannette, 105
Hayford, Casely, 62
Hazlewood, Arthur, 233
Health, *see* Medical services
Hodgkin, Thomas, 35, 53
Hoskyns, Catherine, 239
Human rights, related to regime
performance, 276–9
Humanism, in Zambia, 92, 104
Huntington, Samuel, 17–18
Hyden, Goran, 24, 93, 97, 109, 136, 137,
139, 140

Ibn Battuta, 29
Ideologies, and degree of autonomy,
272–5; and human dignity, 276–9, 289;
definitions, 261–2; economic effects,
261; importance of, 288–93; link with
level of participation, 280–4, 289; main
categories, 262; *see also* Political parties
Ifeajuna, E. A., 162
Ilchman, Walter, 20
Iliffe, John, 30
IMF, *see* International Monetary Fund
(IMF)
Import–export houses, public
ownership, 7
Indebtedness, 291
Independence, as constitutional
monarchies, 71; as prerequisite of
socio-economic improvement, 61–2;
preparations in white settler areas, 38;
slow to come to Portuguese colonies,
40; trends in development, 4
Indirect rule, 36–8, 73
Industrialisation, 47; African capitalists,
87; development corporations, 139; in
Mozambique, 195; preceding
democratic processes, 126; problems, 2

Infrastructural development, 32–3, 34; use of forced labour, 41; *see also* Public works

Institutions, colonial legacy, 284; development, 130; effect of rapid modernisation, 17; for development planning, 148; indigenous, in indirect rule, 36; need to strengthen, 17; state capacity, 284–8; weaknesses, 2–3, 27; western-style, imposition, 51; *see also* Administration

Insurance companies, public ownership, 7

Interest groups, 56–62; sectional groups as, 82, 99; discouraged in Tanzania, 105–6

International Monetary Fund (IMF), 146; influence on Tanzanian policies, 90; influencing assertions of autonomy, 275; privatisation in Mali, 142; standby credits for Somalia, 213

International status, 3; at independence, 2; relations with former colonial powers, 224

Investment, in inter-war years, 42–3

Iron ore, 47

Ironsi, Aguiyi, 158, 163, 164, 168–9, 170

Islam, 54; Mahdist tradition, 56; *see also* Religious associations

Ivory Coast, decolonisation, 44; degree of poverty, 3; exclusively civilian government, 155; human rights record, 276; increasing bureaucratic power, 8; position of private enterprise, 139; state enterprises, 140

Ivory trade, 30

Jeffries, Richard, 61

Jumbe, Aboud, 229

Kampala Agreement (1964), 231, 232

Kano, Alhaji Aminu, 94

KANU, *see* Kenya African National Union (KANU)

Kaplinski, Rafael, 24

Kapwepwe, Simon, 116

Karume, Abeid, 229

Kasfir, Nelson, 127

Kaunda, Kenneth, 5, 83, 116; humanist ideology, 92

Keita, Modibo, 104, 227

Kenya, administration, relations with party, 136–7; attempted military coup, 152, 155–6; clientelism, 119; defence links, 158; East African federation proposal, 228; exclusively civilian government, 155; federal elements, 37; human rights record, 277; intra-ethnic conflict, 86; investment in inter-war years, 43; Kikuyu domination, 81; move away from federalism, 9; one-party system, 4; performance of state enterprises, 142; political parties, 103; position of private enterprise, 139; pre-independence elections, 71; presidential power, 5; trade union politics, 84; union/party links, 58, 60

Kenya African Democratic Union (KADU), 103

Kenya African National Union (KANU), 67, 103, 137; trade union commitment, 58

Kenya Federation of Labour (KFL), political influence, 58

Kenya People's Union, 103

Kenyatta, Jomo, 111; clientelism, 119

KFL, *see* Kenya Federation of Labour (KFL)

Kikuyu, domination of Kenyan politics, 81, 86

Kimbangu, Simon, 55–6

Kotoka, E. K., 160

Labour, *see* Manpower

Labour unions, 7, 56–62; autonomy limited since independence, 106–7; development, 47, 89; factional politics, 90; links with nationalist movements and political parties, 52, 57–62

Lagos, Treaty of, 234

Laitin, David D., 211

Lamizana, Sangoule, 179

Lansana, David, 159

La Palombara, Joseph, 130

Lara, Lucio, 185

Legislative councils, creation, 38

Legislatures, in Anglophone and Francophone countries compared, 75; pre-independence elections, 69

Leopold II, King of the Belgians, 30, 38

Lesotho, 71; exclusively civilian government, 155

Levy, Marion, 15

Lewis, Arthur, 16, 146

Leys, Colin, 20–2, 23, 131, 288, 290

Liberation movements, origin of revolutionary regimes, 191–204; *see also* Nationalist movements

Liberia, military coup, 153

Libya, backing for Chad, 255

Limann, Hilla, 175

Linguistic areas, not coterminous with state boundaries, 9

Linguistic diversity, 78

Lomé Convention, 14, 234, 292

Lonsdale, John, 24

Low, Stephen, 58

Luckham, Robin, 75, 154, 157, 158, 160, 162, 169, 179

Lugard, Lord, 36

Machel, Samora, 5, 69, 95, 183, 184, 192

Malawi, exclusively civilian government, 155; presidential power, 5; *see also* Nyasaland

Mali, 12; constitutional experiments, 5; federal union proposal, 226–7; increasing bureaucratic power, 7–8; military coup, 153; move away from federalism, 9; state enterprises, 140, 142, 143; single-party election held by military regime, 178; trading links, 13

Manpower, allocation, 144; comparison between states, 3; divisions, 90; nationalism of urban workforce, 52; skilled, need in Marxist states, 267, shortage, 48, 88, 132, 220; urban workforce, 89, 93, retain links with rural population, 95; *see also* Migrant workers

Manufactures, imports of, 45

MAP, *see* Muslim Association Party (MAP)

Marcum, John, 184

Margai, Sir Albert, 159

Margai, Sir Milton, 68, 159

Markakis, John, 213

Marketing boards, 88, 139; Somalia, 210, 211

Marxist philosophy, in underdevelopment theory, 25; orthodoxy rejected, 6

Mauritania, human rights record, 278

Mauritius, competition in party politics, 102; exclusively civilian government, 155

Mayall, James, 250, 251, 252, 256

Mazrui, Ali, 96, 99

Mboya, Tom, 58

Medical services, cutbacks in Depression, 42; functional specialists, 43

Mengistu Haile-Mariam, 216

Micombero, Michel, 172

Migrant workers, 88

Migrations, 30

Military assistance agreements, 75, 157

Military coups, 152, 209, 210; ambitions of military personnel, 157; characteristics, 153; conclusions from Nigerian experience, 165–6; economic effects, 156–7; external factors, 165–6; justifications given, 159–60; officers' training, 153–4; reasons, 154–8; related to political skill of leader, 158–9

Military power, compared with developed world, 3

Military regimes, 10; acquisition of civilian trappings, 171; aims, 166–7; allies unrelated to previous regime, 170; characteristics, 11, 168–73; developmental role, 173–4; dissolution of political parties, 121; evaluation of performance, 176–7; initial steps, 166; relations with civil service, 137; revolutionary type, 167–8; stability, Francophone and Anglophone states compared, 157–8; withdrawal, 11, 166, 178–80

Milne, R. S., 138

Minerals, 41; dependence on, 2; *see also* Raw material resources

Mineworkers, as 'labour aristocracy', 93

Mining, 47; development corporations, 139; in Angola, 197; in Guinea, 207; investment during inter-war years, 42; public ownership, 7; use of indigenous labour, 41

Minogue, Martin, 144

Mission schools, 54

Missionaries, 30; in West Africa, 32; influence on colonial governments, 53; Portuguese, 39; seen as government agents, 53

Mohammed, Murtala, 167, 170, 172, 173

Molloy, Judy, 120

Molteno, Robert, 81, 97, 99

Mondlane, Eduardo, 183

Morocco, exclusively civilian government, 155

Mouride brotherhood, 84, 89

Movimento Popular de Libertação de Angola (MPLA), 191; degree of control of Angola, 198; external support, 186; ideological influences, 196; Marxist-Leninist basis, 104; pledge to transform society, 196; support from wide spectrum, 184

Mozambique, border with Rhodesia closed, 13; class not yet political determinant, 94–5; at independence, 192–3; degree of autonomy, 274–5; development planning, 145; development strategies, 112; economic dependence on South Africa, 195–6; educational standards, 3; human rights record, 278; liberation struggle, 191; Marxist-Leninist ideology, 181, 183; policy decisions, 194–5; position of private enterprise, 139; reform measures, 193–4; reorganised public companies, 143; revolution, 183–4; revolutionary regime, 7, 192–6; trading links, 13; *see also* Portuguese colonies

MPLA, *see* Movimento Popular de Libertação de Angola (MPLA)

Mueller, Susanne, 26

Mugabe, Robert, 188, 189, 203

Multinational companies, 13, 42; in Angola, 197, 274; in Guinea, 207, 209, 274; in Nigeria, 273; in Zambia, 23, 272–3

Munslow, Barry, 25, 26, 27, 40, 181–2, 183, 192, 202

Muslim Association Party (MAP), 65

Muslims, *see* Islam

Mwane Lesa, 56

Nasser, Gamel Abdul, 68, 104

National Church of Nigeria and the Cameroons, 55

National Congress of British West Africa, 62

National Council of Nigeria and the Cameroons (NCNC), 63, 64, 161; use of regional power base, 113

National Liberation Movement (NLM) (Ghana), 65; Ashanti support, 80, 115

National Party of Nigeria (NPN), 114–15

Nationalisation, *see* Public ownership

Nationalism, characteristics, 50–3, 76; of bureaucracy, 23; origins, 76; political parties' role, 62

Nationalist movements, in Angola, 184; labour union links, 57–8; leaders as rulers, 79; post-war development, 44; *see also* Liberation movements

NCNC, see National Council of Nigeria and the Cameroons (NCNC)

Neo-colonialism, 45

Neto, Agosthino, 186

Nettl, Peter, 263, 264

New International Economic Order, 291

Niger, election results, 73

Nigeria, ban on political activity lifted, 114; Biafran secession, 81; British Petroleum nationalisation, 13, 273; civil–military relations, 161–5; class consolidation, 12, 94; communal conflict increases, 82; constitutions and constitutional amendment, 9, 37, 71, 178; corruption, 161; decolonisation, 44; degree of autonomy, 273; degree of poverty, 3; expulsion of aliens, 236; factions disrupting military regime, 173; federal structure, 9, 69; human rights record, 276–7; Ibo intra-ethnic conflict, 86; military coup, 152, 153, patterns of behaviour, 163–4, reasons for, 162; military regime, 10, 168–70, economic effects, 173–5, performance, 173; Native African Church, 54; patronage by political parties, 113–15; planning, 147; political associations, 83; political parties, 161, role, 108–9; position of private enterprise, 139; regionally based parties, 102–3; representative government, 38, 43; restoration of multi-party politics, 4; socio-political diversity, 2; state enterprises, 140, performance, 141; unions' fluctuating political activism, 59

Nigerian National Alliance (NNA), dominated by NPC, 114

Nigerian National Democratic Party (NNDP), 63, 113–14

Nkomo, Joshua, 189, 190, 203

Nkrumah, Kwame, 5, 45–6, 64, 68, 76, 104; emergency measures adopted, 80; motives for military coup, 160; view on regional blocs, 224; weakens role of administrators, 135

NLM, *see* National Liberation Movement (NLM) (Ghana)

Nordlinger, Eric, 177

Northern People's Congress (NPC) (Nigeria), 161; dominant party, 103; domination of Nigerian National Alliance, 114; origins, 66; type of party, 67; use of regional power base, 113

Northern Rhodesia, conditions of white workers, 62; pre-independence elections, 71; unions' political activities, 60; *see also* Zambia

Northern Rhodesia African Congress, 63

NPC, *see* Northern People's Congress (NPC) (Nigeria)

Nyasaland, investment in inter-war years, 43; pre-independence elections, 71; *see also* Malawi

Nyerere, Julius, 5, 6, 68, 72; competing with bureaucracy, 8; ideology, 104; manipulated by bureaucracy, 90; on capitalists, 87; policy aims, 91

Nzeogwu, C. K., 162

OAU, *see* Organisation of African Unity (OAU)

Obasanjo, Olusegun, 167

O'Brien, Donal Cruise, 19, 42

Oil, in Angola, 197; effect on international status, 3, 14

Ojukwu, Odumegwu, 169

OLF, *see* Oromo Liberation Front (OLF)

Olympio, Sylvanus, 152

One-party system, 18, 276; clear mandate in some states, 103–4; emergence, 102; intended for Zimbabwe, 203; leader as president, 5; national variations, 4; party subordinate to state, 107–8; reasons for, 103; trend since independence, 4

Opon, Sampson, 55

Organisation Commune Africaine et Mauritienne (OCAM), 229

Organisation of African Unity (OAU), 14, 77, 224, 239–59; Charter weaknesses, 242–3, 245; crisis response, 256; dispute settlement, 250–6; formation, 239–47; human rights commission, 279; institutions, 242; non-alignment principle, 247; non-interference principle, 246–7; breaches of, 252; peace-keeping force, 256; performance, 243; poor attendance at summits, 244; promotion of economic co-operation, 257–9; secretariat, 244–5; structural

and membership problems, 244–6; weaknesses, 259–60

Oromo Liberation Front (OLF), 217

PAFMECA, *see* Pan-African Freedom Movement of East and Central Africa (PAFMECA)

PAICV, *see* Partido Africano da Independência da Cabo Verde (PAICV)

PAIGC, *see* Partido Africano da Independência da Guiné e Cabo Verde (PAIGC)

Pan-African Freedom Movement of East and Central Africa (PAFMECA), 240–1

Pan-Africanism, 51, 76

Parastatal sector, 139–44; need for review, 143–4

Parsons, Talcott, 15

Parti Démocratique de Côte d'Ivoire (PDCI), 103; 1959 election result, 73; loss of power, 8; origins, 65–6; type of party, 65, 67

Parti Démocratique de Guinée (PDG), 58, 103, 136, 205; as mass party, 209; type of party, 67

Parti Progressiste Nigérien, type of party, 67

Parti Republicain de Dahomey, 65

Parti Socialiste Sénégalais (PSS), 8, 9

Partido Africano da Independência da Cabo Verde (PAICV), 202

Partido Africano da Independência da Guiné e Cabo Verde (PAIGC), 108, 191; adaptability, 187–8; link between two states, 199; loss of power, 9; supporters, 187

Patriotic Front Party (PFP) (Zimbabwe), 190

Patronage, effect on state enterprise performance, 142; personal political alliances, 119

PDCI, *see* Parti Démocratique de Côte d'Ivoire (PDCI)

PDG, *see* Parti Démocratique de Guinée (PDG)

Peasant societies, divisions, 88–9; encouragement in Mozambique, 194; from cash crop farming, 46; in Angola, 197; in Senegal, 84; protest against colonialism, 52–3; retaining links with urban workers, 95

People's Redemption Party (PRP)
(Nigeria), 94
Pereira, Aristides, 202
Petras, James, 15
Petty-bourgeoisie, mixed character,
87–8; nationalism, 52
PFP, *see* Patriotic Front Party (PFP)
(Zimbabwe)
Philip, Kjeld, 231, 232
Plamenatz, John, 262
Policy-making, and communication
channels, 120; role of political parties,
110–11
Political characteristics, 1
Political culture, in pre-colonial Africa,
50; unsettled, 2, 156; *see also*
Institutions
Political parties, 62–9, 102–22; decline of
power, 280, since independence,
120–1; degree of support, 70;
differences, 67; ideologies, 68, 104; in
colonial policy, 38; integrative
function, 108–9; labour union links, 52;
leaders as presidents, 5, 105;
legitimising function, 109–10; 'mass'
and 'élite' types, 67; mobilisation and
reconciliation functions, 112–13;
origins, 64–6; patronage function,
113–19; policy function, 110–11;
political communication function,
119–20; recent phenomenon, 3; styles
of leadership, 68; subordination to
state, 107–8; supplanted by
bureaucracy, 7; support from
metropolitan parties, 65
Political power, sought by sub-national
groups, 81; *see also* Power-sharing
arrangements
Portugal, attitude to colonies and
decolonisation, 181; coastal trade,
29–31; early trade, 31
Portuguese colonies, decolonisation,
ideological effects, 181, opposed, 40;
economic and social phases, 40;
economic exploitation, 39–40; forced
labour, 39, 41; neglect, 39; wars of
independence, 45
Poverty, comparison between states, 3;
economic strategies, 17
Power-sharing arrangements, in
independence constitutions, 37; *see also*
Political power
PP, *see* Progress Party (PP) (Ghana)

Pratt, Cranford, 20, 91, 129, 147, 148, 205
Pre-colonial history, 2; organisational
units, 30; political organisations, 50;
sources, 29
Presidents, charismatic leadership, 5, 68;
constitutional position, 71; election,
110; freedom of action, 105; of
Francophone states, 75; party leaders,
5, 105
Principé, *see* Portuguese colonies
Private enterprise, post-independence
position, 139
Professional class, attitudes to nationalist
movements, 51–2; emergence, 87;
safeguarding African rights, 62
Progress Party (PP) (Ghana), 115
Prophetic movements, 55–6
PRP, *see* People's Redemption Party
(PRP) (Nigeria)
PSS, *see* Parti Socialiste Sénégalais (PSS)
Public ownership, 139; in Somalia, 210;
initial results, 141; need for
reorganisation, 142–3; of key
enterprises, 7; over-estimates of
potential, 145
Public service, demand for
Africanisation, 133; expatriates in
senior posts, 87; integrative role, 130;
problems, 137–8
Public works, functional specialists, 43;
see also Infrastructural development
Pye, Lucian, 16

Quedraogo, Macaire, 179

Racial consciousness, basis of OAU
formation, 239
Racial discrimination, in Portuguese
colonies, 39
Railways, *see* Infrastructural
development
Raisman Commission, 231
Ranger, Terence, 189
Rassemblement Démocratique Africain
(RDA), 63, 65, 124
Ratsiraka, Didier, 157
Raw material resources, 21; demand in
Second World War, 43; exports, 45; for
European capitalism, 33; *see also*
Minerals
Rawlings, Jerry, 153
RDA, *see* Rassemblement Démocratique
Africain (RDA)

Regional organisations, functional, 14, 229–30; political unions, 13–14, 225–9

Religious associations, 53–6; related to Marxist philosophy, 6; secession from western-style churches, 54; seen as threat to colonial authority, 55–6; *see also* Christianity; Islam

Representative government, 38, 43

Revolutionary regimes, 168; Angola, 184–6, 196–9; Benin, 209–10; Congo, 209–10; differences, 219; emergence, 7; Ethiopia, 213–19; from liberation movements, 68; Guinea, 205–9; Guinea-Biseau, 186–8, 199–202; initial tasks, 191–2; Mozambique, 183–4, 192–6; originating in civilian movements, 204–9; originating in liberation movements, 191–204; originating with the military, 209–19; Somalia, 210–13; Tanzania, 204–5; Zimbabwe, 188–91, 202–4

Rhodesian Selection Trust, 42; *see also* Roan Selection Trust

Riggs, Fred, 19, 127–32, 150, 264

Roads, *see* Infrastructural development

Roan Selection Trust, 23, 272; *see also* Rhodesian Selection Trust

Roberto, Holden, 186

Roberts, Hugh, 127, 128

Robinson, Kenneth, 35

Robinson, Ronald, 32, 41

Rodney, Walter, 15, 33, 34

Rosberg, Carl, 104, 136

Rothchild, Donald, 175

Ruanda-Urundi, pre-independence election, 72

Rural development programmes, 17; *see also* Agriculture

Rwanda, single-party election held by military regime, 178

SADCC, *see* Southern African Development Co-ordination Conference

Salazar, Antonio de Oliviera, 181

Samoff, Joel, 105

Sandbrook, Richard, 82, 118

Santos, José Eduardo dos, 196

Santos, Marcelino dos, 183

Saõ Tomé, *see* Portuguese colonies

Saul, John, 15, 20, 189

Savimbi, Jonas, 185, 186

Schaffer, Bernard, 38, 132, 138

SCOA, *see* Société Commerciale de L'Ouest Africaine (SCOA)

Sékou Touré, Ahmed, 5, 6, 58, 68, 104, 205–9

Self-determination, within states, 79

Senegal, 30; constitutional experiments, 5, 281; decolonisation, 44; exclusively civilian government, 155; groundnuts, 2, smuggling, 42, 88; human rights record, 276; increasing bureaucratic power, 7–8; organisation of peasant society, 84; perceived threat from Soudan (Mali), 227; presidential power, 5; section of French Socialist Party formed, 65; union with Gambia, 226

Senghor, Leopold Sedar, 68, 155, 227

Seton-Watson, Hugh, 76

Shagari, Shehu, 173

Shaw, Timothy, 22–3

Shils, Edward, 19

Shivji, Issa, 20, 22, 90

Sierra Leone, 30; civil-military connections, 119; decolonisation, 44; delays before independence, 69; inter-party competition, 103; military coup, 153, 158–9

Sierra Leone People's Party (SLPP), army connections, 159; competition with APC, 103; origins, 66

Sisal, 46; increased prices, 43

Sklar, Richard L., 20, 23, 28, 82, 90, 92, 97, 99, 162, 225, 279

Slave trade, 30

Social class, *see* Class

Socialism, basis of most parties, 104; development, 7; discredited by poor economic performance, 221; in Tanzania, 90–1; need for revolution, 13, 25; post-independence espousal, 6–7; variety of interpretations, 204

Société Commerciale de l'Ouest Africain (SCOA), 43

Société Générale (Congo), 42–3

Socio-economic aspects, 20; class determining political change, 86–7; class formation and action, 48, 87–96; colonial legacy, 289; determinants of political behaviour, 27, 97–8; disruption by western-style institutions, 51; of growth, 269–72; social class, relationship with

Socio-economic aspects – continued
communalism, 96–100; stunted
development, 46; variety of process, 27
Somali Revolutionary Socialist Party,
211
Somalia, effect of nationalism on socialist
commitment, 167–8; human rights
record, 277–8; language policy, 211;
military regime, 11; public ownership,
210; revolutionary regime, 7, 210–13;
Soviet influence, 212; sphere for
US–Soviet rivalry, 225; war with
Ethiopia, 14, 212
South Africa, incursions into Angola,
186, 199
South West African People's
Organisation (SWAPO), 199
Southern African Development
Co-ordination Conference (SADCC),
14, 196, 237–8
Southern Rhodesia, UDI, 44; *See also*
Zimbabwe
Southern Sudan Liberation Movement,
10
State companies, 139
Stevens, Siaka, 159
Strikes, resulting in fall of governments,
107
Stryker, Richard E., 269
Sudan, constitutional amendment, 9, 10;
limited impact of revolution, 167; rural
development, 84–5
Sudanese National Unionist Party, 65
Svendsen, Erik, 289
Swainson, Nicola, 24, 286
Swaziland, 71; exclusively civilian
government, 155
Sylvester-Williams, Henry, 239
Szeftel, Morris, 93, 98, 110, 117, 118

Tanganyika, East African federation
proposal, 228; expansion of trade
unionism, 62; one-party system, 103;
peasant protest, 52–3; peasant society,
46; pre-independence elections, 71;
republic, 72; unions' political links, 60;
see also Tanzania
Tanganyika African National Union
(TANU), 4; competing with
bureaucracy, 8, 136; origins, 66; role,
109, 119, in policy making, 111; trade
union links, 60–1, 62; union affiliation,

107; *see also* Chama cha Mapinduzi
(CCM)
Tanganyika, Federation of Labour
(TFL), political non-involvement
policy, 60
TANU, *see* Tanganyika African National
Union (TANU)
Tanzania, administration, relations with
party, 136; anti-government
conspiracy, 156; capitalism in check,
12; degree of corruption, 129;
education, 3, 12; exclusively civilian
government, 155; formation, 229;
human rights record, 276; interest
groups discouraged, 105–6; limits on
union autonomy, 107; Marxist view of
Nyerere's aims, 91; army mutiny, 154;
one-party system. 4; planning, 146–7,
147, 149; political neutrality of civil
servants undermined, 135; position of
private enterprise, 139; power sought
by bureaucracy, 90; reorganised public
companies, 143; revolutionary regime,
204–5; state enterprises, 140;
subsistence farming, 89; war with
Uganda, 14; workers' assertion of
rights, 93
Tarka, J. S., 170
Tea plantations, investment in inter-war
years, 43
Tettegah, John, 59
Togo, electoral coercion, 102; military
coup, 152, 153; single-party election
held by military regime, 178
Togoland Congress, 65
Tongogara, Kumbirai, 190
TPLF, *see* Tigre People's Liberation
Front
Trade, imbalance, 45; terms of, 291
Trade unions, *see* Labour unions
Traders, coastal, 29–30; early contacts,
30; in West Africa, 32
Trading companies, 43
Trading links, 12–13
Transfer of power, 69–75
Tribal areas, not coterminous with state
boundaries, 9, 31
Tribalism, European view of, 30;
framework of sectional conflict, 81
Tribes, integration, 96
Tunisia, exclusively civilian government,
155; political experiment, 5; trade
unions, 107

UAC, *see* United Africa Company (UAC)

UDEAC, *see* Union Douanière et Economique de l'Afrique Centrale (UDEAC)

Uganda, 9; constitution at independence, 71; constitutional amendment, 10; East African federation proposal, 228; federal elements, 37; human rights record, 278; intra-ethnic conflict, 86; military coup, 161; military regime, 10; pre-independence elections, 71; subsistence farming, 89; violence, 109; war with Tanzania, 14

UGCC, *see* United Gold Coast Convention (UGCC)

UGTAN, *see* Union Générale des Travailleurs d'Afrique Noire (UGTAN)

UNCTAD, *see* United Nations Conference on Trade and Development (UNCTAD)

Unemployment, in Mozambique, 193; urban, 12

União Nacional para a Independência Total de Angola (UNITA), ethnic support, 184; external support, 186; uncertain support, 198

Union Camerounaise, 59

Union Démocratique Tchadienne, 65

Union des Populations du Cameroun (UPC), union links, 59

Union des Syndicats Confédérés du Cameroun, political links, 59

Union Douanière et Economique de l'Afrique Centrale (UDEAC), 14, 229

Union Générale des Travailleurs d'Afrique Noire (UGTAN), political influence, 58

Union Progressiste Mauritanienne, 65

Union Progressiste Sénégalaise (UPS), loss of power, 8

Union Soudanaise (US), 104, 226, 227; proscription, 8

UNIP, *see* United National Independence Party (UNIP) (Zambia)

UNITA, *see* União Nacional para a Independência Total de Angola (UNITA)

United Africa Company (UAC), 43

United Gold Coast Convention (UGCC), 63, 64

United National Independence Party (UNIP) (Zambia), 67; intra-party factions, 112, 115–16; loss of power, 9; material benefits of membership, 117; role in local authorities, 10; seen as dominated by Copperbelt, 81, 116–17

United Nations, membership, 78; Third World representation, 14

United Nations Conference on Trade and Development (UNCTAD), 14

United Party (Ghana), competition with CPP, 103

United People's Party (Nigeria), 113–14

United Progressive Grand Alliance (UPGA) (Nigeria), 163

United Progressive Party (UPP) (Zambia), 116

Unity Party of Nigeria (UPN), 114

Universal suffrage, in French Africa, 72

Uphoff, Norman, 20

UPN, *see* Unity Party of Nigeria (UPN)

UPP, *see* United Progressive Party (UPP) (Zambia)

Upper Volta, constitutional experiments, 5; degree of poverty, 3; military coup, 152; Mossi kingdom, 81; multi-party elections, 179

UPS, *see* Union Progressiste Sénégalaise (UPS)

Urbanisation, causing regional imbalances, 12; effects, 18; existence of 'urban proletariat', 89; resulting from mining, 47; results of drift, 11–12; rise of voluntary associations, 56–7

US, *see* Union Soudanaise (US)

Voluntary associations, post-war growth, 56–7

Wallerstein, Immanuel, 25, 57

Warren, Bill, 23

Wars of independence, 7, 66, 76; in Portuguese colonies, 45

Washington, Booker T, 239

Watchtower Movement, 56

Weber, Max, 15

Weiner, Myron, 17

Welch, Claude, 16

West Africa, British missionaries and traders, 32; degree of poverty, 3; European colonisation, 30

Western Sahara, peace plan, 243

Western Somalia Liberation Front (WSLF), 212

Wildavsky, Aaron, 144
WSLF, *see* Western Somalia Liberation
    Front (WSLF)

Young, Crawford, 24, 27, 98, 204, 261,
    264, 269, 278, 280, 286–7, 288

Zaire, constitutional amendment, 9;
    copper, 2; defence links, 158; human
    rights record, 278; position of private
    enterprise, 139; transition to
    independence, 66; urban labour force,
    89; *see also* Belgian Congo
Zambia, administration, problems at
    independence, 125–6;
    anti-government conspiracy, 156;
    attitude to liberation movements, 23;
    civil service, problems of, 137–8;
    competition between parties, 103;
    conflict between sectional groups, 81;
    constitutional amendment, 9; copper,
    2; copper mines nationalised, 13, 23;
    degree of autonomy, 272–3; degree of
    poverty, 3; educational standards, 3;
    élite conflict, 82–3; exclusively civilian
    government, 155; growth of middle
    class, 92; human rights record, 277;
    humanist ideology, 92, 104;
    inter-factional cooperation, 83;
    intra-ethnic conflict, 85–6;
    mineworkers, 93; patronage by
    political parties, 115–19; planning,
    146–7, 147, 149; policy-making, 110;
    political neutrality of civil servants
    undermined, 135; position of
    Barotseland, 37; republic, 71; state
    enterprises, 140, 142, 143; subsistence
    farming, 89; urban labour force, 89;

workers' assertion of rights, 93; *see also*
    Northern Rhodesia
ZANLA, *see* Zimbabwe African
    National Liberation Army (ZANLA)
ZANU (PF), *see* Zimbabwe African
    National Union (Patriotic Front)
    (ZANU (PF))
Zanzibar, *see* Tanzania
Zimbabwe, Africanisation of civil service,
    202; composition of first cabinet, 190,
    203; educational standards, 3;
    guerrillas absorbed into army, 202–3;
    independence, 188–91; influence of
    white settlers, 203; land resettlement,
    203; liberation struggle, 191;
    Mozambique border closed, 13;
    revolutionary regime, 188–91, 202–4;
    steps to aid economic recovery, 202; *see
    also* Southern Rhodesia
Zimbabwe African National Liberation
    Army (ZANLA), 189
Zimbabwe African National Union
    (Patriotic Front) (ZANU (PF)), 68, 71,
    191; success in 1980 elections, 188
Zimbabwe African People's Union
    (ZAPU), 190; competition with
    ZANU, 189; failure in 1980 election,
    191; loses support, 190
Zimbabwe People's Army (ZIPA),
    potential role, 189
Zimbabwe People's Revolutionary Army
    (ZIPRA), 190
Zionist churches, 55
ZIPA, *see* Zimbabwe People's Army
    (ZIPA)
ZIPRA, *see* Zimbabwe People's
    Revolutionary Army (ZIPRA)
Zolberg, Aristide, 15, 140, 280